American Classic Screen Features

EDITED BY
JOHN C. TIBBETTS
JAMES M. WELSH

Foreword by Gene D. Phillips

THE SCARECROW PRESS, INC.
Lanham • Toronto • Plymouth, UK
2010

Published by Scarecrow Press, Inc.
A wholly owned subsidiary of The Rowman & Littlefield Publishing Group, Inc.
4501 Forbes Boulevard, Suite 200, Lanham, Maryland 20706
http://www.scarecrowpress.com

Estover Road, Plymouth PL6 7PY, United Kingdom

Copyright © 2010 by John C. Tibbetts and James M. Welsh

British Library Cataloguing in Publication Information Available

Library of Congress Cataloging-in-Publication Data

American classic screen features / edited by John C. Tibbetts, James M. Welsh ; foreword by Gene D. Phillips.
    p. cm.
Collection of essays previously published in the periodical, American classic screen.
Includes index.
ISBN 978-0-8108-7678-1 (pbk. : alk. paper) — ISBN 978-0-8108-7679-8 (ebook)
    1. Motion pictures—United States—History—20th century. 2. Motion picture actors and actresses—United States—Biography. 3. Motion picture producers and directors—United States—Biography. I. Tibbetts, John C. II. Welsh, James Michael. III. American classic screen.
PN1993.5.U6A85812 2010
791.430973—dc22   2010014976

Printed in the United States of America

Contents

PART III: DIRECTORS

PART IV: FROM SILENTS TO SOUND

PART V: FILMS

Foreword

ARTISTS IN AN INDUSTRY

Gene D. Phillips

"Hollywood's like Egypt," the late producer David O. Selznick, whose film *Gone with the Wind* is discussed in this book, once remarked, "full of crumbled pyramids. It will just keep crumbling until finally the wind blows the last studio prop across the sands. . . . There might have been good movies if there had been no movie industry. Hollywood might have become the center of a new human expression if it hadn't been grabbed by a little group of bookkeepers and turned into a junk industry."[1]

These are bitter words indeed to come from the man responsible for producing films like *Rebecca* and *Gone with the Wind*. Nonetheless, Selznick has accurately expressed the perennial problem that has vexed motion picture makers since the movies developed from their humble beginnings into a full-scale industry: the problem of trying to make motion pictures that are personal, unified works of art which a director can truly call his own, despite the fact that he or she is working in a complicated commercial industry. Yet many a filmmaker has succeeded in this hazardous enterprise, as the following essays, collected from *American Classic Screen*, demonstrate.

In "Periodically Yours," the column he contributed to *American Classic Screen*, Jim Welsh quotes an anonymous film scholar who asserts that most intelligent people he knows "beyond forty go less and less to the movies."[2]

Randy Neil's "Publisher's Letter" takes the occasion to observe that, starting in the late 1970s, the American public witnessed "an emerging new awareness in motion pictures past." The sizeable interest in the classical Hollywood era was grounded to some extent in the increasing availability of Hollywood movies of the past on home video and cable TV. Hence, Neil concludes, the purpose of *American Classic Screen* was to promote "the love, enjoyment, and study of American film past."[3] Although the market for buying contemporary films on DVD has diminished, the films of the past continue to thrive on DVD.

Douglas Brode adds that "the home entertainment revolution" created by the video market can give a new life to "little movies that hadn't a chance in competition with the big blockbusters." On video, such a film can develop "a cult following."[4] Similarly, Melissa Balmain observes that the mushrooming of the video market has sparked a renewed interest in the past films spotlighted in this book. The audience for classic films "has grown through the 1980s and 1990s," she writes; and they are buying thousands of videos by directors all the way back to Chaplin.[5] "In an age of cookie-cutter fare at the multiplex," adds Peter Nichols, video editions of classic films are selling briskly.[6]

In providing articles on films of lasting interest, *American Classic Screen* did not disappoint. Consequently, this anthology of essays from this journal will be welcomed by readers who enjoy the movies of Hollywood's Golden Age; for this book lives up to Neil's promise that *American Classic Screen* promoted an appreciation of "the American film past."

While this book is not meant to be a formal history of cinema in America, it can be considered a work of film history, since the films included in it cover a wide spectrum, ranging from the silent period onward, and represent various trends in filmmaking that have evolved over the years, such as film noir. In sum, the present study is intended not only for the cinema specialist but also for those filmgoers who have enjoyed the motion pictures treated here, to provide them with a context in which they can appreciate the movies more fully.

In the early days of Hollywood, when filmmaking was still an infant industry as well as an infant art, a filmmaker was free to make a motion picture in the way he envisioned it. One thinks immediately of D. W. Griffith, the first auteur, conceiving, producing, and directing *The Birth of a Nation* in 1915, all the while being the only individual involved in the making of the film who had any idea of what the plot was, or how each of the scenes would eventually be integrated into the finished film, simply because it was his custom to work without a written script. Yet the film was carefully made. For example, in the course of the movie, Griffith adroitly utilized extreme long shots to photograph battles scenes of epic scope, as well as close-ups to create love scenes of warm personal intimacy, as suggested in the reassessment of *Birth of a Nation* presented here.

Concerning the essay on Irving Thalberg, George Cukor's *Camille* was the last film to be supervised by Irving Thalberg as chief of production at MGM. After Thalberg died, Eddie Mannix, a studio executive, phoned Cukor and said, "Since *Camille* is Irving's last picture, is there anything you would like to do to improve it?" "Really, it's not necessary," Cukor replied, "but, yes, I suppose I could do a little retouching." So he shot for an additional three days to refine a scene or two as a token of his abiding personal esteem for Thalberg, whom he regarded as "the most brilliant, the most creative producer that I ever worked with. That includes *everyone*."[7]

The essay "Red Alert: Images of Communism in Hollywood" reminds me of what Joseph Losey once told me about *I Married a Communist* (1950): While he was still at RKO, Losey had been offered an impossibly ridiculous script entitled *I Married a Communist* to direct, and he promptly turned it down. It was only afterward that he learned that this script was a touchstone for establishing whether or not a director had Communist leanings. If a director refused to make *I Married a Communist*, he immediately became politically suspect. Losey was the first of thirteen directors to be so tested. The film was finally made by Robert Stevenson and can still be seen on the *Late Late Show* under the title *The Woman on Pier 13*.

Some essays from *American Classic Screen* take on an additional resonance from being published in book form. When I wrote an essay on Stanley Kubrick and film noir for *American Classic Screen* in 1980, I drew attention to *Killer's Kiss*, a 1955 movie of Kubrick's, which had largely been neglected by the critical establishment for some years. Kubrick always dismissed *Killer's Kiss* in interviews as part of his "juvenilia," an amateur effort. By contrast, I believe that *Killer's Kiss* was a promising work by a talented young filmmaker; as such, it deserves consideration.

As time went on, other film historians began to take a second look at *Killer's Kiss* and to take it seriously, most notably James Naremore in his book on film noir, *More Than Night*. In it Naremore highlights *Killer's Kiss* as a "violent, erotically charged thriller," which prefigures later, more mature Kubrick films.[8] *American Classic Screen* was ahead of its time in drawing attention to this underappreciated Kubrick film.

This collection of essays from *American Classic Screen* brings into relief how the films of the past enriched the motion picture medium because they have stood the test of time. By the same token, these essays will live on for years to come in book form.

Notes

1. Ben Hecht, "Enter the Movies," in *Film: An Anthology*, ed. Daniel Talbot (Los Angeles: University of California Press, 1966), 258.

2. Jim Welsh, "Periodically Yours," *American Classic Screen* 5, no. 5 (Fall 1981), 22.

3. Randy Neil, "Publisher's Letter," *American Classic Screen* 4, no. 1 (Fall 1979), 3.

4. Douglas Brode, "Introduction," in *The Films of the Eighties* (New York: Carol, 1993), 13.

5. Melissa Balmain, "Classic Films Prove Golden for a New Set of Filmgoers," *New York Times*, 5 April 1998, sec. 2:17.

6. Peter Nichols, "Making Old Movies Like New," *New York Times*, 17 May 1998, sec. 2:28.

7. Letter to Gene Phillips, August 13, 1980.

8. James Naremore, *More Than Night: Film Noir in Its Contexts* (Los Angeles: University of California Press, 1998), 98.

Prologue
RECAPTURING THE PAST
WITH MARY ASTOR . . .

John C. Tibbetts and James M. Welsh

We would like to begin this volume by highlighting Spencer Berger's discussion of John Barrymore and borrowing an anecdote about Barrymore, from an interview Kevin Brownlow shared with us:

Kevin Brownlow: "When David Gill and I were making the Hollywood series, we found a number of interviewees surprisingly shy of the camera. Alice Terry, for instance, said she had put on too much weight and didn't want to disillusion people who remembered her from the 1920s. I pleaded with her that she would be the only witness for her husband, Rex Ingram, but she was implacable. Joan Crawford was impossible to reach. So we decided to bring a Secret Weapon with us on the next filming trip. Her name was Bessie Love. She had lived in London since the mid-1930s, and had been back to Hollywood very seldom. She had been very popular and we knew that no one would refuse to see her. And so it proved. Alas, Joan Crawford died the very night we flew into New York. When we reached Los Angeles, Bessie looked startled. 'What's happened to the streetcars?' she asked.

"We rented a car and drove over to see Mary Astor at the Motion Picture Home in Woodland Hills. She was still surprisingly beautiful, in that Irish way I find so attractive, even though her real name was Langhanke. She had a very funny 'oh baloney' attitude to the past. She must have been irresistible in her youth—she was irresistible now, in a hospital room. She was very nervous of the recorder and was at first a little hesitant. The name of her first famous lover encouraged her."

Brownlow: "Could you recapture your meeting with John Barrymore?"

Mary Astor: "I should be able to, because I fell madly in love with him. We were asked to go to Warner Bros. He was looking for a young girl to play in *Beau Brummell* [1924]. I was to take a test with him to see how we'd look together.

We went to this horrible wardrobe place and got something that looked a little of the time, with the wig. He had a white wig on and a pair of white flannel slacks, which seemed a little silly, but it was only a test.

"He said, 'I saw a picture of you coming out to the coast to make this picture, on the brink of womanhood,' he said. 'Rather appealed to me.'

"I said, 'Well, I'm just 17.'

"'Good God,' he said. 'No one's ever been 17 before. I'm 41.'

"And I think he was honest about it at that time. He knew I was very nervous for this test and he said, 'What did you think of the script?'

"He expected me to have done my homework and read the script. And I said 'Well, it isn't like Lord Byron's or anything of the real Don Juan of Italy and the Renaissance. . . .'"

Brownlow [I had to interrupt]: "Can you say Beau Brummell, Mary. We're still on Beau Brummell."

Mary Astor: "Oh yes. Sorry. I'm getting mixed up with Don Juan. We made those two together. I said, 'I'm sure there was no Lady Margery Alvanley [Astor's role].' He said, 'Ah yes, but this is the movies, and you are lady-in-waiting to the Queen, and as such' he took me just so that my face was down stage and he said, 'Your servant, ma'am. Let's get the hell out of these lights.' And that was that. After that I couldn't think of anything but Mr Barrymore. He was very kind, very wonderful to me and taught me a great deal."

Brownlow: "Did he actually help with your acting?"

Mary Astor: "He taught me respect for acting. He said, 'Do everything they give you, and do it right. Don't say, 'Oh well, it's nothing' and slough through it. Stick your nose in the air and do the best you can.' [In the breaks] we'd work together on things like Hedda Gabler. He wanted me to go to England and do Lady Anne in *Richard III*. Of course my father said, 'No, no money.' So that was that."

Brownlow: "One gets the feeling from Barrymore's early pictures that he had rather a contempt for the movies."

Mary Astor: "I don't think so. He had a contempt for—well, I don't know. Perhaps you're right. It was a matter of making money, so as to go fishing, because he loved fishing and he bought a yacht and went to Norway and did all sorts of fantastic things. But I don't think he even liked the theatre. . . ."

Kevin Brownlow (concluding): "She signed a photograph 'To Kevin, who can charm one out of a hospital bed. Love, Mary Astor.' But I felt a fraud, because it was Bessie who had persuaded her out of her bed. Being a Christian Scientist, she had no respect for illness. When we got back to London, we stayed in touch and Mary sent a charming note: 'Bessie will tell you, I became famous after the afternoon with you lovely people. Everyone said, 'I didn't know you were *that* Mary Astor.''

ॐ

Editors' note: Though this may seem like celebrity eavesdropping, we would rather consider it oral history. Thank heavens Kevin had the wit and took the initiative to ask such questions while they could still be answered. We can't think of better examples of preserving what Randy Neil considered the nation's "screen heritage." The irony, of course, is that it took Kevin Brownlow and David Gill from Britain to come to Hollywood to take the lead, following the ground-breaking interviews collected in Kevin's book The Parade's Gone By . . . *(1968), followed in turn by his* Hollywood: The Pioneers *book and television documentary series.*

Acknowledgments

Our gratitude goes to the many people who remember *American Classic Screen* and are now helping to bring it to a new generation of readers . . . to Randy Neil, who foresaw many years ago the importance of involving amateur and professional enthusiasts, filmmakers, and historians in the preservation of America's film heritage; to Allyn Miller, who as president of the National Film Society ably managed the magazine's membership and organized the annual awards ceremonies; and to her Kansas City staff and West Coast assistants, including Tom Hartzog, Gene Nelson, John Gallagher, Gary Spink, Vic Pettibone, Romayne Hoffman, Alice Becker, Frank Hoffman, and Frank Edwards; and, of course, to the many contributors who became close and personal friends, along the way, Gene D. Phillips, Frank Thompson, and Stan Singer (who also helped to orchestrate the West Coast Movie Expos) in particular, to name just a few. We especially want to thank three remarkable women at the Digital Media Services Department at the University of Kansas for their unstinting assistance in the preparation of this book. Pam LeRow, Paula Courtney, and Gwen Claasen contributed many hours of their time in scanning and retyping articles from the back issues of *American Classic Screen*. Without them this volume would not have been possible. But our debt of gratitude also extends to our extraordinarily patient and helpful editors, first to Stephen Ryan, our acquisitions editor at Scarecrow Press, who saw the true potential of this material and then worked endless hours helping us to shape it appropriately; and, finally, to our Rowman & Littlefield production editor, Jessica McCleary, who also was splendid in helping to worry us through the production process by staying in good cheer.

Introduction

POLISHING THE BIJOU, ONE LAST TIME

John C. Tibbetts and James M. Welsh

In the inaugural issue editorial for *American Classic Screen* (Vol. I, No. 1, 1976) founding editor Randy Neil wrote: "Film preservation and film collecting have come of age . . . and together, the scholar and buff are beginning to combine their forces to achieve broadly based collating of artifacts, films, and memorabilia that will serve as keystones to the industry's heritage. We intend that *American Classic Screen* will serve the needs of these often diverse interests . . . and bring them together to serve this valuable purpose. It has been brought to our attention that this magazine cannot succeed unless it devotes its pages to scholarly writings and interpretative features. . . . Film historians and archivists must understand that the preservation of the heritage of this industry can only be accomplished if we enlist the help of a legion of other people who would like to seriously study the movies. And the average buff should realize that, without the aid of such scholars, little would be done to keep the older movies alive in our hearts." This was Randy's "Declaration of Principles," suggesting a confluence of interests that was, unfortunately perhaps, only partly achieved over the years.

In a later *American Classic Screen* column called "Periodically Yours" after five years of covering other film periodicals, we at the National Film Society attempted to describe our host magazine. The divided nature of this publication, we wrote, had been a challenge from the beginning, when the National Film Society was known as the Bijou Society. *American Classic Screen* first began as an imitation of *Hollywood Studio* magazine, probably not the best model, since it was a "fanzine," and from the beginning there were those who might dismiss *American Classic Screen* as just another fan magazine, centered upon nostalgia, gossip, and trivia. True, a great deal of celebrity chatter was to be found in our early issues; obviously, the magazine was originally designed for an audience of fans and film buffs, as well as an audience of collectors; but to reach them *ACS* had to compete with Sam Rubin's long-established tabloid, *Classic Images*.

Still another potential audience to be reached consisted of informed films buffs, some of whom had gone on to enter academic departments of cinema studies and had also had experience running local film societies. The orientation for this kind of buff of course tended to be more specialized and increasingly based in film history and in theory derived from other academic fields, linguistics in particular, then, later, psychology, rather than that of fans typically interested in the "stars." A wall was being erected, theoretically brick by brick, to separate the fans from the academics, capped with the razor-wire of inscrutable Theory. The hidden agenda was to kill off any residual enthusiasm for the cinema itself. Of course, not all enthusiastic fans were "silly," though some of them might have been. For egotistical reasons the critic John Simon, an overconfident, Mitteleuropean snob with a gift for nasty rhetoric, warned that film buffs were not particularly well qualified to become good critics. They might write with knowledge and passion, but their critical abilities would always be suspect; we could name academics who wrote biographies of stars so carelessly as to prove Simon's point, alas. But that kind of Simon-snobbery was eclipsed long ago by the Internet and the blogosphere. By the end of the 20th century, for good or ill, *everyone* had become a film critic. It was no longer a profession, but an apparent birthright. With the arrival of video technology, an amazing number of film titles eventually became accessible, from all periods and from all nations.

The coming of the Internet served to dismantle traditional notions of film criticism, since anyone with an ability to blog could enter into opinion formation, weakening the authority of any future would-be Pauline Kaels or Susan Sontags, though in fact few ordinary viewers could approach *that* kind of authority and brilliance; but the Siskel-Ebert thumbs-up/thumbs-down model could easily be eroded by critical Internet bandits. And in addition to that, is the spectre of fan editing of the films themselves. At the 2010 Popular Culture Association Convention held in St. Louis, University of Kansas graduate student Josh Wille read a paper entitled "Han Shot First! George Lucas and the Rise of Fan Editing," concerning the reworking of *Star Wars* footage by someone mysteriously identified as "The Phantom Editor," who turned out to be a Hollywood professional who believed the original Lucas editing and pace could be improved, and then set out to demonstrate how that might be achieved. Lucas himself had changed one confrontation, for example, in which Han Solo had originally shot first to make it appear that Solo was responding to an attack and not simply initiating the violence. The Phantom Editor re-edited the film his way and thereby "inspired" other fans to restructure and create their own personalized versions of their own favorite films, creating a paradigm shift that would seem to suggest that "The Artist is *in* the audience" now, or at least that "The potential *Artistry* is in the audience," now empowered rather than passive. So what might the implications be for conventional notions of "Authority" in a multiplicity of versions of a core text—the studio-approved, original released version? The *auteur* would not therefore be so easily located and identified, for in some cases the "corrupted" film text arguably might be superior to the original, standing on its head the traditional notion of film reception. But back in the 1970s, things were not so complicated.

All along, of course, many collectors and buffs were tremendously knowledgeable, and some of our foremost historians have risen from their ranks. Film collectors-turned-archivists William K. Everson in the United States and Kevin Brownlow in Britain both became published authorities on the silent cinema and beyond, for example, and could not be easily dismissed because of their interests in film collecting, and in film history. One stand-by magazine for informed film buffs was *Films in Review* out of New York City and established before 1950, not quite a monthly at ten issues a year, but a magazine that had long since perfected the form of the career survey, because of the work of Hollywood screenwriter-turned-historian DeWitt Bodeen and others—such as Herbert G. Luft, whose piece on director King Vidor went to press for the December 1982 issue, just after the news that Vidor had died on November 1st, making Luft's first-person perspective all the more significant. Such pieces nicely augmented the tightly crafted up-to-date film reviews that were the main strength of *Films in Review.*

Films in Review was one model to follow, and not a bad one at that. *American Classic Screen* eventually recruited some of the old-timers who had written for *Films in Review*, notably the aforementioned Everson; journalist, translator, raconteur, and feuilletonist Herman Weinberg, who wrote for the *New York Times* and *Variety* and kept a regular column, "Coffee, Brandy & Cigars," for the Canadian magazine *Take One*, before joining *Films in Review* with his column, "The Weinberg Touch," named in honor of his popular book, *The Lubitsch Touch* (1968); and Hollywood historian and biographer DeWitt Bodeen, who began as a stage actor and playwright before becoming an RKO screenwriter for the films *Cat People* (1942 and 1982), *Curse of the Cat People* (1944), *Night Song* (1947), and *Billy Budd* (1962). Bodeen wrote the profiles of Warner Baxter and Boris Karloff, with whom he had worked, and Herman Weinberg did the profile of Victor Seastrom in our second volume. In the present volume, David L. Parker, former technical officer of Motion Picture Section, Prints and Photographs Division of the Library of Congress in Washington, D.C., covered opera on film ("The Singing Screen") for us, while University of Illinois professor Rocco Fumento, who edited the screenplay for *42nd Street* for the Wisconsin/Warner Bros. Screenplay series in 1980, wrote a piece comparing the productions of Busby Berkeley to the dance films of Fred Astaire and Ginger Rogers. But note the mix here: an academic, an archivist, an Industry screenwriter, and, arguably, the most famous film collector in America.

In those days, from 1975 to 1985, film critics ruled and film magazines flourished. On the "academic" side, the dominant magazine was probably *Film Quarterly* (though editor Ernest Callenbach always kept it readable and sensible), followed by *Cinema Journal* and several others: *Wide Angle, Film Heritage, Post Script, Literature/Film Quarterly, The Journal of Popular Film, Film Criticism,* et al. Leading the pack of politically oriented magazines was *Cinéaste,* which proved to be one of the most durable. *Sight & Sound* from Britain and *Film Comment* and *American Film* were the best of the glossy magazines for lovers of film when *American Classic Screen* began, the latter eventually overtaken by *Premiere* (which was not, ultimately, an entirely agreeable substitute) and *Movieline,* a pale imitation at best. And what are the survivors today? *Sight & Sound* and *Cineaste* leading the pack, with *Film Comment* also still there, for those who may still be interested. On the academic side *Film Quarterly* and *Cinema Journal, Post Script, Literature/ Film Quarterly, Film Criticism,* and *Film & History* (invented, reinvented, and then relocated several times) continued on into the 21st century. However, only the limited-circulation academic "niche" journals seemed to be adding titles after the turn of the new century: *Adaptation* (published by Oxford University Press) and *The Journal of Adaptation in Film and Performance* (out of Glamorgan University in Cardiff, Wales). The trend would seem to be towards corporate publishing of film journals, and that may not be reason to rejoice or celebrate.[1]

In his Foreword to *ACS Profiles,* Henry Jenkins is right in expressing the need to establish a useful dialogue between those who love movies and go to them regularly and those who study movies and must have loved them once, but have allowed their natural enthusiasm to be muted (if not perverted) by Theory. The Theory should inform the experience, just as the experience of viewing movies should inform (and perhaps *re*form) the Theory. We hope and believe that many of the "Features" contained in this volume may work towards that goal. Certainly, it is not our intention to be "theoretical" here, merely to be informative and readable. That was always our intent; that was always our goal. These essays are for readers who love films. Period. *Punkt. Ende.*

Note

1. Of those journals that began as independent publications, *Post Script, Film Criticism,* and *Literature/Film Quarterly* have survived as of 2010. *The Journal of Popular Film and Television* is now published by Rutgers; *The Historical Journal of Radio, Film and Television* is published by Taylor and Francis. In Britain, Intellect Books publishes a shelf-load of film journals, many of them new: *Studies in Australian Cinema,* for example, *Transnational Cinemas* (a new start-up in 2010), *The Journal of Chinese Cinemas, New Cinemas Journal of Contemporary Film,* and *The Journal of Adaptation in Film and Performance.* The point is that very specialized academic journals seem to be doing better these days than those geared to more general readers and viewers.

Part I

ACTORS AND ACTRESSES

In the State of California

DE HAVILLAND, PLAINTIFF VS.
WARNER BROS., DEFENDANT

Joanne L. Yeck

Originally appeared in vol. 6, no. 3 (May/June 1982)

Lamb bites wolf? It was rare in the 1940s that Jack L. Warner lost a fight. The public, in fact, thought him invincible. Least likely of all to bring Warner and the whole movie industry to toe was the fleeciest lamb of Warner's flock—Olivia de Havilland.

Her image was meek and mild: she'd played Melanie in *Gone with the Wind* and Maid Marian in *The Adventures of Robin Hood*. She portrayed sweet heroines and handmaidens as opposed to ruthless roles, but beneath this pacific public image, a slow boil was about to burn over.

In the spring of 1943 Miss de Havilland's standard seven-year contract with Warner Bros. was about to run out. De Havilland and the studio had, until 1939, been on fairly good terms. Signing with Warner Bros. while she was still a minor, Olivia had begun her career with *A Midsummer Night's Dream* and went on to costar with Errol Flynn in a very successful series of films, which included the unforgettable *Captain Blood* (1935), directed by Michael Curtiz, and the screen's definitive *Robin Hood* (1938).

Despite her popularity, since all but one of her first sixteen films (*The Great Garrick*) showed black ink on Warner Bros.' ledger, her roles remained small. She was frequently cast in adventure films where her role was strictly the "pretty face" for those romantic moments that kept the women moviegoers happy. Even such fine films as *Captain Blood, Anthony Adverse* (1936), *Charge of the Light Brigade* (1936) and *The Adventures of Robin Hood* (1938) gave the young de Havilland little acting challenge. Personally convinced she could handle meatier roles, she finally had her chance. Loaned to David O. Selznick for his epic *Gone with the Wind*, she played Melanie—the best loved role of her career. She proved to the industry (her peers nominated her for an Oscar) and to the public that she could act!

Enthusiasm high, she returned to Warner Bros. with a fresh outlook, realizing she had reached a new level of artistic maturity. Melanie had been a role with *depth*, a character who had mattered in the film. Melanie was not ornamental—she was essential. And to Olivia, Melanie was real.

To her disappointment the return to Warners' Burbank studio was not what she anticipated. Not only was she assigned the same fluffy parts as before—now they seemed worse. Her increased consciousness about art and her new appreciation of her proven abilities as an actress made the old routine look even bleaker. Her first assignment after her return to Warners was a role in *The Private Lives of Elizabeth and Essex* (1939). She didn't respond to this part the way she had to Melanie; it never came alive for her. The result was a performance she wasn't proud of—a feeling that bothered her deeply. She began to feel sick and nervous when she had to play parts she could not understand.

Insult followed injury, as she continued to be cast in roles she felt were not suited to her ability. With the possible exception of *Hold Back the Dawn* (1941), while on loan to Paramount and an unusual part in *Strawberry Blonde*, which she fought for, her career was not fulfilling the promise made by her portrayal of Melanie.[1]

Her feeling of unsuitability in the roles she was assigned caused many disagreements. So in the spring of 1943, with her contract nearing its end, she determined not to renew it and was eagerly looking forward to working with another studio.

Enter "Suspension." Suspension was part and parcel of the seven-year contract system in Hollywood and it was a well-worn word at Warner Bros. When an actor signed with a studio, he relinquished control of his career. Parts were "assigned," not chosen, and any refusal to cooperate usually meant suspension without pay until disputes were settled. And since these were contracts for personal services, an actress or actor was unable to work—not only at their studio—but at any job.

But suspension meant more than lack of work or pay. Each suspension in turn became an equally long extension which was added to the length of the contract, effectively stretching seven calendar years into seven working years—however long that actually took!

In Olivia's case, 25 weeks of additional work were required as the result of accumulated suspensions. In May of 1943 she accepted the situation gracefully, never doubting her obligation to Warners. At the same time, she was eager to play parts suited to her and to be on her own.

During those weeks of extension she was loaned to RKO for *Government Girl*, a film she didn't care for, but dutifully completed. (Despite her unhappiness with the role, the film was a big box office success in '43.) After completion of *Government Girl*, Warner Bros. loaned her again, this time to Columbia.

With an imminent shooting date, and only a twenty-page script, Olivia knew the production was doomed to fail.

So on extension time, Olivia took a voluntary suspension and left the picture on August 13, 1943—an action hardly appreciated at Warners and certainly not tolerated. It was now clear that completing the extended contract would be difficult and that her unhappy involvement with Warners was likely to stretch into additional months or years.

A few days after Olivia left Columbia's lot, her agent called a meeting in her lawyer's office. They presented Miss de Havilland with an interesting interpretation of the California statute concerning personal service contracts, which appeared to limit such contracts to seven calendar years. If the court upheld this position, her obligations to Warner Bros. would have been satisfied by the previous May.

The contract system as it stood had always seemed a one way street in favor of the studio. The studio could drop a contract player after a year or put them in any part in any film, but the actors were never allowed to exercise their own judgment in the direction of their careers.

Yet a star's career depended directly on the response from two audiences: the public and the critics. An actress could afford to star in a film that was well received by one, and not the other, but two films in a row that pleased neither the critics nor the public could mean the end of a career. This fear, needless to say, was greater than the fear of suspension and a few weeks without pay. So to protect themselves, actors would occasionally refuse scripts they felt were sure to flop.

Some suspensions were due to a difference in judgment: a role would be assigned that the studio thought appropriate to a player, and the actor disagreed. Apparently though, not all suspensions were due to this kind of difference of opinion.

Suspensions were sometimes used as punishment. If actors were not willing to accept the paternal guidance of Jack Warner or their producer or director, they could be suspended for conduct unbecoming a star. Or they might be assigned a role so ridiculous they would refuse it in self-defense, and a suspension would be in order.

Other suspensions, especially at Warners where suspensions occurred frequently, seemed to stem from internal production problems rather than star-studio relations. Jack Warner was accused of improving his cash flow at times by lightening his payroll through suspensions. By offering his more highly paid stars roles they couldn't accept without jeopardizing their careers, he could get them off the payroll for a week or two, with the full knowledge that he would have those weeks of work available at the end of their contracts. This meant that during a box office slump or with no appropriate properties to develop or scripts prepared, the studio could effectively lay off their employees temporarily. Thus the contract, as previously interpreted, always allowed the studio to get maximum work out of its stars. No matter how long or how often they were suspended, the studio could depend upon seven full working years of service.

Consequently, the implications of a favorable decision for Miss de Havilland went far beyond her personal contract problems. The use of suspension as punishment for stars or to solve financial problems would no longer be practical. The studios faced the loss of not only the upper hand, but most importantly the endless services of an actor.

Naturally, Warners could be counted on to do everything possible to protect the old interpretation. The studio executives were very concerned about the possibility of losing the suit. They felt that de Havilland's accumulated suspension time represented at least four pictures in which they could use her at her relatively low contract rate. She had in fact turned down five scripts (after 1939) to accumulate the 25 weeks suspension and the Columbia "walk out" was her sixth.

The meeting her agent and attorney held in August of 1943 was the beginning of a two-and-a-half-year struggle in the California courts. Following a brief hearing on November 4, 1943, the court ruled in Miss de Havilland's favor that contracts in the State of California could not exceed seven *calendar* years.

The studio was, to say the least, dissatisfied with the court's decision and immediately filed an appeal. They prepared a case that attempted to move the court's attention away from a simple interpretation of the law to an accusation against an uncooperative actress.

The transcripts of the appeal report lengthy testimony on Olivia's part. The studio's attorney tried to establish that Miss de Havilland had returned to work at Warner Bros. after making *Gone with the Wind*, too haughty an actress for the parts that Warners had provided her. Olivia denied this and stood her ground admirably in court. She answered time and time again during the long hours of the cross examination that the parts offered were not suited to her and that in her best judgment (and in some cases the judgment of directors like Sam Wood) participation in the films she rejected would have hurt not only her career, but also the film and the studio.

The Warner lawyers continued to insist that Olivia's only reason for turning down scripts was that they were not up to her newly elevated standard. Comparing all films to the caliber of *Gone with the Wind* and all parts to that of Melanie they insisted was ridiculous. No studio could be expected to keep up that standard. Warners' position was that this was simply a case of a star trying to break her contract.

Warners' crucial appeal was lost. The court let the previous decision stand. The suit had been filed to test a point of law and the law was clear. Jack Warner then attempted an additional appeal to the Supreme Court of California, but, finding no new evidence to question the decision of the two lower courts, the Supreme Court refused to review it.

So Olivia was free of Warner Bros. They had lost a fine actress, as well as three months suspension extension work from her which they had counted on.

The impact of the decision on Olivia's career after leaving Warner Bros. was of great importance to her and to her fans. During her seven plus years there, Warners either found no properties that were truly suited for her (which was what she believed all along) or they neither recognized nor appreciated her talent. As soon as the contract dispute was settled and Olivia was free to work again, things changed dramatically. In 1946 she starred in *To Each His Own* for Paramount. It won for her her first Oscar. This was followed by *The Snake Pit* (1948) for Twentieth Century-Fox (the role of Virginia Cunningham remains one of her favorites)—for which she received the prestigious New York Critic's award. Her third film for Paramount—*The Heiress*—won her another Academy Award. She had come a long way from the Warner roles she had played and even further from the ones she had turned down.

The "de Havilland Decision,"[2] as it is recorded in the law books, is still often cited in personal service contract law disputes. It was a decision that marked a crucial turning point in the life of the Hollywood contract player . . . diminishing studio domination and allowing contract players influence over the direction of their careers.

Notes

1. The part of Amy in *Strawberry Blonde* excited Olivia. Though it was not the lead in the production, she felt she understood and could play the role of a wife of a small town dentist. Jack Warner, on the other hand, was far from convinced that she could play a small town girl. This seemed odd to Olivia for she had been raised in a town of 800 and knew the kind of people that inhabited the story. She finally won her argument and persuaded the producers to cast her as the wife of Bif (James Cagney). The performance, directed by Raoul Walsh, was well received by the critics and the public, proving Olivia could succeed in a part that required more than a pretty face.

2. Those who benefited most directly from the "de Havilland Decision" were the actors who had served in World War II. In effect, their time away from the studio would have been considered one long suspension. They would have been expected to continue their seven years from the day they were discharged. Because of Olivia de Havilland's courtroom success, actors like Jimmy Stewart, Robert Taylor, and Clark Gable were relieved of their extensions at M-G-M.

The Lost Movie of Errol Flynn

Wade Ward

Originally appeared in vol. 5, no. 3 (May/June 1981)

In the scenic countryside near Courmayeur, at the foot of Mont Blanc, stands a little village. It was built for a movie that was never completed and was the scene of the downfall of one of the world's best loved actors—Errol Flynn.

Flynn had been one of the top box office attractions in the world since the mid-1930s. But after World War II, the swashbuckling genre he dominated fell from favor with the moviegoing public who wanted more realism in the cinema. To capitalize on the popularity he still enjoyed in Europe, Flynn decided to take his career into his own hands and start making his own films.

His relationship with Warner Bros. Studio, who had put him under contract and made him a star, was always strained. Flynn had recently signed a new contract, but was dissatisfied with the roles he was given and the money he thought insufficient for a star of his stature.

In the early fifties, he started his own production company with his new manager and friend Barry Mahon. A follow-up to his 1948 film *The Adventures of Don Juan* was planned as part of a three-picture deal in Italy. There, his career was on much steadier footing than in the U.S. The resultant picture, *Crossed Swords* was successful, in moderate terms, and Flynn thought, "I will make a mint and show Warner Brothers I don't need them or their studio." [1]

For the second feature in the European deal, the fledgling Errol Flynn Enterprises considered a biographical picture of his old drinking pal King Farouk starring Orson Welles. But the project seemed shaky, as Farouk's life was perhaps too controversial to film. Instead, Flynn decided to film the legend of William Tell. [2]

The project seemed jinxed from the start. There was a labor dispute to settle before any work could be done. The A.F. of L. found out the film was to be made with the labor of the Communist-backed General Confederation and threatened to blacklist the film in the U.S. Flynn used his charm and somehow sweet-talked the labor congress into a more cooperative frame of mind. [3]

Financial backing was also hard to come by. Potential backers thought Flynn a poor risk because of his recent hepatitis bout and his refusal to quit drinking. He had been a heavy drinker for years and there were rumors of his drug abuse. There was fear that this once rugged, handsome he-man might die during production.[4]

Flynn finally found a consortium of Italians and with every penny he had and a little from the Italian government, the financing of the film was charted. Flynn put up $430,000 of his own money, half of the movie's budget. An Italian backer named Count Fossataro agreed to furnish about half that amount and left $50,000 in a joint account with Barry Mahon in good faith. In a credit to Flynn's diplomacy, he talked the Italian government into kicking in 90 million lire, or about $145,800.

Flynn fell into the production with enthusiasm. He hired Jack Cardiff, the cinematographer for an earlier Flynn film, *The Master of Ballantrae,* and the recently completed *Crossed Swords,* to direct and photograph the epic. Cardiff was respected for his work on the earlier films *Black Narcissus* and *The Red Shoes,* but this would be his directorial debut.

Going all out, Flynn decided to use the new wide-screen process, Cinema-Scope. Only one other movie, *The Robe,* had been photographed by this process and it had not been released at the time. Barry Mahon went to Darryl F. Zanuck at Fox to see about using the equipment, but Zanuck refused to turn over the cameras. Mahon, who was a lawyer, threatened a lawsuit, and convinced Zanuck to be more cooperative.

This would have been one of the few roles where the 43-year-old Flynn didn't try to play a young, romantic lead. He cast Italian actors Antonella Lualdi and Aldo Fabrizi, but rejected a young starlet for lacking what he thought was international appeal. Her name was Sophia Loren.[5]

His next big mistake was in choosing the heavy for the film. He immediately thought of his old drinking buddy, Bruce Cabot. They had worked together in Flynn's western epic *Dodge City* and had played together aplenty. He dashed off a cable saying: COME OVER AND PLAY A PART STOP THREE MONTHS FUN AND THE ITALIANS WILL PAY THE EQUIVALENT OF FIVE GRAND. With the promise of a good time and some money, Cabot eagerly responded.[6]

Flynn supposedly wrote the script outline. The final script was written by John Dighton and dramatized the story of Tell. After having been forced to shoot an apple from his son's head, the Swiss hero precipitated a revolt winning Swiss independence in the 1300s. Shooting of exteriors started in northern Italy in June, 1953.[7]

Work was smooth, although Cabot had a habit of running out on the production to party for a few days at a time. However, Flynn never canned him, and Cabot spent many an evening at the Flynn apartment in Rome with Errol and his wife, Pat, who had recently had a daughter.

Most of the money went to build an entire little village through which a stream ran. However, after about three weeks, Flynn was informed that his money had run out. Fossataro's money was needed, but when Mahon tried to draw upon the joint checking account, the bank wouldn't honor his checks.

Fossataro apologized and wrote another check which also bounced. From then on, he could not be reached. The $250,000 he had promised never materialized and the $50,000 he fronted was unavailable.[8]

Flynn was in shock. Every dime he had was sunk into a movie that was barely begun and he was broke for the first time in twenty years.

In the spirit of camaraderie and for the sake of art, Cardiff and the crew worked another six weeks with no pay. But finally filming had to halt. In late August, after two months, *William Tell* was shelved.

Flynn tried to get additional financing, but ran into legal complications. Harry Cohn at Columbia, British filmmaker Herbert Wilcox and *William Tell's* distributor, United Artists, looked into it, but backed away after hearing the Italian's demands. Fossataro still wanted half of the profits and threatened to sue any new investors.

If Flynn thought things were as bad as they could be, he was soon to find out differently. The Internal Revenue Service came down on him for owing $820,000. Flynn was totally ignorant of his tax picture, as that was left to his manager, Al Blum. But Blum had spent Flynn's money in a binge before dying of cancer. Reportedly, his last words were, "Tell Errol I'm sorry."[9]

The shocks kept piling up. Suddenly, Bruce Cabot sued for his salary. He had court officials sequester Flynn's and Mahon's cars and all their wives' clothes. The man Flynn described as "the closest thing I have to a brother," turned out to be a Judas who kicked Flynn while he was down. Errol said of Cabot, "No real man strikes at another through his helpless family—especially after he's been befriended for 20 years."[10]

In his own defense, Cabot explained why he took such drastic measures. When the movie collapsed, Cabot sued because he hadn't received any payment. He claimed he sued Flynn's company, not Flynn. He had noticed a change in Flynn when returning from WWII. Cabot attributed it to Flynn's association with John Barrymore and his group ten years earlier and he thought Flynn's business judgment was affected by drug abuse. He said the incident was part of a larger tragedy—Flynn's gradual decline.[11]

After these stunning blows, Flynn's fragile health gave out. He was bedridden with another attack of jaundice and suffered renal failure. He was told he would die.

But, according to Flynn, he refused to predecease Jack Warner and eventually was on his feet again. In November of 1953 he went to London to seek backing. On the BBC radio talk show *In Town Tonight*, he joked about his financial troubles and spent the rest of his trip hitting up acquaintances.[12]

He returned to Rome claiming he had a promise of 50,000 pounds English money but little of it ever materialized. He tried to see U.S. Ambassador Clare Booth Luce five times to protest his treatment by the Italians, but was never granted an appointment. At about this time he announced that his contract with Warners was cancelled by mutual agreement.

Bailiffs moved in and took all his cameras, film stock and equipment. The crew had no alternative but to leave Courmayeur with unpaid hotel bills of $14,000. Flynn was ensconced in his Rome penthouse and he returned to drink and drugs under the strain.

He returned to California to try to get some more funds. But the only money he could raise was from selling a Gaugin for $50,000. He tried other sources for capital. He sued an Italian vermouth company for $5,000 for using his picture in advertising without his permission; he won $30,000 on the TV game show "The Big Surprise" answering nautical questions; he rented out his yacht, the *Zaca*, to Mary Pickford and Buddy Rogers.

Meanwhile, he sued in Rome courts and got custody of the *William Tell* negative, approximately 30 minutes of edited footage for his movie.[13]

Not everything was breaking badly, though. A friend in from Cuba anonymously donated $10,000 to a Swiss account for Flynn. But that sum was immediately eaten up for debts.

Flynn agreed to take the lead in a film for Herbert Wilcox for $25,000. It was far less than he was usually paid, and Flynn had to take second billing to Wilcox's wife, Anna Neagle, but it was work at a time when no other offers were forthcoming. Flynn had hoped Wilcox would take over *William Tell*, but in vain. He made another European film, *The Warriors*, and then a second for Wilcox for the same price.

Lawsuits were still piling up. Cabot sued for $17,000 in British courts because Flynn lived in Jamaica. However, the suit was dismissed. Cardiff waited two years to start work again while lawsuits, including his own, were bandied about. When he halted work, he was owed nine million lire ($14,580).[14]

Both of Flynn's ex-wives were also after him for money, saying Flynn was behind on his alimony. Through it all, Flynn refused to go bankrupt. In 1955 he was forced to forfeit his beloved Hollywood bachelor pad on Mulholland Drive to his first wife, Lili Damita.[15]

Old debts continued to haunt him. Flynn was sued by his publicists for $1,988.62 for work on an old picture, *The Adventures of Captain Fabian*. His agents at MCA Artists, Ltd. also sued for back compensation of $13,560.

He continued his drinking and drug abuse. In fact, narcotics agents arrested him, but he was never prosecuted. His health was failing, his lungs and liver were about shot by this time.

In 1956 his second wife, Nora Eddington, collared him for $7,000 in back child support and he was in litigation against *Confidential* magazine for libel. But eventually he was out of debt. He would, in fact, leave an estimated $2 million estate when he died a few years later. As poetic justice, Count Fossataro died broke.

But somewhere, thirty minutes of edited Pathé color, Cinema-Scope film never completed or shown still exists. It might have been one of the great epics of the cinema, but all it turned out to be was the downfall of a talented man who was overly ambitious.

Notes

1. *My Wicked, Wicked Ways* by Errol Flynn (G. P. Putnam's Sons, 1959), pp. 7–17.

2. *The Two Lives of Errol Flynn* by Michael Freedland (Arthur Barker, Ltd., 1978), pp. 214–20.

3. Ibid.

4. *Errol Flynn: The Untold Story* by Charles Higham (Doubleday and Co., 1980), pp. 306–10.

5. *The Films of Errol Flynn* by Tony Thomas, Rudy Behlmer, and Clifford McCarty (Citadel Press, 1969), pp. 197–98.

6. Flynn, *My Wicked, Wicked Ways.*

7. Freedland, *Two Lives of Errol Flynn.*

8. Ibid.

9. Flynn, *My Wicked, Wicked Ways.*

10. Ibid.

11. *From a Life of Adventure: The Writings of Errol Flynn.* Edited and with an introduction by Tony Thomas (Citadel Press, 1980), pp. 27–28.

12. Flynn, *My Wicked, Wicked Ways.*

13. Freedland, *Two Lives of Errol Flynn.*

14. Thomas, Behlmer, and McCarty, *Films of Errol Flynn.*

15. Flynn, *My Wicked, Wicked Ways.*

How a Cinema Legend Was Born

THE SCREEN TESTING OF MARILYN MONROE

James Robert Haspiel

Originally appeared in vol. 2, no. 2 (November/December 1977)

Legendary as a film image, Marilyn Monroe made her first known appearance in front of a movie camera at the Blue Book Model Agency in Hollywood. There, in a film test made in 1945, she smiled into the lens over a screen credit announcing her legal/married name then, Norma Jean Dougherty. Actually her birth certificate reveals that Jeane was correctly spelled with an 'e' on the end, as she herself always did throughout her life when signing anything personal. In subsequent months at the agency Norma Jeane appeared in additional film tests: modeling a one-piece swimsuit, walking in a summer dress, in full facial closeups, etc.—all of which became a preparation of sorts for her first motion picture studio screen test the following year.

Norma Jeane made her initial entrance through the fabled gates of the 20th Century-Fox studio on July 17th, 1946. An interview with the Casting Department's Ben Lyon (who'd later be credited with changing her name) resulted in a "test option for contract." She was then given the same test-scene script used earlier by Judy Holliday, a sequence from *Winged Victory*. Fearing that this black and white sound test of a yet inexperienced thespian might not impress studio chief Darryl F. Zanuck into contract-action after all, Lyon decided instead to take another route, namely to capture Norma Jeane's unusual beauty—sans sound—on color celluloid for DFZ's executive consideration. On July 19th Lyon arranged a photographic test to be filmed in Technicolor on the set of a Betty Grable feature then in its pre-production stages, *Mother Wore Tights*. The Norma Jeane Dougherty Screen Test would be lit and photographed by cameraman Leon Shamroy, and directed by Walter Lang. Fox designer Charles LeMaire chose a gown from the Wardrobe Department for Norma Jeane, and the now historical moment in cinema history was committed to celluloid. The camera

13

loaded with a 100-foot roll of silent color film stock, Norma Jeane was given her on-camera direction—upon the command "Action!" she was instructed to: a) Walk across the set. b) Sit down on a stool. c) Light a cigarette. d) Respond to Shamroy's camera as it focused upon her face in closeups—while Lang talked to her out of camera range. e) Extinguish the cigarette. f) Go upstage—Cross— Look out a window. g) Come downstage. h) Exit.

Obviously impressed, the Shamroy-Lang team shot a 2nd 100-foot roll of color film. Viewing the processed footage hours later, Leon Shamroy recalled his reaction for Monroe biographer Maurice Zolotow: "I got a cold chill. This girl had something I hadn't seen since silent pictures. She had a kind of fantastic beauty like Gloria Swanson, when a movie star had to look beautiful, and she got sex on a piece of film like Jean Harlow. This is the first girl who looked like one of those lush stars of the silent era. Every frame of the test radiated sex. She didn't need a sound track to tell her story. That was what made her test so great to me. She was creating her effects visually. She was showing us she could sell emotions in pictures—that's what pictures have to be—moving pictures are pictures that move, not just characters talking."

The following evening the Norma Jeane Dougherty Screen Test was pro- jected in Darryl Zanuck's screening room at Fox. Zanuck told Ben Lyon, "It's a damn fine test . . . gorgeous girl . . ." adding the all-important "Sign her up." For all the initial enthusiasm, Norma Jeane's first contract with Fox—which went into effect on the 26th of August, 1946—resulted in what can only be reviewed as a mostly unproductive year at the studio for the young movie star hopeful. The contract was terminated August 25th, 1947, its single major effect being that the Norma Jean Dougherty who entered the studio 12 months before exited same with a new marquee name, Marilyn Monroe.

Columbia Pictures signed Monroe to a beginner's contract on March 9th, 1948. Garson Kanin claims that while at Columbia Marilyn made a sound test for the Billie Dawn role in the filmization of *Born Yesterday,* a characterization that subsequently won an Academy Award for Judy Holliday. Of the Marilyn Monroe/*Born Yesterday*/Screen Test, Kanin states: "Those who saw it thought it was excellent. But Harry Cohn, the head of the studio, did not trouble to take the six steps from his desk to his projection room to look at her." Marilyn would later lament: "When you're an obscure bit player or starlet, nobody cares whether you can act." Monroe's Columbia contract expired September 8th, 1948—its termination attributed by insiders to have resulted from her refusal to share an "intimate weekend" with boss Harry Cohn.

Marilyn's next screen test venture was one in which the public itself was invited to judge her performance. When the October 10th, 1949 issue of *Life* magazine hit the newsstands, its readers found a Philippe Halsman picture- layout of the current crop of Hollywood starlets. The article was entitled "Eight

Girls Try Out Mixed Emotions." Suzanne Dalbert, Cathy Downs, Dolores Gardner, Laurette Luez, Lois Maxwell, Jane Nigh, Ricky Soma, and Marilyn were featured in a matching series of photographs depicting their reactions to a variety of acting situations: Seeing a monster, Hearing a joke, Embracing a lover, Tasting a drink. It was literally a silent screen test constructed of still photographs aimed at soliciting a write-in response from the magazine's following: "*Life*'s readers can judge for themselves whether the girls have anything to offer the movies besides their good looks." In what now looms as a masterful display of instinct, a Mrs. M. Sakakeeny of Massachusetts wrote the "Letters" column of *Life* (October 31st issue): "Marilyn Monroe is not only the most beautiful, but the one who will no doubt make a name for herself in Hollywood." Looking back, photographer Halsman recalled: "Hollywood's studios furnished me with eight starlets. I set up my still camera to screen-test them." Of Monroe in particular Halsman noted: "Only when she tried to embrace and kiss the invisible lover did Marilyn become an inspired actress. She gave a performance of such realism and intensity that both she and I were utterly exhausted." He added, "I went back to New York, and—except for the one picture in which she made love—forgot about Marilyn Monroe." Some half-dozen years after its publication I mentioned the *Life* article to Marilyn, eliciting a never-to-be-explained gleeful chuckle at the mention of the name of competitor Laurette Luez, star of the 1950 epic *Prehistoric Women.*

By the fall of 1950 Marilyn was the veteran of four years' experience in the motion picture industry, and, in that same period, the casualty of two aborted contracts. During those years she'd played mostly unnoticed parts in a number of studio and freelance assignments. And she was 24 years old—no small handicap in the factories where fantasies were turned into celluloid realities. Most starlets with her same goal had, by that age, become little more than well-used flesh clinging to the perimeter of an already lost dream. While her co-stars in "Eight Girls Try Out Mixed Emotions" were headed towards that bottomless pit of cinema oblivion, and her own earlier screen tests were lying dormant on archive shelves, Monroe pondered the prospect of an opportunity to star in a brand new sound test at the studio that'd dismissed her three years before.

She returned to 20th Century-Fox to film a scene in which she would be required to act the part of a gangster's abused girlfriend. The well established actor-star Richard Conte would play opposite Monroe, as the menacing criminal. This time around, in lieu of a Wardrobe Department costume, Marilyn donned a sweater-dress combo from her own closet—an outfit she'd already worn in several brief movie roles (in *The Fireball, Home Town Story,* and *All about Eve*) pre-dating this latest Fox test.

Given that this new dramatic showcase became the single most influential piece of film ever to capture the Monroe image, despite the fact that it was not produced for mass public viewing, I contacted Richard Conte—as it happened, only weeks before his death in 1975—and obtained an exclusive interview: "I was under contract to Fox and I was asked if I would test with a young girl. I said 'Sure' . . . I think Georgie Jessel was the director." Follow-up research failed to support the Jessel-as-director information. Mr. Conte said that he really didn't know the source of the material from which the test script was gleaned, but he vividly recalled (in actor's jargon) the filming with Marilyn: "She was quite involved and quite free, and concentrated well. She had a natural thing about it—she was quite concentrated." He added, "The quality of the test was concentrated. I have a print of it." So do I. Thus what follows is the actual dialogue and a description of the action of the finale of that sound test in which Marilyn Monroe made her bid for what subsequently materialized into one of the most spectacular motion picture careers in memory—

Marilyn Monroe Screen Test

The scene, one of high intensity, takes place at night in a large living-room. As we join the action, Richard Conte is seated on the edge of a couch facing a very upset Monroe, standing before a huge fireplace.

Fade-in:

RC (agitated): . . . what did you come here for?

MM (pleadingly): To tell you you can't stay here . . . If those gorillas find you here, what happens to them?! (She gestures towards a closed door, indicating other people behind it.) Nothing?— They're just gonna leave them alone? What's the matter with you, Benny? You can't take such a chance.

RC (rising from the couch): How did you find out about this?

MM (angry and in desperation): Two guys came calling on me— looking for you.

RC (in a demanding tone): Who were they?

MM: I never saw them before.

RC: Well, when did they come?

MM (in quick, strong tones): About four o'clock . . .

At this point in the test Richard Conte crosses the living-room to the front door. He peers out from behind the curtains on the door's window, looking into the dark night outside for the men who are pursuing him. Monroe has followed him across the room, and the dialogue resumes as Conte turns back towards MM and addresses her in great anger . . .

RC: You dumb broad! You stupid little . . .

MM (stunned): What's the matter?

RC: They followed you here! Or did you bring them with you?! I oughta . . . (he raises his hand to strike her across the face).

MM (defeated yet defiant): Go ahead! It won't be the first time I've been worked-over today . . . (her voice is trembling). I'm getting used to it . . . (she is apparently referring to the earlier run-in with Conte's pursuers)

A disgusted Conte gets his jacket and puts it on to leave . . .

MM (unsure—desperately): Where're you going?

Conte doesn't answer—he starts towards the door . . .

MM (grabbing his arm, in a plaintive whisper): Benny . . .

Conte exits and there is a slow fade-out on the rejected, helpless girl.

The End

—The director yelled "cut" and it was over; the valuable reel of film on its way to the processing lab. Marilyn waited. In Fox's executive screening room reaction to the Marilyn Monroe Screen Test was positive and on December 10th, 1950 she was signed to her long-term star-making pact with the studio.

Marilyn Monroe is known to have made one more sound test at 20th Century-Fox. It was on June 14th, 1951 that Marilyn joined actor Robert Wagner to work before the test cameras in a "love scene"—one in which stills reveal her back to the camera, his face towards it, suggesting the probability that Wagner was the main focus of the test, and that Monroe was merely assisting in the endeavor. It should be noted that Robert Wagner has publicly indicated that this was Monroe's pre-contract Fox test, but clearly he is in error.

As films featuring Monroe began to reach theaters, the chemistry crystallized and the moviegoing public began to literally flood the Fan Mail Department at Fox with hundreds, and then thousands of cards and letters addressed to "MARILYN MONROE." It wasn't long before she became the most popular star in Hollywood, and eventually the entire world. On the August, 1962 weekend of her death, Marilyn's own comments on the origins of her incredible cinema success were then current in *Life* magazine: "I want to say that the people—if I am a star—the people made me a star—no studio, no person, but the people did." And the rest, as has oft been said, is history.

The Screen Testing of Kim Novak

James Robert Haspiel

Originally appeared in vol. 2, no. 1 (September/October 1977)

So much of Kim Novak's extraordinary youthful beauty was captured on celluloid during the peak years of her movie stardom that from time to time, mostly
through the generosity of television revivals, when one chances upon a replay
of one of her old starring vehicles, one can be instantly caught up in a nostalgic
visit back some two decades—so much a part of the movie media of her heyday
was she. In fact, Kim Novak was a superstar, and this is a glimpse at her earliest
encounters with the motion picture camera.

In the beginning she was called Marilyn—literally. Marilyn Pauline Novak
was born on February 13, 1933, in Chicago, Illinois. Aspirations towards show
business exhibited themselves early: Marilyn Novak made her debut before the
public at the age of 12, appearing fleetingly on a local radio program series,
Calling All Girls. In this medium Marilyn's best feature, her youthful, healthy
beauty, was hidden from view. On the other hand, it was to be the single public
forum in which the actual real voice of Hollywood's future sex symbol, however
immature, was ever to be heard. By the time Hollywood's experts had finished
remolding her later on there would be little to be found—other than in her
non-public early screen tests—of Novak's own voice, destined to be altered to a
sexy, husky tone.

Novak recalls her route to Hollywood: "When I finished junior college,
three other girls and I got the job of touring as demonstrators for Thor electrical appliances. When the tour ended in San Francisco, Peggy Dahl and I had
our train tickets re-routed to Los Angeles, and Peggy's mother hurried out from
Chicago to be with us for three weeks of vacationing. Peggy and her mother
visited M-G-M. They had a letter of introduction and were up in the clouds.
They described everything they'd seen. I didn't feel left out because I've never
been a watcher."

Marilyn Novak's tour had consumed the summer of 1953. Now she was in Hollywood. She made the rounds, winding up at the film factory located on Gower Street. It was an agent, Louis Schurr, who introduced her to the "make-or-break" man at Columbia Pictures, casting director Max Arnow. Arnow's secretary suggested that Novak take up residence at the YWCA's Studio Club, an inexpensive rooming house for young movie-struck hopefuls.

Somewhere in the archives of Columbia Pictures is Marilyn Novak's original screen test. On the night Max Arnow telephoned to advise Novak that she had an appointment to be tested, she was among 93 yet unknown starlets-in-waiting registered at the YWCA haven. "I knew how important it was to the girls around the Club when they were screen-testing for a special part, but I didn't think of myself in that position. I thought it was like when you were a model— you know, drop around, leave some photographs, and 'We'll let you know if we can use you some day.' I wasn't screen-testing for a part. I was screen-testing for—well, nothing. I was two hours late that day! I had no notion of how many people were involved. When I recognized what I'd done, I was in despair."

As Hollywood screen tests of that period went, Marilyn Novak's dialogue test was an elaborate one, a two-parter. First—with the help of Columbia's promising new male screen hope, Robert Francis—she filmed a scene from F. Hugh Herbert's *The Moon Is Blue.* "Bob Francis worked with me . . . reading the off-stage lines." Francis attempted to reassure a faltering Novak: "Good lines make good actresses. You can't miss." Novak recalls, "It was over my head. I was supposed to read a scene that Barbara Bel Geddes had made famous on Broadway, and I knew I wasn't her. I didn't know who I was, or what to do, and I was just terrible. If Bob hadn't carried me through, I never would have finished. I just wanted to hide somewhere. The untold truth is that if I'd had only that test I'd have gotten no place. I didn't register well in it because I was attempting to act for the first time, and I was miserably self-conscious." In an effort to determine Novak's viability as a total screen entity, she next worked solo performing a two-minute monologue in a scene from Benn Levy's *The Devil Passes* (originally presented on Broadway in 1932). For the Levy excerpt it's been said that Novak wore a notable screen costume borrowed from the studio's wardrobe department: an alluring sequined gown worn previously by the Love Goddess herself, Rita Hayworth, in 1952's *Affair in Trinidad.* Novak recalled the second test: "It required an earthy girl who stood before a fireplace and told what she really wanted from life. What she said rang a bell within me. I agreed with her, so I was practically myself." Guiding Novak's 1954 pitch for movie stardom was a then relatively new director, Richard Quine. Within a year's time of these back-to-back tests Marilyn would become "Kim"—and actor Robert Francis' life would end abruptly in a tragic plane crash. Before the decade's end director Quine would find himself almost wed to Miss Novak, as well as guiding her through no less than four more "Leading Lady" cinema roles.

Back at the Studio Club, Novak waited for word from the executive office on Gower Street. Columbia chief Harry Cohn viewed the processed Marilyn Novak Screen Test footage and argued, "She can't act," to which Max Arnow responded, "She'll never be able to act, but that doesn't matter. She's got star quality." Producer Jerry Wald's keen eye for celluloid talent was impressed from a different angle—he told Cohn, "Don't listen; just look." And so it was that Marilyn Novak was signed to a contract at Columbia Pictures, with boss Cohn commanding an all-out effort at the studio to "Make her a Star!"

Novak reflects: "I was just one of those thousands and thousands of kids who come out to Hollywood. You still see those kids, don't you? In the Greyhound bus station and working the restaurants, everywhere. Nobody's told them it doesn't happen that way anymore. It *did* happen to me, but I had no control over that. Gosh, it seems so long ago. I haven't been back to Columbia for a long time."

1954's Marilyn Novak was quickly swallowed up by Columbia's elaborate manufacture-a-movie-star machine. Studio experts went to work to create a "new" Novak. Henceforth her starlet days were virtually consumed with makeup sessions, voice coaching ("My voice wasn't right. I talked without proper breath control, needed clearer tones. I had to become conscious of this, and do something about it"), acting instruction, and publicity orientation. As quickly as they could be processed, visual test films of the enhanced Novak were screened for boss Cohn. Within the confines of the studio Novak continued to develop her celluloid personality in filmed scenes never intended for public viewing. "The truth is I had three months of intensive coaching before I was terrified with the news that I was to be tested for Fred MacMurray's picture *The Killer Wore a Badge*. I had to test four different times, with four different directors, for my first role. I knew experienced actresses were being considered, that all the departments at the studio and the New York office, too, had to be satisfied." She added, "They made me cast as a star, and I didn't know enough to play an extra." While it was Marilyn Novak who reported daily to the set of the Fred MacMurray starrer, it would be "Kim Novak" who'd receive screen credit in the finished film, itself retitled *Pushover*.

Reviewing Kim Novak's official Columbia Pictures debut in *Pushover* (1954), *Variety*'s critic commented: "Miss Novak, who reportedly is being groomed as a possible rival of Marilyn Monroe, shows possibilities in that direction." In quick succession Kim Novak turned up on neighborhood movie screens in 1954's *Phffft*, and in 1955's *Five Against the House*.

With the moviegoing public showing its obvious appreciation of Columbia's new blonde at the box office, it was decided that she should be considered for the stellar role of Madge Owens in the studio's filmization of William Inge's Broadway success, *Picnic.* Harboring a disquieting doubt that Novak—who was quite literally forced on him by studio chief Cohn—was in any way a viable choice to essay the pivotal role of Madge, director Joshua Logan opted for Kim to take a test. "I'd had to test for each previous part at least twice. I tested six separate times for *Picnic* before they were sure I qualified. Josh Logan didn't want any Hollywood actress in his cast full of Broadway veterans." Columbia's Aldo Ray was elected to appear opposite Kim in one of the *Picnic* tests, an emotional love scene. It's been said Logan instructed Ray to "Get some emotion from her any way you can, short of rape." Cohn screened the Novak-Ray sequence for Logan, who reluctantly acquiesced. "After he saw my test run off, he said I might get by on my looks, but that up against true professionals looks aren't enough. I know that only too well!" The subsequent filming of *Picnic*—in which Novak played her love scenes opposite William Holden—was not without difficulty for director and star. Nonetheless, in later years Logan would speak kindly of Kim, and of her thespic qualities.

Kim recollects: "It was push push push back there. I wasn't ready. It's terrible to get so big when you're not ready." During the initial flush of her movie fame Novak commented: "Only a couple of years ago I was lying in my bed, crying my eyes out because of my first screen test. And now look what's happened. I call an old girlfriend on the phone, and do I say, 'This is Kim Novak,' or do I say, 'This is Marilyn Novak'? If I say Kim I'm putting on airs like a movie star, and if I say Marilyn then I'm trying to be overly modest, because they know me now as Kim, and talk about me that way."

Harry Cohn's determined all-out effort to raise Kim Novak to a position of super-stardom crystallized in December, 1956 when *Boxoffice* named her the #1 star in the U.S. In addition to the aforementioned *Picnic,* Novak was currently on view in two high-power films, *The Man with the Golden Arm* and *The Eddy Duchin Story.* Taking his own overview of Kim's popularity with the moviegoing public, Cohn—the power behind her impermanent throne—opined: "The success of Novak is due to great pictures. Any girl who gets six pictures like Novak got has got to be a star." He added, "We've got twelve to fifteen million dollars invested in her." What nobody realized that Christmas, 1956 was that Kim's career in motion pictures had, in fact, just peaked.

Kim Novak's cinema permanence was unsure from the very beginning. She had emerged into the public's conscious on the very heels of Marilyn Monroe's incredible initial impact. Given the Hollywood blondes of Kim's day, Novak seemed more like some unplaceable commodity inhabiting a space off-center of that atmosphere so completely dominated by Monroe, so utterly grounded by the ersatz version, Jayne Mansfield. Kim would continue to make films over the next decade, but at a pace reflective of her declining stardom. In 1966 columnist Ed

Sullivan wrote about Novak's life in the Big Sur region of California, an area to which she had retreated: "She writes song lyrics, paints, writes poetry, and sculpts in driftwood." Kim herself offered: "At this stage of my life, I'm not looking for anything—if it happens, I'm receptive."

With the kind of fame that had spawned *Time* and *Life* magazine cover stories now long behind her, Novak, no longer in the mainstream of the media, seems most responsible for her status as "former" film star. Some years ago, weary of the demands of her profession and of her disappearing public, Kim discussed her affection for life of another quality: "I believe in sea gulls and my horse and my goat who butts those tourists for me. A movie set isn't me. And it never was. I'm a loner. *I have to be.* See, my *real* first name was Marilyn. Don't think I haven't thought about *that.* "She added, ". . . all my animals. I mean they love *me.* 'Kim Novak'—who's that to my horse? Nobody."

The Search for John Barrymore

THE QUEST IS ELUSIVE FOR THE "LOST" BARRYMORE FILMS

Spencer Berger

Originally appeared in vol. 5, no. 6 (November/December 1981)

The days of the high, wide, and handsome Barrymore style are gone, but those who saw the family on stage and screen are the richer in memories. There was Lionel, the great character actor, Ethel of rare beauty and charm, and John, excelling in the widest range of roles. Much as I relished Lionel and Ethel, never have I regretted becoming a John Barrymore addict at age eleven, after watching his 1928 silent, *The Tempest.*

John could play the screen lover or the crazed fiend with equal facility and persuasion—and I will here limit this discussion to his films (his stage work is another long and distinguished story)—and long before the screen found a voice, John's silent films proved his powerful versatility. He could swash and buckle with the best of them as *Don Juan* (1926) and *The Beloved Rogue* (1927) attest; he could make you cringe in fright with his *Dr. Jekyll and Mr. Hyde* (1920); or he could charm you with his wit and elegance in *Beau Brummel* (1924). As he grew older in the 1930s and 1940s, much controversy concerning his alcohol problems and his personal restlessness often threatened to overwhelm his qualities as an actor. Yet, the luster of his name has survived, and we now identify his work as the product of a sharp and theatrically flamboyant personality.

Where does his film legacy stand today? Indeed, it is difficult to place his movie career in a neat perspective. There are, of course, availability problems. The nitrate stock on which Barrymore's films were recorded has, in many cases, deteriorated into highly combustible red dust. Some films seem to have vanished without a trace. Others fell victim to the deliberate destruction of prints for silver salvage. Yet, maybe all is not lost, as long as even a single print or negative can be located. A special problem in the case of Barrymore's first sound films, moreover, is the difficulty in locating the sound discs, as we shall see presently.

23

The Barrymore screen legacy has attracted especially ardent enthusiasts, such as the late John Griggs, an actor who had become enamored of film while playing piano in a silent movie theater. He was able to track down some of the films he had accompanied (including *The Tempest*) and made copies available to other collectors. His special Barrymore films were *Vagabonding on the Pacific* (a personal record of the actor's voyage through Mexican waters) and a reel of deletions from the complete *Beau Brummel*. All the material Griggs gathered became the foundation of the Yale University Film Collection.

The other Barrymore enthusiast is James Card, whose larger holdings launched the motion picture archive at George Eastman House in Rochester, New York, which film scholar William K. Everson considers "quite possibly the best anywhere in the world." Recently retired, Card now cheerfully concedes that the Eastman catalog reflects his partiality for Barrymore.

So, what is missing from the Barrymore legacy? In 1952, when I prepared the first John Barrymore filmography for *Films in Review*, every reference available cited the 1914 Famous Players production of *An American Citizen* as Barrymore's debut. However, in 1969, George Pratt of Eastman House discovered trade paper reviews of three 1912 Lubin Company productions, listing "Jack Barrymore" in supporting roles. Jack, of course, was the Barrymore family's nickname for John. Because of the total lack of hard evidence—films, photographs, publicity—to support that this "Jack" and John were one and the same, I was slow to accept this presumption.

Some theatrical producers considered movie appearances so demeaning that they ordered their leading players to abstain. Since Barrymore was a rather well-established stage actor by 1912, he could have felt safe moonlighting at the Lubin studio in Philadelphia. The fact that his dossier fails to mention a Lubin interlude could be attributed to the fact that Famous Players (the larger and more prestigious firm that he joined in 1914) had reason to expunge all references to his association with the likes of Lubin. No Lubin film with "Jack Barrymore" is known to survive, so it is probable that the negatives of the 1912 productions were destroyed when the company's vaults exploded and burned in 1914.

American Film Institute archivist Audrey E. Kupferberg still holds out hope of solving the mystery of the Lubin prints, as do researchers Linda Kowell and Joseph P. Eckhart, who are reconstructing the Lubin story through company scrapbooks and oral histories they are taking from surviving employees. Thus far, they have found two people who report that they observed Barrymore in the Lubin studio at Indiana Avenue and 20th Street in Philadelphia, although—tantalizing enough—they are not certain whether this "real" Barrymore was there to act or to visit friends. Additionally, after weighing the pros and cons of historians Pratt and Everson, there is more reason than not to begin Barrymore's filmography with the Lubin films.

Here, based on reviews, is a synopsis of these 1912 Lubin films. Their comic plots should be regarded as typical of their time.

Dream of a Motion Picture Director. After reading a scenario to his cast, the director dreams "a startling melodrama," wherein the villain ["Barrymore"] pursues the heroine up and down fire escapes until she jumps into the hero's arms.

The Widow Casey's Return. A newsboy picks up a black sash dropped by a widow and hangs it on her front doorknob with a note saying she has died. A tramp enters her empty home and falls asleep under a bedspread. Mourners gather and mistake him for the widow, until she returns; whereupon she must decide between two suitors [one of which is "Barrymore"].

A Prize Package. A man [the "Barrymore" role is unspecified] finds a marriage proposal in a package of cigarettes and arranges to meet the factory girl who wrote it. After adventures in mistaken identity, all ends well.

Fortunately, Adolph Zukor—who would produce Barrymore's first officially recognized films—realized that American movies had to expand to feature-length format in order to gain more prestige. Working with Daniel Frohman, who represented the American legitimate theatrical establishment, he formed the Famous Players Company in 1912. Together, they distributed the French four-reeler, *Queen Elizabeth,* which starred the international superstar, Sarah Bernhardt. The success of this venture encouraged Zukor and Frohman to film more "Famous Players in Famous Plays."

Barrymore joined Famous Players in 1914 and brought his stage experience and stardom to ten silent farces (1914–1919). His persona was a happy blend of Fairbanks exuberance, Chaplin pantomime, and his own sophisticated charm. The quality of the films were several notches above most other contemporary comedies and attracted large audiences.

In 1915 the Famous Players Studio—atop an old armory—was destroyed by fire. Miraculously, a safe containing the negatives of 17 films that were unreleased and uninsurable (because of nitrate), was preserved. Only one of the films was a Barrymore, quite probably *Nearly a King.*

Today, of the ten Barrymore farces, only the fifth in the series survives: *The Incorrigible Dukane* (1915). There are choppy prints at the British National Archives and Eastman House, and according to film scholar Kevin Brownlow, a "beauty" has surfaced in London. Everson, during authorized visits to the Paramount vaults, has examined each existing print and found none of the missing Barrymores. Nor are any listed on the inventory of surviving negatives. Here, then is a peek at the action in the nine missing farces:

An American Citizen (1914). Barrymore jeopardizes his citizenship by accepting an inheritance on the condition that he marry a Britisher.

The Man from Mexico (1914). Playboy Barrymore tries to palm off a 30-day jail
   sentence as a trip to Mexico.

Are You a Mason? (1915). Bogus lodge meetings give Barrymore an excuse for
   other nocturnal activities.

The Dictator (1915). Wall Streeter Barrymore becomes a South American dictator.

Nearly a King (1916). In a variation on *The Prisoner of Zenda* Barrymore plays
   both a jobless actor and the Prince of Bulwana.

The Lost Bridegroom (1916). Thugs hit Barrymore on the head and induce him
   to rob his fiancee's home.

The Red Widow (1916). Manufacturer Barrymore goes to Russia and "gets mixed
   up with a prima donna and a nest of Nihilists."

On the Quiet (1918). Yale student Barrymore, given to "laugh-provoking
   pranks," wishes to marry a girl, even though she would lose a large inheritance as a result.

Here Comes the Bride (1919). Attorney Barrymore loves the daughter of a
   "wealthy corn magnate" and allows the use of his name in "obtaining settlement of a will."

One film Barrymore made for another company at this time was *Raffles, the
Amateur Cracksman* (1918). It was produced by Weber Photodrama and released
by Hiller & Wilk and provided my first taste of film research, as well as my first
contact with James Card. In 1940 one of the few available prints of *Raffles* appeared at a small New York theater. The manager was willing to sell it after the
run, but I declined the purchase because the quality and condition of the print
was atrocious. I regretted that decision for the next nine years, during which I
repeatedly tried to buy the print from a rental library. At last the print was pronounced unprojectable and made available at a junk price of $5. I phoned James
Card, who offered to professionally diagnose my print. Despite gaping sprocket
holes, scratches galore, mixed and missing sequences, Kodak began the tedious
task of making hand-crafted copies. Midway through the job, Card wrote me:
"What a wonderful souvenir of Barrymore, with all those close-ups! Ironically,
Raffles was made not long after *Intolerance*, which had Griffith apostles swoon-
ing over each close-up as though they were Rosetta stones." Epilogue: A more
complete print—in better condition—surfaced shortly thereafter.

After filming *Raffles*, Barrymore returned to Famous Players for his last two
silent farces (1918–1919). Then, following the trend of his recent stage work, he
concluded his six-year association with Famous Players with two serious screen
dramas. The first is still missing, but the second is safe. The first, *Test of Honor*
(1919), which was Barrymore's last film at the 56th Street studio, tells of a man
who will not reveal that a lie by the woman he loves has caused his conviction for
her husband's death. Highly praised, it was but a harbinger of *Dr. Jekyll and Mr.*

Hyde (1920), which was produced at the Amsterdam Opera House in Manhattan only months before the new studio at Astoria opened. It was his first screen triumph. This film survives.

Still missing today, but patently a let-down after *Dr. Jekyll and Mr. Hyde*, was First National's *The Lotus Eater* (1921). It was filmed on an island off the Florida coast and at the Biograph Studio in the Bronx. It is the story of a millionaire who leaves his wife and heads for China in a balloon. The balloon falls on an island where modern garb is banned (stills show Barrymore in a Greek tunic). Although he finds an attractive girl there (Colleen Moore), he returns to New York. However, before the fade-out, he is back on the island with her.

Flash forward to 1969, when a fellow Barrymore enthusiast—newscaster John Salisbury of Portland, Oregon—wrote me that he'd met a man who claimed to have a print of *The Lotus Eater* and would let him copy it. After many broken dates, Salisbury handed me the torch. The story got even better after I phoned the man who claimed to have the print. It turns out he had not one but *three* prints, as well as some of Barrymore's home movies and letters. He promised to send me full information and a price for the lot. Then, for whatever reason, he suddenly became incommunicado. Next, I read in *Classic Images* that Colleen Moore was looking for a copy of *The Lotus Eater*. The editor forwarded my letter about the print being in Portland to Moore. I merely wanted to find out if she was having better luck locating the print, but apparently she read no further, because she replied: "I'm so excited over your news that if this letter wobbles all over the page, it is understandable!" I regretted the confusion, particularly since she had written in her book, *Silent Star*, that she was "overwhelmed at playing opposite the great Barrymore . . . without doubt the handsomest man I had ever seen."

The quest continued. After pursuing a lead in San Francisco, William Everson recently told me: "I've talked with several people who say they know others who say they've seen *The Lotus Eater*, but the print seems to be guarded by a fanatic." Whither, next? This is typical of the frustrations we face in looking for lost films.

In 1922 Barrymore's 18th and last pre-Hollywood picture, *Sherlock Holmes*, was filmed on location in London and Switzerland, with the interiors filmed in rented space at the Tilford Studio on West 44th Street in New York. This Goldwyn Company release was disappointing to some. Was Barrymore perhaps too detached and preoccupied with his forthcoming *Hamlet* on the stage? Card wrote me in 1954 that the negative of this missing film, lent by Loews, would soon be printed and when was I coming to Rochester to see it? But I had difficulty with the titles, because they'd been cut to a single frame to reduce length and storage cost. Worse, the print was horrendously (and inexplicably) jumbled in sequence.

I had neither time nor expertise to try to make sense of the jumbled 389 shots. Fortunately, this challenge intrigued Kevin Brownlow (whose restoration monument is surely Abel Gance's *Napoleon*). His restoration of *Sherlock Holmes*—unavoidably shy a reel or two—premiered at Eastman House in July 1974. Earlier, in his London flat, he had shown me the work in progress—still with only "flash" titles, but enlivened by his animated reading, commentary, and self-produced sound effects! Wish I had made a tape of that!

In 1920 Barrymore was exhausted after filming *Dr. Jekyll and Mr. Hyde* in the mornings, rehearsing *Richard III* in the afternoons, and appearing evenings on stage with brother Lionel in *The Jest*. Following his second triumph in Shakespeare—as Hamlet in this country and then as the first American to play the part in London (where James Agate of the *Times* wrote that he was "nearer to Shakespeare's whole creation than any other I have seen")—he settled in Hollywood to concentrate on motion pictures.

His third Hollywood film, *Don Juan* (1926), is artistically memorable for his bravura portrayal of the death of the Don's father (also played by Barrymore) and for a splendidly cinematic duel, climaxed by the star's flying leap down a marble staircase to land atop his adversary (Montague Love). Historically, however, *Don Juan* is best known as the first silent feature to be successfully fitted with synchronized music and sound effects. Vitaphone, Warners' sound-on-disc system used on *Don Juan*, was tolerated for a time because, under ideal circumstances, quality was a bit better than the competitive sound-on-film system. It was reassuring that projector and turntable speeds were interlocked and that, when film broke, lost frames were replaced by the same number of opaque frames to keep picture and sound in synch. But audiences were unhappy when synchronization went askew if the projectionist did not count lost frames correctly—and they howled if he started the wrong disc. Adding to the headaches of scratched, chipped, cracked, and lost discs, it's small wonder that Warners shifted to sound-on-film in mid-1930.

Sometimes the sound for an earlier production was transferred from disc to film. Fortunately, an early such transfer was the all-star revue, *Show of Shows* (1929), in which, sandwiched between radio star Ted Lewis and Rin Tin Tin, Barrymore first spoke from the screen. Originally in two-color Technicolor (but surviving now only in black-and-white), his *Richard III* portrayal is a stunning documentation of his theater performance of 1920, when he gave Shakespeare new life by seeming to think out words rather than simply declaim them.

Unfortunately, however, Warners did not go back and put the sound for Barrymore's first two talking features on film. Why they didn't transfer *General Crack* (1929) is a puzzle because it was well reviewed and popular. Barrymore has a dual role—the elderly father and the dashing soldier-of-fortune who becomes a military leader for Leopold II of Austria. The court sequence was his second and last appearance in color. Barrymore's sketches and notes in his copy of the source novel indicate his personal involvement: "All these lines should be acrid and amusing"—"Music—vital, magnificent speech—a stunt!" But the headline for a *Crack* advertisement—"John Barrymore—Yesterday a speech-less shadow—Today a vivid living person thanks to Vitaphone!"—is presently a mockery. Ironically, there was a silent version (prepared for theaters not yet wired for sound) which is in the Czech Archives and the Museum of Modern Art (although still with Czech titles).

Barrymore's second talking feature, *The Man from Blankley's* (1930), was a complete change of pace and marks his first Hollywood appearance in both comedy and modern dress. Initially a sketch in *Punch*, and later a play, this charming spoof concerns one Lord Strathpeffer who, a trifle tipsy, blunders into the wrong dinner party and is mistaken for an extra guest hired to make 14. Much of the public did not know what to make of the mouldy gathering drawn from Dickens—with names like Mr. Pofley, Mrs. Ditchwater, Mr. Gilwattle, Miss Bugle, et al. And some critical reaction was also shortsighted, such as *Photoplay's* review: "It's John's little joke, and we refuse to take it seriously." But, with a coterie of admirers for over half a century, *The Man from Blankley's* remains the most important of Barrymore's missing films.

As we have seen with *General Crack* and *The Man from Blankley's*, the problem with missing sound discs began in 1930. Now, let's cut to 1956, when, for 21 million dollars, Warners turned over to Dominant (an affiliate of United Artists) the television rights to its pre-1949 features and shorts. For a time, Dominant sold life-of-the-print leases to collectors. I was told they had neither picture nor sound for *General Crack* (which proved to be correct), and there were no discs for *The Man from Blankley's* (also correct), but that visuals were available (incorrect). Audrey Kupferberg tells me that this confusion arose because—regarding the questionable legal status of the relatively few titles still on discs—both companies agreed to ignore them. This is a belated confirmation that United Artists never got from Warners any part of either *Crack* or *Blankley's*.

But in 1979, when a posthumous tribute to Jack Warner was planned, it was still believed that Dominant had the film visuals for *Blankley's* and that only the sound discs were missing. I therefore suggested to author Max Wilk that the matching discs be included as part of the search of the Warner vaults. Presto!—all eight had been languishing in a little-used catch-all, together with the eleven discs for *Crack!* Are the picture elements for both in another dark corner in Burbank?

The concept of tailoring movies to a star held sway during Barrymore's years before the camera. Countless magic moments were generated by the personalities who were able to play themselves. Drawing upon the best of both 19th and 20th century stage acting techniques, Barrymore ranged at will from slapstick comedy to classic drama, from dazzling theatrical bravura to a more naturalistic and intimate style. Thus, we recall Garbo's tribute when, in *Grand Hotel* (1932), she kissed him impulsively and broke her silence, saying, "You have no idea what it means to me to play opposite so perfect an artist."

So what is considered his finest work? David O. Selznick maintained, long after the commercial life of his production *A Bill of Divorcement* (1932) was over, that in it, Barrymore gave "the greatest all-time performance on any motion picture screen." Wisely, I think, William K. Everson takes a broader view in his definitive *American Silent Film*: "John Barrymore was a superb and subtle actor, possessed of a magnificent voice, and some of his finest work is to be found in the sound films of the early thirties. But had he never made a sound film, his genius would have been accurately recorded by the silent film."

I think it is impossible to name Barrymore's single best performance; even a "ten best" list is arbitrary and confining. Notwithstanding, here as a centennial salute—Barrymore was born in 1882—are my nominations—two silent and eight talking films—for Barrymore's top ten performances: *Dr. Jekyll and Mr. Hyde* (1920): Split personality illumined; *The Beloved Rogue* (1927): Rollicking François Villon; *Show of Shows* (1929): First Shakespeare spoken on film; *The Man from Blankley's* (1930): Masterful farce; *Svengali* (1931): Chilling, disturbing Du Maurier; *A Bill of Divorcement* (1932): Poignant drama; *Topaze* (1933): Warm, gentle whimsy; *Reunion in Vienna* (1933): Ardent, arrogant royal lover; *Counsellor-at-Law* (1933): Driven, ghetto-born lawyer; *20th Century* (1934): Pioneer screwball comedy.

Yes, John Barrymore's legacy is a gallery of full-length portraits that is both unique in its variety and supreme in artistry.

Innocence Protected

WILL ROGERS AND
STEAMBOAT 'ROUND THE BEND

Peter C. Rollins

Originally appeared in vol. 3, no. 5 (May/June 1979)

Prior to his untimely death by plane crash at Point Barrow, Alaska, on August 15, 1935, Will Rogers had become one of the most important molders of opinion in America. During the last stage of his Hollywood career, he had become the film industry's best paid and most popular male movie attraction at $225,000 per film. His movie persona had undergone several changes since he first stepped before the cameras to make *Laughing Bill Hyde* (1918). From cowboy image he went to that of a rural clown called "Jubilo," who in several pictures loafed through society getting himself into trouble and avoiding work whenever possible. From 1929 to 1932, in films like *Going to Congress, Handy Andy,* and *They Had to See Paris,* he changed to an "innocent abroad" tilting at urban corruption and hypocrisy.

The final Rogers image came with the "Uncle Will" image of films like *David Harum, State Fair,* and *Steamboat 'Round the Bend.* He is no longer cowboy, clown, satirist, or innocent abroad; he is an inland hero spreading salty wisdom and common sense among his rural neighbors. "Uncle Will" was more than just a small town inhabitant. He had special insights into the human heart. Gone is the big city satire of earlier films; in its place are the gentle homilies of provincial life; a provincial life, that is, that became emblematic of an America striving to insulate itself from contemporary strains and pressures.

Plot and Theme

Directed by John Ford, *Steamboat* drops Uncle Will into a characteristic *fin de siècle* setting: the main title is followed by a montage showing a paddle wheeler steaming down the Mississippi; the river is broad and the banks are lined with timber. Just in case viewers might be inattentive to details of rustic *mise èn scene*, descriptive titles clearly identify that we are back in Homeville: "Time: 1890s . . . Place: The Mississippi Valley."

At the bow of the *Pride of Paducah*, we listen to an orotund evangelist (Burton Churchill) who claims to be "The New Moses." By means of a dissolve (indicating a short passage of time), we move slightly aft where we find "Doctor" John Pearly (Will Rogers) selling patent medicine of high alcoholic content. Contrasts could not be more extreme: The New Moses preaches against Demon Rum and Sloth; Doctor John promises that his Pocahontas remedy will exempt consumers from work, "especially at plowing time." Viewers should expect that all characters in this nostalgic tale will be equally eccentric and that the action will contain similar implausibilities.

After selling his entire stock, "Doc" Pearly climbs to the bridge of the ship to talk with Captain Eli (Irvin Cobb), master of the *Pride of Paducah*. In a series of unscripted lines, the two aging humorists introduce the action. Captain Eli learns that Dr. John has purchased "an old mud scow" which he plans to name the *Claremore Queen*.[1] When Captain Eli claims that he will win the annual steamboat race to Baton Rouge, Dr. John takes up the challenge: a bet is made, winner take all. Captain Eli then drops Dr. John and his engineer, Efe (Francis Ford, brother of the director), at a jetty. A short distance away is the deserted *Claremore Queen*, a backwheeler in considerable disrepair.

Plot complications are soon introduced. After sundown, Duke (John McGuire) comes aboard secretively, bringing with him a "swamp girl" named Fleety Belle (Anne Shirley). Doc is dismayed to learn that Duke has recently killed a man while fighting for the "honor" of this ragamuffin. When Doc hears that the homicide was in self-defense, he counsels Duke to surrender in order to clear himself. Duke follows this sensible advice, but an ill-tempered judge condemns the young man to be hanged. Duke's only hope is that Uncle John will find the New Moses, sole witness to the fight, before the scheduled hanging. The law's delays and the challenge of the elements provide Uncle Will with a number of opportunities to work his magical powers.

In these late films of Will Rogers, plot complications are never as important as atmosphere. Early in the film, Duke finds that even the jails of Homeville are hospitable. When Uncle John and Duke present themselves to Sheriff Jetters (Eugene Pallette), they are received as friends seeking lodging. The agent of law and order throws Duke the keys, inviting his "guest" to select any jail cell that looks comfortable. During Duke's incarceration, the prison permits other domestic functions expected in Homeville: Duke and Fleety Belle conduct a lovers' tryst while a chorus of Black prisoners serenade them with a mellow rendering of "There's No Place Like Home." Prior to Duke's departure for execution at Baton Rouge, the sheriff and his family do their best to provide the young lovers with a proper wedding. That the sheriff's sermon is ungrammatical and unnecessarily emphatic about the phrase "'til death do us part," that his daughter can only play "Listen to the Mockingbird" as a processional, only contributes to the quaint atmosphere. Affirmation of authority so pervades the mood of this segment that Duke refuses to escape when Fleety Belle plucks a rifle from the sheriff's hands.

Uncle Will's attempts to find the New Moses become more desperate as Duke's execution approaches. When the *Claremore Queen* heads towards Baton Rouge, Fleety Belle and Uncle John become embroiled in the annual steamboat race. Fortunately, the *Claremore Queen* happens to pass a landing where the New Moses is declaiming against Booze. Drawing on his cowboy skills, the favorite son of Claremore lassos the prophet and drags him aboard. The evening watch also finds use for the improvised lasso: in an effort to conserve fuel, Uncle John ropes a capstan on the stern of the *Pride of Paducah*, with a tow line firmly affixed to the bow of the *Claremore Queen*, Uncle John is able to bank his fires. Not until the next morning does Captain Eli discover ("Holy jumpin' catfish") that he has been pulling a competitor all night.

During the closing miles of the race, the *Claremore Queen* runs so low on fuel that the New Moses proclaims: "Nothing will save us now but the power of prayer." Recapitulating contrasts of the opening scene, we discover that not prayer, but the potent power of Pocahontas will bring victory over the *Pride of Paducah*. Bottles of Doctor John's long-forgotten patent medicine are cast into the flames: humorously, flashes from the wonder-working elixir are shown spurting from the twin smokestacks of the vessel, propelling the *Queen* at unwonted speed. Throughout the excitement, Stepin Fetchit expostulates while others stoke the fires which will bring victory. A concluding reaction shot of Captain Eli shows us that he has been completely overwhelmed by this *deus ex machina*.

Although completely devoid of verisimilitude, this conclusion has the virtue of tying up a number of loose plot elements: Duke is exonerated moments before his scheduled execution; Stepin Fetchit gets the victory cup; most importantly, boy gets girl. In the final shots of *Steamboat 'Round the Bend*, Uncle John lounges on a "back porch" aft of the *Claremore Queen*'s pilot house, smoking one of Captain Eli's favorite cigars. Our avuncular protector deserves his rest: he has resolved the discord around him; life in Homeville will return to its normal placidity.

Acting

Like Will Rogers, Irvin S. Cobb probably assumed that viewers would bring a knowledge of his Kentucky regional style to a viewing of *Steamboat 'Round the*

Bend. It would have been difficult for a contemporary to be ignorant of Cobb: His articles were syndicated in the daily press and scores of his stories had found their way into the pages of the *Saturday Evening Post* and other magazines. Will Rogers' fans would have seen *Judge Priest* (1934), a film which had been adapted from a story by Cobb.[2] Whatever the reasons, a marvelous anecdote conveys the insouciance of the two major actors as they approached the shooting of *Steamboat.* Here is Cobbs's memory of the first meeting between the two regional writers and their young director, John Ford:

> So we went out to make *Steamboat 'Round the Bend.* We had a grand director, John Ford, an emotional Maine Yankee-Irishman, one of the authentic geniuses of the movies. The first morning of "shooting," Will and I were to have a scene together.
>
> "Do either of you two gentlemen by any chance happen to have the faintest idea of what this story is about?" inquired Ford, with his gentle, Celtic sarcasm which can be so biting.
>
> "I don't for one," confessed Rogers, and grinned sheepishly. "Something about a river, ain't it? Well, I was raised at Claremore, Oklahoma, where we don't have any rivers to speak of, so you might say I'm a stranger here, myself."
>
> "I thought so," murmured Ford, who had directed Rogers before. "And I don't suppose, Mr. Rogers, you've gone so far as to glance at the script?"
>
> "Been too busy ropin' calves," admitted Rogers. "Tell you what, John, you sort of generally break the news to us what this sequence is about and I'll think up a line for Cobb to speak and then Cobb'll think up a line for me to speak and that way there won't be no ill feelins or heart burnins and the feller that kin remember after it's all over what the plot was about—if there is any plot by then—gets first prize, which will be a kiss on the forehead from Mister John Ford."
>
> As heaven is my judge, that is how we did the scene, with Ford sitting by, as solemn as a hoot owl.[3]

Director John Ford had good reasons for being so indulgent: What these two regional figures said was not so important, as what, in their accents and colloquialisms, they represented. Cobb and Rogers were simply more important as relics of a bygone era than as actors playing roles. For this reason, the script was designed to be little more than a framework within which these regional humorists could be seen and heard. Fox Pictures was alert to the monetary rewards for such hokum. The American audience was actively interested in seeing more "family films," and Fox was eager to please. Both the general audience and the critics were in agreement about the appeal of films about "Homeville": "Audiences thanked him for his contribution to clean, family diversion. The more analytical saw him as a social factor and a godsend to a stagnant theater."[4] Thus, there were solid economic reasons for allowing Rogers and Cobb to clown on the set.

During location shooting near Sacramento, California, Rogers and Cobb continued their repartee on one of Rogers' regular Gulf radio broadcasts.[5] Audience expectations as to the characters' "innocence" can be extrapolated from the following dialogue. Rogers and Cobb here portray themselves as men from the heartland who have succeeded in Hollywood without becoming tainted by it:

> Rogers: Do you feel yourself, kind of going Hollywood in any way? You know, we all kind of do. It kind of gets us down there. Do you feel yourself kind of?
>
> Cobb: Well, I find that I am talking to myself, and worse than that, I am answering back. And I have been cutting out paper dolls at odd times.
>
> Rogers: And saying your own *yesses*, Hey?
>
> Cobb: Yes, I'm living in yes-man's land, which is worse than no-man's land was during the war. I haven't worn slacks yet. I'm still sticking to my first wife. I guess I haven't gone Hollywood.
>
> Rogers: Do you find that this censorship that Will Hays has got in on us now, does it kind of interfere with you, kind of cramp your emotions in any way?
>
> Cobb: Well, I noticed as a result of Will Hays' campaign they no longer talk about putting a tax on raw film.[6]

The role of innocent had dual functions: Over the airwaves, Cobb and Rogers posed as innocents abroad in America's most liberated city; in *Steamboat*, John Ford was doing his best to establish them as innocents at home in a simpler, rural past.

The contribution of Stepin Fetchit (Lincoln Theodore Perry) to *Steamboat 'Round the Bend* is difficult to evaluate because it is almost impossible to separate his work as an actor from the deplorable history of racial stereotyping in American film. Peter Noble, for example, accuses Fetchit of helping to perpetuate the "popular myth that the American Negro was a happy, laughing, dancing imbecile, with permanently rolling eyes and widespread, empty grin."[7] In a famous CBS documentary, *Black History: Lost, Stolen, or Strayed?* (1968), Bill Cosby similarly condemned Fetchit: "It is too bad he did it so well. It has been planted on the minds of Americans like the memory of a bad auto accident."[8] Criticism along these lines constitutes the conventional wisdom at this time.

A close study of *Steamboat 'Round the Bend* yields additional information. Fetchit's role is not unlike those of other supporting actors: He is a humorous eccentric. Looking directly at performance rather than role, one student of the

Fetchit-Rogers films has observed that: "To determine the *why* of laughter, one might first examine Fetchit's physical appearance on the screen. His image can be described without reference to his race. His bald head, his tall, thin, and angular body, always garbed in torn clothing, always seeming to be in motion, though Fetchit may be sleeping through his own trial. Fetchit's outward image is one of the clown of any color. When Fetchit does move it is in jerks and bounces. His most frequent movement is to lift one arm to his bald head and scratch in bewilderment. Fetchit's maneuvers put one in mind of a trained pantomimist."[9] Fetchit was thus an actor whose humor was not based solely upon racial characteristics.

Fetchit injects a number of incisive remarks as he helps to remodel Uncle John's wax museum. While preparing new exhibits, Fetchit notes that "Little Eva goes with Uncle Tom; she doesn't belong with Napoleon"; when told to move a statue of General Grant, he remarks that the Northern General's uniform "would fit me." That it is Fetchit who plays "Dixie" for a tribute to General Lee seems to classify him as one of the hucksters of the film rather than as a witless underling. When Uncle John fishes a choking New Moses from the river, Fetchit asks him if he is thirsty. This remark has subtle overtones: To a casual viewer, it appears that Fetchit is merely conforming to the stereotype of Uncle Tom, the fawning menial; the attentive observer will note that Fetchit is actually satirizing Uncle Tomism by exaggerating it. All such lines and ploys were of Fetchit's own invention, not the work of scriptwriters and all comment on Black history and Black aspirations. As a character actor of economic value, Fetchit was given considerable freedom for extemporaneous utterance: his contributions were frequently left unscripted, with a general indication that the Black comedian should invent "Fetchit stuff" appropriate to the scene.[10] Thus, while Fetchit wears the costume of a Black menial, he uses physical and verbal comedy to expand his role beyond the stereotype.[11]

The love match between Duke and Fleety Belle takes up a considerable amount of screen time early in *Steamboat,* but, as the film progresses, we discover that the most significant emotional tie in the story is the filial bond between Uncle John and the "swamp girl." Uncle John is at first scornful of the young girl. Gradually, he discovers that she is "a spunky rascal." The last of Uncle John's doubts are dispelled after a confrontation with her "people" from the swamp. In the wake of this test of character, Uncle John supplies Fleety with a feminine costume in place of her rags, making her a true "Belle." Throughout subsequent attempts to save Duke, Uncle John and the young girl work together as a father-daughter team.

If her function in the film is properly understood, Anne Shirley performed admirably as Fleety Belle. Proponents of women's liberation could easily brand the character as just another clinging vine: She is transformed into womanhood with the help of a man (Uncle John); she seems to require masculine guidance. Another view would stress her function as an *alter ego* for viewers. Like many in the Depression audiences for *Steamboat*, Fleety Belle is poor, an outcast longing to be valued for her inherent worth. An accident of birth may have labeled her as a "swamp girl," but we have the opportunity to learn that she is really a sincere and sensitive young person who needs help.

A close reader of the Depression era and Will Rogers' role in it might venture a few additional speculations. Like the audience, Fleety Belle needs the guidance of a father figure. This protector must be above personal or selfish concerns. How much alike were Will Rogers and Franklin Roosevelt in the eyes of theater goers cannot be determined; but it is certain that many who have studied films of the era agree with Andrew Bergman that movies of the thirties conveyed "that the federal government was a benevolent watchman, that we were a classless, melting pot nation."[12] Certainly Rogers' later movies communicated a sense that American values and American character (as embodied by Will Rogers) were sustaining the spirits of the Fleety Belles and the Dukes of this world. As "forgotten men," viewers who had suffered economic setbacks, or had felt the stigma of class, could find reassurance through Uncle Will that the American Dream was still viable.[13] Coming back to the performance of Anne Shirley, it seems clear that she was not merely conforming to a screen stereotype, but serving as a developed symbol representing the needs of a weak and confused nation.

Executives of Fox Pictures seemed to understand that anecdotes about Rogers' off-screen benevolence toward Shirley were good for the picture. According to a release repeated endlessly in the press, Rogers allowed the novice to "steal" scenes from him. Supposedly, Rogers took John Ford aside one day and told him that "I'm gettin' the star's billin' and drawin' down the star's salary, but the star of this picture, man or woman, is the one that can steal it. Come on, John, and have a heart—give the kid a chance."[14] Whether this "real life" scene came from reality or from the Fox publicity department does not really matter: Either way, we have proof that there was an appetite for vicarious participation in the protective influence of Will Rogers. Scenes in the pilot house of the *Claremore Queen* concretize this theme of benevolence: Both Will Rogers and Anne Shirley wear hats inscribed with the word "Captain"; both share the wheel of the ship, a traditional symbol; there is even a bit of bussing from time to time. An involved viewer of these moments of tenderness could interpret that Uncle Will is helping us to steer a course through difficult times, and that he is concerned because our normal hopes and desires have been thwarted by impersonal forces.

Direction

Although *Steamboat 'Round the Bend* is hardly mentioned in available studies of John Ford's career, there are obvious connections between the two men and their work which warrant discussion.[15] John Ford was born near Portland, Maine, just before the turn of the century. Students of Ford's life and work agree that his formative years in rural New England gave him an outsider's view on twentieth-century developments. Like the Oklahoma humorist, Ford felt an attraction for rural life, especially the strong ties cultivated by small communities. Ford also shared Rogers' concern about the future of the American family; as a result, Ford films both celebrate the virtues of family life while portraying the effects of lack of family support when atomized individuals. Ford is also known for his interest in American history—not for antiquarian purposes, but to find a source of affirmation for traditional values.[16]

After Will Rogers' death in 1935, Ford would articulate his world view in such classic films as *Stagecoach* (1939), *The Grapes of Wrath* (1940), and *How Green Was My Valley* (1941). Study of the films made with Will Rogers reveals that Ford must have understood the affinity between his goals and those of Rogers. In *Dr. Bull* (1933), Ford helped Rogers bring to the screen the character of a rural general practitioner who has an excellent bedside manner but a distrust of newfangled ways; *Judge Priest* (1934) was a nostalgic portrait of the old South which drew upon a *Saturday Evening Post* story by regionalist Irvin S. Cobb, Rogers' co-star in *Steamboat 'Round the Bend*.[17] In all the films made with Will Rogers, Ford devoted considerable attention to evoking mood through *mise en scène*. Although they may seem ludicrously sentimental by Age of Anxiety standards, the jailhouse segments of *Steamboat* stress the social harmony of an organic society. Characterizations throughout the film emphasize the quaint: Ford treats rural eccentricities with the same affection found in the regional novels of Harriet Beecher Stowe, or the delicate tales of another Maine artist, Sarah Orne Jewett. Without Ford's precise tuning of mood, the ripostes between Rogers and Cobb would have fallen flat.

More difficult to explain is the *laissez faire* attitude which Ford took toward his principals. Ford would later become known as an auteur who planned his films so carefully in advance of shooting that he was said to edit in the camera. Such a director should not have been happy with stars who appeared for a day's work without their lines memorized. Ford must have known that the subtle obbligato of happiness which the two men generated could not be obtained through normal means: Only if these two entertainers were allowed to play against one another extemporaneously would the right spirit be communicated. Since the goal of most scenes was to evoke a general atmosphere, precision of lines was unimportant. But the right feeling tone (supplied by the actors) within the right setting (supplied by carefully planned photography and painstaking editing) was essential. By allowing Rogers and Cobb to perform without restraints, and by keeping his own presence unobtrusive, Ford achieved the desired directorial objective.

Students of John Ford have ignored his Will Rogers films. *Dr. Bull, Judge Priest*, and *Steamboat 'Round the Bend* have been seen as "bits of work" performed so that Ford could go on to make his auteur films. A closer reading of these rural dramas shows that Ford themes are prominent—the peacefulness of rural life and the simplicity of rural people, the importance of tradition and the family—but they are messages also associated with Will Rogers. In fact, the films are more effective because of the overlapping interests and concerns of these two artists.

Will Rogers and his audience were aware that their world was becoming increasingly perplexing and violent. The most important factor about the imaginary world of "Homeville" created by a Will Rogers film was that the forces and the people were entirely malleable under the workings of the spirit of Uncle Will. Millions of Rogers' fans must have watched such resolutions of conflict with satisfaction. They must have been impressed by what one contemporary reviewer noted was Rogers' power "to set right all the troubles of the impulsive people around him."[18] Given a sympathetic understanding of the forces affecting Americans in the 1920s and 1930s, it is difficult to vouchsafe them their inner need to love such a symbolic man. He meant so much to his people in a time of change and deprivation because he presented them with an image of what Americans had been told to believe was the best in their national character. In preserving this image of humanity and love, Rogers was making no small contribution to the sanity of Americans in a world rushing toward international violence. A reviewer of *In Old Kentucky* hit upon some of the essential positive factors of Rogers' contribution as man and as film image. These late Homeville movies reassured Americans (especially frenzied New Yorkers) "about the solidity and innate common sense of this country." While the reviewer granted that Rogers was probably playing "himself," he felt compelled to add that, as a representative figure, Rogers supplied welcome reassurance in an era of bad news: "Will Rogers has a curious national quality. He gives the impression somehow that this country is filled with such sages, wise with years, young in humor and life, shrewd, yet gentle." Most importantly for the reviewer, "He is what Americans think other Americans are like."[19] After the erosion of values in the twenties, after the economic disaster of the thirties, Americans were indeed fortunate to have such a public person to keep a hopeful image of American values and optimism bright.

Notes

1. Audiences in the thirties would have noted the aging of these two syndicated humorists: Rogers was fifty-six, Cobb was fifty-nine. Also apparent to audiences would have been the significance of the ship names: Paducah is a city located on the Ohio

River where it joins with the Kentucky; Claremore is the major city of Rogers County, Oklahoma, where Will Rogers was born and where the Will Rogers Memorial Museum now stands.

2. Cobb tells his story in an autobiography entitled *Exit Laughing* (New York: Garden City Publishing Co., 1941). Like Rogers, Cobb saw himself in the tradition of Mark Twain, for his regional humor as well as for his journalistic commentary on the times.

3. "His Last Precious Days with Friend Will Rogers Recalled by Irvin Cobb," File Box No. 14.

4. "Screen Loses Star at Peak of Influence," *Dallas Texas News*, 17 August, 1935. File Box 14.

5. Contrasts between Rogers' journalism and his films could be no better illustrated than in this broadcast. While *Steamboat* takes us away from contemporary events, the nationwide radio program addressed such issues as unemployment, a proposed California state tax on the movie industry, prejudice against Indians, the CCC, and the national debt.

6. Gulf Radio Broadcast, May 19, 1935. Both tapes and transcripts of these broadcasts are available at the Will Rogers Memorial.

7. *The Negro in Film* (London: Skelton Robinson, 1947), p. 49.

8. This excellent documentary is available from most audiovisual centers for a minimal rental fee.

9. Harry Menig, "Stepin Fetchit in Will Rogers' Films," an unpublished paper presented to the national meeting of the American Studies Association, 1973, p. 14.

10. Information concerning the treatment of Fetchit was obtained from a Boston College faculty seminar on the Black image in film, sponsored by the American Studies Association.

11. Close viewing of *Steamboat 'Round the Bend* suggests that future scholarship dealing with the Black image in film should attend more closely to specific dramatic contexts, since typed roles can be transformed by gifted actors, among whom Stepin Fetchit must be counted. A recent study by Thomas Cripps, *Slow-Fade to Black: The Negro in American Film, 1900–1942* (New York: Oxford University Press, 1971), is unique for its attention to performances.

12. *We're in the Money: Depression America and Its Films* (New York: New York University Press, 1971), p. 149.

13. Students are invited to explore the relationship between American heroes of the period (on screen, in real life) and the ability of traditional institutions to weather those troubled years. A more extended version of the above quote from Bergman might stimulate discussion and writing: "Movies of the Thirties made a central contribution toward educating Americans in the fact that wrongs could be set right within their existing institutions. They showed that individual initiative still bred success, that the federal government was a benevolent watchman, that we were a classless, melting pot nation."

14. "Cobb Bares Secrets on Film Lot," *Tulsa Daily World*, 5 Sept. 1935, p. 7, Col. 7.

15. *American Visions: The Films of Chaplin, Ford, Capra, and Welles, 1936–41* (New York: Arno Press, 1977) is an excellent study by Charles Maland which makes no mention of films made with Rogers. John Baxter, *The Cinema of John Ford* (New York: A.S. Barnes and Co., 1971) lists the Rogers films in a filmography, but does not discuss them

in the text. Other studies bearing the title *John Ford* by Peter Bogdanovich (London: Studio Vista, 1967), Phillippe Hardiquet (Paris: Editions Seghers, 1966), and Jean Mitry (Paris: Universitaires, 1954) all slight the Ford-Rogers collaborations.

16. In preparing this portion of the essay, I have been particularly informed by Charles Maland's *American Visions,* pp. 99–190.

17. Adoption of regional tales for Will Rogers is examined closely in Peter C. Rollins and Harry Menig, "Regional Literature and Will Rogers Film Redeems a Literary Form," *Literature/Film Quarterly,* 3 (1975), 70–82.

18. Memorial Scrapbook No. 1, p. 31.

19. Rev. of *Life Begins at Forty, New York Sun,* File Box No. 14.

Uncensored Garbo

Charles Affron

Originally appeared in vol. 4, no. 4 (Summer 1980)

When a monarch caresses a bedpost it's not only "pornographic," it's downright "dangerous." Martin Quigley signals *Queen Christina* (1933) among the "Pictures Typical of Wrong Standards."[1] Queens, you see, have "authority, acceptance." Perhaps he feared a nationwide epidemic of bedroom fetishism. Women who had already plucked their eyebrows and bobbed their hair à la Garbo would henceforth spend their time fondling boudoir furniture than silently and invisibly indulging in the "pure love" sanctioned by the Production Code.

Garbo and her films transgress. She made fifteen talkies. In thirteen of them she portrays what used to be called a "bad woman," her badness ranging from sexual dalliance to genteel mistressdom to prostitution. Sex and marriage are compatible in only two of these films, and there the tandem is qualified by the shadiest of pasts (*As You Desire Me*, 1932) and a ploy that invoked the censors' wrath (*Two-Faced Woman*, 1941). Garbo is no naughtier than her rivals, at least according to the Production Code. Aside from Marie Dressler, female stars at M-G-M and elsewhere shone in sexuality. Even the prepubescent Shirley Temple and the virginal Janet Gaynor tease us to a heightened sexual awareness. We often scorn the vulgar "good" taste and manners of Irving Thalberg's hegemony at M-G-M, but during his most active years, the studio's output can be characterized as positively dirty minded. Norma Shearer played a modern "divorcée" (1930) and an exceedingly "free soul" (1931). In fact, two of Mrs. Thalberg's films, *Strangers May Kiss* (1931) and *Riptide* (1934), rate inclusion in Quigley's list of infamy. Joan Crawford was both "possessed" (1931) and "chained" (1934) prior to 1935. Even brave Jeanette was Lubitsch's "merry widow" (1934) and a singing Mata Hari–like spy in *The Firefly* (1937) before sprouting wings in *I Married An Angel* (1942). M-G-M was to become home to Judge Hardy (in *A Family Affair*, 1937) and *Mrs. Miniver* (1942), but only after Harlow had disported herself in its bathtubs and bedrooms, censorably "reckless" (1935).

If we use the obvious norms, Garbo's conduct seems considerably more decorous than that of many other leading ladies of the '30s. In *Grand Hotel* (1932) a flimsy negligee, an exposed knee, in *Mata Hari* (1932) her peek-a-boo dancing regalia—these are exceptions in a cinema wardrobe that consistently drapes every inch of her uncurvacious body. The most damaging effects of censorship on her career had little or nothing to do with the abolition of provocative gestures or risqué attires. The Code seemed more interested in the scripts, in the supposed "ideas" of films, than their potent and not-so-potent subtexts. Censors fussed over the adulterous affair of Marie Walewska and Napoleon, enfeebling whatever spirit there might have been in *Conquest* (1937), and between Garbo and Boyer, a pair of screen lovers whose rhythms ought to have been perfectly matched. In other films Clarence Brown failed to solve easier problems than those presented by an evasive script, a welter of dull, lavish sets, and a heroine whose role was so lacking in definition. *Two-Faced Woman* is notorious in the history of film censorship. It elicited from a particularly enraged Legion of Decency the first blanket of condemnation against a major studio film in several years. It was banned in Australia and Providence, R.I. [2] Cardinal Spellman labeled it as "the occasion of sin and as dangerous to public morals." [3] The Catholic Interest Committee of the Knights of Columbus of Manhattan and the Bronx called it "a challenge to every decent man and woman." [4] Today we need a lively imagination to perceive such resonances in the film. The short scene inserted in the revised version may have cleared up Melvyn Douglas's confusion about which of Garbo's two faces he was looking at, but makes the film neither more or less innocuous, nor more or less boring. (Oh that Garbo had worn one scarred face in another 1941 film of Cukor, rather than the two silly ones that here end her career!)

The paradox of *Two-Faced Woman* is that it stirred such an uproar, and that Garbo was punished for a performance in which the quality of her sexuality was muted, lacking in intensity, almost without suggestive power. I suppose we should be thankful that the guardians of the Code were so busy being alert to white slavery, VD, and children's sex organs that they remained blissfully insensitive to the more disquieting reverberations in Garbo's other films. Perhaps they assumed the public was insensitive as well. It seemed more important to protect the sanctity of marriage, so foully menaced by the polemic of a film as engagé as *Two-Faced Woman*, featuring the radical Constance Bennett and Roland Young, and the inflammatory tribal dance, the "Chica-Choca," led by Garbo herself.

The true perversion of *Two-Faced Woman* is that it vitiates Garbo's sexuality. Everyone knew Garbo was a sex-goddess, perhaps even a love-goddess. The rites befitting a goddess are practiced in mystery. Those films that acknowledge the mystery and abet Garbo in visualizing her secret ceremonies, release her from the purview of the Production Code and detach her from its expectations, its moral standards. There is no provision for a sexuality as personal, as inner-directed, as unrelated to recognizable contexts as Garbo's. Indeed, the Code makes little sense when applied to the individuality of even more obviously "sexy" leading ladies. How do you apply standards to that which, by definition, is un-standard? If Garbo, Harlow, West, Dietrich are stars, they are beyond our poor measure.

But our poor measure is not without value. It functions as an optic, focusing on the star a set of powers that magnify her anomalous aspects, foreign to our experience, and so desirable. Like any strong magnifier not dexterously oriented, it distorts, perhaps obliterates the image under scrutiny. The Code, with its prohibition of sexual explicitness, with its written and unwritten set of strictures, is analogous to the Classical unities and the conventions of bienséance that operate in French tragedy of the 17th century. The Classical Doctrine and its accompanying rules guarantee the intensity of Phèdre's passion; the Production Code, heavy with the trappings of bourgeois prudery and decorum, unleashes Garbo's longing, her belief that sex is a matter of life and death. Yet the degree of stylization demanded by both codes, Classical and Production, is not without its dangers. The relationship between style and experience has a breathtaking delicacy. The intimacy to which Phèdre draws us is perfectly strung on conventions of dramaturgy and versification that lose much of their potency after Racine's last plays. Garbo is sublimely served by the obliquity of representation that is the studio's response to the Code, but with only frustrating intermittency, and ultimately, not at all. Her silent films offer a field of useful comparison. At first, the sexuality of Garbo's pre-Code work is ill defined, almost caricatural, in the vamping of *The Torrent* (1926), *The Temptress* (1926), and *Flesh and the Devil* (1927). Her pervasive orality, aggressively open-mouthed kissing, and interminable puckering over a cigarette and a communion cup are like pale blue illustrations, ones we've seen too often before. The cigarette sequence in *Flesh and the Devil* survives for its historical importance in the Garbo canon, and for its fancy chiaroscuro photography. She is, however, much more provocative in her remaining films prior to her sound debut in *Anna Christie* (1930). Edmund Goulding, Fred Niblo, and Sidney Franklin deck her out in varieties of erotically visual paraphernalia, and their inventions help us distinguish between Garbo, Negri, and other two-syllabled sirens. The shadows, the exotic framing and dressing up in *Wild Orchards* (1929) play a baroque hide-and-seek with Garbo's image. *The Mysterious Lady* (1928) prefigures Sternberg's *Dishonored* (1931) in ways too obvious to mention, and show Garbo every bit as comic a tease as Dietrich would soon be. Yet titillation is peripheral to Garbo's erotic presence. It's a comfort to discover her expertise in ironic modes, but it's a greater comfort to watch as she liberates sensation from irony, clasping it to the core of her imagination.

Garbo's self-centered eroticism emerges clearly in Goulding's version of *Anna Karenina*, *Love* (1927), where the director exploits her refractive presence. She gazes thoughtfully, longingly at an Italian child, caresses his hair, seems to recreate his face, transforming it into that of the son she abandoned in Russia. The child leaves, the actress draws within herself, and with an ineffable cadence transfers this concentration to her love for Vronsky. The time of this config-uration gives Garbo's face the span needed to juxtapose its aspects, to space them for our perusal, and to sum them in her love-filled eyes.

The most extended projection of the star's *innigkeit* occurs in Clarence Brown's pre-Code *A Woman of Affairs* (1929), a cleaned and blocked version of Michael Arlen's *The Green Hat*. Even before the official rules of censorship were formulated, the studio felt obliged to change the heroine's name from that veritable sound of dissipation, Iris March, to Diana Manners. The politely chaste goddess of the chase? Other equally risqué details were modified. The film is not at its most sensational during the several gropings of Gilbert and Garbo. It is the hospital sequence we all remember, and do so, in part, because Garbo so highly eroticizes a context full of non-erotic elements: the corridor, the severe hospital gown, the nuns. Garbo refracts her desire through these elements, isolating it in a space initially alien but eventually hers. Desire is finally lodged in the enor-mous bouquet of flowers that envelops her face. She fondles and devours this proxy-lover, losing herself in it as neither the conventions of lovemaking nor the laws of physics would permit with the lover himself. Her co-star excluded, she appropriates object-referents and exhibits a sexuality basic to art in its obsessive metaphorization—its fetishism. Garbo creates an intimate metaphoric relation-ship between being and object. This relationship is indeed more intimate than one established between two people, unless one of them is objectified. Oblivious to the other characters during this part of the sequence (her progressive discovery of them is a remarkable transition from the register of poetry to the register of drama), Garbo allows us to share her greatest privacy, to enter that secret place where gesture and face and object configure the fullness of passion. Garbo shows us things we were never meant to see. As Phèdre opens herself to the gaze and the metaphoric sword of Hippolyte, so Garbo thrusts herself on us, staggering down the corridor, rapt in longing, and sharing it with her audience on this bridge of flowers. Her screen lover, John Gilbert, is denied the privileged point of view of camera and moviegoer.

In her Code-bound vehicles Garbo transmits similar bounty. In fact, since Garbo never thrived on explicit forms of transmission, it is logical to expect her to flourish in the indirectness of sexual referentiality developed during the '30s.

One immediate benefit of the Code, even in its pre-1934 application, is Garbo's almost complete devampification. Outside of a moment or two in *Mata Hari* and *As You Desire Me*, she doesn't have to indulge in eye-rolling and hip-swinging until *Two-Faced Woman*. Without benefit of the usual signals—winks, leers, funny dialogue, a voluptuous body—Garbo appears to be a woman who enjoys sex, who is eager to make love. Even in *Romance* (1930), one of her emptiest films, Garbo conveys sexual joy, no small feat considering the excessive chastity of her leading man, Gavin Gordon, and the rest of the furniture.

Responding to inventive and sympathetic directors, Edmund Goulding and Rouben Mamoulian, Garbo gives what are arguably her most erotic performances in *Grand Hotel* and *Queen Christina*. A stronger case must be made for Goulding than has been in the past. He is often relegated to the Faith Baldwin–Frances Parkinson Keyes school of directors, yet the visual arabesques of *Grand Hotel*, the interlocking sweep of shots and plot, seem to be more and more his responsibility as we become increasingly familiar with the directorial grace of *Dark Victory* (1939) and *The Constant Nymph* (1943). It is precisely this grace that matches Garbo's rubato, her phrasing of expression and posture. Goulding measures many of the shots to Garbo's extended span of concentration, allowing her to bring together ambiguities of mood and plastique in unfragmented coherence. And it is in these shots, after the ballerina attitudinizing has been gotten out of the way, that Garbo is at her most erotic.

The duration of one brief shot is sufficient for Garbo and Goulding to explore the kind of desire Mr. Quigley would label "impure." After a night of love, the ballerina discovers that the stranger who prevented her suicide is a hotel thief. Despite her full gallery of kept women, for Garbo the essence of sex is not saleable. Her disappointment over Barrymore's confession in *Grand Hotel* gives way almost immediately to belief in the sincerity of his love. The shot in question charts her passage from incredulity to joy. At first withheld, her face, her eyes cross the frame's field, accompanied by a hand caressing the Great Profile and lips sensually exaggerating the nickname, "Flix." A word becomes a kiss, a sexual metaphor if there ever was one. We don't see the kiss she implants on Barrymore—the back of his head is in the way. After the one she has bestowed on us it would be redundant. The back of Barrymore's head is, in fact, an essential element in the shot's dynamics. It sweeps across Garbo's face, and she reappears at the other side of the frame, enraptured, her smile a sign of utter satisfaction. The shot ends when she almost imperceptibly blows on her lover's neck, gently kisses it, and finally nestles her own face there in ecstasy. We were denied the love scene of the previous night. Garbo here gives us a version of her arousal and fulfillment, and in the duration of the shot shows it all, locked in a rhythm that is hers alone.

One of Garbo's telephone scenes offers a variant of this erotic shorthand as well as a reminder of the sexual metaphors of *A Woman of Affairs*. The phone becomes a surrogate lover she addresses in a wide range of tones and fondles with a passion she would be loath to exhibit if the phone were indeed her lover.

Near the film's end she emerges from the door of the Grand Hotel, greets the sun, and, trembling with anticipation, traverses the frame with a movement so sinuous that she seems to be arriving and departing at once, reluctant to leave the sun of Berlin, anxious to be on her way to the sun of Tremezzo and the arms of her lover. It is the ambiguity of this movement, executed in front of a revolving door, that conveys Garbo's eagerness for love, an eagerness that dispels absence, that animates the world around her with the delight of this refracted, stylized sexuality. The obliquity of the referents and the obliquity of her response isolate the thrill of her feeling to such a degree that her lovers often seem in the way, distracting and unnecessary to the erotic design.

This is precisely the case in the *Queen Christina* sequence to which Quigley took such heated exception, although I suspect he reacted to its more explicit yet less erotic aspects. The two-shots are disappointing, and not only because John Gilbert looks so absurd in a caricatural coiffure, moustache, and chin piece. The best parts of the sequence expose Garbo in the solitude of her imagination. The relationship between the cadence of her body and a series of textures creates a pattern more deeply challenging to middle-class morality than the obligatory clinches. Fetishism is not singled out in the Code, but the degree to which it is here displayed would seem threatening indeed.

Garbo has already refined our apprehension of sexuality during the sex-role game she plays with Gilbert. The passage from a lightly worn masculinity to her own version of womanliness is accomplished with signs so faint and tantalizing as to leave us hovering over her identity. The removal of a jacket discloses a shirt less bulging than Gilbert's, a slightly bent knee, a barely tilted head, and a sexuality so rich in variety as to prohibit our most inventive attempts at classification.

After what seems like uninterrupted days and nights of lovemaking, Garbo literally draws the images of love from the textures of the room and reciprocally animates the furniture and shapes with her self-absorption. This appropriation of place and feeling begins with an unusually angled two-shot of Garbo alone, her profile and her reflection in a mirror. She eventually finds Gilbert in that mirror, but not until she has offered us this privileged view of her face, reorganized and newly possessed.

The sequence proceeds with variants of reflection, Garbo impressing herself on surfaces whose degree of tensility constantly modify her presence. The geometry of the spinning wheel tunes us to formality; the wool and the bed yield readily to the touch. At the center of the pattern is another shot analogous to the flower sequence in *A Woman of Affairs*, an extreme closeup of Garbo's face sinking into a pillow, receiving from it and transmitting to it versions of love recollected, present, and anticipated. The final object, the bedpost, is touched by the magic of her face and hand, the wood endowed with the receptivity of the preceding surfaces, and relieved of its banal sexual symbolism. It shares in the richness of sexuality Garbo has imparted to a situation whose introduction was ripe for farce and whose resolution risked being as treacly as its accompanying music. Garbo's lovemaking is projected through filters that organize the experience in a perceptible style while enhancing sensation and presence. It never occurs to us to wonder if sex is simulated. We see Garbo more fully than we ever see Marilyn Chambers or Georgina Spelvin.

If this is perhaps the most fully developed rendition of Garbo's passions, it is happily not the last. In *The Painted Veil* (1934) the baroque orientalia of her liaison with George Brent, again preceded by a moment of literal self-reflection, is properly subsumed by the mosquito-netted, becowled sublimation of her love for Herbert Marshall, her worthiest partner since Nils Asther. *Anna Karenina* (1935) has an unhappy affair with Clarence Brown, who has predictably increased difficulty in coping with the Code's stricter application. However Cukor's *Camille* (1937) is proof that neither actress nor director need feel prohibited by the Code, or more accurately, that prohibitions can be made to work to passion's advantage. In the atmosphere provided by Cukor, Garbo's breathlessness neatly links a consumptive chest and an avidity for sex.

The film and the star function on two levels of sexuality. The first is a luxurious and forthright depiction of the demi-monde that the censors must have excused in deference to the Dumas play's "light classical" reputation. The production values we often find so stultifying in M-G-M films of this period are positive elements in *Camille*, their sumptuousness exciting in radically sensational ways. Garbo on the prowl at the film's opening, suitably displaying her public sexuality in a theatre, reminds us of the way she picked up Robert Montgomery in *Inspiration* (1931); Laura Hope Crews and Lenore Ulric perform with a bawdiness quite remarkable in 1937; an unheard but pointedly laughed at dirty joke is the basis for an extended sequence. The humor and panache, the expensiveness of *Camille* are thresholds for the second level of sexuality, Garbo's hysteria, a highly pitched emotional vibrato scarcely muffled by her worldliness. It breaks through sophistication just as desire breaks through wisdom. She and Henry Daniell collaborate on a laughing duet (he is playing Chopin, *prestissimo*, at the time), during which Garbo's voice, ranging from brittleness to desperation, sings her frustration over her thwarted tryst with Robert Taylor. Wonderfully paradoxical, just before this episode, her gentle laugh at Taylor's ingenuous protestations of love becomes a hysteria made of near-silence, a breathy, whispering voice, her neck extravagantly arched in abandon. This pattern is amplified when she sacrifices Taylor, feigning boredom with her country life and her callow lover. Mercilessly coiffed in corkscrew curls, she mocks Taylor's seriousness, and then, in an anguished embrace, her face visible over his shoulder, she reveals to the camera alone the depths of her longing. We are tempted to forget the sexual core of a film so redolent of bourgeois morality and bourgeois notions of nobility, a film whose decor is so decorous and whose heroine suffers so grandly for her sins. Yet Garbo and Cukor keep the pulse of desire rapidly beating and consistently challenge us with the daring of their gestures. The plot and the dialogue are for the censors; the face, Garbo's ultimate field of sexuality, is for us.

Its suggestive power is never greater than in the shot preceding Taylor's return, near the film's end. A duration of forty-five seconds contains Garbo's joy, her anxiety, her frustration, and above all, her longing. There is something cruelly intimate about the way the camera hovers above, almost pinning her to the pillow, allowing her no area for escape. Her rapidly changing expressions constantly recompose a face the years have taught us to cherish in tranquility. The activity contained in this closeup is rare, and denies the potential of off-frame space. Garbo's face is posited as the locus of all meaning in closeups ranging from *The Saga of Gosta Berling* (1924) to *Two-Faced Woman*, yet never with this degree of exertion. The dynamics of this frame bind us just as tightly as Garbo. Trapped, she shows all, just as Phëdre did, truest in the fullness of desire. She even has her Nanine, a faithful confidante, as befits a tragic heroine. The severity of this shot is emblematic of Garbo at her most effective, opening her being to scrutiny in inverse proportion to her real-life need for privacy. An actress, timid to the degree of banning all visitors from the set, of having the shooting area surrounded by screens, excluding even the director, has no shame in front of the camera. Her superficial reticence is akin to those heroic couplets, and it constitutes a style that leads to equally complete revelations. The rules upheld by the Académie Francaise and the Hays-Breen offices provide a focus for artists whose techniques thrive on indirection, on restriction, on concentration. The Code fails to inhibit an actress whose most cherished fetish is a movie camera, and who gladly shares her obsession with an audience that is figuratively peering through its lens.

Notes

1. *Martin Quigley, Decency in Motion Pictures* (New York City, 1937), pp. 31–40.
2. *New York Times*, Nov. 26, 1941, p. 29.
3. Ibid, Nov. 27, 1941, p. 25.
4. Ibid, Nov. 30, 1941, p. 71.

Will Rogers

THE STORY BEHIND HIS FIRST
TALKING PICTURE

Reba Neighbors Collins

Originally appeared in vol. 6, no. 2 (March/April 1982)

The world eagerly awaited Will Rogers' first talkie in 1929. And Rogers just as eagerly looked forward to a job that would take him back to California where he could spend more time with his family.

For months he had been a "commuter"—between California and New York and on the road in show business. In between his trips, Mrs. Rogers and the children took their turns on the transcontinental trains.

His Hollywood career had started in 1919 when he moved his family from Long Island to California. But after more than 40 silent films, Will failed to reach the peak of success to which he had become accustomed. One critic (Tamar Lane in *What's Wrong with the Movies*) in 1923 blamed it on the "stupidity of the public taste and its unwillingness to take to anything different," adding that Rogers was "ten years ahead of his time in screen acting." In any case, he headed back to New York to the Ziegfeld *Follies*, on the road with lecture tours and into a substitute role for his injured friend, Fred Stone, in a production of *Three Cheers* with Dorothy Stone.

Datelines on his daily telegrams to the papers, as well as tales he tells in his weekly syndicated articles show him as a man-on-the-move, juggling roles as varied as European travel writer, political reporter, columnist, after-dinner speaker and Broadway star. He was already the best known private citizen in America and he loved to be busy. But with the three children growing up, he wanted to stay at home for a while and talking pictures seemed to be the answer.

The *New York Times* reported in March 1929, that—after 18 months of preparation and expenditure of some $15 million—Fox Corporation was ready to produce dialogue and musical pictures exclusively. Fox drew many stars including Will Rogers, William Collier, George Jessel and others. They were placed under contract by Winfield Sheehan, vice president for Fox. He hired entire crews, including musicians, directors and stars to "enable the whole country to see Broadway right in their home town," the *Times* reported. And "the quips of Will Rogers will be heard by audiences gathered in motion picture houses from coast to coast."

On the night of June 1, 1929, Rogers closed the Stone show in Pittsburgh, hopped a tri-motor Ford plane out of Indianapolis then on to the coast where he was met at Glendale airport by a group of celebrities, Fox officials and Mrs. Rogers. Publicity cameras had to catch him on the run before he was whisked away by Betty Rogers for their home in Beverly Hills. From then until mid-September, he was in California—something of a record for such a traveling man.

The *New York Times* announced on June 23 that Rogers would make his first Fox film, *They Had to See Paris*, adapted from a novel by Homer Croy with a screenplay by Owen Davis. It was to be the first of 21 talkies for Fox that took Rogers to the top of the box office in the next six years.

A month later, the *Times* reported that Will was learning to "parley" French for his new venture, taking lessons from the "Parisian dancer," Fifi Dorsay. Louella Parsons described her as "one of the vampiest vamps" to hit the screen in a long time. Claremore, Oklahoma, Will's hometown, also made its debut in the *Paris* film. In a driving rain on June 22, 1929, a film crew arrived in the mid-American town with a baggage car full of equipment and a filming crew directed by J.W. Kaufman.

The book by Croy had used a town in Oklahoma as the home of the main character, Pike Peters. Rogers—always the biggest booster for his hometown and state—insisted that Claremore take its place on the "indelible celluloid" with scenes at the depot and on Main Street—and he got what he asked for. (That same street, by the way, is now called Will Rogers Boulevard and leads up the hill to the Will Rogers Memorial.)

The movie opens with the humble "Pike," a garage owner, hitting the jackpot in oil. His wife Idy (Irene Rich played his leading lady and he often called her his "reel wife") was a socially ambitious mother of two nearly grown youngsters—Opal (Marguerite Churchill) and Ross (Owen Davis, Jr.)—who wanted to expose her newly rich family to the culture of Paris, much against her husband's wishes. Mrs. Peters is finally able to overcome his protests by claiming their son will learn more in one year in Paris than four years in college. Secretly she hopes Opal will find a titled husband.

After the family arrives in Paris, the plot thickens when a Parisian cutie of questionable morals tries to snare Ross and a titled fiancé is "purchased" for Opal. At a fancy party to announce Opal's engagement, Grand Duke Michael ("Mike," as Pike calls him)—the butler and valet—joins the disillusioned Oklahoman in a fun-filled drinking bout. Rogers, hiding in his bedroom with nothing to wear but a dressing gown, finally decides to look in on the party and climbs into a suit of armor to make a sneak appearance. The stairs prove his undoing, and he falls apart, humiliating Mrs. Peters but delighting the audience.

Disgusted, he goes out on the town to try to shake up the family. At the Café de Paris he meets the "vamp," Fifi. While she works at vamping him, he tells her all about Claremore, giving him a chance to use some of his famous quips. When Fifi tries to teach him French, pinching his nostrils together to help him make the proper "n" sound, he says, "French is a great language when you have to hold your nose to learn it."

But his escapades finally convince the family to go home and they rush him back to the safety of Oklahoma.

Frank Borzage, who directed the film, said the cast and crew had so much fun it was more like a vacation or a "refreshing adventure." According to Borzage, Will was so shy he kept pushing the younger actors closer to the camera and turning his back as he delivered the lines. When they ran rushes after the first week's work, Rogers was finally persuaded to watch them, but he stayed only a moment and got up to leave. When asked what was wrong, Will mumbled, "Oh, I dunno. Except that maybe I don't quite think that that face on the screen looks like me . . . and the voice is not me. It can't be. Not that voice!"

After that he refused to go near the projection room.

"The face that launched a thousand quips," as the *New York Times* called it, wore no makeup in the film, "as his wife sees him at breakfast, so the camera sees him later on." His face "undergoes no tinkering, no kalsomining, no hand decorating. The Will Rogers grin operates without any lubrication from grease paint. The famous forelock of unruly hair has never been disciplined by Brilliantine. The comedian has yet to pluck an eyebrow or hide a wrinkle."

In his own article about the film Will said, "I sure do hate those close-ups. When those old wrinkles commence coming and the old mane is turning snowy, why we don't want either cameras or people to commence to crowd us." He was soon to be 50 years old.

He dodged photographers and avoided interviews in Hollywood. Some claimed he would not give interviews because he was saving his material for his own columns. But more than likely, he worried about the fabricated stories that were often used to build up stars, usually with more fiction than fact.

But a few articles cropped up in the fan magazines anyway.

Jimmy Fiddler wrote about his past experiences with Will. He lauded Rogers' return to Hollywood and said the screen had finally found a way to capture the charm and personality of Will's voice. He noted the "comments of wit and wisdom that fairly roll off his tongue." Relating that Rogers refused to use the pretty Spanish-style bungalow that Fox had fixed up for his dressing room, Fiddler said Rogers told them "I come to work in my picture clothes and I don't wear make-up. I ain't going to spoil that pretty house slopping around in it."

When someone remarked that Will seemed to do his acting with ease, Will said: "Well, if you're doing what you like to do, and people like what you are doing, it just ain't no trouble at all to anybody."

In a later article, Conway Felton wrote: "Will Rogers makes no pretense at being an actor." Felton told how nationally famous people would come to the studio, including royalty and millionaires, and interrupt Rogers during the shooting. Most stars were protected from fans, but with such fans as those calling for Rogers' attention, the studio usually made an exception and let Rogers have time to visit with his friends. Sometimes he would ask them to stay and have lunch with him in the commissary. And then "there would be a million laughs," commented co-star Marguerite Churchill. She also told about Will's love for chili and onions—which he ate, disregarding close-up scenes with the other actors.

Rochelle Hudson—a Claremore native who went to Hollywood at age 16— in a story "as told to" Reginald Taviner for a film magazine, said "every Rogers picture is scheduled to start when Rogers is ready, not when the studio is. He is the only star in the industry who can hold up pictures already prepared until it suits him to begin on them."

Will would not do a scene until it seemed right to him. Rochelle said he tried out his "gags" on the electricians in the rafters. He listens, she said. "If the laugh doesn't come, Bill discards the line. This method of his may spoil the first take, but if he gets the laugh Bill doesn't need to know what an audience will do. The electricians have already told him. . . ." She said all the workers on the set called him "Bill" and followed him around just as did the stream of dignitaries who came to see him.

Rogers was impatient with the little details that preoccupy directors, such as which way the coat was buttoned when the shooting stopped for the day, so it could be done the same way when they started again the next day. Will's stock answer when the director worried about such things was: "It'll never show on a big screen with loud music!"

In his columns for the papers, Will called the new talking films "Noisies." He said, "Everybody that can't sing has a double that can, and everybody that can't talk is going right on proving it. . . .Everything is 'annunciation.' I was on the stage 23 years and never heard the word or knew what it was."

Was Will Rogers an actor? Or was he simply "being himself"?

Magazine and newspaper writers disagreed, and the question has not been settled to this day. Spencer Tracy in an article for a movie magazine about his friend Will had an answer: "What's the difference?" he asked. "The whole idea is to be natural. Hell, Will *has* to be a great actor, why, he's acting even when the camera's not there. He has to act just to be able to keep talking the way he does with all that colloquial speech when he knows better, and after all the proper talking he's been exposed to." Tracy said he had tried for years, but never could develop the knack: "I can't do what Will does," he said.

Tracy was taken over by Rogers who saw his potential as an actor. Will introduced him to Winfield Sheehan and Frank Borzage and both became important in Tracy's career. Tracy was invited to join the select group who had so much fun at the lunch table with Will and then accepted Rogers' invitation to come watch a Sunday polo game. When Spencer fell in love with the sport, Rogers couldn't do enough to help him. It was Rogers to whom Tracy went for advice in his film career and he found a real champion. Tracy noted: "The longer and the more intimately I know Will Rogers, the more I admire him—and more convinced I am that much of his charm lies in his boyishness. In spite of his amazingly wide contacts with world affairs and with the men who bring them about, in many ways he has never 'grown up.' A strange paradox—he is, at the same time, one of the best known, and one of the least known men in the world. By inclination he is a grand 'mixer.' By instinct, he is as retiring as a hermit." Tracy described his friend as "painfully shy," and most reluctant to talk about himself. He said Rogers was to be admired for the extensive charities and even more so because he didn't tell anyone about them. He also noted that Rogers never ceased to feel pride in his roots in Indian Territory and Oklahoma, and the fact that he dined with presidents and industrial giants, wearing his plainest clothes, "with such pride that it is dignified. There is not one drop of hypocrite's blood in his body. One of the chief symptoms of his boyishness is his insatiable curiosity. Another is his enthusiasm. I've never known a man who was more interested in finding out what makes the wheels go round. I've never known anyone who could throw more enthusiasm into everything he does, into his play and into his work. Behind a rather lazy mannerism, he hides a school boy's energy. . . . Of course, he is always in the pink of condition. He neither drinks nor smokes. He is not a heavy eater and he keeps regular hours. Every morning at the crack of dawn, he is in the corrals, grooming and riding his horses, and roping calves. He could still qualify as a top hand on anyone's cattle ranch."

Will's close friend Irvin Cobb said Rogers "never went Broadway when he was a hit in Ziegfeld's *Follies*, never went Hollywood, after he began to mop up in the movies. . . ." He described Rogers as the man "who dashes away from Yes-Man's land with . . . its barbwire entanglements of studio intrigue and its front-line trenches full of conniving executives, to climb into a pair of two-dollar overalls and hunker on a corral fence and contemplate the beauties of beef critters for hours on a stretch. It is the Will Rogers who still at heart is an Oklahoma cowhand, and as generous in his appraisals of human beings, tolerant in his judgments and not too bitterly satirical about the things and movements which he dislikes." Continuing, Cobb wrote: "There is a chain upon the gate down by the highroad to keep out the crowds that otherwise would make life a burden to the dwellers here, but there is no latch on Bill Rogers' soul and no lock on the cockles of his heart."

In an article about Hollywood and "sex appeal," Harry Steele wrote: "I still can't believe it. Here we have Gable, Garbo, Crawford, West, Lombard and even Mickey Mouse to bring the censors down on our necks and Will Rogers, who up to few months ago wouldn't even wear a tuxedo, brings home the bacon." Steele described Rogers as having about as much sex appeal as a "specimen of bread mold," adding that psychologists who tried to explain Rogers' magnetism were wasting their time. He credited Rogers' success to his ability to speak forceful truth that could be understood. "He is a plain-spoken man communing with plain-spoken listeners." Comparing him with Lincoln and Twain, he said Will belonged with this "group of geniuses." He also referred to Will's keen sense of observation, a product of early environment—his Indian heritage and the ability to gauge the temper of a man. An insight that not too many writers discovered during the Hollywood era.

Louise Dresser, a co-star whose friendship with Will dated back to their vaudeville days in New York, called Will "the most humane person" she had ever met. "I only wish it were so that all newcomers to the screen could play their first picture with Will Rogers, for with him to help them, that camera panic would be as nothing at all. Kindness and consideration for his cast, for everyone connected with the picture is a creed with him. It is always a genuine regret when the day comes for the last shot to be taken."

The Rogers family began a whole new way of life with Will on the coast again and keeping somewhat regular hours. They were living at 925 N. Beverly Drive in Beverly Hills—in the "house that jokes built," as Rogers called it, which had a riding ring and plenty of playing space. But he was fixing up the ranch in Santa Monica Canyon—off Sunset Boulevard—that summer of 1929, and the whole family moved out into a sort of summer home while their house in town underwent extensive remodeling.

Every Sunday, Rogers played polo with the Uplifters team, and usually he was top scorer. He played just as hard as he worked, and he took his polo seriously. Competing against the "Hollywood Sheiks," headed by Guinn "Big Boy" Williams, Rogers played with his old friends Jim Minnick, Hal Roach, Claire Brunson and Snowy Baker. Fred Stone and his family came to visit in August and spent some time with the family, having picnics and rides through the canyons. In late August, golfer Bobby Jones was in town and Rogers visited with him. Both of his sons, Will Rogers, Jr., and James B. Rogers, played polo, too, and on some occasions daughter Mary and Mrs. Rogers played as well.

Will continued writing his weekly columns and his daily "piece for the papers," which was datelined Beverly Hills for most of the summer. But he was running out of new material and getting restless with the same routine.

Plans were made for a grand Hollywood preview of *They Had to See Paris* and many big names were to appear at the extravaganza. But Rogers shocked the studio heads by announcing he would not be there! He was "going home."

On the morning of September 17, he flew out of Santa Monica, and that afternoon flew from Wichita, Kansas to Claremore—his "real" home. He saw the new six-story hotel that was going up with his name on it, visited his sister, spent time at the old Rogers ranch near Oologah where he was born, then started a wandering trip to the west coast, via homes and ranches of old friends. Mrs. Rogers wired him: "Preview is over. You can come home now." And he was ready.

Part II

GREAT PAIRS

Those Bubsy Berkeley and Astaire-Rogers Depression Musicals

TWO DIFFERENT WORLDS

Rocco Fumento

Originally appeared in vol. 5, no. 4 (July/August 1981)

By now everyone knows that Warners' *The Jazz Singer* was not the first to break the sound barrier. Hollywood had been experimenting with sound since the earliest days of filmmaking, and *The Jazz Singer* was merely a part-talkie, with not more than five minutes of running time given over to dialogue, and its extraordinary success was because the electrifying presence of a singing Al Jolson. Between 1928 and 1931 there were literally hundreds of musicals or non-musicals with singing and dancing interludes, like Mamoulian's *Applause* and the von Sternberg–Dietrich films. When *42nd Street* came along early in 1933, musicals were supposed to be dead. The public had tired of posturing heroes and prissy heroines, of cramped, smothered-by-sets stagings, of witless dialogue and the preposterous plots of *Dixiana*, *Bride of the Regiment*, *Her Majesty's Love*, and *Footlights and Fools*.

By 1933 the Depression had cut moviegoing attendance in half (from 110 million between 1927 and 1930 to 60 million in 1933) and Warners was in serious debt. Like the other majors, Warners had over-extended itself, mainly by breaking into the distributing and exhibiting of films through the acquisition of three hundred theaters. It was impossible for the studio to meet its long-term indebtedness. Warners managed to pacify the Depression wolf, barely, with the films of that tough-guy trio of giants, Edward G. Robinson, James Cagney and Paul Muni, with such fluke box-office hits as the William Powell–Kay Francis sudser, *One Way Passage*, and with the tight-budgeted comedies of loose-mouthed comedian Joe E. Brown. And if the prestige films of Miss Ruth Chatterton and Mr. George Arliss erased not one penny of Warners' huge debt, that was the price the studio paid in order to give it some class. They were Warners' answer to M-G-M's Garbo and Paramount's Dietrich.

The Warner Bros. formula for its non-musical hits, beginning with *Little Caesar* and continuing with *The Public Enemy* and *I Am a Fugitive from a Chain Gang*, was applied to *42nd Street*: quick pacing, lots of action, little dialogue. The studio that had taught the screen how to talk was now teaching it how not to talk too much. Though *42nd Street* was not Warner Bros.' salvation, it was, like Columbia's *It Happened One Night* (released the following year), a surprise smash hit, a big moneymaker, and a sleeper that practically no one expected would be a frontrunner flick. The movie would serve as a model for dozens of subsequent films including Ken Russell's *The Boy Friend*, which tried to satirize it but ended as an exercise in tedium. Later in 1933, with the success of *42nd Street* as inspiration and incentive, RKO made and released *Flying Down to Rio* starring Dolores Del Rio and Gene Raymond and featuring, in subsidiary roles, Fred Astaire and Ginger Rogers. In that film Astaire and Rogers burned up the screen with a dance number called "The Carioca" and, by so doing, grabbed the brass ring of stardom and the hearts of movie audiences throughout the world.

If *42nd Street* had been a failure, *Flying Down to Rio* might never have been made and the team of Astaire-Rogers might never have been born. Nor would we have had the string of Warner Depression musicals that followed (*Gold Diggers of 1933, Footlight Parade, Dames*) or the string of Astaire-Rogers Depression musicals (*The Gay Divorcee, Roberta,* and *Top Hat*). From the above, one might assume that the Warner musicals had a great deal in common. They didn't. What they had in common, mainly, was that they were all made in the darkest days of the big Depression, from 1933 to 1935. That isn't to say that one set of musicals is better than the other; they are simply different from each other.

Warner Bros.' musicals met the Depression head-on. The Depression was an integral part of these films. Ruby Keeler, Joan Blondell, and even Ginger Rogers, who appeared in two of the Warner movies before her pairing with Astaire, looked like they wore off-the-rack clothes, lived in squalid rooming houses, worried about runs in their hosiery, and schemed about ways of keeping the wolf away from the door. Warner films, even their musicals, were topical and had the gritty look of realism about them. The Astaire-Rogers films were anchored in no particular time and totally ignored the Depression as Fred and Ginger whirled off to such exotic lands as Brazil, England, and Italy with Astaire attired in top hat, white tie, and tails and Rogers feathered, sequined, and furred in gowns by Bernard Newman. Both delighted us with frothy, witty, Prince Charming–Cinderella romances while dancing to the melodies of Broadway's top composers, Jerome Kern, Cole Porter, and Irving Berlin. Two things the Warner and Astaire-Rogers films did have in common were amusing, often biting, wisecracks and wonderful supporting casts of comedians. In terms of locale, scripts, and clothes, the Astaire-Rogers films gave us a lovely, charming fantasy world and the Warner films gave us the sleazy world of backstage theatre life, where, often as not, a poor chorus girl, with the wolf huffing and puffing at her door, invited him in to insure herself a good meal.

But there is a schizophrenic quality about both sets of Depression musicals. While the Astaire-Rogers films take place in a delightful never-never land of the imagination—a Rio or London or Venice that exists nowhere but on the silver screen—their dance numbers are realistically staged or as realistically staged as dance numbers ever have been. Conversely, while the Warner scripts were grubby with realism, Busby Berkeley's production numbers were as bizarre and as feverishly phantasmogoric as a Franz Kafka short story.

The best dance numbers in the Astaire-Rogers films are the "little" ones, the dance duets. Like dialogue in a good short story or play, they help to advance the situation and to reveal characters. The "Isn't It a Lovely Day" number from *Top Hat*, for instance, is a wryly humorous revelation of character and of plot advancement, with its comprehension of at least ten minutes of dialogue into five minutes of song and dance. In a London park, the never-say-die suitor, Jerry, has forced himself upon the supposedly disinterested Dale. Before Dale can rid herself of him, a thunderstorm comes up, Dale and Jerry take refuge in a covered bandstand, and he sings "Isn't it a lovely day to be caught in the rain?" Grinning, he glides into the second line: "You were going on your way, now you'll have to remain." Though the sentiment expressed is entirely in keeping with Jerry's role as determined pursuer, he seems also to be rubbing salt into a wound. In spite of this, Jerry's essentially charming, good nature shines through. Dale listens to him sing and is affected in such a way that her responses become less and less hostile. The dance that follows, during which thunder frightens Dale momentarily into Jerry's arms, is explicated, perhaps a bit too enthusiastically, by Arlene Croce in her *The Fred Astaire and Ginger Rogers Book*:

> Is there anything in movies more wonderful than thunderstorms and lightning? Rain numbers are always fun, but what can match that *second* clap of thunder that shifts the rhythm into double time, or the moment when we see the bandstand through the rain and the whirling pair alone on their private stage?

The Berkeley numbers are called "production" numbers rather than "dance" numbers because, in the main, there is very little dancing in Berkeley's films. Berkeley had been a non-musical actor and director on the stage. It was merely by accident that he was put in charge of directing a musical. He admits that he knew nothing about dancing, that "I never took a dancing lession in my life," and that what he learned about dancing, he learned from chorus girls. This is why Berkeley, the non-dancer, rarely directed *dance* numbers. In many of his biggest production numbers, there is either no dancing whatsoever, or else very little. Instead of dancing, what Berkeley gives us is movement: girls forming snakelike, phallic patterns either on solid ground ("Young and Healthy") or in water ("By a Waterfall"); chorus boys and girls marching in military fashion ("Shanghai Lil") from *Footlight Parade*, "Remember My Forgotten Man" from *Gold Diggers of 1933*, and "All's Fair in Love and War" from *Gold Diggers of 1937*); girls bending their bodies to form human harps, which other girls are strumming ("Spin a Little Web of Dreams" from *Fashions of 1934*); girls seated at baby-grands as the baby-grands form intricate patterns ("The Words Are in My Heart" from *Gold Diggers of 1935*); girls with scores of normal-sized neon-lit violins forming one giant neon-lit violin ("Shadow Waltz" from *Gold Diggers of 1933*): girls with boards on their backs fitting them together to form a gigantic puzzle of Ruby Keeler's face ("I Only Have Eyes for You" from *Dames*). The girls move, the camera moves, baby-grands glide across the floor, the floors revolve, and all combine to form astonishing kaleidoscopic patterns. A few critics complained that Berkeley's production numbers might be squeezed into Yankee Stadium but not within the tight confines of any Broadway stage. Berkeley had had years of stage experience before he went to Hollywood. Apparently these critics never stopped to think that Berkeley was the first to know that his numbers could not be performed on any "real" stage. Instead, from the very real, stage-bound world of the rehearsal hall, he plunges us into a fantasy world with no boundaries.

However, in the Astaire-Rogers films, the production numbers are also *dance* numbers, both for the stars and for the chorus boys and girls: "The Carioca" from *Flying Down to Rio*, "The Continental" from *Top Hat*. Not only are they dance numbers, but they are also more firmly grounded in realism. They are not so fantastic that they could not be performed where, on the screen, they are shown to be performed, i.e., in hotel ballrooms or nightclubs, albeit gigantic ballrooms and nightclubs. Berkeley's influence is certainly seen in these numbers, most notably in the kaleidoscopic configurations of the chorus boys and girls, but at the same time they are too stage oriented to be Berkeley. The Astaire-Rogers musicals could easily have dispensed with these "grand finales" and in subsequent films they *were* dropped.

The camera work in the non-musical sections of both sets of films is not particularly inventive. It is typical of the thirties with the usual tricky wipes and dissolves, and the use (sometimes the overuse) of montage, particularly to compress time, to depict the passage of time, or to fling us into a new setting. But the musical numbers are something else. Berkeley, most often working with cameraman Sol Polito, uses a constantly moving, audaciously probing, leering "Peeping Tom" camera that shows us his stars and his chorus from every conceivable angle, including between their spread-eagled legs. In the midst of a dance we get a close-up of Ruby Keeler's smiling face and then another close-up of her dancing feet and, mixed in with her dancing feet, we get a close-up montage of chorus lovelies. In the "grand finale" numbers of the Astaire-Rogers films, when the stars are off stage, the camera may not be as daring as Berkeley's, but nevertheless it does weave in and out, slip up and down, and glide back and forth. But when he was dancing alone or with Rogers, Astaire would not allow this sort of tricky camera work. He and Rogers took off into space, *not* the camera. A dance number was a dance number and the camera should *always* see and follow the dancers in full figure. That was Astaire's order and it was obeyed. Berkeley, who didn't direct dance numbers and who loved a constantly moving camera, could never have obeyed such an edict. Perhaps this is why, years later when both Astaire and Berkeley were under contract to M-G-M, they never made a movie together.

"Lovely Day" is a "story" song and dance number. In the Warner Bros. musicals, Busby Berkeley also used "story" production numbers. The "Shuffle Off to Buffalo" number from *42nd Street*, the "Pettin' in the Park" number from *Gold Diggers of 1933*, the "Honeymoon Hotel" number from *Footlight Parade*, and the "Girl at the Ironing Board" number from *Dames* are all "story" songs. Yet, unlike "Lovely Day" they are not *a part of* the script's main story line; rather, they are *apart from it*. They are complete little stories incorporated into the large stories of backstage life. Even the very topical politically and socially conscious "story" songs ("Shanghai Lil" from *Footlight Parade*, with the sailors and their Chinese girlfriends doing configurations of the American eagle, the Stars and Stripes, and the face of newly elected President Franklin D. Roosevelt, or the "Remember My Forgotten Man" number from *Gold Diggers of 1933*, with Joan Blondell singing of the men who fought in the big war and were now reduced to standing in breadlines) aren't used in production numbers which have any bearing on the films' plots. And, in spite of the topicality and the realism of the "story" songs, Berkeley presents them surrealistically rather than realistically—the Depression depicted in pop Dali-esque images.

It is a popular myth that Depression audiences wanted merely escapist entertainment—entertainment divorced from everything that reminded them of their own hard times. If this were true, then the sheer escapism, the total fantasy world of Paramount's lavish, all-star *Alice in Wonderland* (1933) would have insured its popularity. Instead the film bombed at the box office and with the critics. It is revived on college campuses today as a supreme example of high camp. Nor did Depression audiences want the opposite extreme: a topical, solemn, and socially aware mirror of their own miseries. King Vidor's *Our Daily Bread* (1934) did receive, however, good reviews and is revived today for its earnest, well-intentioned social realism. The formula for the successful Depression film was to mix fantasy with a dash or more of realism and come up with a winner named *It Happened One Night*—or *Little Caesar*, or *Scarface*, or *42nd Street*, or *Top Hat*.

The Screwball Satirists

WHEELER AND WOOLSEY

William M. Drew

Originally appeared in vol. 2, no. 4 (March/April 1978)

They frolicked across the screen—two funny little men, one a sad-faced little fellow with a boyish, quavering voice, the other a skinny character with horn-rimmed glasses, a huge cigar and straight black hair parted in the middle. For eight years, during the depths of the Great Depression, this pair of outrageously zany satirists of pretension made millions laugh throughout the world, attaining a popularity comparable to their contemporaries, Laurel and Hardy and the Marx Brothers. Then, in 1938, one of the pair died. In the succeeding years, their films, although fondly remembered by veteran filmgoers, were seldom revived and this team, once a synonym for wacky humor, was virtually unknown to a later generation. Although they received their share of favorable reviews in their day, many critics did not appreciate their antics, with the consequence that they were ignored and forgotten by most film historians. It was forgotten that the popularity of their films had helped to establish RKO-Radio as a major studio and had provided excellent opportunities for newcomers to the cinema like Joseph L. Mankiewicz, George Stevens and Betty Grable. Forgotten was the fact that the team and their films retained their hilarious vitality and appeal long after more pretentious and once-acclaimed productions of the same period had faded. Yet the three greatest comedy teams in the history of the American cinema are Laurel and Hardy, the Marx Brothers—and Bert Wheeler and Robert Woolsey.

Wheeler and Woolsey were among the few comedy teams that did not combine a straight man with a comic and their films were accordingly permeated with a sparkling, often satirical madness that was seldom found in the works of such later teams as Abbott and Costello and Martin and Lewis who adhered doggedly to the stereotyped "straight man–comedian" formula. Like Laurel and Hardy, Wheeler and Woolsey evolved individual comic characters who provided an excellent contrast and were likable as well as amusing. Bert Wheeler was a parody of the traditional romantic lover with his wavy brown hair and his round, pretty but wide-mouthed face. While his characterization often displayed, in its naiveté and foolishness, the classic screen innocent, he still possessed an underlying roguishness which harmonized with his partner. Bob Woolsey, the self-proclaimed mastermind of the team, was a lecherous, scheming, boastful, but good-natured con-man. The cigar, horn-rimmed glasses, penchant for loud clothes, skinny physique, mincing and swaggering walk and hair parted in the middle enhanced his characterization.

Since, for all their zaniness, their characterizations were believable and had more warmth than many other teams, it was possible for Wheeler and Woolsey to have love interests in their films. Wheeler's feminine counterpart, often played by Dorothy Lee, combined the innocence of the ingénue with the roguishness of the flapper, creating a perfect match for Bert's personality. Woolsey's feminine partners, on the other hand, were worldly-wise and boldly flirtatious, complementing his characterization. There was a consistency in the characterizations of the team. In most situations, Wheeler and Woolsey insisted on remaining Wheeler and Woolsey—the romantic Bert and the more realistic Bob. Even when confronted with a dangerous situation, they usually managed to preserve their oddly dignified, wisecracking insouciance.

A leading characteristic of the team was a steady stream of nonsensical dialogue with puns and wisecracks. Like the Marx Brothers, Wheeler and Woolsey used this nonsensical dialogue to undermine the reality of any situation by reducing it to absurdity. "You mean you shot him in self-defense," the detective said. "No," Woolsey replies, "I shot him through the heart." "He was shot through the head," states the detective. "Well, his heart was in his mouth," is Bob's comeback. In *Cockeyed Cavaliers* (1934), Bert is a kleptomaniac. In the same film, Thelma Todd describes her lowcut dress as "the coming thing," to which Bob remarks, "It must be coming because there's a lot of it that hasn't arrived yet." In *Half Shot at Sunrise*, Bob says to a woman, "I can't recall your name but I've forgotten your face" and, in the same film, when the two comedians are masquerading as waiters in a cafe, a customer asks them, "Have you a wild duck?" to which Bob replies, "No, but we could take a time out and aggravate it for you." In *Cracked Nuts*, the boys have considerable difficulty in pronouncing the phrase "twenty miles as the crow flies." This results in a whole routine centering around the mispronunciation of this phrase, during which Bob exclaims, "Don't you know the king's English?" to which Bert replies, "No, is he English?" The two comedians' many years of experience in vaudeville and on Broadway contributed to their excellent timing in such exchanges. They were also masters of the insult. When a woman angrily demands of Woolsey in *Peach O'Reno* (1931), "How can you look me in the face?" he rejoins, "I'm just getting used to it, I suppose." And when Bob calls a man a "weasel" in *Kentucky Kernels*

(1934) and the man indignantly protests that he has never been so insulted in his life, Bert comments, "That's your fault. You don't get around enough."

Not only were they skilled in verbal humor, the team also used many hilarious sight gags in their films. One of these is a slapping routine in *Rio Rita* (1929), performed as they are perched next to their fiancées on a ship's railing overlooking the water. The routine begins as the duo affectionately pinch each other's face while their girlfriends sing "Sweetheart, We Need Each Other." It proceeds, gaining in tempo, to the point that they are soundly slapping each other in the face with the momentum causing both of them, along with their fiancées, to fall off the railing into the water. In a scene in *Cracked Nuts*, Bert has come to visit Dorothy Lee in the apartment she shares with her aunt, played by Edna May Oliver. Miss Oliver, who does not approve of Bert's romancing Dorothy, returns to the apartment unexpectedly. Bert, to avoid being caught by her, hides in the shower. As Miss Oliver prepares to take a shower, she turns on the water, not knowing that Bert is there, whereupon Bert, trying to avoid getting wet, launches into a pantomime using an umbrella with ballet-like grace. *The Nitwits* uses elaborate sight gags when Bob attempts to induce Bert to escape from the surveillance of the police. Bob mistakenly thinks that Bert is a murderer and the police are out to "get" him. Bert and Bob are on the ground floor of the building where the murder took place when a policeman arrives to prevent any possible suspects from leaving the building. Bob tries to distract the policeman so that Bert can escape by grabbing the policeman's hat and tossing it into the street. Instead of using this stratagem to flee, Wheeler goes into the street, comes back with the hat and obligingly returns it to its owner. Throughout this sequence, Woolsey makes liberal use of pantomime in an attempt to outwit the policeman and to try to get his message across to Wheeler who remains oblivious to Bob's anxiety.

Their directors, most of whom were graduates of silent screen comedy, included Edward Cline, William A. Seiter, Norman Taurog, Mark Sandrich and George Stevens. (Stevens' first major successes as a director were his films with Wheeler and Woolsey.) Several of the team's writers were also distinguished veterans of silent comedy including Tim Whelan who had been a leading gag-man for Harold Lloyd and Harry Langdon, and Ralph Spence, the celebrated writer of humorous titles for many silent comedies. Wheeler and Woolsey, skilled writers themselves, worked with such expert screenwriters as Herman J. and Joseph L. Mankiewicz, S. J. Perelman, Bert Kalmar and Harry Ruby, Norman Krasna and Al Boasberg—most of whom also worked with the Marx Brothers during the same period.

The *New York Times* film critic, Mordaunt Hall, said that "Mr. Wheeler and Mr. Woolsey are almost as mad as all the Marx Brothers together" and wrote of their *Girl Crazy* (1932) that "it offers a brand of humor that few could resist." Quinn Martin of *The New York World* said that the team "attains a pitch of hilarity comparable to that of the Marx Brothers" while the prestigious film magazine, *Photoplay,* consistently praised their works.

From their screen debut in 1929 in the hit musical, *Rio Rita,* to *The Nitwits* directed by George Stevens in 1935, Wheeler and Woolsey reigned supreme as RKO's most popular box-office stars, appearing in a succession of sparkling, zany comedies. But beginning in 1935, the team was affected by changes which were taking place within the film industry. In 1934, after years of harassment by pressure groups like the Legion of Decency, the film industry established the Motion Picture Production Code to regulate its product, a situation which inevitably affected the performing styles of comedians like Wheeler and Woolsey and the Marx Brothers who were well known for their risqué gags and double entendres. Wheeler and Woolsey's peak period of popularity, the early '30s, was a cynical era hardened by the worst years of the Depression while continuing to be influenced by the legacy of the free-and-easy '20s. When the New Deal began to take effect in the mid-'30s, resulting in a more hopeful and confident outlook in the nation's mood, Hollywood began to make films that stressed traditional virtues, designed for the American family. At the same time, the studios made expensive productions that were designed to gain intellectual prestige for the industry. The industry tended to spurn or ignore the allegedly "lowbrow" slapstick and broadly farcical humor, an attitude which had grievous consequences for the later films of the three great comedy teams of the 1930s. Various other complicating factors caused Wheeler and Woolsey to become the first comedy team to be adversely affected by the changing times. For one thing, they were replaced in 1935 by Fred Astaire and Ginger Rogers as RKO's most popular stars. The Wheeler and Woolsey films, now much less important to RKO, were turned out as second features, no longer receiving the care that they had once been given. Their performances as a team may also have been affected by the fact that Bob Woolsey suffered from a series of illnesses during the making of their last films. These illnesses culminated in his death in 1938 from kidney disease at the age of 49. Like the later efforts of Laurel and Hardy and the Marx Brothers, Wheeler and Woolsey's last five films, made from 1935 to 1937, are generally quite weak. While they contain a number of amusing scenes, these later works are slow paced and uninspired compared to their previous films. Like Laurel and Hardy and the Marx Brothers in their later films, Wheeler and Woolsey's characterizations are much less vivid and sympathetic in their last efforts. Even if Wheeler and Woolsey had lasted longer, it is doubtful that they could have regained their former position in the cinema, since the climate of the industry had become less favorable to broadly satirical comedy.

With Wheeler and Woolsey, the basis of their world of comedy lies in the belief that the whole world is a crazy place where anything can happen and where every institution is essentially screwy. The result is that the comic view of their films emphasizes the absurdities of the institutions with which we live and which we take for granted as normal. Divorce suits, the prison system, the military, ineffectual peace conferences, South American coups d'etats, big business, the genre of African exploration documentaries—all are targets for satire in Wheeler and Woolsey's comedies. In their antics, the team was ably assisted by a talented roster of supporting comedians, headed by their perennial leading lady, the beautiful, petite and vivacious Dorothy Lee, who appeared in 13 of the team's 21 features. In many ways, the collective characterizations of the three great comedy teams of the '30s are reminiscent of the three great solo comedians of the silent era. The Marx Brothers resemble Charlie Chaplin in their continual battle with the establishment, Laurel and Hardy are similar to Buster Keaton in their stoic resignation to a world with which they cannot cope and Wheeler and Woolsey recall Harold Lloyd in their boundless buoyancy and triumphant pursuit of success. As befits the cynicism of the Depression era, however, Wheeler and Woolsey's formula for getting ahead in the world is customarily quite dubious, often involving outright deception. Only once, in *Diplomaniacs* (1933), are Wheeler and Woolsey completely defeated when the craziness of the war-mongering nations of the world combines with the greed of arms manufacturers to defeat the idealistic peace movement represented by the comedians and succeeds in bringing on the ultimate insanity—a holocaust in the form of a world war. Usually, however, when pursuing more immediate and worldly goals, Wheeler and Woolsey triumph through a combination of bluff, calculation and sheer luck.

Peach O'Reno, Cracked Nuts and *Diplomaniacs* are representative of the team's use of satire and the unique style of crazy comedy they brought to the screen which produced a succession of consistently excellent and hilarious films.

Peach O'Reno was directed by William A. Seiter, who directed one of Laurel and Hardy's finest features, *Sons of the Desert,* and written by Tim Whelan and Ralph Spence. It satirizes the Reno divorce industry, showing it to be a big business like any other. Divorce lawyers Wheeler and Woolsey have become rich through divorce suits and a special streetcar takes divorce-seeking clients to the duo's office. By night, Bert and Bob's office serves as a casino and, as Woolsey remarks to the guests, "It's certainly good to see so many happily divorced couples here tonight." Interviewing one woman client, Woolsey pulls down a patented rapping shade containing a list of the unpleasant attributes of the unwanted spouse. The woman angrily recites them all ("a cheat," "a souse," "a preposterous prevaricator," etc.) and Bob comments, "You don't want a divorce. You want a firing squad." Like any other big business, there is cut-throat competition in the divorce industry. The rival firm of Jackson, Jackson, Jackson and Jackson starts a price war on divorces by lowering their rates. Wheeler and Woolsey retaliate by pricing their divorce rates even lower. The next move of Jackson, Jackson, Jackson and Jackson is to have one of the Jacksons appointed judge so that he will be in a capacity to rule against every suit represented by Bert and Bob. Further complications arise with the appearance of a gunman who is determined to kill Bert for getting his wife a divorce. In an attempt to escape the gunman, Wheeler disguises himself as a woman despite his reservations about being able to pass for a woman since, as he says, "I don't look masculine enough." Into this scene come two attractive young sisters played by Dorothy Lee and Zelma O'Neal, in an attempt to halt their parents' divorce. The boys fall for them and decide to help them. The courthouse where this case is tried is a circus with food vendors hawking their wares in the aisles of the courtroom and radio station GIN, "the breath of Reno," broadcasting the proceedings. All ends happily as Wheeler and Woolsey succeed in having the suit dismissed by playing on the emotions of the judge and jury and thus reconciling their girlfriends' parents.

Cracked Nuts was directed by Edward Cline, renowned for his association with Buster Keaton and W. C. Fields, and written by Al Boasberg, Ralph Spence and the former silent film comedian, Douglas MacLean. Most of the film takes place in the mythical South American kingdom of El Dorania as it satirizes the constant coups d'etats in Latin America in its depiction of the military in alliance with corrupt politicians continually overthrowing the reigning sovereign. King Oscar, the latest ruler, is determined to escape the fate of his predecessors who have all been assassinated by the military. He gambles away his crown in a dice game with Zander Ulysses Parkhurt (Bob Woolsey) and luckily escapes from the country with his life while Bob becomes King Zup, the new king of El Dorania. (His name is derived from the initials of the character he portrays in the film.) He also acquires a woman named Carlotta who informs him that she has been a favorite of all of the 12 kings who have reigned in El Dorania during the past year. "You're not a wife," Woolsey observes to her. "You're a calendar." Bert Wheeler portrays Wendel Graham who is down to his last $100,000 and is hotly opposed in his courtship of Dorothy Lee by her aunt (Edna May Oliver). With his remaining funds, Bert purchases a revolution from an El Doranian politician, played by Boris Karloff on the eve of his success in *Frankenstein*. Karloff, in league with General Bogardus, plans a coup d'etat to overthrow the current monarch and make Bert the new king of El Dorania. Bert sails for El Dorania on the same ship as his sweetheart, Dorothy Lee, and Edna May Oliver who has extensive land holdings in the South American nation.

When he arrives, Bert discovers that the present king is his old friend, Woolsey, and he is naturally reluctant to shoot Bob in order to become king himself. When Bob expresses a wish to be executed by a novel method if he has to be killed, General Bogardus decides that Woolsey will be bombed from the sky by an airplane. "It will be remembered for years," the general says. "Yeah, but not by me," remarks Bob. There is a large crowd on the big day and the aviator turns out to be cross-eyed Ben Turpin who, as Woolsey notes, "is so cockeyed that he spent three years in the southeast trying to join the Northwest Mounted Police."

In the crazy climax, Bob, seated on a throne, narrowly escapes the exploding bombs. Finally, an explosion from one of the bombs strikes oil and El Dorania is suddenly a wealthy nation. The country becomes a republic and Bob, as the first president, appoints Edna May Oliver the Secretary of War. This satirical farce may very well have inspired two other satires set in mythical nations ruled by cigar-smoking comedians: *Million Dollar Legs* (1932) starring W. C. Fields and Jack Oakie, which Cline also directed, and the Marx Brothers' *Duck Soup* (1933).

Diplomaniacs, directed by Seiter and written by Joseph L. Mankiewicz, is the team's most extraordinary satire. The film depicts the disastrous Geneva Peace Conference that had convened in 1932 and which had failed to halt the rearming of the various powers, a situation which eventually led to the Second World War. In its satirical presentation of these events, *Diplomaniacs*, an excellent early example of black humor, is the most surrealistic in form and, at the same time, the most bitterly realistic in point of view of Wheeler and Woolsey's comedies. For once, Wheeler and Woolsey are completed defeated in their goals, ending up as victims of a nightmarish insanity which they are powerless to control. As the film opens, Bert and Bob are barbers on an American Indian reservation whose business is failing because Indians do not need to shave. The peace-loving Indian nation, newly rich from the discovery of oil on their land, hire the boys to be representatives to the Geneva Peace Conference in order to induce the nations of the world to sign a treaty renouncing war.

Wheeler and Woolsey set sail for Europe and encounter formidable opposition to their peace mission from the High Explosive Bullet Company which depends upon continuous warfare for its profits. The general manager of this corporation, played by Louis Calhern, is constantly scheming to wreck Bert and Bob's mission. He hires a wisecracking Chinese assistant (Hugh Herbert) who is unable to get along with Calhern, and refusing to take his villainous plans seriously, eventually quits the conspiracy to return to China. Calhern also hires a young woman named Dolores (Marjorie White) to seduce Wheeler and Woolsey and steal their briefcase. (As she says: "I've got what it takes to take what they've got.") The captain of the ship on which they are sailing gets drunk and they spend eight months crossing the Atlantic. In Paris, Dolores succeeds in stealing Bert and Bob's briefcase but the duo continue on to Geneva where they survive many attempts on their lives by the directors of the High Explosive Bullet Company. They finally arrive at the Peace Conference where they find the delegates fighting on the conference floor. When Bert and Bob attempt to discuss peace, they are driven out by the war-loving delegates. However, they return and through their showmanlike appeals for an end to warfare, they temporarily win the delegates over to the side of world peace. But soon the businessmen of the High Explosive Bullet Company succeed in sabotaging Wheeler and Woolsey's peace mission completely by forging the names on the peace treaty intended to be signed by the delegates from the various nations of the world. Bert and Bob, thinking the signatures on the treaty to be genuine, depart for what they envision will be a triumphant reception back home. "We'll be the greatest heroes the world has ever known!" they exclaim. Instead, the nations of the world become enraged when it is discovered that the treaty has been forged. As a result, the Second World War breaks out and Wheeler and Woolsey are unfairly blamed for it. When the boys step out of their airplane, after returning home, they are met by soldiers which Bert and Bob mistake for a heroes' welcome by the Indians. "Fellow redskins," Bob proclaims, "this is the greatest moment of your lives. You see in me another Sitting Bull and my little pal here, sitting pretty." They are interrupted by a tough sergeant who hands them guns and gruffly orders them to shut up and fall in line. "Now look here, my good man," protests Bob, "I don't like the tone of your voice nor your ugly face." "Better get used to both of them," the sergeant replies. "America's at war and you've been drafted. You're in the army now!" And so the film ends on an absurd and hopeless note with Wheeler and Woolsey being marched off to war, victims of greedy capitalists and intolerant nation-states. Many films have exposed greed and the self-destructive insanity of the human race as the principal causes of war but what is unusual about *Diplomaniacs* is that it uses the medium of broad farce to express these grim truths. Like *Duck Soup* (produced the same year), *Diplomaniacs* was too offbeat to be properly appreciated in its own time but it remains a trenchant and uproarious commentary on the darkest aspect of human existence and a testimony to the freedom which many filmmakers enjoyed in the early '30s.

Perhaps when there are more studies of this period, Wheeler and Woolsey's films will be more frequently revived for audience viewing. Then, instead of being the most underrated of American film comedians, sad-faced Bert Wheeler and horn-rimmed Robert Woolsey will be regarded as one of the three greatest comedy teams in American film history.

Part III
DIRECTORS

Kubrick, *Killer's Kiss,*
The Killing, and Film Noir

Gene D. Phillips

Originally appeared in vol. 4, no. 3 (Spring 1980)

The sober look at life presented in the post-War "film noir" was in keeping with the movement toward greater realism in the cinema that followed the Second World War. Audiences had grown accustomed to the realism employed in wartime documentaries and fiction films about the war, and continued to expect this same brand of realism in postwar films as well, not only in pictures that dealt directly with the war, but in other kinds of movies too, such as crime melodramas. These films were frequently shot on location and called forth more naturalistic performances from the actors in order to match the authentic settings. Stanley Kubrick's Killer's Kiss *and* The Killing, *in the mid-1950s, came near the end of this cycle.*

Paul Schrader has enumerated several elements that were usually evident in film noir, of which the following are noticeable in *Killer's Kiss:* The film takes place almost entirely at night, often in murkily lit rooms, alleys, and side streets. The actors move about in this hopeless, dark, brooding atmosphere. "There is nothing the protagonist can do," writes Schrader. "The city will outlast and negate even his best efforts," and this is why the hero and heroine of *Killer's Kiss* flee the city at the film's end.

Killer's Kiss, originally titled "Kiss Me, Kill Me," was co-scripted by Kubrick and Howard Sackler. They built their story around some exciting action sequences which would carry the weight of the film and not be costly to shoot, including two key fight scenes and a chase through some lower Manhattan warehouses. Kubrick shot *Killer's Kiss* in the shabbier sections of New York, which gave the film a visual realism unmatched by the post-synchronized sound track.

The hero of the story is a young fighter named Davy Gordon (Jamie Smith) who is already a has-been. We discover him pacing in the waiting room of Grand

Central Station, awaiting the departure of his train. Over the sound track we hear his voice as he begins to recount the events of the past few days in an effort to sort them out for himself. "It all began just before my fight with Rodriguez," he muses, and we cut to a poster advertising Davy's fight, then to Davy examining his face in the mirror of his cheap furnished room. There are photos stuck all round the edges of the mirror which show his Uncle George and Aunt Grace on their farm near Seattle. The pictures represent the cleaner life which Davy has left behind but not forgotten.

His only companion seems to be his pet goldfish, which he dutifully feeds, indicating a softer side to his nature. Davy is the type of film noir hero who is hard-boiled on the surface in order to hide from the brutal world around him the more human, emotional side of his personality. There is one shot of Davy seen through the fishbowl as he peers into it, symbolizing that he is imprisoned in the narrow life which he leads as is the fish in its bowl.

In his loneliness he has taken to staring at Gloria Price (Irene Kane), the girl who lives across the way, whose window is just opposite his. That she is equally lonely is reflected in the fact that at other times she snatches looks at him from her vantage point. They are two isolated individuals whose ability to watch each other from a distance only further emphasizes their separateness. Later they leave their building at the same time, their paths crossing in the lobby as Davy makes for the subway on his way to his fight and Gloria meets her boss Vince Rapallo (Frank Silvera), who is waiting at the curb to driver her to Pleasureland, the dance hall where she works as a hostess. Vince's possessiveness is immediately apparent when he inquires how long she has known Davy. "He just lives in the building," Gloria replies in a bored tone of voice.

The scene shifts to the arena for what Peter Cowie calls in *Seventy Years of Cinema* "one of the most vicious boxing matches ever seen on the screen." Kubrick photographs much of the fight through the ropes to make the viewer feel that he is witnessing the bout from ringside. At crucial moments the director moves his hand-held camera into the ring, first showing Davy's opponent Kid Rodriguez lunging at the camera as if at Davy's jaw, and then showing Davy slumping to the floor in a daze. At this point Kubrick turns the camera upward to catch the overhead lights glaring mercilessly down on the felled fighter.

While Davy broods in the darkness of his room about his final failure to make it as a fighter, he sees Gloria enter her room across the way and begin to undress for bed. Davy watches with undisguised interest until his phone rings. It is Uncle George, offering his condolences over the bout and inviting Davy to come back to Seattle to live and work on the farm. The camera is on Davy as he talks; behind him is a dresser, in the mirror of which we can see Gloria's reflection as she gets into bed. In a single shot, perfectly composed, Kubrick shows us Davy's erotic interest in the girl registering on his face as he talks distractedly to

Uncle George, while at the same time we see the dreamlike image of Gloria in the mirror, who is the true object of his attention at the moment.

Later Davy is awakened by a scream and sees through the window that Gloria is being assaulted by Vince. Her assailant flees when he hears Davy coming, leaving him to comfort Gloria. She explains that Vince had come to ask her to become his mistress and when she sneered at the idea he became violent. Davy assures her that Vince will not come back; Gloria falls into a childlike sleep as the camera cuts to a close-up of the doll which hangs atop her bedstead, suggesting that, despite her present life, Gloria is still an innocent at heart who has been tarnished by the corrupt atmosphere of big-city low life.

In Grand Central Station once more, we see Davy still nervously awaiting his train for Seattle, recalling now how he told Gloria of his plans to return to the family farm: "Looking back, I wonder why I believed her when she said that she would come with me," he says to himself. "She was so scared that she would have grabbed at anything." Thus the viewer at last learns the source of Davy's anxiety while he paces the station floor; he desperately hopes that Gloria will arrive in time to go with him as she had promised. This is a nifty suspense hook on which to hold the filmgoer's interest as Davy goes on with his story:

After Vince kidnaps Gloria, Davy tracks down Vince with a gun and forces the gangster to take him to the warehouse loft where Gloria is being held. At the warehouse Vince's men overpower Davy, but he escapes by jumping through a window to the street below.

Davy runs down streets and through alleys, up a fire escape and across rooftops in his efforts to elude Vince and his hoods. At one point Kubrick stations his camera on a flat rooftop and watches Davy jog from the farthest edge of the roof toward the camera pursued by the racketeers, thereby giving the viewer the feel of Davy's exhausting run without ever moving the camera. Finally Davy takes refuge in a warehouse storeroom filled with department store mannequins. Vince finds him, nonetheless, and the two men face each other for what both of them know is going to be a struggle to the death.

The partially dismantled dummies grotesquely prefigure the violence that the two protagonists are likely to inflict on each other. Vince hurls a torso at Davy, then grabs a fire ax from the wall. Davy fends off his assailant with the broken bodies of the mannequins until he is able to seize a pike-tipped window pole. The opponents viciously battle among the debris like two gladiators, flailing at the camera with their deadly weapons. Finally Davy delivers the death blow off camera. There is a close-up of the smashed head of a dummy as the sound of Vince's scream of pain elides into the screech of a train whistle in Grand Central Station.

Davy brings the story up to date by recounting that he was cleared of Vince's death because he acted in self-defense, but that he has now lost Gloria, probably for good. Up to this point in the film the exterior scenes have taken place mainly at dusk, at night, or at dawn, in true noir fashion. This dark, brooding atmosphere is quickly dispelled as the camera cuts to a bright, sunshiny day outside the station, where a cab is just drawing up to the curb. Gloria gets out and rushes inside to join Davy in his flight from the city to the fresher life on the farm. They embrace and kiss as the camera pulls away, losing sight of them in the congested crowd of passersby hurrying through the station.

In their departure from the brutal big city, which has proved a harsh and unpleasant place for both of them, one can see early indications of Kubrick's dark vision of contemporary society that are further elaborated in his next film. *The Killing* is a tough and tightly knit crime thriller about a racetrack robbery carried out by a group of down-at-the heels small-time crooks who hope to pull off one last big job to solve all their individual financial crises. Like *Killer's Kiss*, *The Killing* comes at the end of the film noir cycle.

"After ten years of steadily shedding romantic conventions," Paul Schrader writes, "the later noir films finally got down to the root causes" of the disillusionment of the period: the loss of heroic conventions, personal integrity, and finally psychic stability. The last films of the trend seemed to be painfully aware that "they stood at the end of a long tradition based on despair and disintegration and did not shy away from the fact." Certainly *The Killing* does not.

Furthermore, *The Killing* also reflects another element of film noir that Schrader points out as endemic to that type of movie: it utilizes a complex chronological order to reinforce a sense of hopelessness and lost time in a disoriented world. Based on Lionel White's novel *Clean Break*, Kubrick's tightly constructed script follows the preparations of the makeshift gang bent on making a big pile of money holding up a racetrack. They have planned the robbery to coincide with the actual running of the seventh race, and Kubrick photographs the heist in great detail with all of its split-second timing. He builds suspense with great intensity by quickly cutting from one member of the gang to another in a series of flashbacks that show how each has simultaneously carried out his part of the plan. All of these parallel lines of action lead inexorably to the climactic moment when the ringleader gets away with the loot.

Pauline Kael, who agrees with Kubrick that *The Killing* marks the real beginning of his career, says in *Going Steady* that robbery pictures tend to be terribly derivative of earlier robbery movies, but that it is still possible for a director to bring a fresh approach to the project: "to present the occupational details of crime accurately (or convincingly), to assemble the gang so that we get a sense of the kinds of people engaged in crime and what their professional and non-professional lives are like. A good crime movie generally has a sordid, semi-documentary authenticity about criminal activities," she concludes, "plus the nervous excitement of what it might be like to rob and tangle with the law."

All of these elements are evident in *The Killing*. In giving us a glimpse into the seedy lives of each member of the gang involved in the robbery, Kubrick has given the film a touch of sleazy authenticity that raises it well above the level of the ordinary crime movie.

The director elicited a high order of ensemble acting from a group of capable Hollywood supporting players who rarely got a chance to give performances of such substance. Sterling Hayden plays Johnny Clay, the tough organizer of the caper. Jay C. Flippen is Marvin Unger, the cynical older member of the group; Elisha Cook, Jr., is George Peatty, the timid track cashier who hopes to impress his voluptuous wife Sherry (Marie Windsor) with stolen money, since he cannot otherwise give her satisfaction; and Ted De Corsia is Randy Kennan, a crooked cop. They and other cast members help Kubrick create the brutal atmosphere of the film.

Kubrick was confident that his method of telling the story by means of fragmented flashbacks would work as well on the screen as it did in the novel. "It was the handling of time that may have made this more than just a good crime film," he says. Another thing that attracted him to White's book, Alexander Walker points out very perceptively in *Stanley Kubrick Directs*, is that the novel touches on a theme that is a frequent preoccupation of Kubrick's films: the presumably perfect plan of action that goes wrong through human fallibility and/or chance.

It is clear from the outset in *The Killing* that the tawdry individuals whom Johnny Clay has brought together to execute the racetrack robbery comprise a series of weak links in a chain of command that could snap at any point. Add to this the possibility of unexpected mishaps that could dog even the best of plans, and the viewer senses that the entire project is doomed from the start. Nevertheless, one is still fascinated to see how things will go wrong, and when.

During the credits of *The Killing*, the film cuts from these documentary shots of the track to shots of the preparations before a race: the starting gate is brought into place, the horses line up in their positions, etc. It is a tribute to Kubrick's naturalistic direction that when in the betting area, few filmgoers suspect that the action has shifted to a studio set. The voice of the narrator further contributes to the documentary air of the picture. He introduces each of the characters, describing why each is implicated in the plot.

Some of the strongest dramatic scenes in the film are those between mousy George Peatty and his sluttish wife Sherry. George is hopelessly in love with Sherry and is constantly afraid that she will two-time him with another man, something she has already done repeatedly. Kubrick gives us a thumbnail sketch of their ugly, unhappy relationship in just a few lines of dialogue.

Maddened by her constant condescension, George blurts out that he is involved in a big operation that will make them rich. Sherry shrewdly tries to pry more of the details from him; but George, aware that he has already said too much, becomes evasive. "My own husband doesn't trust me," she pouts. Sherry later tells her love Val (Vince Edwards) what she has been able to wheedle out of her husband. Ironically, she is as submissive to this cheap crook as George is to her.

At the meeting Johnny has called with his fellow conspirators, he goes over the intricate plans which he has laid. A single overhead lamp illumines their worn, defeated faces as they talk, leaving them surrounded by a darkness that is almost tangible. It is this darkness that seems to hover around Kubrick's characters in many of his films and which they desperately seek to keep from engulfing them—usually without success.

Tension begins to mount as the day of the holdup dawns. "Four days later, at 7 a.m., Sherry Peatty was wide awake," says the narrator. Badgering her nervous spouse at the breakfast table, she gets him to admit that today is the day. The only possible weakness in the film is the implausibility of George's being quite as naive and ineffectual in dealing with his wife as he is portrayed to be. But the two performers breathe a great deal of credibility into their handling of these scenes, particularly Elisha Cook, Jr., whom Penelope Houston describes in *Contemporary Cinema* as "the prototype of all sad little men."

"At the track the favorite, Red Lightning, was given only half a portion of feed, and Johnny Clay began what might be the last day of his life." Ironically, it will be that last day of life for just about everyone involved in the project but Johnny.

From this point onward Kubrick begins to follow each separate strand of the robbery plot through to its completion, doubling back each time to show how each of the elements of the elaborate plan is implemented simultaneously with all of the others. Kubrick repeats the shots from the credit sequence of the horses getting into starting position for the seventh race each time he turns back the clock to develop a different step in the complex robbery plan, thereby situating the viewer temporally.

Kubrick thus builds his film from the beginning toward the peak where all of Johnny's meticulous planning suddenly converges on the moment when he enters the cashiers' office and scoops up $2 million. Johnny passes George Peatty's window as George gives him a frightened, furtive look. George opens the door, Johnny moves by him and enters the locker room, where he gets a rifle and puts on a rubber mask and gloves. With typical Kubrick irony, the face on the mask is frozen into a perpetual grin.

Thus disguised, Johnny bursts into the cashiers' room and orders them to fill his large laundry sack with all the money it will hold. Then Johnny makes his getaway.

Kubrick begins to draw the last threads of the plot together as Johnny's companions in crime assemble in Marvin's shabby living room to await Clay's appearance with the money. The men sit around drinking nervously and listening to radio reports of the "daring holdup" at the track. George's hand, anxiously nursing a glass, is in the foreground, suggesting the tension that permeates the room.

"Where is Johnny?" George whines. "Why does his timetable have to break down now?" There is a knock at the door, but instead of Johnny and the cash it is Val and one of his mobsters. They force their way into the room, expecting to grab the swag for themselves. A shoot-out ensues that leaves everyone in the room dead — except George, who is mortally wounded. For a moment Kubrick trains his handheld camera on the pile of corpses spread around the room, recalling for an instant the clump of mannequins in the climactic sequence of *Killer's Kiss*. The room is silent, except for the sound of bouncy Latin music pouring from the radio, providing an ironic counterpoint to the carnage of the scene.

George Peatty has enough life left in him to struggle toward the door. The camera, assuming his point of view momentarily, sways with him in the direction of the door, and George's hand enters the frame to twist the knob. Johnny has just pulled up outside. The camera is now in the back seat of Johnny's car and follows George as he comes out of the building, sprawls across the hood of Johnny's auto, pulls himself together, and forces himself to continue across the street, where he gets into his own car and drives away.

George is moving with the determination of a man who knows he must accomplish something before he takes his last breath. Once home he finds Sherry packing to go away with Val, as he suspected he would. She tries to mollify him with a prefabricated alibi, but for once in his life George is not to be forestalled by his scheming wife. "Why did you do it?" he asks plaintively, already knowing the answer. "I loved you, Sherry." He then blasts away with his pistol, the impotent husband finally penetrating his wife with bullets. As George himself falls forward toward the camera he knocks over the birdcage, symbol of his pitifully narrow existence, which is now at an end.

Johnny, aware that something terrible has happened, drives to the airport to meet his girl Fay as planned. En route he buys the largest suitcase he can find and stashes the loot in it. He finds Fay and they proceed to the check-in counter, passing two men who are quite clearly sizing up everyone who enters the air terminal. With nervous nonchalance Johnny demands that the airline allow him to lug his huge suitcase on board with him rather than stow it in the luggage compartment. Throughout his bickering with the airline personnel, which Kubrick records in a single take, the bulky bag stands inertly in the center of the frame, as Johnny tries to minimize its size. Realizing that he is causing a scene,

Clay capitulates and watches apprehensively as the bag is tossed onto a conveyor belt and disappears from sight.

Johnny and Fay arrive at the departure gate just in time to see the baggage truck drive out onto the windy airfield. They watch in mute horror as the ramshackle case falls off the top of the mountain of luggage and springs open, flooding the airstrip with stolen bills that blow right at the camera. The fate of the money in *The Killing* recalls how the gold dust in John Huston's *Treasure of the Sierra Madre* (1948) blows across the desert sands. In that film the men who have slaved to acquire the gold can only laugh hysterically when they contemplate how it drifted away from them.

But Fay and Johnny are in a daze. She supports his arm as they walk to the street and hopelessly try to hail a taxi before the two FBI agents who have been watching them all along can reach them. Fay tells Johnny to make a run for it, but he can only murmur, almost inaudibly, "What's the difference?" Resigned to their fate, Johnny and Fay turn resolutely around to face the two men advancing toward them through the glass doors of the flight lounge. Like Davy and Gloria in *Killer's Kiss*, Johnny and Fay had hoped to escape the corrosive atmosphere of the big city by flight to a cleaner climate. But for Johnny, brutalized by a life of crime, it was already too late.

The Killing is the kind of crime melodrama that Pauline Kael had in mind when she wrote of the sort of film that has a "sordid, semi-documentary authenticity about criminal activities" and exudes "the nervous excitement of what it might be like to rob and tangle with the law." The occasion of her remarks was the 1968 Jim Brown vehicle *The Split*, which imitated *The Killing* in an uninspired way that makes one appreciate Kubrick's film all the more. When *The Killing* itself was released a decade earlier, Miss Kael saw it as "an expert suspense film, with fast, incisive cutting," and "furtive little touches of characterization." *Time* applauded Kubrick for having shown "more imagination with dialogue and camera than Hollywood has seen since the obstreperous Orson Welles went riding out of town."

In his treatment of the film noir cycle in American cinema, Paul Schrader pointed out a triple theme inherent in these films: "a passion for the past and present, but also a fear of the future. The noir hero dreads to look ahead, but instead tries to survive by the day, and if unsuccessful at that, he retreats to the past. Thus film noir's techniques emphasize loss, nostalgia, lack of clear priorities, insecurity."

Similarly, in his two noir films Kubrick shows us modern man gradually being dehumanized by living in a materialistic world in which one man exploits another in the mass effort for survival. In his later films like *Dr. Strangelove* which probe into the future, Kubrick further suggests that man's failure to master the world of the present can only lead to man's being mastered by the world of the future.

It is clear, then, that the tenets of film noir were congenial to Kubrick's developing personal vision in his early career. Consequently, it is not surprising that at least two of his first films fit so neatly into the film noir genre.

Material in this article has been drawn from the author's book Stanley Kubrick: A Film Odyssey, *where it appears in a completely different form.*

The Twilight World of Roland West

A FORGOTTEN MASTER OF THE MACABRE

Scott MacQueen

Originally appeared in vol. 7, no. 2 (March/April 1983)

In the annals of Clutching Hands, Hooded Figures, and Old Dark Houses, the name of film director Roland West might not figure as prominently in the minds of viewers as James Whale or Tod Browning—but be not deceived: Roland West in his day was a master of his craft and one of the best technicians in the genre of the horrific. This Master of the Gothic style was himself something of a Faustian man. His career would abruptly end for reasons inexplicable today. His life was at times shrouded in mystery. And his penchant was obviously toward "things that go bump in the night."

Of all his films, at least two deserve the status of "classic." One of them was a police thriller that stood at the forefront of sophisticated early talkies. It was called *Alibi* (1929), and it deserves to be seen by more of today's viewers. The other was a preeminent entry in the list of Gothic exercises so beloved by Hollywood in the 1928–30 period. Even its title positively reeked of bone-chilling atmosphere—*The Bat Whispers.*

What do we really know about this odd and elusive man? He was born in Cleveland, Ohio in 1887 and, from the age of twelve, worked with theatrical stock companies and vaudeville. Like D. W. Griffith, his films forever after were to be influenced by the traditions of the melodrama. With his former manager, Joseph Schenck, he made his first movie, *Lost Souls* (1916), and went on to *Deluxe Annie* (1918), *The Silver Lining* (1921), *Nobody* (1921), and *Flaming Love* (1924). *The Unknown Purple* (1923) and *The Monster* (1925) were his first filmed thrillers. By the time of *The Bat* in 1926, Schenck was chairman of United Artists and his company distributed it and West's subsequent films, *The Dove* (1928), *Alibi* (1929), *The Bat Whispers* (1930), and *Corsair* (1931).

West, a wealthy dilettante, made films mostly for his own amusement, then devoted more of his time to a new avocation, a seaside restaurant called "Thelma Todd's" (named after the actress, his mistress and part owner of the establishment). Following a lover's quarrel with West in 1935, Miss Todd was found dead of carbon monoxide poisoning. West was implicated in a murder charge, though the official coroner's verdict was "accidental death." West never returned to films. He died in Santa Monica on March 31, 1952, survived by his second wife, the actress Lola Lane.

The man was odd and elusive and it is equally difficult to form conclusive opinions about the larger body of his work. None of his silents, save one, have survived and they are poorly documented. *The Unknown Purple* is his earliest antecedent of *The Bat Whispers*, adapted from a 1918 stage play by West and Carlyle Moore. Originally written as a motion picture scenario, *The Vanishing Man*, it told the story of an inventor of a "purple light" of invisibility who uses his creation for revenge on his scheming wife and her lover, who had sent him to jail for a crime he didn't commit. Reverting to haunted house formula, West's ghostly use of the light was highlighted by purple tinting in release prints.

The Monster (1925) is the only surviving example of West's silent films. It is a turgid, obvious parody with comic effects achieved lazily and routinely through banal gag titles and situation comedy. In a rural Midwestern town the disappearance of a prominent citizen causes the biggest excitement since "the grocer's wife ran off with the milkman." Johnny, played by effeminate milquetoast Johnny Arthur, receives his detective's certification from a correspondence school when a title informs us that he has ambition, which in Danburg is "like having eczema." Lon Chaney plays Dr. Ziska, an asylum inmate masquerading as the institution's director who arranges automobile wrecks on the lonesome nighttime highway and extracts the survivors for his "scientific work": transferring souls between men and women. West arranges most sequences as though for a stage proscenium, using spotlights and dimmer lights to emphasize characters and events within these tableaux. Ziska's first appearance is impeccably staged: shadowy fingers writhing on the wall herald his descent of a steep staircase into a pool of light. While drawing on an elegantly mounted cigarette that wreathes him in wisps of smoke, Ziska casually resurrects a dead man with some artful hand gestures. Beyond this, Chaney plays the character as pure parody. His performance and the movie are failures.

The 1926 version of *The Bat* is missing. Its reputation as a good, important thriller is enhanced by the presence of William Cameron Menzies as art director and Arthur Edeson on camera, but its unavailability for appraisal, along with the rediscovery of *The Monster*, make it impossible to repeat the hazy estimations of an earlier generation. Assuming its similarity to *The Monster*, West probably improved his remake. Sound and wide-screen photography were available to him in 1930 but, more importantly, he had profited from the atmosphere and distorted set architecture of German expressionist silent films, such as the work of Paul Leni and F.W. Murnau. One senses that West must have been both familiar and dissatisfied with Paul Leni's American film, *The Cat and the Canary* (1927), for he seizes on Leni's fluent devices in the same context—the camera roaming through the old house, cutting to already moving camera shots, exploitation of expressionistic décor, and invariably improves on them. The silliness of the melodrama is acknowledged and then transcended to create genuine terror. West's sensibility is closest to another German director, the Fritz Lang of *Das Testament von Dr. Mabuse* (*The Testament of Dr. Mabuse*), evoking a black nightmare which is never visited by sunlight, naturalism, or reason, and which is not dissipated even after the threat has been removed and order ostensibly restored.

West's infatuation with the possibilities of his medium mature in his first sound film, *Alibi,* one of the few early sound features that tries to combine the visual eloquence of late silents with material bound completely to dialogue and the stage.

Alibi opens with the shadow of a prison guard on a stone wall, in front of which moves a policeman's nightstick. We hear the dull ring of the stick impacting against the stone. In a series of dissolves, a bell rings, and the listless feet of convicts march past; a guard watches, his shadow looming behind him, and the trudge of feet merges rhythmically with the sound of the nightstick striking the wall. Dissolve to a huge perspective shot of the cell block: Prisoners appear from their cages and mechanically form ranks. Another dissolve to the Warden's Office, then a typed paper identifying "No. 1065" as "Chick Williams." Williams, in civilian clothes, quietly examines his release form while a guard sorts his discarded prison clothes in the dim light seeping through a barred window. A final dissolve, and Williams appears, a free man, on the steps outside of the prison.

The very next sequence in *Alibi* opens with an expansive dolly shot of Bachman's nightclub, the lettering on the canopy taking prominence as we dolly under the awning to the front doors. We dissolve to another dolly shot, in perspective, across the hallway as the camera picks out the name BACHMAN written in huge tiles across the floor. Reaching the end of the hall, we hear merrymakers and music. Dissolve to another dolly across the floor of the nightclub, up to a chorus line and, in a final dissolve, to one particular chorine.

The camera movements in *The Bat Whispers* make those in *Alibi* look like mere rehearsals. For $400 technician Charles Cline constructed a lightweight, twenty-four-foot long camera dolly that could send a camera "zooming eighteen feet in a fraction of a second." [1] In press releases West touted the achievement and, without naming names, gloated over its alleged superiority to the mammoth crane that Paul Fejos and Hal Mohr had spent thousands of dollars developing at Universal for *Broadway* (1929). Though it could never achieve the dizzying speed the Cline dolly *appears* capable of (these sequences in *The Bat Whispers* are executed in miniature sets) the *Broadway* crane more than justified its cost with the tremendous versatility it extended to subsequent Universal productions.

In *The Bat Whispers*, West unshackled the camera from the weighty blimped housings and immobility typical of early sound films. Additionally, a scaffold was constructed thirty feet high and three hundred feet long, from which the camera was suspended by steel cables and sent zooming on tracks through space. Though it would be several years before the moving camera would completely re-attain both the beauty and logic that it had mastered in late silents like *Sunrise*, West's fluid camera movements justify themselves by their mere existence—though perhaps they impart a "bat's eye view" to the proceedings.

The story about The Bat terrorizing the tenants of a gloomy old mansion in his search for stolen money was already old-fashioned in 1930. While Mary Roberts Rinehart's story had concerned itself with spinster Cornelia Van Gorder's calm penetration of the mystery, West chose to make The Bat's exploits the subject of his chronicle, with appropriately fantastic visual syntax to tell the story. Some images convey this sense. The film's first shot is a pullback from a tolling clock tower at night that dissolves to a rapid forward tracking shot as the camera dives into an open window to discover The Bat's intended victim, Mr. Bell. A shot of Bell looking out of the window is taken from outside, over his head, accenting the height and inaccessibility of his apartment by revealing the sheer face of the skyscraper and the city streets below. We cut to a head-on exterior shot to reveal The Bat dangling within the window frame as he reaches down and throttles his victim.

To convey the criminal's flight to the countryside, the sound of a tolling bell returns us to the clock tower, then the noise of a locomotive and a shot of rolling train wheels. This too segues to a rapid panorama of the city as seen from the moving train. These three moving shots climax with a fourth, rolling down the railroad tracks as the train approaches a sign announcing the town of Oakdale. Just as we appear moments from hurtling into the sign, the tracks swerve to the right. With another dissolve, we are speeding in a car down a country road. As the headlights strike the facade of the Oakdale Bank in front of us, The Bat's shadow sweeps fleetingly across the front of the building. The chase leads to the Fleming estate where the story proper is begun. The Bat continues to be exploited as a disembodied phantom, his shadow stalking about outside the house. Flashes of lightning reveal him perched in the treetops, wings spread majestically as he drops on his unsuspecting victim, or looming malevolently at the window of the darkened study.

After establishing the uncanny manifestations of The Bat, West takes us into the mansion. We approach from a great distance as the camera races through the air over the manicured lawns of the estate and picks out a window on an upper floor. Thunder rumbles and lightning flashes, the darkness between the bursts of light cunningly masking the juncture of two distinct shots as the camera moves up to the window sill and into the house, gliding autonomously along the ancient corridors, as it approaches a pencil of light bleeding under a slightly ajar door. We hear voices, faintly at first, then louder as we sneak up to the door and dissolve into the room to discover Mrs. Van Gorder speaking with her maid.

Later, the Bat's presence in the house becomes more tangible. Lightning flashes illuminate him in the treetop beyond the window. As the flash subsides, the room is thrown into darkness. Another flash reveals him now on the balcony, moving toward the window. Again darkness. In the next bolt of lightning we are aware of the now-open window and the certainty that The Bat is in the house. Cut to the wall, where The Bat's hunched shadow slowly pivots with hands outstretched. A closer tracking shot, and the shadowy fingers seem to bleed along the wall, a la Murnau's *Nosferatu*.

Fears of a fluid, ever-present menace reach a crescendo when the heroine, Dale, separates herself from her companions to investigate a hidden room where we know The Bat is hiding. Carrying a lone candle to light her way, Dale takes no notice as the false front fireplace inexorably closes behind her. She is sealed in with the monster in a single, perfectly calculated take marked by the exaggerated groaning of the closing wall. Dale rifles through papers on a desk, then senses another presence in the room. Silhouetted against the wall, The Bat spreads his cloak regally in the silence and darkness. Dale's terror is conveyed in a close-up, but the expression immediately changes to incomprehension. As we cut back to The Bat, he is slowly folding his wings about him and shrinking back into the darkness. Thunder rolls on the soundtrack as he becomes an amorphous black shape diminishing into a pool of umbrage. Then suddenly, with an uneven, halting gait, the crouching figure lurches from the shadows. "Quiet! Quiet!" he whispers, "Not a word—not a sound!" Dale's candle flickers out and The Bat closes in on her. "I'm gonna getcha, do ya hear?" he whispers. "Stand still! Till I put my hands around your lily white throat and *squeeze* and *squeeze* until you're dead!"

Though discovering the identity of The Bat is secondary to the verve of his exploits, West plants ample visual, if not dramatic, clues that focus our attention on Detective Anderson. Well before the denouement, when The Bat is unmasked, Anderson is introduced in silent-film style by a close-up of his calling card, which dissolves to a long shot of Anderson and Mrs. Van Gorder, before pulling up to a tight shot. This kind of a dissolve, existing in real time rather than elapsed time, is used at several points in the film to highlight details or to move into a scene. Unlike a match cut, it provides a languorous flow to events and, in this instance, causes the moment to stand out in our perception. With each subsequent appearance, Anderson is presented with unusual style. As he eavesdrops on Dale's telephone call, the composition is much like a split screen, with Anderson on the left and Dale's shadow cast on the right, the two figures separated by a band of shadow falling diagonally across the frame.

This visual decadence climaxes with The Bat's unmasking, when the ersatz detective is revealed in all of his hollow-eyed splendor beneath the villain's black mask. "There never was a jail built strong enough to hold The Bat," he declares, "and after I've paid my respects to your cheap lock-up . . . I shall return . . . at night!" A final close-up of his face, awash in flickering light from the burning garage, ends the film. "The Bat always flies at night," he grins broadly, displaying his teeth, "and always . . . in a straight line!" He laughs hideously to himself, and tossing his head back, cackles as we fade to black.

Unlike James Whale's *The Old Dark House* (1932), and others which would cap the story with an epilogue dispelling the hallucinogenic horrors, *The Bat Whispers* ends with the demon still holding sway over a world of perpetual night. By allowing the clichés to breathe easily with their own naïve charm, West freed himself for the much more difficult task of remaking the stock elements into something genuinely frightening. That after fifty years, *The Bat Whispers* still has the power to engender terror, speaks for the validity and efficacy of his principles.

This is not a film one remembers for performances, though there is a certain outrageous conviction in Chester Morris' Bat who exclaims "I've got the greatest brain that ever existed!" Maude Eburne, usually anathema to any film she appeared in, is surprisingly restrained in her provision of comic relief, since probably for once the nervous staccato of her role is derived from the play rather than imposed on it. Gustav Von Seyffertitz, as the odious Dr. Venrees, is such a skeletal, unwholesome-looking individual that he seems quite at home amid the medieval armor, marble pillars, and shadowy recesses of Paul Crawley's spacious, brooding sets.

This is a film to revere for its visual look, the responsibility of two talented, creative cameramen: Ray June and Robert Planck. The soundtrack, though respected and used with invention, never dominates their visual storytelling. It is a long, deathly silence punctuated by dire threats, fearful pronouncements, and thunder, in which we are constantly straining for screams and noises in the night, and the inevitable whisperings of The Bat.

The film's one misfortune was in opening at the wrong time to an audience indifferent to both its subject and its highly inventive technology. The 1928–1929 period was crammed with other "old house" films like *The Last Warning, The Haunted House, The House of Horrors, House of Secrets*, and *The Terror*. As *The Bat Whispers* went into production in the summer of 1930 (its title stressing that The Bat will now be seen *and* heard), the industry was still experiencing the changeover to sound. With the First National remake of *The Gorilla* already in release, that first week of November 1930 must have seemed unbearable with a remake of *The Cat and the Canary*—*The Cat Creeps*—opening the day after a special preview of *The Bat Whispers* on the sixth. *Variety* favorably reviewed *The Cat Creeps* and dismissed the preview of *The Bat Whispers* as "One of those mystery-mellers with 90% of the action in dimly lit interiors."[2] However, when *Variety* properly reviewed it again the following January, its production and camera qualities were noted along with the bitter truth that it ". . . must follow all of the other mystery-haunted house films. Needs and can stand plenty of heavy exploitation."[3] One disillusioned critic was moved to title his review, "The Bat Groans . . . with Age."

Yet when Universal sent out *The Cat Creeps* on November 7th it had been preceded by a saturation promotion in its key opening dates, which made the film a moderate box office success. United Artists simply did not consider *The Bat Whispers* in the same league as *Hell's Angels* and *Whoopee*, and sold it accordingly. To complicate matters, *The Bat Whispers* was distributed in two formats, conventional 35mm and a special 65mm widescreen version.

October had already seen the debut of several other incompatible widescreen processes with Fox's "Grandeur" 70mm for *Happy Days* and *The Big Trail*; Warners' "Vitascope" *Kismet*; RKO's "Natural Vision" for *Danger Lights*; and M-G-M's "Realife" *Billy the Kid*. Only the M-G-M format was viable for exhibitors, since existing equipment could be modified with a lens for $200, as opposed to the Fox system, which cost the exhibitor $4000 to install, or custom "Natural Vision" projectors costing $12,000. The industry believed that widescreen would be standard by Christmas, without reckoning on harried theater owners recovering from the trouble and expense of converting for sound. Some could not fit the equipment into their projection booths, more voltage was needed for a stronger arc lamp, and some processes had a dual system for sound with chain drive motors synchronizing two machines.

As *The Bat Whispers* went into its first run on November 29th, the exhibitors' reservations were shared by a public who did not think much of widescreen at the inflated price of two and three dollars a seat. For all practical purposes widescreen was dead and the Hays Office made it official in December when it ruled against further 70mm productions, forbidding ". . . by word or gesture . . . [to] permit the public's curiosity to be aroused about any new [motion picture] invention for at least two years."[4]

Of the twelve films West made, only four survive. *The Monster* was salvaged at M-G-M in the early seventies, and *Alibi*, though withdrawn is protected. *Corsair* is available for rental and legal purchase. Though reissued twice and shown on television in video's infancy, only a precious few 16mm prints of *The Bat Whispers*, deriving from the Atlantic Pictures reissue, exist in private hands. Though original leaders on the 16mm print under study indicate it as ten reels, it runs a bare 71 minutes, while the pressbook describes the film to be nearly 8,000 feet in ten reels —or 89 minutes. Contemporary reviews indicate that there was a brief epilogue—missing from the study print—in which the audience was addressed by a voice from the black screen, after which Chester Morris reappeared as himself to ask that the ending not be divulged to future patrons.

Though a copyright renewal was secured in 1958, the existence of preservation elements is not confirmed. A duplicate 16mm negative prepared in Europe—dark and grainy with a wretched soundtrack—is the only assured posterity. Teasingly, a pristine 65mm nitrate print donated in the early 1960s by Mary Pickford to the doomed Hollywood Museum does not appear to have made the transition to The American Film Institute, where the failed museum's film holdings were consolidated. If intact, that unique 65mm print survives on volatile and unstable nitrate film stock. Unless it is located and copied, *The Bat Whispers* may remain in the limbo of lost films.

Notes

1. *The Bat Whispers* exhibitors' pressbook.
2. *Variety*, November 12, 1930.
3. Ibid.
4. "Wide Film Is Ruled Out," *Variety*, December 17, 1930.

William Wellman

THE PARAMOUNT YEARS (1927–1930)

Frank Thompson

Originally appeared in vol. 4, no. 4 (Summer 1980)

William A. Wellman is known for a handful of films that must rank among the classics of the American film: Beau Geste, A Star Is Born, Nothing Sacred, The Public Enemy, The Ox-Bow Incident, The High and the Mighty. *What of the balance of his career, though? It seems to me somehow unfair to judge an artist only by his masterworks. The formative, immature and failed works are surely as important to an understanding of the oeuvre as the mature and successful ones. In some ways, these formative works hold an even greater fascination for the discerning viewer for they show the false steps, the developing interests; they are masterpieces in embryo.*

The films listed above are familiar indeed, but the following titles from the early Paramount years probably do not mean much to you: Chinatown Nights, The Man I Love, Woman Trap, Dangerous Paradise *and* The Young Eagles. *These films are forgotten, yet today they constitute a respectable and interesting part of Wellman's growth as a director. They were Wellman's first five sound films, produced between his great success with* Wings *(1927) and his prolific period at Warner Bros., from 1930 to 1933.*

స్

Although prints of Wellman's Paramount films of 1927–30 exist and are available for viewing, these films have fallen into an anonymity that they don't entirely deserve. Certainly there's not a masterpiece among them but there is much in each to admire and much to learn about their director's interest, strengths, flaws and obsessions. They are fine, tough little films and need no apology. The five are most valuable, however, for the air of prescience with which they are imbued. They foreshadow the mature Wellman of the mid-to-late thirties.

In this way, the relationship between two brothers on opposite sides of the law in *Woman Trap* predates that of another pair of brothers two years later in *The Public Enemy;* The understanding wife of an egocentric, disaster-bent boxer in *The Man I Love* serves as a blueprint for Vicki Lester in *A Star Is Born*; the heavy, muggy, tropical atmosphere of *Dangerous Paradise* informs the characters' actions and attitudes in a way that looks forward to other Wellman films in which landscape is as important as any other facet: *Beau Geste, The Call of the Wild, Track of the Cat, Island in the Sky; Young Eagles* concerns itself with Wellman's greatest love, flying, a subject that he would return to again and again, even to his very last film.

One of the most striking qualities of the films is their movement. Produced at that legendary time in film history, the switch to sound, none of these films has the talky, stagebound look that we have come to associate (mistakenly, perhaps) with the early sound film. On the contrary, Wellman moves the camera about to a much greater extent than he was ever to do again. The fluidity of the camera, coupled with the careful, controlled lighting, links these films more to the late silent film than to the early sound film. Wellman refused to give up the beauty that he had found in such films as *Wings, Beggars of Life* and *You Never Know Women.*

His major fondness of the period seems to have been reserved for the moving camera. This in itself wasn't very unusual for the time. The late twenties saw a great deal of UFA-influenced camera work in Hollywood films. Wellman, like many other directors (John Ford and Howard Hawks, for instance) took to his baroque style immediately, only to give it up later in the thirties when he realized that it was at odds with his style.

"Camera movement I loved," said Wellman, "and then I got awfully sick of it." In his best films, he seems to have honed down camera movement to the bare essentials and used it in a manner more utilitarian than stylistic.

In the twenties, though, he pulled out all the stops, and this style seems to have been born of ego rather than artistic choice. He was out to prove that nothing so inconsequential as a little microphone was going to hamper his work. An arrogant man, he was always out to prove himself in one way or another. If everyone else was having their films stagebound by the microphone, then, by God, he'd "track" till the cows came home.

He said, "When we first started [sound], the booms were camouflaged. They hung from chandeliers or something and you had to get your action underneath there. That burned me up—you can't make pictures that way—you've got to have some flow. So I came in and said, 'I got news for you sound men this morning. I'm moving that Goddamned mike.' And I got my grips, got me a big ladder and went and took [the mike] and put it on the end of a broomstick. And I moved it and it worked."

While not quite the technical innovator that he makes himself sound (virtually every director who was working at the time claims to have invented the moving boom mike), it does seem to be true that Wellman was among the first directors to resume more or less normal film-making technique after sound had temporarily nailed everything to the floor. He took sound in stride and used it naturally and unobtrusively just as he was to become an early master of Technicolor and Cinemascope.

About sound he "didn't have an opinion one way or the other." "My reputation was based on making films very quickly. Whether a film talks or not is immaterial anyhow. I prefer [the term] 'motion picture'—a picture that *moves*, and movement is the most important thing."

Wellman's pictures did move, his early sound ones even more than his silent ones. In fact, one finds only a single major stylistic difference after the conversion to sound: with the new informational possibilities of dialogue, he was able to dispense with what he believed to be an overused technique—the close-up. To Wellman, close-ups were exclamation points, elbow nudges to the audience. While necessary in the silent films, where the face must hold more dramatic responsibility, the close-up could be used with more discretion when dialogue was available. He explained, "You use close-ups to bolster a sequence, to get a point over. Cut in to a close-up and it means something." In fact, so relieved did he seem to be when rid of the constant necessity of the close-up, that his early sound films are almost completely devoid of them. Rarely does he move in closer than a medium shot, even in the most dramatic moments.

Wellman wanted to evoke emotion, not from tight close-ups of tear-stained faces, but from the skillful manipulation of the camera, editing and dialogue. No matter how unjustified his faith turned out to be, Wellman always trusted the story and used his considerable skills in ways that best told it.

Wellman told Kevin Brownlow in *The Parade's Gone By*, "I don't know what made me begin to move the camera around. I'd seen fights and I wanted to get closer to them so I'd move forward. Then I thought I'd do that with the camera. But what I loved most was composition. I used to get some wonderful odd angles, but then everybody started using odd angles—shooting through people's navels—so the idea was destroyed. Then I realized that the best thing was to make the picture the simplest way you could; if you wanted movement or anything like that, use it where it really meant something."

Though he was never to completely shake his penchant for "odd angles," Wellman spent these years at Paramount unifying his vision and reconciling the extremes in his nature. While still a sucker for a good tracking shot, it's obvious that he was becoming more concerned with making his technique more invisible.

For example, there is a scene in *The Man I Love* in which the camera follows a boxer into a locker room, through it to a dressing room. It stands outside as the boxer and his manager enter the dressing room arguing, their faces appearing periodically at a window in the door. Then it follows the two back through the locker room, into the fight arena and down the aisle. As the boxer enters the ring, the camera tracks along the front row to the opposite side of the ring to bring the boxer's girlfriend into a medium shot—all in one take!

The length and complexity of this scene is breathtaking and, as an example of Wellman's virtuosity, exceeds even the famous Folies Bergere crane shot in *Wings*. A shot of this type (it takes place in three separate rooms and goes places that it would seem impossible to lay track) would be difficult in a silent film. But with the extra problems of dialogue and sound effects, it seems nearly superhuman.

The most important point about this scene, though, is the way Wellman practically throws it away. The scene is strictly functional. It was done in one take, not because he felt like being brilliant that day, but because that was the way the story could best be served at that point. Though it doesn't have the trappings of a *tour de force,* it is one. As Wellman told Brownlow in the quote above, he used movement where it really meant something.

This tendency toward simplicity had farther-reaching effects than merely a paring down of his visual style. It also affected his choice of stories. The personal story in *Wings* is vital, of course, but the star of that film is World War I, not Buddy Rogers. But Wellman's next films were devoid of the spectacle that, for better or worse, defined *Wings*. Characters and relationships became more important. Consequently, performances became more nuanced and suggestive. If the dogfights and battle scenes are what one takes from *Wings*, the portrayal of Tom Powers by James Cagney in *The Public Enemy* is what one remembers from that film.

The progression is an important one. The period from 1928 to 1930 at Paramount is where it evolved.

Obviously, to many, there seems to have been a regression. *Woman Trap,* on the surface, must seem like a step down from *Wings*. After all, how could the director be equally adept and committed to both genres? Perhaps the attitude that all of Wellman's films between the acknowledged classics are mere filler, inconsequential and trivial, helps to explain the obscurity into which these films have fallen.

Yet Wellman's career is full of such contradictions. How odd, for example, to follow the grim, solemn, important film *The Ox-Bow Incident* with the seemingly frivolous *Lady of Burlesque*.

Yet, to wonder at these juxtapositions is to deny Wellman's wide range of concerns and to ignore his position as a contract director. As such, he had relatively few choices about what projects he would be assigned (at this stage in his career, that is; later, of course, he was given a considerably freer hand).

The fact is that, whether they were studio assignments or personal projects, Wellman's films are all of a piece. *Woman Trap* is as close to Wellman as *Wings*. Closer perhaps, for the smaller, more unassuming project, almost by definition, leaves more room for the director's personality to project itself. No matter how slight the film seemed to be, no matter how trivial the story, Wellman was somehow able to leave his imprint on the finished film.

In his self-deprecating way, Wellman confirms this: "Frankly, if you review my whole background, it's not very good. I can tell you that for every good picture, I made five or six stinkers. But I always tried to do it a little differently. I don't know whether I accomplished it, but I tried." He succeeded better than he knew, perhaps. The way Wellman did things "a little differently" translates to style and how strong and original that style is becomes more apparent with each viewing of one of his films.

Charles Barton, assistant director to Wellman during this period, puts it this way: "Well, let me tell you something; my conception: I don't think Wellman ever made very many bad films. I really mean this. Even at the start, he always had some little thing in his films. He was real. He was honest."

Barton sums up these Paramount films pretty well. Sometimes shaky in premise, underdeveloped, poorly motivated, the films still work. It's as if they are propelled forward on the amazing strength of Wellman's convictions. Where the scripts or actors provided no life, Wellman infused his own into the films until they seem to sing with pace, enthusiasm and energy. What Charlie Barton said about Wellman can be equally applied to his films: they are real, they are honest.

Let's take a look at each of these five films individually. I have avoided synopsizing them for reasons of space, but synopses can be found in *The American Film Institute Catalog—Feature Films 1921–30*.

Chinatown Nights (1929)

Chinatown Nights is a curious film. Sort of an inverted *Broken Blossoms*, the film creates a genuinely creepy vision of Chinatown society. Wellman, by the way, returned to this locale three years later in *The Hatchet Man*, a fascinating, much maligned film.

As with the other films discussed here, *Chinatown Nights* is far better at creating a mood than in conveying much believability. The events are cursorily told, the acting is wildly variable and the ending lacks conviction. Yet it remains consistently interesting.

Many have cited this film as Wellman's first full talkie, but actually the dialogue is only partially synchronized. The tricks are often in evidence: characters speak with their lips obscured or facing away from the camera. The musical score is a constant undercurrent which links the film strongly with the silent period as does the variable camera speed which stylizes the action to a degree that the full talkie would not allow for a while.

Oddly, these potential faults are actually the film's salvation. The disembodied dialogue, caused by dubbing onto a scene shot silently, adds greatly to the film's overwhelming sense of isolation and confusion. Perhaps it's coincidental, but the use of partial sound could hardly have been used in a more apt vehicle. The picture's theme is dislocation: that of an entire city in the midst of an American metropolis; that of a white leader of a Chinese Tong faction; that of a prim society woman with a perverse taste for squalor. The emphatic, deliberate rhythm of dubbed speech heightens the hallucinatory mood and conveys this sense of separation swiftly and effectively. Dark and ugly and good in ways that Wellman probably didn't consider, *Chinatown Nights'* essence is that of a nightmare.

The Man I Love (1929)

This was Wellman's first full talkie and a worthy effort it is. One particularly intriguing scene has been discussed elsewhere in this article, but there is much more to recommend the picture. The story is a time-honored one (a boxer alienates his wife as he attains celebrity, gets and loses an exotic mistress, finds his wife to be loyal and faithful through it all, wins the big fight) but Wellman infuses it with imagination and wit and makes it seem less clichéd than it really is.

Dum Dum Brooks (Richard Arlen) is a rather perplexing protagonist for a film, mainly because he so thoroughly lives up to his name. He is stupid, arrogant and an opportunist. He drops his wife at the first opportunity and only takes her back after he's been rejected by the respectable society of which he longs to be a part.

Though the plot is moth-eaten and the hero is not quite sympathetic, the film is engaging on many levels. Much credit must be given Herman Manckiewicz for a witty script. The dialogue has a lowlife charm and most of the characters seemed to have learned to say "Duh" at their mothers' knees. Wellman, of course, was always at home with thugs like these. He had a particular way with depicting bored men who spend their lives moping around until an act of violence or sex breaks the monotony. The locker room scenes in *The Man I Love* look forward to other gatherings of Wellman thugs in *The Public Enemy*, the reporters waiting around for a hanging or a card game in *Woman Trap*, the tense, hot Legionnaires awaiting another Arab attack in *Beau Geste*, the melancholy soldiers in *The Story of G.I. Joe*. While Wellman's films are filled with staccato action, rapid feet and tongues, often his most representative scenes are those when his men merely stand and wait.

If *The Man I Love* is among the first of Wellman's films to explore these tableaux of ennui, it's also the origin of another, farther-reaching Wellman tendency: that of the provocative suggestion. The big championship fight, the climax of the film is hardly seen at all: we simply see Dum Dum's wife listening on the radio or the ringside announcer describing the action.

Another example is that of Dum Dum and Celia's (Mary Brian) wedding night on a boxcar full of horses. Unable to afford a ticket to New York, Dum Dum has arranged for them to ride in a car with some racehorses. Celia is being a good sport about the less than desirable circumstances and Dum Dum tries to create a romantic mood with the Victrola that is Celia's wedding present. As she sings along with "their song," Dum Dum kisses her in mid-verse. The camera rises discreetly above this action to rest on the sober, unmoving face of a horse. He is completely disinterested in the scene on the boxcar floor and for a full minute, until the song ends, the screen is filled with a picture of this calm horse. When the song ends, the camera cuts to the spinning turntable until we know that no one is thinking of turning it off.

Dozens of eccentric little touches like this make *The Man I Love* a delightful picture. Though we are always a step ahead of the plot, the film accurately points the way toward the filmmaker that Wellman was to become. Where *Wings* was the product of a gifted youngster with the resources of a huge studio, a phenomenal budget, a squadron of photographers and an entire army base (complete with army) to help him along, *The Man I Love* is a perfect example of Wellman's ability to make something of nothing.

A nothing-of-which-Wellman-could-barely-make-anything was Richard Arlen, who appears in these Paramount films with alarming frequency. Inexplicably, he appears to have been a favorite of Wellman's for he appears in *Wings*, *Beggars of Life*, *Ladies of the Mob*, *The Man I Love* and *Dangerous Paradise*. His earnest good looks get him by in the first three films for they are silent, but when he is called upon to talk, his performances are sadly inadequate.

Wellman was fortunate in pairing Arlen with a remarkable succession of leading ladies and it's hard to look bad opposite the likes of Clara Bow, Nancy Carroll, Mary Brian and Louise Brooks. And, too, at least in *The Man I Love*, he's called upon to act woodenheaded and thick-tongued so the effect is not inappropriate (it's still, however, not pleasing). In a film like *Dangerous Paradise*, however, he's nearly intolerable as a world-weary intellectual. Luckily *Dangerous Paradise* has much to divert our attention from Arlen's embarrassing presence, notably the enchanting Nancy Carroll and a movie full of the slimiest villains on record.

Dangerous Paradise (1930)

In an apparent attempt to deflect criticism for its rather cavalier treatment of Joseph Conrad's novel *Victory*, *Dangerous Paradise* carries a credit that reads,

"Based on incidents from a novel by Joseph Conrad." This never fooled anyone, though, and *Dangerous Paradise* has usually been regarded as bad Conrad and bad Wellman. It's neither, really, in that it captures a certain Conradian atmosphere even while it scuttles the book from which it extracts its "incidents." The muggy, tropical attitude of the film is wonderfully brought off and shows again how much Wellman could add to an impossible project.

One of the enormous riches of *Dangerous Paradise* is its vast and varied assortment of villains. In what must be the most lecherous cast ever assembled, the slavering honors are tied between the eternally weasly Clarence H. Wilson as Zangiacomo, leader of an all-woman orchestra and the fat and oily Warner Oland, in whom lust and drool are synonymous, as the hotel owner Schomberg.

If Wellman was discreet about sex and violence in *The Man I Love*, he is much more so in *Dangerous Paradise* as is evidenced by the death struggle of Zangiacomo and Schomberg.

They accidentally meet in the room of Alma (Nancy Carroll) whom they both covet. With a grunted threat, Schomberg hulks toward the wiry Zangiacomo who screams in fear and picks up a large candlestick with which to defend himself. The candle falls from the holder onto a dresser-top where it lies, still lit, on its side. Instead of following the action of the fight, the camera continues a slow track toward the candle. When the candle fills the frame, we hear a scream . . . the sound of a body falling downstairs . . . silence. The candle's flame goes out. Fade out.

The candle is made to stand in for Zangiacomo and this is one of Wellman's most persistent and enduring devices. Wellman most often presented death indirectly and most often by using an object that has been identified with the character at some point during the film. He seemed to avoid showing a dead body on screen for more than a brief moment and his epitomizing objects bring home a sense of death or loss far more efficiently (and often more gruesomely) than if he had filmed the death scene head-on.

This candle is an early example (not the first) of this trait and the list could go on for pages. Among the most poignant examples are: the airplane propeller that slows to a stop as Richard Arlen dies in *Wings*, the bathrobe being buffeted by the waves in *A Star Is Born*, the trumpet being buried in the sand in *Beau Geste*, the artificial leg lying abandoned in the mud in *Wild Boys of the Road*, a rocking horse floating briefly, then sinking in the flood-swollen river in *The Great Man's Lady*.

In each case we are only briefly (if ever) shown the death. There is something infinitely more sad and touching in that rocking horse than in being shown the drowned bodies of the two children that it represents. Wellman makes us participate, imagine, work, believe.

Of course the candlestick is not as worked out as a symbol as the other examples I've named. Though it effectively conveys Zangiacomo's death, it's not an object that he is identified with at any other point in the film. In 1929, Wellman was possessed of the instinct, but was not quite at the point in which to use it to its fullest potential.

A discussion of *Dangerous Paradise* would certainly not be complete without mentioning the marvelous performance by Nancy Carroll. She was such a sure-footed actress that she remains natural and compelling and believable even in the midst of the outrageous hams that surround her. To my mind, one brief moment in the film stands as an apotheosis of screen acting. As Alma and Heyst (Richard Arlen) stand listening to a native song wafting across the bay, Heyst begins to translate the words for her. The look of admiration and interest (concentration, even) on her face is both profound and impossible to describe. She is so completely listening to what Heyst is saying that it ceases to be acting and becomes a convincing reality. What may seem like a small point seems to me a memorable moment and brings home how unjustly neglected this actress has been and continues to be.

Young Eagles (1930)

Concerned as it is with the great love of Wellman's life, flying, it's hard to understand how *Young Eagles* could turn out to be so lackluster and insincere. In many ways, it can be considered the last film of an unofficial trilogy about World War I aviation with *Wings* and *Legion of the Condemned* (1928).

There is little aviation footage, but what there is of it, lifts the film a notch or two. One can almost feel Wellman's relief at getting far above the trivial story told with acting that Buddy Rogers and Jean Arthur are probably anxious to forget. In all of Wellman's films about flying, there is an exhilaration felt every time he is airborne that takes the film to another, higher level of expression. Wellman's men with planes form a unique coterie in the American film. No other director was so eloquent on the beauty and freedom of flight. That great love is very much in evidence here and it is what lifts *Young Eagles* out of the mire.

There is an amiable, casual spirit to the barracks scenes in the film. It's one of those classic Wellman places, like the gym in *The Man I Love*, men bursting with energy and rambunctiousness and nothing to do. Wellman men love a good fist fight because it's the perfect vent for this boredom and those that don't indulge in practical jokes (as many, many Wellman citizens do) hang around trying to get slugged on the jaw.

The constant joking, bickering, ukelele strumming in the barracks has the flavor of having been put on film by someone who knows what barracks are like and who knows the nature of fighting men. Even in a film that ultimately shows little interest and affection from its director, he can't resist leaving a little of himself on the screen.

Woman Trap (1930)

Where *Young Eagles* is filled with promise and ends in disappointment, *Woman Trap* is a film that succeeds far beyond any reasonable expectation. A simple crime saga, this is Wellman's most skillful film of the period and among the most accomplished of his early career. Tough, brisk, funny, the film is in many ways the prototype of the better known *The Public Enemy* in its depiction of two brothers on opposite sides of the law and the circumstances that separate them. Unlike *The Public Enemy*'s antagonistic brothers, Dan and Ray Malone (Hal Skelly and Chester Morris) have an easy, genuine affection for one another. Their tender horseplay in the beginning of the film establishes their love for one another and the film's tension arises, not from their diverging views on law but from their eroding relationship.

The labyrinth of relationships gives the film its substance but the pervading sense of irony gives it its style. Scene after scene is played to a contrapuntal emotion.

When the Malones' mother is accidentally blinded, they stand in a hospital corridor awaiting word. They are grief-stricken and worried and a little embarrassed by their public display of emotion. No one notices them, however. As they stand awkwardly in the corridor, a couple of young orderlies tell a dirty joke. As they approach the punch line, a nurse noisily drops a tray and is loudly reprimanded by a head nurse as the orderlies roar with laughter.

Dan, who feels responsible for the accident, wanders down the street, looking for solace. He meets his girlfriend Kitty (Evelyn Brent) and they step inside a hotel lobby to talk. This scene (played, incredibly, with both principles' backs to the camera) is interrupted several times: a little boy asks his mother, "Why is that man crying like that?"; a couple of secretaries giggle over a recent proposition: " . . . so I kissed him where it would do the most good; on top of his bald head!" By playing this sad scene to an accompaniment of everyday sounds, Wellman compounds the sentiment. As a character says in *Roxie Hart*, "Laugh and the world laughs with you. Cry, and you look like a chump." Dan *feels* like a chump and this awkwardness makes his sorrow all the more genuine. How much more effective this approach is than if the same conversation had been backed by tremulous strings. The contrapuntal strains of laughter continues through the film accompanying scenes of murder, treachery and sorrow.

The film is so well thought out that it never becomes melodramatic. The multi-layered emotional tensions keep the film brisk, meaningful and entertaining and the ending is at once tragic and optimistic, a trait it shares with *Wings, Beau Geste, A Star Is Born, Wild Boys of the Road, Roxie Hart, The Great Man's Lady, The Ox-Bow Incident, Lady of Burlesque, The Call of the Wild, Men with Wings, The Light That Failed* to name but a small number. There is ever-present

in Wellman's films an underlying solemnity and pessimism that informs his attitudes and colors his themes.

Woman Trap makes use of an identifying phrase motif, a Wellman practice
that first appears in *Wings* and continues throughout the balance of his career.
Ray calls Dan "Beanpole" in a mock-taunting way as a sign of brotherly affection. His use of the nickname helps to define the tensions of any given scene
wherein he uses it and, at the end, when he calls out "Goodbye . . . you Beanpole" as he is about to kill himself, the use of the nickname makes us aware of
the impending death as it conjures up images of their happier past. This device is
an identifying tag on the characters who use it. It helps us to know them better
and faster and tells us things about the changes in their lives with economy. In
Wings ("All set?"), *Beau Geste* ("I promise you."), *A Star Is Born* ("Do you mind
if I take just one more look?"), *Other Men's Women* ("Have a chew on me."),
Battleground ("That's for sure. That's for dang sure.") and on and on, Wellman
supplies his characters with a verbal or physical calling card. One would be hard
pressed to think of a Wellman film in which this doesn't occur. It supplies a
crucial thread throughout each film and, in a larger sense, the whole of his career.

One must be careful not to attribute too much symbol-mongering to Wellman. As he once expressed surprise when it was pointed out to him how often
it rains in his films, so he probably never considered the identifying phrase mo-
tives, the epitomizing objects, the litany of catchphrases that run like a chalk
line through his films. He was an instinctive artist. Yet an instinctive artist has
as much a claim on our attention and respect as has the meticulous planner, for
instinct comes from the heart and soul as well as from the brain. One who works
with true instinct puts a great part of himself in his work.

All of these traits of Wellman's films, all of these attitudes, all of these
interests appear first in these forgotten films. The remarkable personality that
Wellman infused his films with was developed in these short, unpretentious
films that no one sees anymore. That he was a superb craftsman shouldn't be
contested; that he was also an artist of stature should come to be realized. *Chinatown Nights*, *The Man I Love*, *Woman Trap*, *Dangerous Paradise* and *Young Eagles*
show how Wellman learned to be both artist *and* craftsman and how he enriched
his work by letting each facet of his nature have equal rein. These five little films
may not grace film history books or late-night movie spots on TV or revival
house marquees or college courses, but, as a group, they stand for a remarkable
period of growth and development of one of America's finest film directors.

The Wellman Westerns

AN APPRAISAL

Frank Thompson

Originally appeared in vol. 4, no. 2 (Winter 1980)

In the light of westerns like *The Robin Hood of El Dorado* and *The Ox-Bow Incident*, it is surprising that William Wellman did not make more Westerns than he did. A tough, uncompromising "man's man" whose predilections included studies of male groups in conflict, it would have seemed that a large percentage of his approximately ninety films would have been Westerns. In fact, he directed only nine films in the genre and acted in one more. Nonetheless, they constitute an important part of his career and demonstrate a surprising variety of tone and texture on their own. Some of the most important, in this writer's opinion, will be examined here—*The Robin Hood of El Dorado* (1936), *The Great Man's Lady* (1942), *Westward the Women* (1951), *The Ox-Bow Incident* (1943), *Buffalo Bill* (1944) and *Track of the Cat* (1954).

William Wellman certainly got his start in a Western-infested atmosphere. Wellman had made friends with Douglas Fairbanks Sr. when Fairbanks had appeared in Wellman's hometown of Boston in a stage play, *Hawthorne of the U.S.A.* Fairbanks would come to see Wellman play hockey with his high school team and they kept in touch when Wellman was in France during World War I. At war's end, Wellman found himself invited out to Hollywood where Fairbanks offered him a role as the juvenile in Fairbanks' film, *The Knickerbocker Buckeroo* (1919). Wellman always insisted later that he hated acting, hated the way that he looked on screen, that, indeed, he had rushed out of the theater to vomit while *The Knickerbocker Buckeroo* was showing. It is more probable that Wellman found the idea of acting slightly effeminate, disliked putting on makeup, and (probably most important) did not like taking orders. He much preferred giving orders and actively sought out the job that would put him in charge of things. Wellman, however, told the story this way: "I said to Doug, 'Look, I don't want to speak disrespectfully of actors, but I just don't want to be one.' Doug said, 'Well, what do you want to do?' I pointed to Albert Parker [the director] and

103

asked how much he made. Doug told me and I said, 'I want to be a director.' It was purely financial."

Even Fairbanks' influence went just so far, though, and Wellman had to start on the bottom rung of the studio ladder, beginning as a messenger boy. Little by little, he worked his way up through the various jobs on the lot, property boy to assist director. As assistant, he had the opportunity to work with such action directors as T. Hayes Hunter, Clarence Badger and, most importantly, Bernard Durning.

Durning was a powerful influence on the young Wellman. He was a large, handsome man with a penchant for drinking and fighting. In fact, Durning's drinking gave Wellman his first opportunity to direct a film. While on location, Durning went off on a blinding drunk and turned the half-finished film over to his assistant, Wellman. When the film was screened for studio executives (who praised it as one of Durning's best) Durning admitted that Wellman could take the credit for saving the film from an untimely end and that he should be made a full director.

Soon, Wellman was given Dustin Farnum to direct. *The Man Who Won* (1923) was Wellman's first film. Interestingly, it also appears to be the only Western that Wellman made during the silent years, despite a six picture association with cowboy star, Buck Jones.

Of the fifteen silent films that Wellman directed, no more than three are known to exist so it's rather difficult to tell how influenced he was by the standards of the day. Although we don't know his approach to *The Man Who Won*, one thing is certain: by the time Wellman got around to directing another Western, he had developed a dark and serious side that few of his films would ever completely escape. By 1936, when he directed *The Robin Hood of El Dorado*, it was clear that Wellman had found his niche not in the wide open spaces of the American West, but in the crime-ridden streets of the big city, the sweaty dressing rooms of two-bit boxers, and the cramped, dingy hide-outs of killers on the run. His early films are more inclined to be bleak affairs, more hard-bitten melodramas than frothy comedies or musicals (Wellman can probably claim fewer happy endings than any director in Hollywood besides Erich von Stroheim).

After the introduction of sound to the movies, Wellman made several fine, tough movies at Paramount before moving to Warner Brothers in 1930 for a remarkable two and a half years. It's been said that Wellman would not refuse a script while at Warner Bros. and that is probably true. But that doesn't alter the staggering productivity of his stay there, for between 1930 and 1933, Wellman had directed sixteen films for Warner Bros. (plus two more for Paramount and one each at RKO and M-G-M). Some were potboilers, to be sure, but all were well directed and some retain their power and originality to this day. Such films as *The Public Enemy* (1931), *Night Nurse* (1931), *Heroes for Sale* (1933) and the stunning Depression drama, *Wild Boys of the Road* (1933) are fine enough on their own but it's startling to think that Wellman was turning out films like these every two months or so.

He made them fast, and, seemingly, without effort but this run of films still remains powerful and angry, full of violence, social protest and searing personal drama.

The point is that Wellman may have started out in the optimistic, man-kisses-horse West of Dustin Farnum, but by the time he came around to directing another Western, that type of innocence was gone for him and what remained in the West was racial bigotry, rape, murder, lynching and betrayal. Of course the centerpiece of Wellman's Westerns is that dark and brooding work, *The Ox-Bow Incident* (1943) a scathing indictment of lynching and mob rule. A peculiar film to have been made during the Technicolor Betty Grable, Patriotism-and-Cleavage War years, *The Ox-Bow Incident* has lost none of its simple, profound power. Often attacked for the artificiality of its sets and the dubiousness of its premise (after all, wouldn't the lynching be just as morally reprehensible if the victims were guilty?), it needs to be understood that Wellman's claustrophobic view of this terrible act is exactly what is called for. The dark leanings of the men are provocative in this slightly unreal setting in a way that would certainly have been less effective on location. *The Ox-Bow Incident* is archetypal Wellman, containing in microcosm the personalities that inhabit all of his films: victimized innocents, sadists, ordinary people easily swayed by the loudest voice. But this was nothing new for him. Wellman had explored this territory before in his first sound Western, *The Robin Hood of El Dorado* (1936).

Enter *Robin Hood*

Apparently in 1936 the M-G-M executives wanted to recreate the great success of 1934's *Viva Villa* with Wallace Beery. (Interestingly, as a footnote, Wellman did some uncredited work on *Viva Villa*, as did Howard Hawks.) The legend of Joaquin Murrieta was deemed a good prospect so the studio turned to Walter Burns Noble's romanticized biography of Murrieta for their source material.

The film softens Murrieta's character a great deal and he is played by Warner Baxter as a kind and gentle man driven to violence, despite the truth that the actual Murrieta was a sadistic robber and gleeful murderer. Where Baxter is allowed to expire on the grave of his wife, the real Murrieta was shot in the back by one of his own men. Then he was decapitated, and his head was placed in a jar to be shown around the territories that he had once terrorized. After his death, rumors began to grow that he was never killed, that he was living in hiding, biding his time for a spectacular comeback. Soon the rumors turned to legend and Murrieta became another character from folklore.

Although Wellman felt that the film was misnamed, *The Robin Hood of El Dorado* accurately sums up the kind of mystique that had grown up around this famous bandit. Like the real Robin Hood, Murrieta is presented more as victim than criminal, filled with hatred until he is driven to bring the same grief on his persecutors that they have brought on him. The outlaw-as-victim idea has always been a very attractive one, and the movies are full of bloodthirsty killers that we have brought to our hearts, like Butch Cassidy and the Sundance Kid, Bonnie and Clyde. Just think of the many times we have cheered on Billy the Kid and Jesse James. Wellman, like other good directors, has used the character as something more than an outlaw, as the personification of the ills afflicting the society that the outlaw thrives in.

The story is briefly told: In the mid-1800s, California has become the focal point of the nation's attention when gold is discovered there. Every day brings more settlers who carry with them the Might Makes Right spirit of the American abroad. The Mexican natives of California are tolerant of the influx at first but soon begin to chafe under the overbearing attitudes of the white men who seek to drive them off their land. Every stream, for the white settlers, exists only to be panned for gold, every inch of land to be dug up in search of a rich vein. Isolated acts of violence have begun to break out so that American troops have been brought in to quell any Mexican uprisings that might be imminent.

The film opens on a happier note. It is Joaquin Murrieta's wedding day. He is to be married to his childhood sweetheart, Rosita, and the entire village has joined together in laughter and song to celebrate the happy occasion. A brief dark cloud is brought over the proceedings when Joaquin is questioned about a friend of his who has been taking potshots at some of the white settlers. But this moment of tenseness soon passes and the marriage goes on. Joaquin and his new bride move into a small house after the wedding and prepare to live happily ever after.

Soon after the wedding, Joaquin is walking through the woods when he sees the friend, about whom he has been questioned earlier, about to take a shot at two approaching settlers. Joaquin distracts him and a brief shootout occurs during which Joaquin's friend is killed by the settlers. The two men, Bill Warren and his brother Johnnie, are grateful to Joaquin for helping to save their lives and he takes them to his home to tend their minor wounds and to have them meet Rosita. Joaquin and the Warrens soon become close friends and they all express a wish that the differences between the Mexican and the whites could be settled soon.

Soon after this, four prospectors find a small amount of gold in a stream on Joaquin's property. They come to Joaquin's house and order Joaquin and Rosita to leave immediately. Joaquin refuses and a fight ensues. The men easily overpower Joaquin and knock him out. When he awakens, he finds that the men have raped Rosita and beat her to death. Bill Warren arrives on the scene and begs Joaquin to let the law take care of the four murderers.

Joaquin knows, however, that the law is negligible in the territory and the sheriff is inept and unwilling to bring the four men to justice, so Joaquin searches them out and kills them one by one. He is seen during one encounter by a notorious Mexican bandit, Three-Fingered Jack, who senses that Joaquin would be good bandit material. Jack offers to let Joaquin ride with his band but Joaquin refuses.

Now with a price on his head, Joaquin is forced to go into hiding at the farm of his brother. There, he is in the process of healing his broken heart and spirit through hard work and peace and quiet. One day, he takes his brother's mule into town for some supplies and is accosted by a group of drunken white men who are looking for a fight. They accuse Joaquin of stealing the old mule that he is riding, even though they know he is innocent. When Joaquin's brother Tomas arrives to protest Joaquin's innocence, the drunken group (which is rapidly becoming a mob) seize the two brothers and demand that they be punished for mule theft. They tie Joaquin to a tree and flog him until his back is raw and lynch Tomas from a tree in the town square. When the mob leaves, some members of Three-Fingered Jack's band come and take Joaquin to their camp.

Now consumed by hatred of the whites and ruled by an obsession for revenge, Joaquin quickly takes over as leader of the outlaw band. Their first mission is to locate the ringleaders of the mob that lynched Tomas and kill them. Having accomplished that, the outlaw band begins to terrorize the white towns and army posts. All the while, the band grows larger and larger.

Finally, through information provided by a spy, a large posse has located the outlaw band's hideout. Whipped into frenzy by the accidental killing of a young girl (who had been arriving in California to marry Johnnie Warren), the posse, led by Bill Warren, attacks Joaquin's camp and kills his entire small army. Joaquin, though gravely wounded, escapes and is able to reach the grave of Rosita, where he dies.

This is the barest synopsis of this bleak story but it gives an idea of what an angry, violent film *The Robin Hood of El Dorado* is. Although Wellman claimed that M-G-M tried to insert too many prettified incidents in the film, it remains nearly uncompromisingly told. In the guise of an action-packed Western (which it certainly is), Wellman has made a stronger attack on racism and intolerance than appeared in the spate of Hollywood films of the forties and fifties such as *Gentleman's Agreement.* What is admirable about this film is that the blame is never one sided. There are good and bad Mexicans just as there are good and bad white people. Though the film's sympathies are more with the Mexicans, everyone must take part of the blame for the carnage that ends the film.

There is a telling scene midway through the film, soon after Joaquin has joined Three-Fingered Jack's band. As the two men sit by a campfire, Joaquin notices a long string of something hanging from a tree. When he asks what it is, Three-Fingered Jack replies, "Oh, that's a string of Chinaman's ears. I don't know why, but every time I see a Chinaman, I want to cut his ears off. I *love* Chinamen." Thus does the roundelay of racial hatred go on and on—the Mexicans are as guilty of bigotry as the Americans and though an occasional alliance may be formed (as with Joaquin and the Warrens) when the final conflict comes, they all side with their own colors again.

Certainly, *The Robin Hood of El Dorado* anticipates the "revisionist" Westerns of the sixties and seventies by its mixture of sentimentality and violence. The massive battle at the end of the film prefigures the appalling violence of Sam Peckinpah's *The Wild Bunch*, but these two films are linked by more than that. Both have a strong undercurrent of nostalgia and regret for a way of life that is being forcefully torn away and both refuse to show good and bad in the traditional white and black hat manner of many Westerns. In addition, there is another striking echo from *The Robin Hood of El Dorado* to *The Wild Bunch* and that is the use of the Mexican folk song "La Golondrina." Joaquin's people sing it as a farewell to him in a scene near the end of the film that immediately precedes the battle with the posse. Similarly, the Mexican villagers sing it as a farewell to the Wild Bunch as they ride out of the small town they have rested in to go on to the large fortress/city where they will eventually lose their lives.

The sentimentality as a prelude to violence is striking and poignant and it is interesting that the same song is used to such similar effect in two films from such different points of view. There is not much point in making many comparisons to the two films, but one finds echoes from one in the other.

As I mentioned above, Wellman had many arguments with the executives at M-G-M regarding the filming and casting of *The Robin Hood of El Dorado*, not the least of which was the presence of Warner Baxter in the title role. Wellman felt that Baxter was too old for the part and wanted to get Robert Taylor. For whatever reason, the studio refused and Wellman was forced to go along with Baxter. Despite Wellman's misgivings, Baxter brings a sincerity to the role that Robert Taylor could not have. Though Taylor could physically be conceived as Murrieta, in 1936, he simply was not actor enough to handle the role. Baxter may seem too old for the part but his superior skills as an actor stands him in good stead. There is one grave mistake in Baxter's portrayal of Murrieta and that is the appearance of Baxter's Cisco Kid suit near the end of the film. This, unfortunately, stretches credibility quite a bit and one's head swims at the idea of some hapless executive trying to beef up the commercial possibilities of this grim tale by implying that it might be a Cisco Kid movie.

Baxter, in addition to his age, also rubbed Wellman the wrong way by being afraid of horses. Four stage hands had to hold a horse still (while they crouched out of camera range) when Baxter was shown astride it. The veteran stuntman Yakima Canutt doubled for Baxter in all of the long shots in the saddle.

Filmed at Strawberry Flats in the Sierras, the location seems to have been a typical one for Wellman. Yakima Canutt later stated that the image that Wellman had made for himself as a brawler par excellence was not quite factual and that he had once talked Wellman out of a fight rather than beat him to a pulp. Many assistant directors and various technicians have stated otherwise, however, and virtually anyone who ever worked for Wellman has a story of getting punched by him or punching him. Charles Barton, Wellman's assistant at Paramount in the late twenties and early thirties, told me that Wellman had once socked him in the jaw in anger at some mistake that he had made. Impulsively, Barton punched him right back and Wellman said, genuinely hurt and puzzled, "You son of a bitch, you'd do that to *me?*" Suffice it to say that whatever were Wellman's brawling habits in the studio, they tended to broaden somewhat in the camp-like atmosphere of location.

Wellman's Western Women

Wellman's next trip West was somewhat less bitter but *The Great Man's Lady* (1942) casts a jaundiced view of the pioneer spirit and reveals the sense of personal loss that accompanies the forging of new trails. More than any other feeling, this sense of the price, in human lives, of conquering a frontier fills all of Wellman's Westerns (indeed, nearly all of his films). Hannah Semplar (Barbara Stanwyck) helps her husband Ethan Hoyt (Joel McCrea) to build an empire, but loses him, her children and, finally, her own identity in the process. As the picture is framed by a modern unveiling of a statue of "The Great Man—Ethan Hoyt," the reminiscences of 108-year-old Hannah questions the entire motive behind American empiricism (as *The Robin Hood of El Dorado* also does). Contemporary reviews of the film were taken aback by this angry look at our noble pioneer heritage, refusing to believe that America could have been founded and built by money-grubbing opportunists. Today, we find this an awful lot easier to believe and *The Great Man's Lady* seems much cannier a picture of the building of the West than it did upon its original release.

One point that the picture makes is that the building of the West was a time when a man needed a strong wife and Hannah Semplar not only provided the brains and ethics, but most of the brawn behind "Hoyt's" empire.

For all of Wellman's reputation as a "man's" director, it is very interesting to note how many of his films (particularly his Westerns) show women to be the stronger, more intelligent and principled sex. From Hannah Semplar to Louisa Cody and Dawn Starlight in *Buffalo Bill* to the wagon train load of mail-order brides in *Westward the Women,* the women provide the moral and emotional center of the films' events. Of course there are points when Wellman's women have grown too strong—Ma Grier in *The Ox-Bow Incident,* and Ma Bridges in *Track of the Cat,* for instance. These women's strength has left them devoid of humanity and their characters are parodies of ambition and iron will.

Interestingly, these latter two characters are both the creation of Walter Van Tilburg Clark (both named "Ma"), which may tell us more about Mr. Clark than about Wellman, but that is the stuff of another study.

Wellman often complained that he didn't like working with women, that they took too long getting ready for a scene, that they were too particular about how they looked and didn't want to appear messy, even if their refusal ruined the integrity of a scene. But like many of Wellman's complaints, only someone who has never seen any of his films could believe that he didn't like working with women. Time and again, the women in Wellman's films come away with the finest performances when the men often emerge looking more than a little stodgy and wooden. Barbara Stanwyck's role in *The Great Man's Lady,* for instance, is one of her finest portrayals. In it, she must age from sixteen to one hundred and eight and she brings a firm conviction and high style to every stage of the aging process.

Because of the oft-repeated claim that he didn't like working with women, many eyebrows shot up when Wellman announced that he would film Frank Capra's story, *Westward the Women* (1951), a heroic saga of the trek across dangerous deserts from Chicago to California by nearly two hundred women, heading west to become brides for a colony of male settlers already there. Capra has said that he got the idea from a magazine story about South American women who had undergone a similar trek across the Isthmus. He transferred the story to the American West and tried to get Columbia interested in filming it. But, he said, "Columbia was no place for Westerns, they didn't have the background and the people for it. They weren't equipped to make Westerns. No horses." Wellman became enthusiastic when Capra told him the story and said, "That's a hell of a story, I'd like to do that. Maybe I could do it at M-G-M."

M-G-M liked the idea and gave Wellman the go-ahead.

Capra said, "It was basically the 'Taming of the Shrew.' It was about one strong-willed woman who had to have her way. There were twenty thousand other women around but *she* had to have her way and the man had to knock her down. Then she finally learned her lesson."

In one sense, the story is the "Taming of the Shrew," but on a larger scale. Along the way, it paints a picture of heroism and stamina that few Westerns attempt with men. Of the women who start out, nearly half quit or die on the trail but the half that live are immeasurably stronger for the experience. A very fine work, it contains many wonderful moments. One of the most beautiful moments in any Wellman film occurs after a devastating attack by Indians (typically, for Wellman, the attack is not shown, only the aftermath). The wagon master (Robert Taylor) asks for a roll call of the women who have been killed. As a survivor calls out each name, her voice is echoed about the canyon as the camera rests its gaze somberly on the still form of each dead woman. It is a ghostly, elegiac moment and acts as a quiet tribute for all those who have died blazing new trails. Parenthetically, there is a companion piece in Wellman's last film, *Lafayette Escadrille* (1958). While describing three new recruits' first night in the barracks of the Lafayette Flying Corps in France, the camera moves from one sleeping face to another as the narrator (Wellman himself) quietly describes their eventual fates. For his deserved reputation as a hellraiser first class, Wellman became a much quieter cinematic voice in his last films in the fifties and the mood of *Westward the Women* as it would be later in *Lafayette Escadrille* is one of tribute and respect.

The location work on *Westward the Women* turned out to be nearly as grueling for the cast and crew as for the fictional women in the film. Near the beginning of the movie, Robert Taylor addresses a roomful of women who are volunteering for the trek westward. He describes in harsh terms how arduous a journey it will be, that they will need to be well versed in leading a team of horses, roping cattle and shooting guns. He advised that any women who did not feel equal to the task of crossing a hostile desert would do better to quit immediately. Whether he took his cue from the script or vice versa, Wellman gave an almost identical talk to the cast of his film before they started shooting.

The women were put through a three-week course where they were trained in the art of riding, roping, shooting and anything else that a pioneer woman might need to know. In addition, they did strenuous calisthenics and generally got used to living in a Spartan environment. This was to aid them immeasurably when the location work began at a place called Surprise Valley in the Mojave Desert.

Apart from interiors, virtually no shooting was done at the studio. Wellman had been ecstatic when cameraman William C. Mellor chose Surprise Valley because of the beauty and unpredictability of the terrain. He found that they could shoot the entire film in a relatively small area of ground and give the illusion of having covered many miles of desert. Wellman instructed Mellor to use no filters (or as little as possible) to give the film a stark, glaring look. It works beautifully for one almost feels the white heat of the desert sun in this shadowless land.

There is one parenthetic point for the auteurist. At one stage of the filming, Robert Taylor was a little unsure as to how he should approach his character for the rough wagon master who falls for a high-spirited woman on the trail. He went to Wellman (who, as a rule, did not like to verbalize things like motivation) and asked his advice. Wellman thought for a moment and then replied, "Be me." Taylor took the advice and played the wagon master as if he were Wellman directing the film.

Westward the Women is too seldom seen now. It deserves a wider audience, not only because of its inherent qualities as a great action Western but because it is that rare commodity, a monument to women, to the pioneer spirit and to the indomitability of the human will. Rarely does it fall into the sexually condescending trap of so many films of its period (although male chauvinism has its advocate in John McIntire, who continually spouts such sentiments as, "Women'll go through a lot when there's a wedding ring in sight," after some amazing scene of bravery and strength). It is important, though, that we do not confuse the sentiments of a character with the sentiments of the filmmaker and Wellman's admiration for these women is evident in every frame of this great film.

Later Westerns

Another type of monument was attempted six years earlier and this one didn't fare so well. But to tell the story of *Buffalo Bill* (1944), we must first backtrack a little to *The Ox-Bow Incident* (1943).

When Wellman first read Walter Van Tilburg Clark's anti-lynching novel, *The Ox-Bow Incident,* he was completely enthralled. He recognized that the quiet, profound simplicity of the book could be transferred to the screen with a minimum of changes and could end as a great film. He was ecstatic when the man who owned the rights to the book approached him to direct a film based on it; but his delight soon withered, for it became apparent that the would-be producer had no idea what to do with this grim book. He considered it too depressing for the wartime audience and at one point even considered filming it with Mae West! Wellman was outraged that the man could not see what he had and finally bought the rights himself. He later claimed that it was the only time in his career that he had ever spent his own money on a property. He brought the book home and read it to his wife from beginning to end, even though it took most of the night to do it.

Still, Wellman found himself in much the same predicament as the former owner of the property. He could interest no one in filming the story. He had just completed a five-year contract as producer/director at Paramount and was currently at liberty. After approaching several studios with the project, he decided to go to see Darryl Zanuck.

Zanuck and Wellman were never on the best of terms. They had made many films together and had apparently fought through every one of them. In fact, once (legend has it) when he had to use Zanuck's studio for some miscellaneous scenes of *A Star Is Born* (1937), Wellman walked on the lot, paused at a large picture window, picked up a rock, shattered the pane and walked on in, saying, "That's to let Zanuck know I'm back." Still, their mutual dislike was underscored by a considerable professional respect. When Wellman called Zanuck to tell him about *The Ox-Bow Incident*, Zanuck immediately asked to read the book.

The next day Zanuck called Wellman in and told him, "I don't think it'll ever make a dime but I think it'll be a film that we'll both be proud of. Make it." Wellman was elated but Zanuck had an ace up his sleeve. He would give Wellman carte blanche to do *The Ox-Bow Incident* at 20th Century Fox but, in return, Wellman must agree to make two more commercial films for the studio, sight unseen. Wellman agreed. The first, *Thunderbirds* (1942), was filmed before *The Ox-Bow Incident* and the second was *Buffalo Bill.*

Filming *Buffalo Bill* did not seem like much of a penalty to Wellman. He thought he could make a fine film of it and knew that his friend Gene Fowler had been working for some time on a screenplay exposing Buffalo Bill for the charlatan and faker that he was. Wellman went to him and for several weeks they worked on a script. "And boy," said Wellman later, "when we got into that thing, it was true."

Then something went awry. Wellman told Richard Schickel in his *The Men Who Made the Movies* interview, that Fowler, one day, called Wellman to come up to his house. "It was in winter and he had a lovely den, and a little fireplace going there. He said, 'Bill, you know, you can't stab Babe Ruth, you couldn't kill Dempsey, you can't kill any of these wonderful heroes that our kids, my kids, your kids, my grandchildren, your grandchildren, everyone else worships and likes. And that's what we're doing. Buffalo Bill is a great figure and we cannot do it. What do you say? What do we do?'" Wellman replied, "Let's burn the goddamned thing." "So," he went on, "early in the morning we got drunk and we put it in, page after page. And burned up the most wonderful work I've ever done with a writer in my whole life. And he was right."

If the story has the feeling of "The Big One That Got Away," it must be remembered that Wellman was, at heart, a storyteller and more than a few of his tales were embellished from telling to telling. There is undoubtedly some truth there, though it is worth considering that Wellman was getting studio pressure to do a more heroic biography that would be in tune with the war effort. Certainly, he had his hands full trying to bring *The Ox-Bow Incident* to the screen and can be excused for avoiding another fight at this point in his career.

Buffalo Bill as a film (and as a Wellman film) often leaves something to be desired. Not quite the shameful artistic flop that Wellman was wont to describe it, it often enough has the ring of truth and at least two scenes of undeniable beauty and grace.

Although Bill is presented as a rather full-blown hero from the beginning of the film, it becomes apparent very soon that he is more than a little boyish and naive and not terribly intelligent. The film attempts to compare Bill's simple, homespun innocence with the disease-ridden constrictions of civilization that his wife comes to champion. Seeing this as the basic conflict of the film excuses a lot of the other faults in execution and gives *Buffalo Bill* a sense of sadness that goes far toward ennobling some of the film's cruder excesses.

It must be admitted, however, that the most memorable points in the film are those of action and humor. When Bill is invited to a fancy dress party by his wife-to-be (Maureen O'Hara), the invitation ends, "R.S.V.P." Bill is puzzled by this and goes to the Indian schoolteacher, Dawn Starlight (Linda Darnell) for an explanation. She tells him what the initials mean and helps him to write a note of acceptance. Dawn writes the note on the blackboard of the schoolhouse while Bill laboriously attempts to copy it in his own handwriting. Several times Dawn thinks of better words for the note and erases what she has written. Bill must be content to scratch out what he has written to accommodate Dawn's improvements and his note ends as a total mess.

This is a very funny and charming scene and also an important one. In one stroke it shows us many things: Bill's respect for the Indian as teacher, his basic childlike earnestness to do the right thing (emphasized by his sitting in a ridiculously small desk in the schoolhouse), his innocence of the ways of the civilized world. Most importantly, though, it foreshadows the difficulties that Louisa will have adjusting to frontier life, for what use is there of an R.S.V.P. in the midst of the wilderness?

The centerpiece of the film is the amazing battle scene at War Bonnet Gorge. Wellman had a particular talent for filming battles in such a way that the action is felt rather than seen. Here, the fight takes place in the middle of a river and the action is often obscured by water and mud. This battle was so well shot, in fact, that it was used in its entirety in *Pony Soldier* (1952, d. Joseph M. Newman) and *Siege at Red River* (1954, d. Rudolph Mate). William Everson, in his marvelous book on Westerns, notes that in reviewing these latter two films, critics unanimously praised the battle scene, stating how much better the widescreen was able to capture such battles!

As the prelude to the battle, Bill indulges in hand-to-hand combat with the Indian chief, Yellow Hand (Anthony Quinn) to buy time for more soldiers to arrive on the scene. I have alluded earlier to Wellman's penchant for implying action rather than showing it and this fight is a prime example of this style of his. The two men fall from their horses and into the river. The camera tracks slowly down the river bank showing only the surface of the river. Occasionally a hand will burst through the surface, an upraised knife, a face. Soon, the camera slows to a halt and rests on the river's surface for a moment. Then one body stands up in the river and the other floats slowly to the top.

Moments like this nearly redeem *Buffalo Bill* from the rest of its excesses. Even the inevitable train of events that follows sounds a great deal more compelling than they turn out to be on screen: Bill's rise to popularity via the outrageous dime-novelty of Ned Buntline (Thomas Mitchell), his subsequent humiliation and fall from grace when the public is led to believe that he lied about his role in the War Bonnet Gorge Battle, his separation from Louisa and the subsequent death from diphtheria ("It's a crowd disease, a disease of civilization.") of his son.

I have dwelt on the more positive aspects of *Buffalo Bill* but its faults are many. Though it has a serious side there is an overall air of carelessness about the production as if one can sense that it was not a film that held Wellman's interest very long. Worth seeing for the grains of good ideas (and, approached with nothing but fun on your mind, it is a cheerful little movie), the film is a strange hybrid—part fiction and part fact, part conviction and part humbug. In its review of the film, the *New York Times* said, "William Wellman has directed the action in a magnificently exaggerated style. Buffalo Bill's was a fantastic legend and 20th Century Fox has done nothing to tear it down." That really sums up the strengths and weakness of *Buffalo Bill.* Wellman's "exaggerated style" gives the film flair and life and the vivacity of a Remington painting, but the insistent hero worship of the script finally robs the film of much integrity.

The last Western that Wellman directed was certainly the most unusual. *Track of the Cat* was based on the novel by Walter Van Tilburg Clark, author of *The Ox-Bow Incident.* Reacting against the gaudy, garish Technicolor films of the day, Wellman had long carried the idea of filming a story in color in which only black and white would make it onto the screen. He wanted to strip the visuals down to the bare bones and create a stylistic exercise with the simplicity of a line drawing. When he read *Track of the Cat,* he felt that he had found the perfect property for his experiment.

Excitedly, Wellman called photographer William Clothier and described the story and the color scheme that he wanted; they would photograph the sky only when it was grey, back-light the trees so they would photograph black, all clothes would be black, white or grey. The only colors that appear in the film are red and yellow, the colors of a mackinaw and a scarf. In addition, a bit of blue sky appears at the end, otherwise only unavoidable colors are used (flesh tones, the brown of logs, the yellow of a fire). The result is gorgeous—stark, bleak, an overall look that perfectly complements the story. It is one of the rare instances when style and content carry equal weight in a Wellman film, because he was more often than not interested in getting the story on film and getting it over with.

Wellman (like many directors of his era) did not admit to caring much for art. He thought that was better left to pretentious foreign directors and that it was more than a little silly to afford too much serious study to an entertainment like the movies. This is not to say that he was a careless filmmaker—far from it. He was always a superb craftsman who sincerely cared about his stories and wanted only to make an entertaining and commercially successful movie. That is why *The Ox-Bow Incident* and *Track of the Cat* are so very important to Wellman's body of work. These were the only two films that Wellman seems to have made completely for himself, when he cast all thoughts of commercialism aside, because of an artistic urge that had to be fulfilled.

Despite how successful these two films are commercially or artistically, they remain almost undiluted Wellman. He made better films and he made films that he had to fight harder for, but *Track of the Cat* and *The Ox-Bow Incident* are the two films that, for me at least, lift Wellman out of the rank and file of Hollywood directors, for few other studio directors of his time ever took that kind of risk.

Wellman was very saddened by the commercial failure of *Track of the Cat*. He had assumed (foolishly perhaps) that the audience would see what he was getting at, that they would catch the bleak beauty of the color scheme, would appreciate the subtle symbolism of a vicious cat that is never seen and seems to represent different terrors to the different characters in the film. The audience, however, did not appreciate the film. The color scheme went unnoticed, they felt cheated by Wellman's refusal to show a big, scary cat, they were depressed and displeased by the somber drama.

This film needs to be seen again, for what an earlier generation missed should not determine the unjust neglect of this minor masterpiece. Though it has long been maligned by critics as slow moving and talky and dismissed by people who have only seen it on television (where the stunning Cinemascope photography is mangled beyond repair), *Track of the Cat* should come as a surprise to those who are unfamiliar with it, upon seeing it as it should be seen.

Though the script has reminded many of Eugene O'Neill, and the odd camera angles (including one from the viewpoint of the grave showing a coffin being lowered into it) recall Carl Dreyer, the style is Wellman's and Wellman's only (via William Clothier, of course) as can be verified by viewing many of his other films. That the bleakness and isolation of his characters, the starkness of locale and the lofty ambitions of the style reach a certain fruition in *Track of the Cat* does not mean that these elements have not always been present in Wellman's work.

William A. Wellman was a studio director, a man who made films that were assigned to him—with rare exceptions—and a man who was proud of his good commercial track record and the diversity of subjects that he covered. But even he had to admit, toward the end of his life, that maybe there was a little of the artist in him after all. Take for example the framing device in *The Ox-Bow Incident*: The two protagonists ride into town at the beginning of the film and an old dog crosses their path. At the end of the film, they ride back up the same road and the old dog also retraces her own steps. A minor touch, but one that gives a wholeness and life that perhaps a less caring director would not take the time with.

Track of the Cat was the last Western that Wellman directed. After his autobiographical *Lafayette Escadrille* was tampered with and marred by the studio executives, Wellman lost heart in his film career. The last two films that he worked on were *Flight of the Phoenix* (later taken over by Robert Aldrich, who had earlier served as assistant to Wellman in 1945's *The Story of G.I. Joe*), and *The Rounders*, a comedy Western that was later filmed starring Glenn Ford. Wellman complained that the studio didn't see any point in making a funny Western and wouldn't back him on developing *The Rounders*, so he quit and never made another film. We can only wonder what Wellman would have done with a Western comedy after the bleak, serious series of Westerns to his credit. But we need not take the time wondering about things that might have been, for we can devote that energy to rediscovering the fine Westerns that he did make, among which are some of the finest Westerns of all time.

For an action director, Wellman did not go West as often as we could expect him to, but when he did, he did so memorably.

Part IV

FROM SILENTS TO SOUND

The Squaw Man Returns

Roger Holden

Originally appeared in vol. 7, nos. 5 and 6 (November/December 1983)

*One of the most prized of all Hollywood artifacts is the famous "Barn" in which Cecil B. DeMille and Jesse Lasky made the first Hollywood-produced feature film of more than three reels—*The Squaw Man *(1914). The story of that pioneering effort and of recent efforts to protect and preserve the barn makes for fascinating reading. It is told with the special assistance of Ms. Josephine Royle, daughter of playwright Edwin Royle, who herself appeared in the play that was the subject of the DeMille-Lasky production.*

ॐ

Imagine for a moment, a movie about the making of a very special movie. In our movie of the mind, we have four heroes: a director who has never made a movie before, a glove salesman who wants to sell this movie to the public instead of gloves, a vaudeville producer who is risking a small fortune on the film's production, and a Broadway playwright who envisions that the cinematic medium might allow his famous play to be portrayed in new and intriguing ways.

Mix into our plot a series of events surrounding the making of this special movie that can only be paralleled by the afflictions of Job. In what appears to be a clear attempt to sabotage the film's production, the director is the subject of hidden gunfire and a negative of the film is almost destroyed when it is trampled by unknown feet. Add to this another misfortune: during the movie's world premiere the film jumps up and down uncontrollably in the projector. Soon, one can only feel tremendous sympathy for our heroes, for the film's director as he now envisions bankruptcy and jail if this movie venture bombs. Money acquired from selling state rights to the film has already been spent in production of the now uncontrollably jumping film. It seems as if all is doomed.

But wait! As in most fairy tales, there is a happy ending. The film is fixed a few days later and jumps no more in the projector. More importantly, the playwright's story, as presented by the film, captivates the imagination of the

American public so much that the movie is a tremendous success and the movie industry is itself changed forever.

The aforementioned was not a fairy tale. It is the actual history of Hollywood's first successful feature movie. The director who had never made a movie before was Cecil B. DeMille. The former glove salesman was Sam Goldwyn. The vaudeville producer was Jesse L. Lasky and the Broadway playwright was Edwin Milton Royle. The movie was *The Squaw Man,* an entertaining story which dealt with such controversial topics as racism and social injustice. It had all the elements necessary for movie success—romance; western and cowboy culture; satire on aristocracy; laughter, tears, excitement; and a previous Broadway success. Try now to imagine what would have happened to Hollywood history if this 1914 movie had flopped with the studio going bankrupt and DeMille and Goldwyn out of the movie business.

If current efforts by certain individuals and organizations succeed, then the importance of this movie and the story of its making will be securely preserved for future generations. Josephine Royle, whose father was Edwin Milton Royle, is now making efforts to publish for the first time her father's autobiography. Upon publication, this promises to shed new light on the pioneering contributions her father made to the birth of Hollywood as the motion picture capital. Also a remarkable preservationist organization in Hollywood has taken the barn which was used by DeMille and Goldwyn as the studio for *The Squaw Man* and is converting it into the Hollywood Studio Museum. The organization called Hollywood Heritage has restored the barn to its original studio look and relocated it near the Hollywood Bowl. The museum is scheduled to open in May of 1984 and is to attract worldwide attention with the opening gala. Josephine is an honorary member of the museum's board of trustees. This was accomplished as a result of both she and myself contacting Hollywood Heritage during the summer of 1982.

In May of 1982, I asked Josephine Royle if we could explore together the possibility of a movie remake of her father's play, *The Squaw Man.* We are currently examining ways through which this might be accomplished.

Josephine Fetter Royle is a remarkable woman. She is a playwright, drama teacher, and lyricist. Her sister, Selena Royle, who recently passed away, was a veteran actress of stage and screen including the classic WWII movie, *The Sullivans.* Growing up with the Royle sisters as friends of my family was an incredibly enriching experience. My mother, Bernice Holden, moved to the Hollywood area in the early '50s. There she met Josephine, or Jo Jo as she is affectionately referred to, and an incredible prolific songwriting partnership soon emerged. The songwriting duo of Royle and Holden produced numerous songs, some of which were arranged by Lyn Murray, George Cates of Lawrence Welk fame, Haakon Bergh, Walter Samuels, and Elmer Bernstein. It is my hope that someday Josephine's and my mother's work might be explored and revived since much of it has withstood the test of time in terms of style and quality.

But alas the realities of raising two children in Hollywood when you're a talented but poor songwriter caught up to my mother. She made the decision that the family came first and we would have to move to my grandmother's farm in Kansas. After moving, my mother started out as a newspaper reporter and was eventually promoted to assistant editor. She now works as a professional typesetter for a printing firm. Josephine and my mother kept in touch throughout the years and remained the best of friends. Every Christmas and birthday, my sister and I would receive wonderful gifts from both Jo Jo and Selena. Occasionally, there would be a movie on TV in which Selena played and my imagination would go back to those first five years in Hollywood.

I remember one day at the age of eleven or so that I was browsing through one of my mother's trunks in which she kept things special to her. There I came upon a book entitled, *The Squaw Man.* As it had the Royle name on it, I was curious to see what it was about and if it was famous. My mother told me that it had been made into a movie a long time ago. Now at the age of 31 years, I am finally discovering what an important story Edwin Milton Royle wrote in 1904. That was the year he wrote it as a one-act play in New York. A few months later it was presented by the Lambs Club and soon after in 1905 opened on Broadway.

DeMille and Lasky, realizing the success and popularity of *The Squaw Man* during the first decade of the 20th century, wisely chose it as their premiering film endeavor. DeMille respected the story so much that he remade the film twice more, once in 1918 and again as a "talkie" in 1931. DeMille was quoted as saying in the early 1930s that *The Squaw Man* is a film that he would remake every 10 years. It has been over fifty years since DeMille made that remark. Now that we are approaching the middle of the '80s, one feels that the time is ripe to consider Mr. DeMille's statement.

The Squaw Man is a beautiful story that should be revived for our generation. In its treatment of Native American characters, *The Squaw Man* was ahead of its time. The play incorporated genuine Ute dialect in the dialogue and the 1914 film starred Red Wing, a native American actress in the leading female role of Nat-u-ritch. The story portrays her as a woman of great courage, inner strength, and love. The leading male role is that of a white man of aristocratic background who marries Nat-u-ritch. He is then shunned wrongly by society as a "squaw man." The plot then explores the harsh realities that this unique couple experience. Can their marriage work in a world which opposes their love?

The Squaw Man is a classic romance and western that is full of intrigue and excitement. In these days when movie executives are grasping at straws for feature film ideas, why not remake Hollywood's first successful feature film?

Save the Barn

In December of 1913, Cecil B. DeMille rented part of a barn located near an orange grove at Selma Avenue and Vine Street in Los Angeles. The barn was used as the studio in which *The Squaw Man* was filmed. After the huge success of the film, the Jesse L. Lasky Feature Play Company expanded and part of the barn was demolished; the rest was used for storage. In 1926, it was moved to Paramount's Marathon Street lot and was used as a gymnasium. When the Jesse L. Lasky Feature Play Company evolved into the Paramount Pictures Corporation, the barn became part of Paramount's western set. A porch was added and railroad tracks built outside and the barn became part of the set in the *Bonanza* television series.

In December of 1956, the barn was designated a California landmark as Hollywood's first major film company studio. Film dignitaries, including DeMille, Goldwyn, and Lasky attended the dedication ceremonies. In 1979, Paramount donated the barn to the Hollywood Chamber of Commerce who turned it over to their Hollywood Historic Trust Committee, chaired by actor Buddy Ebsen. It was moved to a parking lot near the Hollywood Palace.

On March 13, 1982, the Hollywood Historic Trust turned possession of this historical treasure over to the Hollywood Heritage. Hollywood Heritage, in their efforts to convert the barn into the Hollywood Studio Museum, turned over the first shovelful of dirt for the museum's foundation on November 12, 1982. On February 15, 1983 the barn was moved to its new home outside the Hollywood Bowl.

Buddy Ebsen once remarked to members of the National Film Society: "In the picture business, or any business, we can learn a great deal from what the pioneers did. . . . Their studio was just an old barn. It's still here, and I think it should be protected. It reminds us of how Hollywood began and our children should have the chance to see it." Mr. Ebsen is so right in his view that the "Barn" studio is of the utmost historical significance.

The Birth of a Nation

AN ASSESSMENT

Seymour Stern

Originally appeared in vol. 5, no. 1 (November/December 1980)

Noted Griffith historian Seymour Stern examines the triumphs and the controversies surrounding The Birth of a Nation. *For the most part, these notes have never before appeared in print. They reveal Stern's lifelong preoccupation with Griffith's masterpiece. All materials are printed by permission of the Stern Estate, Ira Gallen, Executive Director.*

ॐ

Griffith's gigantic spectacle of the American Civil War and the Reconstruction Period in the Old South was the first world-famous picture, and remains to this day the great landmark in film history. This is the film with which the motion picture is universally regarded as having established itself as a medium of expression, and as having proven itself for the first time a fine art. Neither the future of the motion picture nor Griffith's career beyond this point can be viewed in its proper perspective without understanding the nature and significance of *The Birth of a Nation.*

Early in 1914, Griffith broke with Reliance-Majestic when the company refused to vote the sum of $50,000 for the production of a book, *The Clansman,* by a Southern clergyman, Thomas Dixon, Jr. It was a romantic and violent story of the American Civil War and the Reconstruction Period in the South. The company officials were shocked at Griffith's proposal to make a film at nearly twice the cost of *Judith of Bethulia* or greater than the largest sum expended on any film since the industry began. Bitter sessions led to bad feelings. Griffith in high anger resigned. The heads of Reliance-Majestic and of the affiliate company, Mutual, convinced that he had become unbalanced, gladly tore up the contract.

Griffith canvassed the industry for a backer. He received a cold shoulder from every producer. In many instances he met with caustic criticism for daring to think of basing a film on what was generally termed "that nigger book."

Accordingly, Griffith and Harry Aitken, without benefit of either the industry or the banks, formed a new independent company, the Epoch Producing Corporation, to produce the film; later, when the industry also refused to distribute it, they formed the Epoch Distributing Corporation. Both companies were formed exclusively for *The Birth of a Nation* with cameraman G. W. Bitzer.

The Birth of a Nation was produced at a total cost of $110,000. By today's financial standards, this sum was trifling, but by the standards of 1914, it was staggering. Aitken succeeded in raising only about half of the originally estimated budget of $50,000, but Griffith would not wait for the balance. With unrestrained enthusiasm, and in a mood of reckless gambling, he began work with Thomas Dixon and Frank Woods on the scenario and, when this was completed, he cancelled all leaves and vacations for the staff and company, stepped up the working schedule to sixteen hours a day and flung himself with unbridled energy into the task. Bitzer tells of the "tremendous zeal, energy and genius Griffith put into having its timing just so, its tempo right to a hair. I remember how hard he worked in the day, and then far into the night. . . . Of all motion pictures ever produced, none ever was more beset with difficulties than *The Birth of a Nation,* and only [but] for the belief and indomitable spirit of Griffith, to carry it to a successful conclusion, would it [n]ever have been finished."

After six weeks of rehearsals, "shooting" or actual production began on July 4, 1914, America's Independence Day, in the countryside near Los Angeles. The first scenes photographed were battles of the American Civil War. Actual production or "shooting" lasted nine consecutive weeks. Additional scenes were taken later, and the total "shooting" schedule ran, roughly, from July to October.

Interiors were shot at the Fine Arts Studios at the outskirts of Hollywood— then a mere countrified village. The exteriors were taken throughout Southern California, the principal locations being the pine forests at Arrowhead, Idyllwild and Big Bear Lake; the San Fernando Valley; Imperial Valley (plantation and cotton-picking scenes) and the hills beyond Whittier to the south, and near Calabasas and Ojai to the north.

Sherman's march to the sea and at least one major battle scene—the Union attack on the Confederate trenches at Petersburg, were filmed in the San Fernando Valley. The locations for these sequences were the sand washes and open fields, where Universal Studios now stands.

Griffith hired "extra" players by the hundred, including Civil War veterans for types and "atmosphere"; hundreds of horses; and an arsenal of artillery pieces. He took action in the major battle scenes four miles from the camera; and he leased the southwestern portion of Whittier County, some eighty miles south of Los Angeles, along the inland route to Mexico, so that roads and highways could be closed off for filming the far-flung ride of the Clansmen. *The Birth of a Nation* marked the real beginning of modern film production.

An unexpected crisis forced him to hurry. When World War I broke out in August, 1914, the price of horses rose, and then came a shortage of horses, as the European governments began buying them for the slaughter. Griffith, exasperated over possible frustration, bought or rented horses from corrals, ranches, stables and trading posts throughout California and Arizona.

The cost of production soared far beyond the original estimate. Again and again, the project was threatened with abandonment and extinction. Bitzer had always felt the highest admiration and respect for Griffith, and never more so than now, but as he watched him grapple with this seemingly impossible film, he relates that his admiration turned to awe and his respect to pity. By way of personal tribute to Griffith, he put up $25,000 which, as he relates, he never expected to see again. (At the end of the next fifteen years, the investment brought him back over half a million dollars.) But even this was far from enough. Griffith, Bitzer, Griffith's secretary, J. D. Barry, Lillian Gish and the other leading players now made frantic efforts to raise further capital among their friends and acquaintances. Their campaign reached a bizarre climax when they took two days off for house-to-house soliciting in the wealthy suburb of Pasadena. *The Birth of a Nation* finally cost $110,000, but some of the money was not raised until the final week of shooting.

Griffith's zeal reached a peak-point of fanaticism during the final weeks of "shooting," when the schedule was tightened to twelve hours before the cameras, from sunrise to sunset, and eight hours in the cutting room for preliminary editing or, in all, twenty hours a day.

When "shooting" was completed, three and a half months were spent on editing the film. Hence, the overall time of production came to about six months (the average feature film at the time was completed and made ready for release in four to six weeks).

Finally, in January, 1915, Griffith engaged Joseph Carl Breil, a composer and orchestral leader, to adapt to the finished film a complete symphonic score. Griffith himself, who knew composition, arranged passages of Negro and Southern folk music. Breil composed the famous Clan-call, a weird blend of reed-whistles and horn-blasts, played during the scenes showing the birth of the Ku Klux Klan, the summoning of the Clans and the ride of the Clansmen.

The initial run began on February 8, 1915, at Clune's (now the Philharmonic) Auditorium, Los Angeles, where the picture ran for seven months under the original (book) title, *The Clansman.* Soon afterwards, at a press preview at the Rose Gardens (now the Winter Garden), New York City, the original title, *The Clansman,* was changed by Dixon, who found it "too tame" and gave the film its new and permanent name.

Late in February, 1915, advertisements, heralding the arrival in New York of the Griffith masterpiece, claimed the "Dawn of a New Art Which Marks an

Epoch in the Theatres of the World." This pronouncement was no mere press agent's blurb. It was the very nearly unanimous opinion of the intellectual and theatrical world of all America. Sir Herbert Tree, over here on an acting tour, declared the picture signified "the birth of a new art—and a new artist," and less than a month after the New York premiere, a critic, Richard Barry, writing in the magazine section of the *New York Times,* hailed Griffith as "a producer without a rival . . . a generalissimo of mimic forces whose work has never been equalled . . . a triumphant Columbus of the screen." A special showing was held in the East Room of the White House for President Wilson, his family and members of the Senate. Wilson, from whose *History of the American People* Griffith had quoted extensively in subtitles introducing the second half of the story, contributed the oft-quoted comment: "It is like writing history with lightning, and my one regret is that it is all so terribly true."

On March 3, 1915, at 8:05 p.m., *The Birth of a Nation* had its "official" world premiere at the Liberty Theatre, New York City. Here it ran for 44 consecutive weeks as the first two-dollar attraction in screen history; also, as the first film accompanied with a "full orchestral score," played by a symphony orchestra. It was the first film presented in standard theatrical form, twice daily, at scheduled performances, and divided like a play into (two) "acts," with an intermission between the acts. As thus projected, *The Birth of a Nation* in its complete original form consisted of 1,375 individual shots.

During the first few days of the Liberty Theatre run, the print is said to have totalled 1,544 shots. Due to embittered liberal and Negro objections, however, Griffith, to prevent the film from being banned in its entirety, agreed at a conference with Mayor Mitchell and the Chief of Police of New York City, to delete certain scenes and sequences, showing white women at an Abolitionist rally commenting contemptuously on the alleged body odor of Negroes; Negroes chasing white girls down alleys and Negroes lynching white men to telegraph poles and otherwise running amuck through the town of Piedmont in the grand climax; also, certain scenes in the original epilogue, showing American Negroes being deported back to Africa and groveling there in the wilderness before a primitive black god. The results of this conference were published in the *New York Times,* and the deleted scenes were permanently omitted from all showings north of the Mason and Dixon line. The remaining 1,375 shots have been ever since universally accepted as the official or complete original print. This running time came to two hours and forty-five minutes. This original, nationwide "first run" remains in many respects perhaps the most unique spectacle on record. For, although it appeared at a time when the machinery of projection still was primitive, and the means of distribution still inadequate, Griffith's masterpiece nevertheless launched a sudden, sweeping revolution in the technique of theatrical presentation. It startled the world with new methods of exhibition and "atmospheric effects." A fresh strategy of psychological appeal, a new method of putting a film on, which we accept today, without, perhaps, suspecting its origin, here sprang into being.

Such familiar practices as the sale of tickets, weeks in advance; reserved seats; scheduled performances; souvenir programmes; costuming of usherettes (according to the period costumes shown on the screen); orchestral accompaniment; symphonic overtures; stage prologues; dimming or elimination of half-lights, and total darkening of the house interior during the showing; modulated or variable projection; intermissions—in a word, the whole modern system of deluxe motion picture presentation, suddenly emerged here, full blown and quite literally unprecedented as "added attractions" to what was in itself a film exhibition, without likeness in the history of the screen.

The Birth of a Nation struck at the vested interest of the theatre in the two centers where the blow hurt the most: at the box office, and in the domain of public opinion. So great, indeed, was its triumph, that a legend arose, which persisted for many years afterwards, that *The Birth of a Nation* had itself given birth to the new medium. Be that as it may, it advanced the motion picture in one giant stride from its former position as the "tag-end of a vaudeville show" up to a point of vantage, from which the film could and actually did threaten the older arts with commercial competition and with a wholly unforeseen bid for esthetic superiority.

The film made heavy inroads on all counts into theatrical domain. It inspired the leading stage producers to cite it as a standard. An example of this was an advertising billboard in Times Square, which proclaimed the third act of a co-contemporary Broadway play, *Common Clay*, as an achievement that "surpasses in sheer dramatic intensity any scene in *The Birth of a Nation*." This was the first time that a movie was used as the yardstick of comparison for judging a stage play.

The motion picture had arrived. The entire American film industry was jubilant. The "masterminds" of New York and Hollywood, who had less than a year before turned down Griffith and the story, now hailed the picture and Griffith as their personal discovery. Griffith tells that some producers rationalized their rejection on the ground that they felt it was his patriotic duty, and also in his best interest, to produce and release the film himself. With such touching consideration as has rarely if ever been manifested by the American film industry, Hollywood was setting the pattern for a technique of anti-creative and anti-experimental suppression, followed by tactical "apologies," that was to dominate its production policies during the next twenty-five years. On one point only were all agreed, the professional personnel and the producers alike: namely, the fact that, thanks to Griffith, the film as a medium, a fine art, had at last become a reality.

Overnight, the principal players of *The Birth of a Nation* became famous. Some were made "stars"—notably, Henry B. Walthall, Lillian Gish, Mae Marsh, Wallace Reid, Elmo Lincoln, Miriam Cooper and Ralph Lewis.

The outstanding character portrayals were those given by Josephine Crowell, Donald Crisp, Joseph Henabery, Elmo Lincoln, Raoul Walsh, Walter Long, Howard Gaye, George Siegmann, Mary Alden and Jennie Lee. Of the latter group, Mary Alden and George Siegmann gave the best performance of their careers, creating two rather unforgettable and extremely forceful characterizations—Lydia Brown, the Hon. Austin Stoneman's sex-crazed mulatto mistress; and Silas Lynch, mulatto leader of the blacks, respectively.

But the acting honors of *The Birth of a Nation* have historically been accorded to Henry B. Walthall and Mae Marsh. Walthall in the role of Col. Ben Cameron (the "Little Colonel") set a new standard in silent-film pantomime. Griffith pronounced him years later the greatest of film actors, and cited the Little Colonel as representing in his judgment the most distinguished male performance in the annals of screen-playing. Among the actresses, Mae Marsh in the role of Flora, the "little pet sister," won the acclaim of critics and public alike for the best female performance. Eight years afterwards, in 1923, her work here still was used as a yardstick of appraisal for her final noteworthy screen role, in Griffith's *The White Rose*.

Other members of the cast, notably Elmer Clifton, Joseph Henabery, Raoul Walsh and Donald Crisp, became directors. Clifton died in 1949; Henabery, Walsh and Crisp remained in the field, both as actors and directors.

The portrayal of Elsie Stoneman by Lillian Gish introduced a new type of heroine to the screen; it marked the beginning of what a contemporary critic, Herb Sterne, describes as an "entirely new fashion and standard in American beauty," which he designates as the type of the "Griffith Girls." The type, as it evolved in the whole gallery of portrayals created afterwards by Griffith and the girls, derives from this initial, historically significant portrait-image, of Lillian Gish, designed to create the "flower and symbol" of white female virginity and to project the quintessence of female white beauty.

As already stated, the theme of *The Birth of a Nation* is the American Civil War and the Reconstruction Period in the Old South. In effect, it may be summarized as a definitive screen-portrait of the Southerners, projected as the image-symbol of an emotional and racial (tribal) tradition.

Griffith, himself a son of the Old South, took the view that slavery, not the rise of Northern industrialism, was *the* issue of the Civil War. He further contended, that, basically, the issue was not economic or even political but racial and sexual (in the early days of the conflict over *The Birth of a Nation*, he used the terms "emotional" and "moral" as synonyms for these). Throughout the film the private feels and dreams, the societal principles and values—in short, the emotion-culture—of the Southerners are stressed as the motive of behavior and the source of drama. This approach dominates the story during its Civil War episodes no less than it does the epic of Reconstruction, in the second half.

Structure of the Film

The picture falls into two major divisions ("acts"), formally entitled on the screen, Part I and Part II. Part I dramatizes the American Civil War of 1861–1865 up to, and including, the surrender of Lee and the assassination of Lincoln. This part also includes a screen-prologue, which picturizes the introduction of Negro slavery into America in the 17th century, together with slave auctioneering, and the rise of the Abolitionist movement in New England, a century and a half later. But the feature of Part I is the spectacular and realistic battle scenes of the Civil War.

Part II, which begins after the sequences of Lincoln's assassination and its depicted effect on the South, traces the exploitation of the newly emancipated Southern Negroes by Northern bankers and industrialists ("carpetbaggers"), and by political fanatics of both North and South ("scalawags"). It dramatizes the struggle against, and ultimate defeat of, an allegedly vengeful movement by these elements to "crush the White South under the heel of the Black South," as a subtitle puts it, and to rule the defeated Southerners through a Northern-controlled cultural, economic, political and racial dictatorship.

It is the second half of the film, also, which depicts on a tremendous scale the attendant growth, and eventual triumph, of the old Ku Klux Klan, or Invisible Empire (1868–1871). The film, in a series of subtitles introducing Part II, quotes Woodrow Wilson as stating in his *History of the American People* that this post-bellum secret organization saved the Old South from anarchy, and quite possibly from annihilation.

The Birth of a Nation ends with an allegorical epilogue, which, in its original, complete, uncensored form forecasts, and indeed urges, the deportation of all members and descendants of the black race from America to Africa, and prophesies that in the wake of this "solution" we may expect the coming of the Prince of Peace, the free intermingling of the world's peoples, and the victory of love in Christ. (In the mutilated, 9-reel, sound version, released in 1930, the epilogue, together with much other material from the original print, was omitted.)

It is especially noteworthy that *The Birth of a Nation*, in the narrow, conventional sense, has no "heavy." There are a number of villains, but each is the embodiment or projection of an ideological and political doctrine. Some examples are Stoneman, representative and spokesman of the carpetbaggers, scalawags and Northern industrialists (white); Silas Lynch and his henchmen (black); Gus, the renegade (black) and others. But the true menace or "heavy" is the political and racial dictatorship, concretely and vividly personalized. The racial issue bursts out in all its fury, when Lynch tries to force an intermarriage with Elsie. Thus the major tragedy of the film—"the agony which the South endured that a nation might be born," as Griffith expresses it in a subtitle—is brought home through the more familiar and intimate characters. There is a certain quality of fateful inevitability, inherent in the historic drama and mass action, which underlies and dominates the personal stories and private tragedies, giving the film an epic quality.

The Controversy

From the start *The Birth of a Nation* touched off bitter controversy and bloody conflict. The history of the film after its release is without parallel in stage or screen annals. Its anti-Northern interpretation of the American Civil War and of the Reconstruction Period in the South; its vitriolic censure of a great American radical statesman, Thaddeus Stevens; its treatment of the Negro and of the political and social problems stemming from his emancipation; its wild and stirring picturization of the activities of the original Ku Klux Klan, or Invisible Empire, from 1868 to 1871 and, above all, the bitter import and bold challenge of its anti-democratic and anti-liberal ideology—more specifically, its passionate insistence on biological inequality, white supremacy, segregation and states' rights: all this stunned the American public as no other theatrical presentation had ever done. The storm of controversy that rose in its wake soon very nearly had the whole country fighting the Civil War over again. Like a cyclops with a blazing torch, the film traveled swiftly, igniting arsenal after arsenal of human emotions. As Cecil B. DeMille recently reminisced, it "burst upon the world with atomic force." It was sweepingly successful with all types of audiences throughout the country. It took city after city by storm, dazing the immense audiences with its gigantic dimensions and its overpowering emotional impact. But it was neither its miraculous popular appeal nor its signal artistic merit and physical magniture that stirred up the tumultuous waves of emotional excitement and external commotion among the people; rather, it was the aggressive and arrogant attack on liberal democracy. The idea that fifty years after the Civil War, in the America of 1915, the history of the conflict and its aftermath should be or even could be interpreted by an avowed American from what appeared a militantly anti-democratic and anti-Negro Southern viewpoint, had apparently not occurred to anybody, and dumbfounded everyone north of the Mason and Dixon Line.

Griffith together with Dixon was passionately denounced by such well-known liberals as Oswald Garrison Villard, Jane Addams, Lillian Wald, Eugene V. Debs, Frederic C. Howe, Francis Hackett, Upton Sinclair, Dr. Charles W.

Eliot, head of Harvard University, Stephen Wise, W. E. B. Du Bois, Albert Bushnell Hart, the historian, and others. Griffith was accused of having "deliberately humiliated and libelled 10,000,000 American citizens, portraying them as nothing but beasts"; and he was attacked in a five-column newspaper tirade by Hart for having "made a mockery of the Union victory in our Civil War." He was also pronounced guilty of having sabotaged the progress of interracial relations in America. Indeed, one newspaper editorial suggested that the film in effect was a Southern post-Gettysburg counterattack, and that it should be retitled, "Victory of the Confederacy."

The National Association for the Advancement of Colored People, in collaboration with various "Booker T. Washington Clubs," and with the vigorous support of *The Nation, The New Republic,* the *New York Globe,* and other liberal magazines and newspapers, launched against Griffith and the film a nationwide campaign of boycott and denunciation, which lasted over a year, the echoes and repercussions of which have been heard for decades.

Mass demonstrations and riots broke out in a dozen cities, reaching a high pitch of fury in Boston and Philadelphia. The race riot that swept the New England capital was the first of many such riots that broke out anew when *The Birth of a Nation* was revived during the 1920s.

In Boston, 5,000 Negroes led by white liberals and sympathizers stormed the State Capitol Building, demanding the film be suppressed and threatening "mass action" and reprisals if it was permitted to continue. Anti-Negro mobs countermarched on Boston Common and threatened lynchings. Beatings, fist-fights, knifings, mob-clashes, shootings and violence of a seemingly organized type, coupled with damage to both Negro and white property, flared throughout the city. In consequence, to avoid having to ban the film, and at the same time with an eye to the Negro vote which he sorely needed, Mayor Curley requested Griffith to delete the entire sequence of Gus chasing Flora through the woods and of Flora leaping to her death to escape rape—the sequence to which the most violent exception was taken. Negro-newspaper editors, including the well-known William Trotter, who protested against this ruse to keep the film on exhibition, were fined or jailed for disturbing the peace.

In Philadelphia, while the film was being unreeled to frenzied audiences inside the Forrest Theatre, 3,000 Negroes, milling outside the lobby, battled in the streets with 500 police. Heads were cracked; police and citizenry alike were knifed; Negroes were beaten, kicked, shot or jailed; and the riot spread until it engulfed a large part of Philadelphia's Negro population.

During the 1915 run, inside and outside the Liberty Theatre in New York, clashes and other disturbances broke out; Negroes were arrested for hurling eggs at the Liberty screen, and thereafter Griffith had the house put under police guard. He sprinkled each audience with Pinkerton detectives.

The Boston demonstration and the Philadelphia riot put *The Birth of a Nation*—and thus the motion picture—on the front page. Time and again, the European war was forced to share space with Griffith's atomic masterpiece. Thus did the world first become movie-conscious.

What clearly emerges from the conflict and confusion over the issue is the overwhelming evidence of lack of intention on the part of American ruling circles to do anything about it. Assurances and even promises were made to Negro organizations or representatives, by top churchmen and politicians, that the film would be banned or else drastically censored to eliminate its more inflammatory effects. But nothing was done. The evasion pattern was always the same: assurances were invariably followed by a period of silence and stalling, and then, when the surface commotion evoked by the initial impact had died away, the matter was dropped on the grounds that since there were no further riots, there was no further need for suppression. It was an ingenious and insidious tactic, for although the external commotion waned, the poisonous effect of the picture in generating new contempt and new hatred of the Negro race, both among those whites already infected and those infected here for the first time, continued unchecked and did its work for further hate and future conflict. Only when the United States entered the First World War did *The Birth of a Nation*, as if by magic, disappear from the nation's screens. Negro blood, Negro labor, Negro money and Negro support were needed to "make the world safe for democracy."

However, conservatism did not win a complete victory. For as a result of the vast commotion, *The Birth of a Nation* inadvertently generated some sympathy for the Negroes even among those people who might otherwise be regarded as categorically illiberal. The indignation and protest came from a minority, but the minority was articulate and gave signs of increasing. Due to this fact, as well as to the organized pressure and wrath of the liberals, the film was banned in Ohio and, subsequently, in a number of other states and cities, where it has never to this day been shown. Censorship of the screen began in America in a serious way with the legislation that followed in the wake of *The Birth of a Nation.*

To combat screen censorship, which he hated, Griffith wrote, published and distributed a pamphlet, *The Rise and Fall of Free Speech in America.* Copies by the thousand were circulated wherever the film was shown. "It is to be admitted," wrote Terry Ramsaye, "that part of Griffith's ardor grew out of the fact that he had money at stake in the picture, but it would be unfair to believe that this was the source of more than half of his zeal. There is considerable evidence . . . that Griffith would rather make pictures than make money. It was indeed this very fact which so early set him apart from the commonplace in motion picture production . . . Griffith issued statements, made speeches and wrote letters proclaiming fundamental rights of expression which he said should be self-evident.

His fight for *The Birth of a Nation* was really a fight for the whole institution of the screen."

Throughout the tempest Griffith stood his ground. He contended that the real villains of the piece are not the Negroes, but white politicians, who mislead the Negroes and use them as pawns. All this was based, he said, on historic fact, which he had documented with research in government archives, citing, in particular, the report of a congressional investigation into the "Condition of the Last Insurrectionary States." He cited with telling effect Woodrow Wilson's *History of the American People*. He defended his right as a free American citizen to dramatize history in the light of his own understanding. And he argued that if the screen could not stand the acid test of free speech on controversial subjects, then it was not free and something should be done about it.

But the Griffith company (Epoch), reactionary almost to a man and taking its cue from Dixon, in 1915 attacked the censorship and defended the film along quite other lines than free speech. It is tragic to record that it was with Griffith's full knowledge and public approval that Epoch issued malicious and militant statements to the press, branding agitation against the film as a deliberate attempt by what it called, variously, an "intermarriage conspiracy" and the "intermarriage crowd" to foment trouble. It implied or openly stated, according to the circumstances and the community, that the National Association for the Advancement of Colored People or its liberal sympathizers had hired "hooligans" to create turmoil in the theatres, wreck the screens, provoke street fights, incite riots; or, in a word, to foment interracial strife, which then could be blamed on the picture. Finally, it boldly avowed that one of the aims of the film was to awaken the American people to the "menace of mongrelization." This aspect of the controversy raged virtually unabated up until America's entry into the First World War and reappeared when the post-war revivals began.

As a masterpiece, *The Birth of a Nation* has withstood the test of time, and looms increasingly as the immortal landmark of the screen. It has both the integrity and the massiveness of a true epic. It is of primary importance in the cinema, not only as a powerful influence on all subsequent production, but as a work of art in its own independent and intrinsic right. The qualities of the film as a conscious creative work are many and definite. Structurally, it exhibits a singular clarity, symmetry and proportion of parts. There is a wonderful flexibility and coherence in the pattern of the action. Episode and sequence are interwoven admirably—with a fluent naturalness and simplicity—in a moving and breathingly natural story.

Innocence Abroad

HEARTS OF THE WORLD

James M. Welsh

Originally appeared in vol. 2, no. 3 (January/February 1978)

As a celebration of American "innocence" (and innocence abroad, at that), particularly in terms of old-fashioned values and domestic virtue, David Wark Griffith's *Hearts of the World*, made in 1918, just as the First World War was in its concluding stages, must be considered a minor masterpiece. It is also, of course, potentially a work of propaganda, though the film's propaganda was apparently toned down before its final release by deleting a great deal of rather heavy-handed anti-Hun material. In his book *D. W. Griffith: His Life and Work* (Oxford Press, 1972, p. 187), Robert M. Henderson reports that the film was reduced from twelve reels to eight (a substantial reduction), partly to reflect the changing world situation after the armistice, but partly also for artistic reasons. The extant version is still obviously anti-German, reducing a complex political conflict to a morality play of black-and-white absolutes—and this, indeed, is the film's most serious flaw.

The print of *Hearts of the World* now circulated by the Killiam Collection runs to just two minutes over two hours. In this version the action is broken down into three major movements: 1) The Village in Peacetime; 2) War and the German Occupation; and 3) Liberation and the restoration of order. Fully one-third of the film (subtitled "The Story of a Village") is devoted to the first movement, as Griffith takes his time to establish the nature and character of this particular, anonymous French village. In fact, the first portion of *Hearts of the World* could easily stand on its own as a self-contained vignette telling the story of young love and courtship as it develops between "The Boy" (Bobby Harron) and "The Girl" (Lillian Gish), both of whom are transplanted Americans living on the "Rue de la Paix" in this peaceful, idyllic, French village.

Seldom has Griffith's naive charm worked so well as in the beginning of this motion picture. One needs only to consider, for example, the way in which Griffith represents the first meeting of the lovers, as Lillian Gish innocently follows a wandering gosling who leads her to the Boy, or the jealousy that the Boy's youngest brother (about three or four years old) develops for the Girl (to be reconciled just before their intended marriage). This little tale of courtship is complicated by the designs of another girl, "The Little Disturber" (marvelously played by Dorothy Gish), on the Boy, whom she embraces on the street just in time for Lillian Gish to see them. Meanwhile, all the villagers are of course ignorant of the machinations of the German General Staff, an irony which Griffith suggests by taking the audience directly into their planning room at staff headquarters.

The film starts with a "Prologue" that shows Mr. Griffith at No. 10 Downing Street, shaking hands with Lloyd George; it then shows him "in the British front line trench at Cambrin, fifty yards from the enemy's lines." Such *tableaux vivants* as we find in this film have an eerie authenticity, as when, for example, we see Lloyd George, Winston Churchill, Asquith, and Gray waiting dramatically in London, on the brink of war. We witness documentary footage here and there that has an indisputably authentic "feel" and are forcefully reminded thereby of the chronological closeness of the artifact to the event.

Ultimately, of course, Griffith shows us how the War affects ordinary people, suggesting in broad dramatic terms how it indiscriminately destroys villages and villagers. In telling this story of death and destruction, Griffith is at his most powerful. As the War comes to "The Village," the Girl, having witnessed the death of her mother, goes into a state of shock. She wanders off, unhinged, into the blue-tinted night. Approaching the battle zone, she discovers the wounded body of the Boy and spends the night, locked in a pathetic embrace with her unconscious lover who has fallen "under the risen moon" and appears to be dead (though he will later recover). After some hours pass, the wounded soldier is discovered and taken away for medical treatment. Still in a state of somnambulant shock, the Girl returns to the Village, not totally aware of where she has been or what she has experienced.

The story is told effectively and with a great deal of restraint. In Griffith's world the sacred family is threatened by War, which gradually claims its casualties, one by one. The survivors respond heroically, attempting to hold the family together. When the Boy's mother dies, for example, his younger brothers, mere children, bury her, performing this "sacred rite" themselves. The acting is generally understated, and all the more touching for that. Beyond the rather ponderous opening, subtitles are used minimally and efficiently.

Ultimately, the brutality and inhumanity of the war is presented more as background than foreground in this film. It provides a continuing source of menace and destruction that efficiently complicates the plot and sustains tension; it separates and endangers the young lovers, whose potential for happiness is linked to the liberation of the Village and the restoration of peace and harmony. As in *Intolerance*, both the thematic and melodramatic issues are effectively resolved by the last-minute rescues at the end, when first Bobby Harron saves Lillian Gish from the lecherous designs of the German Officer Von Stroheim; then, soon afterwards, when both of the principals, on the brink of committing suicide out of desperation—death before dishonor—are rescued by the arrival of the Allied armies.

Thus the two lovers, who once lived in innocence and harmony on the "Rue de la Paix," are safely reunited, Americans in France saved by Americans in France. This happy conclusion is overseen by the smiling portrait of Woodrow Wilson, as Griffith seems to give his moral benediction to the eventual American commitment to the Allied cause. At the end victorious troops march under the flags of France and the United States, and the final montage concludes with a shot of the lovers, arm in arm, under a halo of light. An improved new world is dawning for the young, their parents now dead and buried, victims of the holocaust. The serious lovers and their comic counterparts, as well as the Boy's younger brothers, are not only the survivors, but the builders of new era.

It is interesting to compare Griffith's *Hearts of the World* to Raoul Walsh's *What Price Glory*, made some eight years later in 1926 and based on the stage treatment by Maxwell Anderson and Laurence Stallings, for these two films reflect values that are worlds apart, as the innocence of Griffith's "old-fashioned" story gives way to the sophistication and worldliness of the middle 1920s. *What Price Glory* therefore reflects a considerable difference in substance and tone, though both films certainly reflect the experience of the Great War and both are carried along by a melodramatic romantic involvement. The Griffith film, however, is mainly "about" the Boy, the Girl, and the Village; the Walsh film, on the other hand, is mainly "about" the Marine Corps, and although the romantic element is present, and strongly so, it is always secondary to the rivalry between Captain Flagg (Victor McLaglen) and Sergeant Harry Quirt (Edmund Lowe). Both films present a dilemma of love and honor, but in *What Price Glory* the emphasis is more squarely upon honor. At the end of the film Flagg and Quirt march off into battle together, leaving the girl who loves them both behind. Quirt is under no formal obligation to go: he has been wounded in action, and he has bested Flagg in their personal battle over Charmaine (Dolores Del Rio). Having finally made her choice and claimed him, Charmaine clearly wants Quirt to stay. But he has a weakness for bugles; he is driven by a strong sense of personal honor and esprit de corps. His very being resists inaction and domestication. The character is so well defined that he cannot stay, even though the film ends with Charmaine's dire prediction that neither comrade will return a third time from the front.

In *Hearts of the World*, Griffith takes well over forty minutes to establish his characters and create an impression of village life during peacetime. Walsh also opens his film with establishing "business," but what he wishes to establish is the intense rivalry between Flagg and Quirt, the one a "man's man," the other a "ladies' man." Walsh takes us into the brothels of Shanghai so as to show the two men fighting over a prostitute named Shanghai Mable. Thence to the Philippines, where, again, Quirt takes advantage of Flagg and steals his girl. Can there be any question, then, about what will happen with Charmaine when Quirt finally shows up in France? Even so, Walsh somehow creates the impression that Flagg is indeed capable of winning Charmaine's love as well as her heart.

What Price Glory is perhaps as lopsided in the macho world it presents, where men are men and women are used, as *Hearts of the World* is in the old-fashioned world of naive sentimentality it presents, where women ought to be honored, respected, and defended. *What Price Glory* effectively mingles chivalry with compassion and comedy with tragedy. After the brusque comedy of the opening sequences set in Shanghai and the Philippines, Walsh quickly makes his transition to the war in Europe: "France, 1914. Aflame with War—civilization dedicated to destruction—fields of production drenched with blood—" a terse, laconic subtitle announces, as we see a symbolic Roman soldier, sword and shield in hand, marching toward the camera. "Then, in 1917," the subtitle continues, "America joined the Allies and the old Marines were in the biggest war of all." The comic tone of *What Price Glory* is reestablished, however, whenever Flagg and Quirt leave the front lines and resume their rivalry over Charmaine. In Griffith's film the comedy is exclusively confined to the peaceful opening sequence.

What Price Glory never questions the need to fight, as, nearly a decade later Ernst Lubitsch's *Broken Lullaby* was to do. But it does establish a sense of pity and compassion for the youthful victims: "Cannon fodder. Young and green replacements. Boys from every walk of life." Their first entry into battle is dramatized, as Captain Flagg leads his raw recruits into their baptism of fire.

Yet this and later silent war pictures fail to capture quite the same atmosphere or the haunting contemporaneity of Griffith's *Hearts of the World*, and all of them enter into a sort of mythification of the war experience, as one would expect to find in a genre picture. In *Wings*, for example, the enemy assumes a sort of exotic nobility, as symbolized by the Count Von Kellermann, who refuses to take unfair advantage of David Armstrong when he realizes the American pilot's machine gun has jammed. As the subtitle emphasizes, "There was a chivalry among these knights of the air." *Hearts of the World*, on the other hand, springs from the passions of the moment, and the Germans Griffith presents are, almost entirely, ignoble, barbaric brutes. D. W. Griffith was not out to make a genre film; the war in his film is more background than foreground, though frequently a tangible and convincing background. Mr. Griffith succeeds because he is reworking the materials—the characters and the formula—he knows best, fashioning a melodramatic story, as only he could, about a boy, a girl, and a village. *Hearts of the World* is recognizably a Griffith picture, and for that reason it is unique.

The Big Parade

A STANDARD FOR THE FUTURE

Lawrence H. Suid

Originally appeared in vol. 2, no. 3 (January/February 1978)

Following every war, a nation tries to forget about the conflict as quickly as possible. The disillusionment after World War I further alienated the American people from any positive thoughts about our participation in the conflict. As the 1920s progressed, the isolationist impulse deepened with the result that appropriations for the Armed Forces dried up and the Services shrank in size. In such an atmosphere, Hollywood found little reason beyond isolated efforts like *The Four Horsemen of the Apocalypse* and *The Merry-Go-Round* to produce a serious film about American involvement in the Great War. Nevertheless, war remained one of the subjects worthy of a major screen effort. A good story and proper timing rather than the subject itself, therefore, became the governing factors as to when the first post-war war film would be made.

King Vidor, a young and promising director in the mid-twenties, thought it "would take ten years to evolve a true War Picture. Propaganda and the passions of the struggle blind the participants from seeing it sanely; then satiety and a cynical reaction follow, no less blinding or distorting." Because war was "a very human thing," he believed it would take ten years' perspective for the human values to take predominance and for the rest to sink into insignificance. By 1924, Vidor, however, was seeking to make his first major film, one which "comes to town and stays longer than a week." Consequently, when he brought his aspiration to Irving Thalberg, head of M-G-M, he suggested that "War, wheat, or steel" would provide a suitable subject for such a major film.[1]

After discussing the possibilities of steel and wheat, Thalberg asked if Vidor had a particular war story in mind. While he had no specific idea, the director later recalled that he "wanted to make an honest war picture. Until then, they'd been all phony, glorifying officers and warfare. There hadn't been a single picture showing the war from the viewpoint of ordinary soldiers and privates, not one that was really anti-war." He told Thalberg that he would like to show the

140

reactions of a typical young American who goes to war and reacts normally to all the things that happen to him.

This approach interested the studio head and he immediately directed the M-G-M story department to send Vidor all the synopses they could find of war stories about World War I. However, according to the director, "they all looked the same after a while." He told Thalberg that the stories had an "unreal, almost musical-comedy flavor about them" and so lacked any sense of the realism he envisioned for his film. He wanted the audience to "share the heart beats of the doughboy and his girl and mother and folks." The director did not want to ignore "the huge surrounding spectacle" of war, but wanted to show it through the eyes of the common soldier. In such a film, he hoped the viewer would see how the "human comedy emerges alongside the terrific tragedy. Poetry and romance, atmosphere, rhythm and tempo, take their due place."

While Vidor continued to read story ideas at M-G-M, Thalberg went to New York where he saw the play *What Price Glory* which had just opened to "some of the wildest applause" Broadway had ever seen. He immediately hired Laurence Stallings, one of the co-authors, to go to Hollywood and work on a story with Vidor. The ex-Marine captain, who had lost a leg at Belleau Wood, arrived with a five-page story entitled "The Big Parade." His scenario focused on three young men who join the Army and become friends despite their divergent backgrounds—the son of a millionaire, a riveter, and a bartender. They go off to France where the rich doughboy falls in love with a French girl and loses a leg in battle while his two friends die in combat. Unlike most war stories, "The Big Parade" portrayed the lives of ordinary soldiers who tried to survive in a situation not of their own making. Stallings had no heroes seeking glory and no officers strutting around winning the war all by themselves. This was the sort of story Vidor had been seeking and the studio purchased it immediately. In order to provide additional material to fill out a screenplay, Stallings settled into Vidor's house where he proceeded to tell the director more about the war than he had gotten out of all the synopses and books he had been reading.

According to Vidor, Stallings "had more knowledge to communicate— more knowledge for my purpose—than the Committee on Public Information's 750,000 feet of stored films through which my agent pored in Washington." Nevertheless, despite his obvious help to Vidor, the playwright had no desire to remain in Hollywood, to write a screenplay based on his story. Consequently, when he headed back to New York, the director and a young studio writer, Harry Behn, accompanied him to get as many more of Stallings' ideas as possible. After reminiscing with him across the country and when they could catch up with him during the following week in New York, Vidor and Behn returned to Hollywood. Writing all the way back, they turned in a completed script three days after their arrival.

Once this had been completed, Vidor faced the task of recreating the authentic ambiance of Army life during wartime. Like virtually every maker of war movies over the years, the director believed he had to obtain accuracy of detail because so many men had taken part in the events he was portraying. Consequently, in addition to his conversations with Stallings, Vidor spent long hours looking at combat footage, which the War Department had sent out from Washington, in order to compensate for not having been in combat himself. At the same time, he hired two ex-soldiers as technical advisors to help insure accuracy. Moreover, in the course of shooting the film, he was to go to extraordinary lengths to secure the authentic atmosphere of conditions at the front. In one instance, a long debate took place over whether an officer's car being used in an important scene had the same type of wheels such cars had had in France. Finally, the research department called Washington to check the facts. The director also got firsthand information from unexpected sources. In trying to construct a number of German gun emplacements, Vidor discovered that his technical advisors had only seen blown-up gun nests. A laborer listening to the discussion spoke up, offering to describe the proper alignment. The man had been a German non-com during the war and he ended up commanding the German machine gun position in the film.

In turning to the United States Army for assistance in shooting the large-scale scenes of whole units of men advancing to the front, Vidor followed already developing procedures. Since the earliest days of the industry, the military had participated in movie making with advice, personnel, and equipment. In 1911, for example, Hap Arnold, later to command the Air Force in Europe during World War II, recalled that he "picked up a few extra dollars" by performing in a movie being shot on Long Island. In preparing to film *The Birth of a Nation* in 1915, D. W. Griffith asked West Point engineers for technical advice in preparing his Civil War battle sequences. West Point also supplied some Civil War pieces for close-up shots. Having established such contacts, Griffith turned to the Army for help in making *America*, his recreation of the Revolution.

For *America*, filmed in the summer of 1923, the War Department loaned Griffith more than 1,000 cavalrymen and a military band to help stage the crucial battles of the revolution. Secretary of War Weeks ordered the Army to provide Griffith every reasonable assistance. Reportedly, the cavalry units given to the director constituted the largest number ever assembled outside actual war maneuvers. The War Department justified such assistance on the ground that the combat sequences gave observers the opportunity to study the Revolutionary War battles with a precision never before possible because of the expense involved. According to Griffith, he received thousands of dollars worth of assistance because President Coolidge and Secretary Weeks believed the film would have a "wholesome and quieting effect" on the American people.

With this sort of assistance in mind, Vidor asked the Army for two hundred trucks, three to four thousand men, a hundred planes, and other necessary equipment to help portray large-scale troop movements to the front. When the War Department approved assistance, Vidor sent a second unit to Fort Sam Houston near San Antonio to film the needed scenes. Vidor had wanted the men and trucks to move in a straight line away from the camera and into the horizon with the planes flying over at a specified moment. Unfortunately, the assistant director got caught up in the Army's bureaucracy and, accepting the generals' claim that there were no long, straight roads in France, allowed the commanders to stage the maneuver on a curved road. While Vidor found the performance "magnificent," none of the 25 reels of film contained the effect he was seeking.

While relatively limited in scope, the Army's help proved essential in enabling Vidor to give his film a feeling of openness and size. In acknowledging the importance of this cooperation, Vidor said the military "cannot be overpraised." Except for the scenes shot in Texas, however, Army assistance was limited to providing a small amount of Signal Corps combat and training footage for a few of the battle sequences. The director filmed the rest of the combat scenes in and around Los Angeles with most of the shooting taking place on a tract of land about a city block square. All the soldiers in these scenes were extras and most of them had served in the Army even if they had not been overseas. Because of their military experience, Vidor did not have to train them to act like soldiers as future filmmakers often had to do when using extras in their war movies.

Vidor did face the problem of working with only a limited number of men and trucks during his Los Angeles filming. Consequently, when he had to create the illusion of large troop movements, the director had the men and trucks move in circles (out of camera range) to sustain the action for the desired length of time. More important, Vidor's immersion in the Signal Corps combat footage, his long discussions with Laurence Stallings, and the advice of his military advisors enabled him to capture on film the authentic atmosphere of combat. In at least two cases, however, he recreated reality better than his technical advisors remembered it. In one instance, he photographed men going into battle in columns of twos; in the second, he had the troops start walking straight ahead and then spread out as they deployed for battle. Both advisors argued that these maneuvers had never occurred in France. Vidor used the scenes anyway because he "just figured that nobody could have seen the whole front." Later, he found several sequences in the Signal Corps footage showing troops actually advancing in columns of twos. Likewise, despite his advisors' opinions, the director had wanted to have the advancing soldiers open up for dramatic effect following the title "Attack Formation." In this case, the War Department itself confirmed the accuracy of the maneuver when it wrote to Vidor that everything in the completed movie was technically accurate.

Although *The Big Parade* did contain an essentially anti-war theme, Vidor said that the military never made an objection to the film's content. He personally thought the film had "an anti-war feeling, definitely . . . But I don't know if you can call the whole film an anti-war film." Nevertheless, the director recalled that before the film opened, he had "anticipated an attack from militarist factions. But there were none." The reverse proved to be the case. When one of the Duponts, the manufacturers of large amounts of war materials, visited the set during shooting, he liked what he saw so much that he told Vidor he would supply a tent in which to show the picture if exhibitors refused to handle it. Such worries also proved unfounded as the film met with instant acclaim and box office success.

The Big Parade focused on the common soldiers and their reactions to the situations in which they found themselves through no fault of their own. Vidor said he tried to show "that all people concerned are affected alike, that they are just the same in habit and living, with similar hopes, loves and ambitions." Moreover, none of his characters are heroes, not even the film's star, John Gilbert, who played the millionaire's son. While he is young and good looking and falls in love with a beautiful French girl, he goes off to battle and loses a leg. To Vidor, the big message was that he "lost his leg instead of coming home a hero . . . He laughed at anything heroic, overly patriotic." In these terms, Gilbert, as the common man, "was neither a pacifist nor an over patriot. He just went in and experienced what he experienced and then reacted. You couldn't call him an activist."

Similarly, Vidor does not attempt to create an anti-war feeling by strewing the screen with blood and gore in order to show that war is hell as many filmmakers have done over the years. In the process of attempting to use violence in this manner, a movie usually ends up suggesting that war is an exciting adventure filled with romance and good times. In contrast, Vidor pictures the unglamorous side of combat. Gilbert's buddies die; he comes home with only one leg; and the girl he left behind has fallen in love with another man. (In itself, this plot twist is almost unique in the history of war films.) Even though Gilbert does return to France to claim the girl with whom he had fallen in love, the audience comes away with the impression that war really offers few rewards. According to Vidor, in all Gilbert's "war actions, all of the praise and the hospital bit and the killings of his buddies, he is cynical about the war thing. It was a great adventure as far as the girl goes, but not as far as the war goes."

Whatever effect the story had on the martial spirit of the audience, The Big Parade did attract record-breaking audiences because of Vidor's direction, the quality of the acting, and the authenticity of the combat sequences. According to the film critic of the Boston Transcript, The Big Parade gains "sweep and pathos and a certain boisterous humor through the directorial acumen of King Vidor. To watch it unroll is to realize anew all the shallow bombast, all the flatulency and all the saccharinity with which previous picturemakers have encumbered the trade of war."

Not all critics saw The Big Parade as totally realistic, however, especially when compared to What Price Glory. One writer argued that Vidor's film was not a cinematic equivalent to Stallings' play: "There is in the picture none of the matter-of-fact bitterness, none of the professional disillusionment, little of the humdrum sordidness that characterizes the spoken play." Despite Vidor's intent to make a realistic movie, the critic further said that audiences would find "sentiment" in *The Big Parade* because filmmakers are "distrustful of too much realism." Nevertheless, he conceded that the film "goes farther toward honest naturalism than any preceding film of the German war. It indulges in a minimum of affected flag-waving and makes no bones about allowing the unpleasant to intrude."

These efforts by Vidor, his crew, and the actors produced a film that may not have been a literal reproduction of combat, but at least created a superb illusion of what war actually consisted. The ultimate judge of such authenticity are the soldiers who were there, who rolled in the real mud and were maimed by the real bullets, the 2,000,000 men Vidor intended to satisfy when he said, "I did all that was humanly possible to insure accuracy on this picture." An ex-sergeant who had been there agreed after seeing the movie: ". . . it is all there, good people—incredibly real, incredibly tragic, and therefore true to nature." While watching the soldiers eating, the ex-doughboy "could actually smell those beans and that amazing coffee, so useful in getting gravy or grease off your mess kit." To him, *The Big Parade* was "a war film. And when I say 'war' I do not mean a sham battle in the suburbs of Peekskill either. This means that some folk, and particularly our women folk, won't like it but it will 'get' them, just the same." It was war "with all its horror and its comedy, its agony and its gayety, its ruthlessness and its infinite love and sacrifice."

A man sitting behind the ex-sergeant agreed: "This is no picture. This is the real thing." Both men thought the actual war scenes "were so obviously true that if you forget for an instant you were only looking at a picture you caught your breath and wondered how the Signal Corps ever did it, and how King Vidor ever got these films released for his picture." That soldiers believed they were viewing actual combat footage instead of a recreation is perhaps the ultimate compliment to the filmmaker. Nevertheless, for the studio, the ultimate compliment remained the box office success. *The Big Parade* ran at the Astor Theater on Broadway for two years, taking in a million and a half dollars in the process. It played for six months at Grauman's Egyptian Theater in Hollywood. And, in a few years, it had grossed over 15 million dollars on an investment of only $245,000. Clearly people were ready to accept Hollywood's recreation of the Great War.

Note

1. Editor's note: Vidor only considered war the theme of *The Big Parade*. Steel was the theme of *The Crowd* (1928), and wheat the theme of *Our Daily Bread* (1934).

The Jazz Singer
A COMMENTARY ON THE FILM'S 50TH ANNIVERSARY

Rosalind Rogoff

Originally appeared in vol. 2, no. 1 (September/October 1977)

The Jazz Singer was more than just another sound novelty. It was more than just Al Jolson performing a few vaudeville numbers. It was more than just better tone and better synchronization. All of these already existed in the Jolson Vitaphone short of 1926. While this short had been well received, it did not rock the moving picture industry. *The Jazz Singer* was unique in the long struggle to put sound and film together. It was the first feature film to use synchronized, internal sound creatively within a cinematic framework. As such it set a new precedent for what a sound film should be.

What is meant by creative sound within a cinematic framework? Well, all previous sound films (except newsreels and educationals) used theatrical, operatic, or vaudeville subjects filmed essentially as they were presented on a stage. *The Jazz Singer* was also a theatrical subject. The play had opened on Broadway September 14, 1925, to good reviews. At the time Warner Brothers bought the rights to the play, it was not considered as a potential sound movie. If Sam Warner had wanted to make an all-talking movie out of *The Jazz Singer*, in the same way that Edison and de Forest had filmed their theatrical subjects, he would have just re-enacted the play on the sound-equipped stage of the Manhattan Opera House and intercut a few different camera set-ups. This had been done with the earlier Vitaphone shorts. Instead, *The Jazz Singer* was given an original scenario in much the same way as any silent film adapted from a stage play. The film's scenario considerably opens up the original play. In the play there were only two sets: the parlor of the Rabinowitz apartment, and backstage of the theater in which Jack Robin was performing.

The show was not really a musical. In fact no musical numbers were performed on stage, although several took place off-stage, and the singing could be heard by the audience. Many scenes in the film were never in the play, and were only suggested by passages in the dialogue.

More than a month was spent in New York City filming location scenes of the Jewish Ghetto and the Winter Garden Theater. The film opens with a montage of shots taken on Orchard Street, setting the mood of Jewish culture. These shots were filmed in documentary fashion, unbeknownst to the people of the neighborhood. Director Alan Crosland hid his cameras in the back of an old moving van in the Orchard Street scenes. Through a slit in the burlap covering, the business of the Ghetto could be photographed unknown to its citizens.

Not only were documentary scenes filmed in this manner, but several action scenes were, too. Early in the film, Warner Oland as Cantor Rabinowitz angrily drags his young jazz-singing son out of a saloon, through the street, and back to their apartment. This was filmed using the residents of the neighborhood as unwitting extras, thereby obtaining naturalistic and occasionally unexpected reactions from the passersby.

The first voice heard in the film is not Jolson's but Bobby Gordon's, playing Jolson as a youth. From the very beginning, the sound sequences are handled in a striking manner. In the earlier sound films, precise synchronization was one of the key selling points of the novelty. In order to prove that the performer's lips were moving in exact accord with the sound of his voice, the actor rarely turned away from the camera and vice versa. With the very first song by Bobby Gordon, the old belief that audiences would be confused by the disjuxtaposition of picture and sound was shattered. The sound was not merely a means in itself, in this early scene as well as throughout the film, the sound was used to further the action and add dimension to the characters.

While the character of young Jake Rabinowitz is singing, the camera cuts to old Yudelson drinking a beer in the next room. Yudelson, enticed by the music, looks into the other room to see who is performing. Upon recognizing the boy as the son of his friend the cantor, he leaves in a rush to tell the old man. Throughout this sequence the picture cuts from various distance shots of Gordon singing, Yudelson listening, and even a caption of dialogue. Yet regardless of the shot, Gordon's song can be heard until Yudelson exits onto the street, where presumably the sound would not carry.

After Cantor Rabinowitz is notified by Yudelson of Jake's whereabouts, the cantor rushes to the saloon. He pauses at the entrance of the saloon, where young Jake is seen in long shot singing another song. The camera then cuts again during this number; first to the cantor opening the doors of the saloon, then to a close-up of his angry face, then to a shot of the piano player drinking a glass of beer, and then to the boy catching sight of his father and stopping his song. All of the sound sequences in the film are handled in a similar fashion. Thus the sound is used as counterpoint to the action. If the only point to sticking singing sequences into *The Jazz Singer* was the drawing power of Jolson's voice, then why bother with recording Bobby Gordon at all? Jolson was not even the first voice to star in *The Jazz Singer*. George Jessel was supposed to repeat his stage success, but he withdrew over a salary dispute.

The next vocal sequence in the film was still not Jolson. After young Rabinowitz has been brought back to the apartment and duly punished, the cantor must sing for the holy days in the Synagogue. Warner Oland, not being a real cantor, had to be made to appear singing the *Kol Nidre*. Dubbing, or adding the vocal after the filming, was not done at that early date. Cantor Josef Rosenblatt, who also appeared in the film, probably sang into a microphone just off screen while Oland mouthed the words. This was how voices were dubbed until 1929.

The singing of the ancient prayer in the Synagogue is intercut with the scene of young Jake upstairs preparing to leave home. Jake, and the audience, can hear the cantor's singing. This underscores the boy's unhappy plight and makes the scene far more effective than if it had been done silent. It is interesting, however, in the prior scene when the cantor punishes Jake (done off screen), there are no sound effects (e.g. boy's cries, or spanking noise), only background music. Even during the singing passages, there are no sound effects in those scenes with which the singing ones are intercut.

The next musical sequence takes place in Coffee Dan's, a popular starting place for young performers. This scene, like all the preceding ones, is original to the film. For the first time the sound effects, dishes clanking, hands applauding, and mallets being tapped on the tables are all audible. The Coffee Dan's scene marks the first appearance in the film of Al Jolson. Playing the part of the adult Jake Rabinowitz, Jolson has changed his name to Jack Robin and become a professional entertainer. With the small combo, Jack sings "Dirty Hands, Dirty Face." Throughout this number Jolson is photographed mostly in three-quarter shots, which give full inclusion to his expressive hand and body movements. The song is intercut with shots of May McAvoy, as the heroine Mary Dale, entering the restaurant with her friends and admiring Jack's singing. At the end of Jack's first song, there is a long shot from the audience, and their applause is heard.

The camera cuts to a three-quarter shot of Jack again, but instead of starting another song right away, he addresses the audience:

> Wait a minute, wait a minute, you ain't heard nothing yet! Wait a minute, I tell you. You ain't heard nothing! Do you want to hear "Toot, Toot, Tootsie"? All right, hold on! (Al turns his back to the audience, walks a few feet back to the musicians behind him. The camera has cut to a full shot to take in this action. Al gives the following instructions to the musicians.) Listen, Lou, play "Toot, Toot, Tootsie," three choruses, understand? In the first chorus I'll whistle, all right? (He

turns around, walks to the front of the platform, the film cuts to a three-quarter shot again, and he starts to sing "Toot, Toot, Tootsie.")

This was a first for a sound movie. Previously, and for a long time after *The Jazz Singer*, dialogue was delivered in an awkward stagy fashion. This dialogue bit in *The Jazz Singer* seemed realistic, because in all probability it was. The "Wait a minute, you ain't heard nothing yet!" was a popular trademark of Jolson's stage performances. He frequently interrupted his numbers with this catch phrase. If the real Al Jolson were singing some songs at the real Coffee Dan's, he would probably at some point say "You ain't heard nothing yet!" and give some instructions to the band. For this reason, it is not likely that this snatch of dialogue had been written for the film. All the pre-production announcements about the film specified that it would not have spoken dialogue. "Songs will be introduced only at those points where they come in naturally and there will be no talking."

In the original method outlined for interpolating the song sequences into the picture, there was no margin for ad-libs:

> To begin with, it must be borne in mind that one reel of film is accompanied by just one sound record. The film can be cut, rearranged, shortened or anything desired—when not accompanied by Vitaphone—but since the record cannot be altered, once a thousand feet of film has been synchronized with a disk it must remain in precisely that form and length.
>
> First, all those portions of the reel which do not call for singing will be filmed. Then the reel will be assembled and cut, titles and all. The singing scenes will have been carefully rehearsed and timed to the second, and in the places in the reel where these are to go, blank film of an equivalent length will be placed.

This was not the method that was finally used, however. Perhaps in rehearsing Jolson, it was found that he could not be held within the tight confines of times sequences. The film, which ran only 88 minutes, was ultimately released on fifteen reels. "Louis Silvers gets credit for having arranged the Vita synchronization with the projection booth switching machines for Jolson's songs, the change-over generally coming on a title."

Jolson's ad-libs in the Coffee Dan's scene had a strong impact on Sam Warner. His brother Jack recalled the situation like this:

> It is ironic, I think, that *The Jazz Singer* qualified as a talking picture only because of a freak accident. Sam was supervising the song recording when Jolson, in a burst of exuberance, cried out: "You ain't heard nothin' yet, folks. Listen to this."
>
> Jolson had often used these words on the Broadway stage as a sort of trademark, and when Sam listened to the phrase on the playback

he realized that the singer's speaking voice could have a shattering wallop.

He had Al Cohn write a soliloquy in which Jolson stops singing after the first chorus of "Blue Skies" and talks to his mother. . . .

Jack Warner is not the most reliable source of information. However, the length and intricacies of the "Blue Skies" scene seems to indicate that it was at least partly written. Jolson may have embellished the dialogue he was given to say, but Eugenie Besserer and Warner Oland also have lines in that scene.

After the scene at Coffee Dan's and before the dialogue scene with Al and Eugenie Besserer, the film contains another original and imaginative sequence. Jack goes to a theater in Chicago to hear the famous cantor Josef Rosenblatt. There is a long shot of Rosenblatt on stage singing. This cuts to a close-up of Jack sitting in the audience. After several establishing cuts, the scene dissolves from Cantor Rosenblatt singing in the theater to Cantor Rabinowitz singing in the synagogue. The same voice is heard throughout. One-half shots of Oland as Cantor Rabinowitz are intercut with close-ups of Jack remembering his father. Then the scene returns to the theater and Cantor Rosenblatt. He finishes his song and the whole scene fades out.

After a short scene in a railroad station, Jack Robin returns to New York. Now begins a scene in the cantor's apartment which leads into the famous dialogue scene between Jack and his mother. A mother-son scene similar to this is included in the play. The teasing mood of the dialogue is the same, but the actual lines are different. The scene in both the play and film begins with some business about Cantor Rabinowitz's sixtieth birthday. The film cuts to a very nice tracking shot of Jack running through the Orchard Street throngs to his old tenement. Jack enters the apartment, with a prayer shawl for his father. Some of the captions used in this scene are taken from the dialogue of the play, but the spoken lines used later are original to the film. In the play, Jack and his mother go off stage, where Jack plays a song on the piano and sings it "jazz" style for his mother. This scene comes fairly early in the play, and does not have as much of an impact as it does in the film. In the film, the piano is on screen. Jack sits at the piano and begins to play. He is seen and heard in a half shot, singing and playing "Blue Skies." The camera cuts back to a half shot of both Jack and his mother after the first chorus, and the following dialogue exchange begins:

Jack: (Playing left-handed vamp on the piano) Did you like that, Mamma?

Mother: Yes.

Jack: I am glad of it. I'd rather please you than anybody else I know of. Oh, darling, will you give me something? (Stops playing piano)

Mother: What?

Jack: You'll never guess. Shut your eyes, Mamma, shut them to your little Jackie! I'm going to steal something, Ha! Ha! Ha! and I'm going to give it back to you some day, you see if I don't. (He kisses her.) Mamma darling, if I make a success in the show, we're going to move from here.

Mother: Yes?

Jack: Oh yes, we're going to move up in the Bronx, lots of nice green grass up there, and a whole lot of people you know, the Ginsbergs, the Gottenbergs, and the Goldbergs and oh, a whole lot of bergs I don't know at all. And I'm going to buy you a nice black silk dress, Mamma. You know Mrs. Friedman, the butcher's wife, she'll be jealous of you.

Mother: Oh, no.

Jack: Oh, yes, she will. And I'm going to give you a nice pink dress that'll go with your brown eyes.

Mother: Oh, I don't know.

Jack: What do you think you don't know? Who's telling you? What? She's telling you what? Yes, you wear pink or else! Or else you wear pink. And darling, I'll take you to Coney Island and we'll ride in shooting the chutes, and we'll go through the Dark Mill.

Mother: Yes!

Jack: Have you ever been to the Dark Mill?

Mother: Oh, no.

Jack: Well, with me it's all right. I'm going to hug you and kiss you . . . (she pushes him) Now, Mamma, Mamma stop that! You're getting kittenish. Mamma listen! I'm going to sing just as I will when I'm going on the stage, you know, in the show. I'm going to sing it really jazzy. Now get this! (He starts playing the piano and singing "Blue Skies" again. The shot which had been a half shot of both Jack and his mother during the dialogue sequence, cuts to a half shot of only Jack at the piano for the song part. He slaps the piano at one point in the song.) Do you like that slap better? (He continues singing. The picture cuts to a close-up of Cantor Rabinowitz entering the apartment, back to Jack singing at the piano, then back to the Cantor reacting in a half shot.)

Father: (Angrily) Stop that!

At this point the film reverts to silence, with *Romeo and Juliet* music swelling in the background. By carrying it to a logical end, though, and giving Warner

Oland the last line, the scene builds up a great deal of power. The following scene, consisting mostly of dialogue captions, seems something of a letdown by comparison.

Jolson's acting in the film was a little self-conscious. He was at his best singing. His dialogue delivery in the scene with Eugenie Besserer is a little over-played, but it had a more natural quality than that contained in most previous sound films. The use of a medium close camera angle also added the necessary intimacy to the scene.

The film contains three more song sequences. Again all are integrated to further the action of the film. Jack's father becomes critically ill, and his mother and Yudelson go to the theater where Jack is preparing for his big chance on Broadway. It is the time of the Jewish holy days, and they want Jack to return to the Synagogue to take his ailing father's place as cantor. A short scene of Mary Dale dancing with a chorus line is inserted here, but it contains no source music nor sound effects.

Jack is torn between going back to do his religious duty, or staying with the show. The producer and Mary persuade Jack to go on in the dress rehearsal. Jack dons the famous blackface, and goes on stage to perform "Mother of Mine." This is intercut with scenes of his mother and Yudelson watching him from the wings. After seeing and hearing her Jackie on stage, Mrs. Rabinowitz says in a caption to Yudelson, "He's not my boy any more. He belongs to the World." She and Yudelson then leave before Jack has finished the song.

After the song is over, the producer's applause is heard. He runs to the stage to congratulate Jack. Jack is still tormented by the decision he must make. He says in a caption, "It's a choice between giving up the greatest break of my life or breaking my mother's heart." Such lines are better read than said. Jack makes the decision to go home, and the show is postponed. What a simple solution after 15 minutes of teary melodramatics!

The sound in the next scene is used very effectively. Cantor Rabinowitz lies dying in bed. Jack's voice can be heard singing the *Kol Nidre* with the choir, from the Synagogue downstairs. His father rallies, and sits up in bed upon hear-ing his son's voice. The doctor opens a window, and the sound pours in louder. Scenes in the dying man's bedroom are then intercut with those of Jack in the Synagogue. In a caption the cantor says, "Mamma, we have our son again." He dies happy. There is a trick shot of Jack still singing the *Kol Nidre* with the specter of his dead father behind him.

The scene cuts to Broadway. The bright lights and the excitement of the street are pictured. A shot from behind shows Jack walking out on stage. He is in blackface, and over his shoulder his mother and Yudelson are visible in the audience. Jack breaks into a spirited rendition of "Mammy," shot from differ-ent angles (including behind) and intercut with close-ups of his mother in the audience. At one point in the song, Jack goes down on one knee. The camera tilts smoothly to take in this action. When Jack rises again the camera tilts to keep him in the frame. Jack, his arms outstretched, finishes the song, and the picture ends.

Reviewers had high praise for the Vitaphone, but were somewhat more reserved with regard to the silent portions of *The Jazz Singer.* The Warner brothers were businessmen. Rather than make the film so that it could only be shown in the 140 or so theaters equipped for sound at that time, a silent version was also distributed to the thousands of theaters not yet willing to install Vitaphone equipment. The film, as it is constructed, can be shown silent without much loss in the continuity of the story line. The sound sequences are important, not as a novelty in themselves, but because they add to and reinforce the pictorial actions in the film. All previous sound films, with perhaps the exception of *Dream Street,* depended entirely on the sound for their appeal. These films could not be shown silent without losing whatever coherence they had. The general attitude toward the sound film was summed up by Espes Winthrop Sargent in 1918:

> It may be predicted that the talking picture will never replace the photoplay. It may become an established form of amusement, but in this connection the motion picture camera will merely support the talking machine and supply appropriate action to the song or speech recorded. The phonograph is unlikely to be used as a device to heighten the effect of photo-play.

The Jazz Singer turned this attitude completely around. Many factors probably entered into the success of *The Jazz Singer.* The technological improvements made in sound recording and reproduction helped. Greater public interest in sound helped. Jolson's presence helped. The dedication and work of Sam Warner (who died from pneumonia the night before *The Jazz Singer* opened) helped. But above all *The Jazz Singer* was a movie using long established motion picture techniques.

From Silence to Sound

THE TRANSFORMATION OF THE MOTION PICTURE INDUSTRY

Rosalind Rogoff

Originally appeared in vol. 1, no. 4 (March/April 1977)

Despite such earlier sound film efforts as the Kinetophones of 1913–14 or the Phonofilms of 1923–26, the transition to sound began with the opening of the Vitaphone synchronized, Warner Bros. release, *Don Juan* on August 6, 1926. Although nobody knew it at the time, this was the start of a gradual, and in retrospect almost systematic, phasing in of sound and phasing out of silence. In only three years less than 5% of the feature films produced in the United States were silent. Nobody, not even William Fox nor the Warner brothers, could have foreseen that!

Harry Warner was not attracted to the Vitaphone system because of its artistic possibilities. To him it was strictly a promotional gimmick.

> The thought occurred to me that if we quit the idea of a talking picture and brought about something the motion picture theatre of the present day really needs—music adapted to the picture—we could ultimately develop it to a point at which people would ask us for talking pictures.

So Harry offered theater managers the chance to provide large orchestral accompaniments with their films without having to pay a lot of musicians. In fact many Vitaphone records not intended to accompany any film were distributed to theaters, including overtures, exit music, and the national anthems of various countries. Working from this angle, Harry Warner was shrewdly able to persuade many theater managers to install Vitaphone equipment in the first half of 1927:

> We wanted to prove that there was a public that wished to see good pictures with good music, that the vitaphone helped the picture by

154

its orchestration, and, if so, they ought to put it in. Well, we convinced them one at a time, until today—the wire I had Saturday was one hundred and forty convinced theatre people. That is quite a lot, because when we made the contract we agreed only to install one hundred and sixty the first year.

Harry's arguments in favor of synchronized music convinced not only theater owners but other motion picture producers. William Fox already had an active interest in sound films, as well as his own sound system, the Movietone, when he released the musically accompanied version of *Seventh Heaven* (1926). On the other hand Paramount used an outside system—which was later bought by RCA—for its musically accompanied version of *Wings*.

The Studios Gain Control of the Score

Both of these films exemplify another advantage to the producer of using recorded sound. Even though important films were often distributed to theaters with elaborately composed and orchestrated scores, these were still left open to interpretation and variation by the individual conductors at the theaters. On lesser runs, the local piano player could certainly never capture the desired orchestral or organ effects of the first run. By recording the music, the studios had real control over the score. This was immediately put to good use. Theme songs like "My Buddy" in *Wings* or "Diane" in *Seventh Heaven* could swell up on the sound track at just the right psychological moment. In all other respects, however, these musically accompanied films were silent. They were made using the same techniques and style that silent films always had.

For the film *In Old San Francisco* released in July of 1927, Warner Bros. recorded not only the music but sound effects of an earthquake for the climactic scene. While this was another step forward in the transition to sound, it was not particularly innovative in film presentation.

Almost from the beginning sound effects and music went hand in hand in motion picture exhibition. By the mid-twenties first run theaters had large orchestras and choruses playing especially for movie theater use, had keys which could produce a variety of sound effects as well as musical accompaniment. Sound effects machines, such as were popular before World War I, did not remain in vogue. However, sound effects men were kept working in many theaters to provide realistic noises with the films:

> In a pit in front of the screen, like a miniature theatre orchestra, sat a man and a boy who between them had invented or improved upon the various "instruments" they played on. A large rattle with the

ratchets placed unevenly, imitated the crackle of rifle or machine-gun fire . . . A quantity of sand spread on the top of a big drum produced . . . a good imitation of the sea washing the shore or a train gathering speed from a station— . . . depending upon the action of the hand that did the swishing. Most remarkable of all, perhaps, were the sounds the junior member of the "orchestra" produced by blowing through various-sized glass lamp funnels. The whistling of the wind, the roar of lions, the growl of tigers, the howls of dogs and wolves— all seemed to come easy to him.

Such elaborate sound effects make it easy to understand why Hilda Doolittle ". . . was not particularly impressed" by the ". . . buzz and whirr of the plane wheels" in the Movietone newsreel of Lindbergh's flight, ". . . as we have been so long familiar with the same sort of thing adequately represented 'off' at the average cinema." What did impress people were the small, everyday, taken-for-granted noises captured almost subliminally by the Movietone's live action recording. The scrunch, scrunch of George Bernard Shaw's footsteps on a garden path or other ". . . ordinary noises—a stalled engine or the honking of horns—are funny because they are so completely true to life."

The Development of the Sound Film

The Movietone News shorts were often simply photographed interviews of famous men. Occasionally they showed a greater fluidity of movement as when following Bobby Jones in cuts and pans around the golf course. Both Movietone and Vitaphone were also producing vaudeville-type shorts in 1927.

Brian Foy directed a short for Warner Bros., which featured William Demarest as the Master of Ceremonies in "A Night at Coffee Dan's." Al Jolson and Cantor Josef Rosenblatt were each starred in vocal shorts. Later that year variations of these Vitaphone shorts were integrated into *The Jazz Singer*. It was this kind of merging of one form into another that especially marks the development of the sound film.

The Jazz Singer was both an extraordinary film and a very ordinary one. As a silent film it was average. The plot was sentimental. The directing only adequate. It was a pleasantly entertaining film without being anything special. The integration of the sound sequences into the cinematic framework of the film was however nothing short of amazing. Except for D. W. Griffith, who had tried unsuccessfully to interpolate a song into *Dream Street* in 1921, no one had ever tried using vocal sound creatively in a feature film. The vocals are not merely novelty insertions, but add dimension to the characters and further the plot. For example the scene of young Jake Rabinowitz preparing to run away from home is intercut with shots of his father singing the ancient prayers in the Synagogue. Jake, and the audience, can hear the Cantor's singing. This underscores the boy's unhappy plight and makes the scene far more effective than if it had been done silent.

The Singing Fool, Warner Bros.' somewhat non-sequential sequel to *The Jazz Singer,* brought greater sophistication to the construction of the part-talkie. A score was specially composed for it, including several good song numbers by top pop-music composers DeSylva, Henderson, and Brown. The film opens, in silent style, with a highly mobile camera trucking through a speakeasy until it reaches Al Jolson who plays a waiter. The film then wavers back and forth between the traditional silent method of telling the story through pictures and captions and the new sound method of songs and speeches. One scene which was exceptionally well received by audiences at that time was of Jolson talking and singing to child actor, Davy Lee. *The Singing Fool* was about 40% sound sequences and despite highly sentimental dialog and very static talking passages, the film became the highest grossing picture of the decade.

The Rush Is On

Other producers rushed to emulate the success of the part-talkies by grafting sound sequences into otherwise silent films. This was handled with varying degrees of success. A film like *Lonesome,* which is such a perfect example of the silent movie at its best, became ridiculous in its two talking passages. The film was a delicate, romantic, sensitive story interrupted with mundane aphorisms spoken woodenly and obviously filmed at another time and place. More common was the tacking on of sound scenes at the beginning or the end of a film, as in Lionel Barrymore's 1929 *Mysterious Island.* Almost entirely silent, *Mysterious Island* has one long dialog exposition scene at the beginning which adds little to the film.

By 1929 the clamor was on for sound in some fashion in all films. Exhibitors demanded talkies because audiences wanted them. Even before the release of *The Jazz Singer* silent film attendance had begun to fall off. There was a new fad in the air keeping people home nights: radio waves—voices in ether! Suddenly sound had become all important. Any sounds—staticky, feeble, distorted voices heard through uncomfortable headphones—were keeping people out of the theaters. If the film industry were to keep its audience it had to develop an effective sound system. It was the radio industry which supplied not only the technological equipment for the improvement of cinema sound recording and amplification; it also created an audience ready and eager for sound. To people willing to sit in their homes listening to the squawks emanating from an Atwater-Kent, the better sound quality of even the early sound films was an improvement.

The Feature-Length Talkie
Becomes a Success

Those films that had gone into production as silents now had musical tracks, sound effects, singing, or speaking scenes stuck on. New films were written as part-talkies, and vaudeville routines and playlets were still being made as one and two reelers. In 1928 while Jack and Harry Warner were in Europe, Brian Foy decided to expand such a two reeler into a feature film. When Jack and Harry returned to the studio, they found Warner Bros. had produced a barely feature-length, 100% talking film *The Lights of New York*. According to Brian Foy, the Warners were not too pleased and did not want to release it. Foy convinced them to release it and when it became an immediate success Foy became the fair-haired boy at Warners for his ability to produce sound films.

The Lights of New York is a curious, often unintentionally funny little movie. Foy is supposed to have made the movie for $40,000, which even in 1928 was extremely cheap. The actors, most of whom never made it in sound films, clearly did not know what they were expected to do. The fear of forgetting a line, of not knowing where to stand to be near the microphone, and the curse of speaking with intelligibility all contributed to the overall ineptness of the performances. In an early scene in a barber shop Eugene Pallette's voice fades in and out while he walks between two fixed microphones. The most famous and oft shown scene is where Wheeler Oakman as the chief gangster carefully enunciates each word of "Take—him—for—a—ride," to his two rather half-witted henchmen. This kind of slavishness to the microphone is what gave the early talkies their bad reputation. Nevertheless there were some good points in camera angles, cross cutting, tension building, and counterpointing of gunshot sounds with shooting shadows that made *The Lights of New York* exciting to many people in 1928. The sound added a heightened sense of reality to some of the scenes, and there are stories that women fainted during the shooting scene in the barber shop.

By the end of 1928, Fox and Paramount also released their 100% all talking pictures. An ancient Oriental sage once said that a picture is worth 1000 words. For some reason the inscrutable Occidental minds in the motion picture industry inverted this and tried to put 1000 words with every picture. At least that's how some of the 100% all talkies seemed. It was actually computed that only 1000 words could fit in a reel, and scripts were written on this basis of "words per reel."

Paramount's entry into the talking picture sweepstakes, *Interference* (1929), was a well mounted, slick picture taken from a play about marital problems of the upper crust. The cast was vastly superior to that of *Lights of New York*, with both Clive Brook and William Powell successfully surviving the transition to sound. In fact, probably on the strength of his performance in *Interference*, Powell graduated from supporting parts to leading man. Despite the high quality of production and acting, *Interference* appears today as stagy and stodgy. Indeed it is certainly 100% talking and very little else.

The Fox newsreels and shorts of 1927–28 gave the Fox technicians and directors experience in open air location filming. Fox wanted to capitalize on this ability for its first feature—*In Old Arizona* which was shot on location. This at least freed the camera from the studio and introduced sound into that most cinematic of genres, the Western. Warner Baxter won an Academy Award for his (from what I have seen) rather hammy, Mexican accent performance of the Cisco Kid.

The Fixed Camera

The all-talkie, by the very restrictions on the camera movement and microphone placement of 1928–29, tended to be verbally long-winded and pictorially confined. Acting had either the woodenness of rote line reading, or the cutsie-pieness of overacting. Stage actors, like Ruth Chatterton, were imported to Hollywood in droves. Miss Chatterton had beautiful speech and a slightly ponderous acting style. One of her first all talking films was that old stage chestnut, *Madame X*. This weepy, fallen woman melodrama got excellent reviews in the *New York Times*. Directed by Lionel Barrymore, the film appears campy and ludicrous today. There is one scene in which Lewis Stone is talking to a friend. When the friend angrily jumps to his feet, the camera tilts up about a fraction of a second too late and the actor's head goes out of the frame for a moment. After delivering a few lines the friend sits down, and again the camera tilts too late to smoothly capture this action. It was this sort of clumsy camerawork which should have been simple enough that made silent movie lovers fear sound was going to be the ruination of cinematic art.

> Eight or ten cameras were used to photograph an entire scene: long shot, medium, and close-ups. Each camera operator was instructed as to what part of the action he was to photograph, so the editors were well supplied with angles for editing the scene. One thousand foot film magazines had become a necessity, for many of the scenes ran between eight hundred and one thousand feet. All cameras were interlocked with the motor running the sound-cutting head, and everything was synchronized to start rolling together. Once started, all cameras ran without interruption through the entire scene. To cut out one, that perhaps might be photographing only a shot that was going to be used for as little as twenty feet, could cause a surge of power and spoil the entire take.

Working under conditions like that, cameramen could not always keep alert and had even been known to fall asleep.

Yet the myth of the moving camera has put the transitional sound film into a position of unfair comparison. Transitional sound films have always been criticized because of the fixed position of the camera. However, most silent films did not have a moving camera. Only a few German films of the mid- and late-twenties, most notably *The Last Laugh*, used almost constant camera motion. After the release of *The Last Laugh* in this country, many American directors borrowed some of the mobile camera ideas for their films, but most silent films of the late twenties had only occasional camera movement. People moved across a stationary camera set-up, or were tracked or followed with a pan. Frequently the picture just cut back and forth to different scenes, situations, and faces. Many dialog scenes in the silents consisted of cross cutting between two heads talking with dialog captions in between. There was very little difference between a long talkie silent passage and a long talkie talkie passage, except that captions were used instead of spoken dialog. The main advantages in these silent scenes were that they were usually kept short; the captions, if well written, could be amusing and concise; and every reading was perfect since the audience gave its own inflections to it and did not have to listen to an inept actor.

The "Transitional Sound Film"

The inability to have camera movement in the all-talkie annoyed many creative people. So once again several existing elements were merged into a new entity— "the transitional sound film." The part-talkie used long silent passages in which action could be filmed unhampered by a microphone. Yet it was already known that sound effects could be added to parts of these silently filmed passages. Directors thought, why not drop the silent style and captions from these passages, keep them shorter, and add in more realistic sound effects. *The Cock-Eyed World* (1929) is a very good example of this treatment.

Raoul Walsh interspersed many shots of marching soldiers, complete with band music and crowd noises, in between the static dialog scenes. In this way the film hops back and forth between sluggish dialog scenes and nicely paced sound effects scenes. Eisenstein, Pudovkin, and Alexandroff expressed the joint fear that spoken dialog would slow down pictorial action and destroy the effects of montage. They recommended using sound only as counterpoint to the visual images. The split personality of *The Cock-Eyed World* seems to support this point of view.

However writers quickly began to realize that a special kind of quick dialog could be adapted to the needs of film, without hampering the pace of the editing:

Let us assume that a play and a picture run for the same time, two hours. The play has three acts, each with two scenes. Probably each scene has no more than three sequences. This makes a total of about eighteen sequences. Look now at the sound picture. It may have anything from fifty to a hundred sequences; and, unlike the play, within its sequences we have many shots. Each picture sequence, therefore, is much shorter than a play sequence. Hence, the number of words and other language effects must be much smaller than in the play. Each word must convey a maximum of meaning and emotional effect. And it must also be so selected as to complete the requisite phrase of meaning in an exceedingly brief time span.

In many ways the dialog in *The Cock-Eyed World* was better than many of its contemporary sound films. It was delivered naturally and off-the-cuff. The acting was not stiff and wooden. Unlike the high-class filmed stage plays, *The Cock-Eyed World* was full of slang expressions and coarse humor which brought audiences to see it in droves. It is the excess verbosity of the dialog that makes the picture seem to drag so when viewed today. It violated Walter B. Pitkin's highest principle of time. "That is, the dialogue must advance apace with the visible action and under no conditions be allowed to slow down the latter, *unless, by so retarding it, the speech intensified plot or character in some important way.*"

Yet even this excellent rule has its exceptions. If the content of what is being said is interesting enough, even the harshest critics are willing to forgive bad filming or sluggish pacing. For example *The Coconuts* (1929) and *Animal Crackers* (1930) are both horrible films, but are accepted as classics because of the Marx Brothers' routines contained therein.

Both of those Marx Brothers' movies were adapted from stage musicals. Music and vocal numbers were considered the perfect material for sound films. The first sound features were simply those with musically synchronized scores. The part-talkies however, had background music only in the silent sections. Since the silent films were basically unrealistic pantomimes, it was felt that music helped to establish a mood for the film. Yet background music would seem incongruous coming out of nowhere in a realistic talking sequence. In order to find a believable excuse to have music in the film, source-music from a radio, a barbershop quartet, the dance orchestra in the nightclub, someone whistling in the shower, or anything else that could be palmed off as "realistic" was inserted into every possible scene.

This was why background music took so long in returning to films; not because of some technical difficulties in recording. In 1929 Al Christie produced a popular two-reeler called *Faro Nell*. The film, a parody of the old fashioned Western melodrama, contained dialog, sound effects, and continuous background music. The reason for this probably goes back to those early films of which *Faro Nell* is a parody. Since these all had highly melodramatic musical accompaniments, the musical track of *Faro Nell* parodies that old-style music.

Films based on Broadway musicals and operettas followed the conventions of these forms, and had music come in for a song without rhyme or reason. However, musicals written especially for the movies tried to maintain this facade of realism. Hence the great popularity of the backstage musical. Production numbers could be introduced logically as part of the show or a rehearsal for it. Even non-backstage musicals like *Sunny Side Up* introduced the songs as part of a block party, a charity show, or just singing at the piano.

Ernst Lubitsch was one of the first to use music as an integral element of the film. In his segment of *Paramount on Parade* (1929) an entire scene is cut and structured to the tempo of the Apache music. In this way something as simple as cloths being thrown on the floor became elements in a dance pattern; in *The Love Parade* (1929) many of the songs stemmed from the situations and were used to further the action. After Jeanette MacDonald has had her first dinner with Maurice Chevalier she starts playing the piano. The camera then cuts to members of her court, who, knowing the Queen has finally decided upon a husband, take up on the song. For those who complained of lack of camera movement in transitional sound films, there was no shortage of it in *The Love Parade*. In fact that 1929 film had a far more active camera than Lubitsch's 1932 film *One Hour with You*.

The Best of 1929

The year 1929 was a year that had just about every kind of sound and silent film: stagy all-talkies, elaborate part-talkies, goat-gland talkies (those silent films with sound scenes awkwardly implanted), musically synchronized silents (very few, and mostly from minor production companies or Europe), total silents (primarily shorts and serials), sound cartoons, Movietone News, vaudeville shorts; the stringing together of musical and comedy shorts to make those 100% all-talking, all-singing, all-dancing, all-wide-screen, all-color, all-star monster reviews, and even a surprising number of *good* transitional sound films.

The rapidity with which sound took over Hollywood can be exemplified in Mordaunt Hall's ten best pictures lists of 1928 and 1929. In 1928 not a single "talkie" was listed, and ". . . those among this number that were synchronized with sound effects cannot be said to have gained anything by the new device." Hall did, however, make a short list of what he considered the best sound films of that year. These were *Interference, The Singing Fool, The Home Towners,* and *Napoleon's Barber,* a half-hour short directed by John Ford, in which "Incidental sounds and flashbacks of Napoleon's thoughts serve to enhance this episode . . ."

In 1929 Hall's ten best films were:

The Love Parade
Disraeli
Hallelujah!
The Passion of Joan of Arc
The Taming of the Shrew
Bulldog Drummond
They Had to See Paris
The Sky Hawk
The Virginian
Sally

The only silent film on the list was the imported *The Passion of Joan of Arc*. Hall also had a runner-up list, which included most of the popular musicals of the year.

This lightning revolution left Hollywood in a spin for about two years. Producers were madly experimenting with styles, techniques, and genres. Films became redundant as sound techniques, which should have supplanted silent ones, were used in conjunction with them. Fox discovered the use of voice-over narration in its Movietone News. It used this technique to introduce *Just Imagine* (1920), but had an identically worded caption projected at the same time.

Naturally there was a great deal of concern over how the change to sound would affect the hierarchy of established movie stars. Movie director Monta Bell confidently predicted:

> While unquestionably there will be, for a time, a certain stimulated demand for actors with ability to speak dramatic lines, I do not believe that the public is going to throw over Clara Bow, Mary Pickford, Buddy Rogers, Jack Gilbert, and Charlie Farrell, nor any other of the motion picture stars who have arresting personalities. Nor do I think that the public is going to throw over Emil Jannings, and Pola Negri, and Greta Garbo, and Ramon Novarro, because they have accents.

But the panic was on in the ranks of silent stars. While screen actors were rushing around looking for vocal coaches, who had sprung up like mushrooms on the Hollywood landscape, stage actors were rejoicing. Peggy Wood wrote in 1930:

> . . . when *Variety,* the actor's Bible, began to run scare heads such as "Film Stars in Panic," "Flicker Careers Ruined by Sound," "Legits in

Demand," "Foreign Stars 30 Per Cent Flops," the nonpicture actors
of America slid anticipatory tongues over their lips and wondered
if this might not be their meat . . . Heretofore the ability to project
emotion with the voice had been useless; dark brown eyes and plenty
of crisp curly hair were worth many thousands a week more, . . . now
they really didn't know what would go, and at least he [the stage ac-
tor] would have the advantage of knowing how to say lines.

This did not prove to be as much of an advantage as she at first thought.
Saying lines to a microphone was completely different from speaking to a theater audience. Stage actors were looked upon with more confidence by movie
producers, but they too had a lot to learn.

For all their experience, these same Broadwayites are really petrified.
Though they may have had years of saying lines back of the footlights,
that protective as well as illuminating barrier, here they know they will
have to perform before a cylinder hanging within a few inches of their
heads and knowing that at the other end of the wire running from that
microphone sits a deity called the mixer, up in his little room, listening with appalling coldness to their histrionic efforts.

So Broadway actors came and went, and a few established film stars failed
to make the transition. Undoubtedly studio executives used the voice scare as an
excuse to get rid of troublesome performers, or to cut salaries of those they felt
were overpaid. Still, they had an investment in the star system, and stood to lose
a great deal too. Foreign accents were a great source of nervousness. Emil Jannings who spoke very little English, simply returned to Germany. Vilma Banky,
who had a heavy Hungarian accent, retired. Paul Lukas, who also had a Hungarian accent, made some early talkies, but not using his own voice. An actor named
Lawford Davidson received ". . . $500 a week as Paul Lukas' voice double."
There was genuine fear as to how the public would accept Greta Garbo's heavily
accented Swedish voice. Great care was taken in choosing a script for her first
sound film. *Anna Christie* was not released until March 1930. By that time much
of the panic had subsided as the public accepted foreign actors. Even Paul Lukas
was using his own voice by then.

Garbo's leading man during the 1920s, John Gilbert, was the most famous
casualty of the talkies. Gilbert was the most popular leading man of his day. To
millions of women, he epitomized virile romanticism.

What about the voice of the man who is virile as a steel mill, lusty as
Walt Whitman, romantic as a June moon? Gilbert's voice! You heard
it in *His Glorious Night.* It is high-pitched, tense, almost piping at
times . . . Jack's great art is pantomime. Remember those remarkable

closeups of intense eyes? . . . It was tremendous on the silent screen. He spoke through his eyes.

This was a common problem among many silent film actors. They spoke through their eyes. The penetrating stare, flaring nostrils, batting eyelids, and other exaggerated facial and body movements that seemed so exciting in silent films, were superfluous, even silly, in sound films. Acting styles for the talkies had to be subdued. Some actors lost out because they could not adjust to this acting style. Others because their voices were just not in keeping with the characters they had been playing.

Commenting on a Phonofilm in 1924, Iris Barry was shocked to "Imagine Chaplin talking. His whole talent is immediately wasted." Charlie Chaplin agreed. He knew that his cultured sounding English accent would never sound right coming out of the little tramp. He refused to kowtow to the tyranny of dialog, and made two of his best films during the sound era by simply not talking. Buster Keaton, on the other hand, could not have had a more appropriate voice for his character if he had had it made to order. However, his style of comedy just didn't play well with dialog. Only Raymond Griffith could be literally described as having no voice. He spoke in a hoarse whisper.

Many silent film actors like Ronald Colman, Marie Dressler, Wallace Beery, and Fay Wray moved from silent film roles to identical counterparts in sound films. Their voices were so right that when seeing silent films of these performers one can almost hear them speaking the captions.

The transitional period also gave birth to its own short-lived stars, who seemed to flare brightly for a while and then fizzle away. Laura La Plante was considered so important in 1929, ". . . that Universal . . . insured her voice for $40,000." However, she soon disappeared from the industry.

It must also be remembered that the transition from silent to sound films occurred simultaneously with the transition from the Roaring Twenties to the Depression of the thirties. Many stars who passed the mike tests and even had a couple of successful sound pictures were unable to survive the Depression. Flappers like Alice White, Clara Bow, and Colleen Moore were victims of the changing times. Only chameleon-like Joan Crawford was able to transform herself from the quintessential jazz baby of *Our Dancing Daughters* in 1928 to the hard-boiled Depression sister of *Grand Hotel* in 1932.

Sound Equipment

Most of the equipment used for sound films was originally designed for phonograph recording, radio broadcasting, and public address systems; except for sound-on-film, which was barely out of the experimental stage. Therefore it did not matter to the radio and phonograph industries that the microphone was connected directly to a rather large amplifier box, making it difficult to move and conceal. Until new microphones better suited to motion picture work could be designed, sound film producers had to find ways to work around the equipment. Hence the early practice of hiding microphones in furniture, and the awkward immobility of the actors. Extraneous noises had to be blocked out or the microphone would pick them up. Filming was done at night until expensive soundproof double-walled studios could be built. Special lighting that would not crackle like the current arc lights had to be devised. Camera noise had to be kept from the microphone. First cameras were placed behind windowed walls, then in specially built soundproof booths. Although these booths were always built with small wheels, moving one of these one-ton buildings was another matter. It took six husky men to push the camera booth down the corridor in the convent scene in *Applause* (1929), and still the camera could not keep pace with the actors. Finally, sometime in late 1929, sound-absorbing material was put directly around the camera and soundproof blimps were designed.

Other unexpected problems, like the sound absorbency or reflection of sets, multiple camera setups using lighting that would be appropriate for all angles, and the shadows cast on the set by the microphones hanging overhead, all had to be met as they arose.

Editing and mixing of sound presented a whole new area for conquest. George Groves, head soundman at Warner Bros. for about 40 years, used six different microphone set-ups for the scoring of *Don Juan* (1926). This gave quite a noticeable and pleasing balanced effect to the resulting musical accompaniment. Although optically recorded sound, printed on a separate film from the picture, could be placed on ganged wheels for side-by-side cutting, the absence of early optical sound readers made this difficult. Discs, therefore, had the editability advantage during the transitional years. As early as 1927, sound cuts were made by using ". . . the original recording and, by taking two or three pressings of that particular part of the score and playing down to a certain part of another we made a music cut to conform to the picture cut . . ."

At first four turntables were used. The first one had an indicator that counted once every revolution for ten minutes. This was used to determine the starting and stopping point of each record. Records were started and stopped by hand, and the picture was recut after all sound cuts to re-establish synchronization. As sound became more complicated, 50 to 100 records were being combined on a single reel and automatic switching devices were designed.

By 1932 most of the problems had been solved. Sound films were as brilliant and diversified as the verbally witty *One Hour with You* and the taut and violent *Scarface*. In *One Way Passage* the dialog is kept extremely sparse, the camera very fluid; and what could have been a maudlin story of doomed lovers becomes a sparkling, sophisticated romance.

The revolution to sound dramatically changed the structure of the industry. Inroads were made into the great domains of the movie moguls by banks and large corporations like Bell Telephone and RCA. William Fox, not Gilbert, was the biggest casualty of the period. Wiped out by the Depression, not the introduction of sound, Fox eventually served six months in prison for bribing a federal judge. For the most part, however, the industry adapted quickly to the audiences' demand for sound. In the space of a few short years, as far as the American public was concerned, the silent era was gone and forgotten. While a few aficionados may have longed for a return to the silent film, economics, as always, dictated Hollywood's future.

We would like to thank the Los Angeles Film Calendar *for permission to print this article. The editors regret that the notes for this essay, published over three decades ago, have long since gone missing. The essay was extracted, however, from Rosalind Rogoff's USC thesis, "The Long Engagement: From Silence to Sound," which includes her original documentation.*

Important Words from a Film Pioneer, Made at the Beginning of the Era of Sound

Irving Thalberg

Originally appeared in vol. 1, no. 5 (May/June 1977)

In the spring of 1929, the University of Southern California teamed with the Academy of Motion Picture Arts and Sciences to present a special filmmaking course, "Introduction to the Photoplay." Courses like this, of course, have been staged for years . . . but not with the uniqueness of this one.

The teachers were the pioneers of the industry. And in one of the only pieces of personal writing ever released by Irving Thalberg, we present a sample from this provocative course.

Thalberg was the "boy genius" of the industry. Leaving Carl Laemmle, his early mentor, he headed production at M-G-M and built its record of premier quality. He died at age 37, and he is still missed.

ॐ

My friends, as you have probably already observed, or as you will know before I am through, I am not a lecturer, but the opportunity of speaking to you and presenting a subject that is as close to my heart as the modern photoplay was one that brought me out of my shell. A lecture with the modern photoplay for its subject is very broad in its scope, and in the short time I have to speak, I can only touch on some of the most vital and fundamental aspects of it.

In order to understand the modern photoplay, in my opinion, which is based on about twelve years of experience during which time I have made fifty or more pictures in each of those years, one must understand the meaning of the word 'entertainment,' for entertainment is the purpose and end of the photoplay. The definition of the word 'entertainment,' as given in the dictionary, is that something which engages and holds the attention agreeably. There seem to be two essential points in this definition—that entertainment engages the attention of people, and that it brings about a pleasing response in them. Entertainment is the objective of the photoplay and we must keep in mind that as entertainment it must appeal to the varied tastes of all people. Other arts generally appeal to a selected group, but the motion picture art, and it is an art, must have universal appeal. This is fundamental, for the motion picture industry, with its investment of hundreds of millions of dollars, is based on the hope that it will appeal to the people of a nation and of a world, and if it did not have this appeal, it could not have reached its present state of development.

We have seen that the foundation upon which the whole motion picture industry is built is the desire to provide entertainment. Therefore, when we are judging or criticizing what we see on the screen, we must first consider it from the standpoint of entertainment value. We can also judge it from an artistic or technical viewpoint as well, but its entertainment value must be the first criterion.

I have read over the lecture made by my good friend, Mr. Glazer, and it has been suggested to me that you would probably be interested in an expression from me on any differences of opinion I might have with the things he said. In Mr. Glazer's discussion of dialogue, he made the point that *In Old Arizona* could have been told just as effectively in silent form, and that the dialogue was only an embellishment. I don't quite agree with him. I think the dialogue in this picture was a distinct entertainment feature. The voice of Warner Baxter, the trained voice of a very fine actor, possessed entertainment value without which the story would not have reached the success that the film did reach. His voice meant the difference between mediocrity and success.

Mr. Glazer also mentioned *The Broadway Melody* and called it a "glorified vaudeville show." I don't know whether he meant that as a compliment or not, but anyway, he found fault with its form. I must disagree with his criticism; but you, of course, can form your own opinion. The very fact that it didn't follow any pattern and that people break into song with orchestral accompaniment just out of nowhere, is only bad if the effect is bad. If the effect on the minds and sensibilities of the listeners is unpleasant, if it destroys the continuity of the story, then, of course, it is bad. I think it has distinct entertainment value. How can we tell when such an interruption will be entertainment or when it will be bad? This question can be answered the same way one would answer the question: How does a painter paint an arm so that it looks like an arm? It is intuitive, instinctive—some do and others do not have it. I think in his criticism of *In Old Arizona* and *The Broadway Melody* Mr. Glazer did not give the entertainment factor as much consideration as it deserves.

Mr. Glazer's criticism brings to mind one of the fundamental facts regarding motion pictures, and that is that the public wants the change, the looseness, the flexibility that is possible in this medium. It, as you know, is based on a tremendous investment and is supported by the weekly attendance at the moving picture theatres of a number of people equal to the population of the United States. It has grown along with various other forms of art and the world has had the same opportunity to become interested in sculpture, in painting, in literature, and in every form of art, but the motion picture art has attracted the attention of the world to a degree far surpassing the others. Now, as I have already said, a medium of art, of expression, that so clearly satisfies so great a number of people must not be judged on the same forms and same fundamental lines that other arts are judged by, because it is very clear to me that the very number of people who find enjoyment week after week, year after year, in seeing the thing, want the looseness, the change, the various methods of presenting a film that this industry and art has had an opportunity to present to the public. The very methods by which it tells its stories, the very change that each type of film brings about are in themselves of interest, and have distinct box office value. The great popularity and interest in talking pictures, which up to this time have been only fairly good and some quite bad, has been their novelty. Thus, we have a medium in which difference, in which change of form is in itself an entertainment asset.

Even more basic than the change in form in accounting for the tremendous popularity of screen entertainment is the fact that pictures themselves have been a source of interest from time immemorial. Today the periodicals and newspapers that specialize in pictures are tremendously successful—there is an interest in just picture. People are interested in news reels that tell no story at all, and in films, like *Nanook of the North* in which the interest is chiefly in the geographic background and pictorial beauty rather than the story. Many photoplays that have sheer beauty of picture have been successful for this reason, and certainly any picture that has that for an asset has its story embellished by it. People are also fascinated by motion on the screen and an interesting example of this is one that came to my attention just recently. The company that made *White Shadows of the South Seas*, when they returned from the South Seas where the picture was taken, said that there, the picture theatres have to hang a screen in the middle of the house to separate the blacks from the whites. This screen makes the pictures appear out of proportion and backwards to the blacks, but they are still interested and come all the time, mainly because the movement on the screen is interesting.

We have seen that motion picture audiences are interested in pictures, movement, and changes in form, but even more important than these is the necessity of having the subject matter of photoplays correspond closely to current thinking—they must be topical. One of my chief functions is to be an observer and sense and feel the moods of the public. When I am asked to pass on the expenditure of huge sums of money and decide whether one kind of picture should be made or another kind, the greatest problem to be settled is that of judging whether or not the subject matter of the story is topical. What is accepted by the public today may not be accepted tomorrow. One of the finest examples I can give you of this is that war pictures in one period and another, in order to be successful, have had to be presented in an entirely different flavor.

During the war, various patriotic pictures were produced with success, showing war as a glorified thing in which no sacrifice was too great to make for your country, and having all the various forms of patriotism that could be gotten into a picture, including titles such as *The Kaiser, The Beast of Berlin*. The people were stirred up and were thinking along those lines, and war photoplays capitalized on that thought. After the war, however, the war pictures were not successful, at least that was the common belief. However, we produced a picture called *The Big Parade* which to a great extent has made history along the lines of pictures, and the only difference between it and the other war pictures was the different viewpoint taken in the picture. We took a boy whose idea in entering the war was not patriotic. He was swept along by the war spirit around him and entered it but didn't like it. He met a French girl who was intriguing to him, but he wasn't really serious about her. The only time he was interested in fighting was when a friend, who was close to him, was killed. It was a human appeal rather than a patriotic appeal, and when he reached the German trenches and came face to face with the opportunity to kill, he couldn't do it. In other words, a new thought regarding the war was in the minds of most people and that was the basis of its appeal.

What Price Glory is an excellent example of the entertainment possibilities of a loose construction, and also of a treatment of a current topic. Men who had absolutely no relation to each other were picked up in China, in the South Seas, and then in France, and people were interested in them because they represented a type of character and a mode of living that had been introduced to the American public through the war. During the war, many people who would never have been in contact with professional soldiers developed an appreciation of their talk, their ideas, their ideals or their lack of them, their philosophy of life, and it became a subject that people were thinking of. It became a topic in current thought and for that reason it was an excellent subject to make.

I could go on with many more illustrations on that subject, but now I want to bring out the relationship between pictures and the stage in regard to the matter of currency. Close attention to what the public is thinking about at the moment cannot be applied to the stage, because stage audiences are not the normal audiences that the picture ones are. They are a centralized group of people, exotic, as a rule far better educated than the masses, and a different form of psychology and attention must be applied to them than to the picture audiences. The great successful plays never made any attempt to carefully correspond to the current thought of the moment and we find some that have run for generations.

However, the spirit of modern life, the attitude of modern life, the attitude of children toward parents, the family life or the lack of it, is so quickly and so normally and clearly brought out in pictures. Of course, in each picture of the kind in which one thought is given the predominating position, there is an exaggeration, but nevertheless, there is a resemblance to the current thought of the day.

The motion pictures present our customs and our daily life more distinctly than any other medium and, therefore, if we were to come back a thousand years from today and tried to find some form of expression that would more clearly, more perfectly explain how we live today, it would have to be the motion picture, because there is no medium of today that so universally must please as great a number of people, and to do this it must be current in its thinking and in the processes by which its heroes and heroines do things. It couldn't be the magazines or the newspapers because they only use unusual subjects; and our literature appeals to an exotic or a sentimental group.

Right there is another side to this question. I have often been asked, "Do you think that the modern pictures, the great pictures, will endure forever?" While no one can state with any authority what will happen; in my opinion, the modern picture will not live forever as an artistic production, because one of the most important features of pictures is currency—the immediate fitting in with current thought. Now, of course, there are exceptions and at all times, a great story or a great work of genius will overcome any obstacle. We have the work of a master artist like Emil Jannings. At times he has been successful in overcoming all obstacles of ordinary standards of acceptance by the public. A great director like Ernst Lubitsch, through his cleverness and his genius will and has at times overcome the general lack of acceptance of his type of thinking. In short, I believe that although the modern picture will not live forever as a work of art, except in a few instances, it will be the most effective way of showing posterity how we live today.

I don't know enough about sculpture or painting to give you an expression of those subjects, but while I was in Europe, I had the opportunity of studying the work of the great painters and sculptors in the Vatican and the many other galleries of Europe, and the thing that struck me as a motion picture producer was the fact that it is difficult to distinguish between the different painters in various periods. They all tried to get things along certain patterns and to follow certain schools. You find artists who are accredited with thousands of paintings, but many of these are undoubtedly the work of the students who worked under their direction. The fact that paintings go in periods or schools, each with a style of its own, applied also to the motion picture and is something that should be observed in thinking of the motion picture and the modern photoplay as you students are at the present.

The various directors and stars are examples of style and we can very easily trace their popularity up and down on the style of the moment. For instance, it is no accident that Clara Bow with her representation of the flapper of today, is a star. If it hadn't been her, it would have been some other girl of exactly her type. The directors, I think, are probably a more interesting group of men in our art than any other group, because they have in their command and within their powers the ability to tell stories and are more responsible, in my opinion again, to tell stories than almost any other group—the writers, the stars, or any one else. It is their style, their manner of telling stories that is so interesting. I hope that anything that I may say for or against any director will not be taken seriously because I am just expressing opinions that other people will probably disagree with. I am merely giving you what I think and want you to use your own judgment.

I think it is entirely fitting that I should start with D. W. Griffith, who is certainly a master director and one whom we remember with great awe and appreciation of the many things he accomplished. He is an idealist and his love scenes on the screen were idealistic and things of beauty—nobody could direct such scenes with as much appreciation for them as Griffith. His heroine, Lillian Gish, his heroes, Richard Barthelmess and Henry B. Walthall, and others, were the epitome of everything that was fine, noble, and glorious; but his pictures are not successful today because modern ideas are changing. The idealistic love of a decade ago is not true today. We cannot sit in a theatre and see a noble hero and actually picture ourselves as him. William Haines with his modern salesman attitude of go and get it, is more typical. The other thing becomes abnormal and, therefore, is less interesting.

In contrast to D. W. Griffith is Cecil B. DeMille, who is a very excellent example of a director who is not interested in art for art's sake. I have heard him discussed in various terms by critics, but I know his attempt to appeal to the current thinking of the day, is not haphazard. It is not because he doesn't understand sheer art or the conventions of other types of art proper, for as a matter of fact, he is more keenly attuned to those things than other directors; but he knows his medium and is deliberate and tries to make his pictures as close as possible to current thinking.

King Vidor is as much a realist as Griffith is an idealist, and his pictures have been an attempt to mirror life of today as it really is. I have discussed scenes with him many times, and have advised him to do this or that to heighten the dramatic effect, and his greatest fear has always been to make any character do anything that was not natural for him to do.

There are other directors who have entirely different styles, are equally successful, and tell their stories with equal strength. Mr. Murnau's *Sunrise, Faust*, and the various pictures he made in Germany certainly were fine achievements, regardless of their commercial success. He does not mirror life from the moment, but from a mood. If his mood is oppressive, his characters are oppressive, his lighting is oppressive. If a flower were growing in a scene he wants to make oppressive, he would not permit it to be there unless it were drooped over. His whole thought in each scene is to represent a mood. Lubitsch has the George Bernard Shaw quality, if he doesn't mind the observation, of trying to turn each thing into a point of amusement. He sees life from an amusing standpoint and his whole effort in direction is to turn each situation into a laugh.

I could go on indefinitely giving examples, but I want you to know that all the men in pictures have tried their best, and if the medium has not realized its possibilities it is because of our not knowing what to do with it. The principle is there, the medium is there, and it will eventually take its place as the art, because there is no other medium that is of interest to so many people. You have seen that change in form and change in subject matter are of great importance to the motion picture. Indeed, one may truthfully say that change is the lifeblood of the art and this doesn't only apply to the form, but also to the people employed in the industry. The favorites of yesterday are gone and the favorites of tomorrow come up. Where new material is to come from we do not know, and although we are drawing on the stage, from the writers of literature, and other sources, there are not enough people to make the thing as it should be made. Perhaps we will get some material from this class. At any rate, the field is open because it isn't like the electrical business or the shoe business and cannot get along without any one group of brains that is in it at the moment—it must be supplemented. It is bound to develop because it satisfies the emotional needs of the people and the satisfaction of those needs is perhaps one of the most vital problems of our civilization. I do not know what would happen if pictures were taken from the world. It would not make much difference for a week or a month, but if they were completely and permanently taken away, think what everybody would lose—those in rural communities and those piled on top of one another in the cities—without the motion picture theatres to go to.

There is no greater subject, and that goes for all subjects, than the motion picture. It is the art of arts because there is no other medium that appeals to so many people. There are others who think just as I do and I am going to quote a few lines from an article written by Aaron Horn in *The Educational Review*, under the title, "Teaching Appreciation of the Photoplay": ". . . For the common people, a course in photoplay appreciation is more needed than a course in literature because it is a much larger and interesting factor in the life of the average person than literature is."

Part V

FILMS

King Kong and the Military

Lawrence H. Suid

Originally appeared in vol. 1, no. 6 (July/August 1977)

Despite all the early publicity pictures and posters, Air Force jets did not shoot King Kong off the World Trade Center in Dino De Laurentiis' remake of the 1933 classic.

In announcing the production of his film in December, 1975, Di Laurentiis took out full-page advertisements in newspapers and magazines showing King Kong battling jet fighters just as his ancestor had slapped Navy biplanes out of the sky from the Empire State Building. Unfortunately, the artist who created the drawing had failed to look at a script or consult the producer.

Modern jets simply fly too fast for even a super ape to pluck out of the sky. Reflecting this reality, the script which De Laurentiis submitted to the Pentagon, accompanying his request for military assistance in making the film, called for attack helicopters like those used in Vietnam to shoot down Kong atop the Trade Center.[1]

To satisfy the expectations created by the publicity pictures, the producer did include in the script a sequence in which Air Force jets are ordered to attack the giant ape but are recalled shortly after takeoff.[2] In the released film, however, the jets have been consigned to the editing room floor, leaving the owners of the original poster to wonder what happened to the Air Force planes.

Although new to Hollywood, De Laurentiis' request of military assistance for *King Kong* showed that he had quickly learned about the long-standing relationship between filmmakers and the Armed Forces. From the infancy of the industry, producers have sought assistance from the military in the form of technical advice, men, and equipment. Such cooperation is most visible in Hollywood's combat spectaculars beginning with *Wings* (1927) and extending through *The Longest Day* (1962), *The Green Berets* (1968) and *Tora! Tora! Tora!* (1970), to most recently, *Midway* (1976). The military believed providing such assistance to commercial films aided recruiting and helped inform the American people of its activities and procedures.

Nevertheless, over the years, the Armed Forces has just as regularly assisted on non-military films in which their presence was often not even visible. In 1923, for example, the War Department loaned D. W. Griffith more than 1,000 cavalrymen and a military band during his filming of *America* (1924). The movie portrays the American Revolution, and the soldiers took the roles of both the colonialists and the Redcoats. The Army justified its help on the grounds that the combat sequences gave observers the opportunity to study the Revolutionary War battles with a precision never before possible because of the tremendous expense involved. Griffith claimed he received the assistance because President Coolidge and Secretary of War John W. Weeks believed the film would have a "wholesome and quieting effect" on the American people.[3]

Such high ideals or political ends (the Teapot Dome scandal still hung over the Republican Administration when *America* was released) have not usually been prerequisites for assistance. The Navy loaned director Robert Wise an instructor to teach Christopher Plummer the art of blowing a bosun's whistle so he could call his children in *The Sound of Music* (1965).[4] More often, "out of uniform" aid takes the form of equipment and facilities loaned to a filmmaker when he cannot find commercial sources.

The Navy allowed Walt Disney to build a set representing the superstructure of Captain Nemo's *Nautilus* on a submarine and then gave it a piggyback ride during the filming of *20,000 Leagues under the Sea* (1954).[5] When Billy Wilder could find no other way to transport the reproduction of Lindbergh's plane from one location to another during the filming of *The Spirit of St. Louis* (1957), the Air Force provided the director with a huge cargo plane.[6] And when Twentieth Century-Fox needed a location on which to build a church for the wedding scene in *Hello Dolly!* (1969), the Army gave permission to use a site at West Point.[7]

More often, the Armed Forces have cooperated on non-war films in which a service is portrayed responding to an emergency situation as it would do in an actual crisis. De Laurentiis' new *King Kong* is only the latest example of such assistance. In the original version of the film, Navy biplanes shoot Kong off the Empire State Building. In the 1951 science fiction classic *The Day the Earth Stood Still*, Robert Wise was able to use Army and National Guard men and equipment because the military would be expected to challenge a flying saucer which would land in Washington.[8]

Following the same guidelines, the Department of Defense extended cooperation to two recent disaster films. Nevertheless, like combat pictures, such non-war movies must portray the military accurately and provide benefit to the Services by informing the public of its operating procedures or in the case of science fiction films, of its possible operating procedures.

In *The Towering Inferno* (1975), Navy helicopters are portrayed answering a request to assist in rescuing people from the burning skyscraper. The Navy felt its appearance on the screen would help inform the public that a military emergency assistance network does exist to meet such situations. The Department of Defense did request that the filmmaker include lines in the script describing the emergency network. While the explanation did not get into the movie because the request was not made mandatory, the credits did acknowledge the Navy for its assistance.[9]

Before agreeing to give help to *Airport '75*, the Air Force conducted a test to see if one of its helicopters could actually fly as fast as a 747 jet under conditions portrayed in the film. It then ascertained that a man could actually be lowered from the helicopter to the "stricken" airliner. Only then, did the Air Force approve use of its aircraft and personnel to simulate the rescue.[10]

Because of the criteria for accuracy, the Air Force refused to assist Steven Spielberg, the director of *Jaws*, on his film *Close Encounters of the Third Kind* which deals with human contact with flying saucers. The Air Force felt it would be counterproductive to cooperate on a film which treated flying saucers as "scientific fact" rather than science fiction.[11]

In contrast, the military did not take De Laurentiis' *King Kong* seriously. To be sure, when the original publicity picture appeared, some Air Force officers did express some concern that the Service would seem to be the ultimate villain in the film for killing Kong. Nevertheless, when the producers first approached the Pentagon to lease a Navy research vessel and then to secure the use of helicopters and men, the military found the script suitable for assistance with only a few corrections. For example, the screenwriter had indicated that the helicopters used in the final attack on Kong belonged to the Air Force. In fact, the Army flies attack helicopters while the Air Force uses its whirlybirds for non-combat missions.[12]

On another level, the Defense Department did object to an inference in the script that the President of the United States had given the oil company secret pictures in return for a bribe. According to Paragraph V A of the Instruction 5410.15 dealing with cooperation to the media, a production receiving military assistance must not only benefit the Department of Defense, but it must be "in the national interest." Furthermore, the script must comply with "accepted standards of dignity and propriety in the industry." Under that guideline, the Pentagon's Public Affairs Office felt that the explanation that the "super-classified" satellite pictures of the mysterious island came "via a donation I made to someone in Washington, D.C. No names, but I think he lives on Pennsylvania Avenue" became "objectionable."[13]

While a reference to the White House being the source of the photos appear in the movie, the military did ultimately provide the necessary helicopters for the climactic scenes. Despite feeling that the military participation in the ground attack on Kong was "a jumble" in the original script, the Pentagon permitted the producer to seek limited assistance from local National Guard units.[14]

If the Department of Defense has recognized its potential role in defending the citizenry against super apes, the Navy Department did not recognize similar responsibility in December, 1932, when RKO Studios requested assistance in making the original *King Kong*. According to producer David O. Selznick, he requested the use of four Navy Hell Divers for one day with a total flying time of two and a half hours per plane. He noted that the planes were located in Long Beach and would not have to leave their base. According to the letter, the Commander of the Eleventh Naval District had assured RKO full cooperation if the Navy Department gave permission.[15]

In response to the request in a memo to the Chief of Naval Operations, the Navy Review Board noted that the story "has nothing whatever to do with Naval scenes. Use of Navy planes would compete with civilian aviation." The Board, therefore, recommended against cooperation. As a result, the Chief of Naval Operations wrote to RKO that the script "Does not fulfill Department's requirements for Naval Cooperation in that there is nothing pertaining to the Navy and use of planes as requested would compete with the civilian airplane industry. Department compelled to disapprove of Naval cooperation in this project."[16] Despite this official turndown, Selznick managed to obtain use of four Navy biplanes from Floyd Bennett Field on Long Island when he went East for the film's location shooting. He gave $100 to the Officers' Mess Fund and $10.00 to each pilot. While not a great sum by today's standards, the Navy flyers were more than satisfied to take part in the film, given their Depression-period salaries.

The pilots provided the film's director with aerial shots of planes over New York City flying in formation, peeling off, and diving at an imaginary target, then looping and attacking from the other direction. Ultimately, 28 scenes of real aircraft were intercut with process shots and miniatures to create the attack on Kong atop the Empire State Building.[17]

Such unapproved assistance has been rare since Hollywood always wanted to avoid alienating the military against future requests for help. Nevertheless, because filmmakers have considered military equipment so essential to creating an authentic ambiance, they have on occasion resorted to out-of-channel means of securing footage, as in the original *King Kong*. Of course, since the film was all in good fun, the Navy manifested little if any unhappiness with RKO.[18] This was not the case with the unauthorized assistance which the producer of *Seven Days in May* (1964) obtained.

The Department of Defense wanted nothing to do with the adaptation of the best-selling novel into a film, since it portrayed the Chairman of the Joint Chiefs of Staff attempting a coup against the President. Although some efforts were made to secure military assistance by Columbia Pictures which first held film rights to the book, Twentieth Century-Fox ultimately decided to make the movie without cooperation.[19] This presented producer Edward Lewis with a problem since the script called for shots aboard an aircraft carrier.

Taking a chance that officers in the field might be unaware of the Pentagon's position in regard to the film, Lewis talked his way onto the *USS Kitty Hawk* berthed in San Diego and obtained the needed footage of actors boarding the ship, crossing the deck, and then departing from it. He even utilized on-duty sailors to give added authenticity to the sequences.[20]

The Department of Defense thought that Lewis acted "unethically" and thereby "involved the Navy in a situation that is embarrassing." Maintaining that the producer and director were aware of the military policies on cooperation and had discussed other assistance with the Pentagon, the DOD Public Affairs Office asked the Motion Picture Association to look into the matter and take appropriate action.[21]

According to the producer, however, he acted as he had done during location shooting for his previous films, simply inquiring "as to whether or not the wishes of the director could be fulfilled." He claimed he had not discussed possible cooperation with the military and said he assumed that because the book had been a best seller, the Navy officer had had full knowledge of the subject matter.[22]

Even if the officer had read the book, of course, he had no immediate way of knowing that the Defense Department did not want to be involved with the film. Moreover, the government itself was not of one mind about the contents of the book. President Kennedy liked it and thought it would make a good movie. Consequently, the White House had given the producer and director full cooperation by permitting them to tour the Executive Mansion, stage entrance and exit scenes on the grounds, and even to conduct a riot outside the gates on Pennsylvania Avenue.[23]

The military, however, has always been more restrictive in granting cooperation than other agencies (with the possible exception of the FBI), since it has viewed commercial films as information vehicles which return benefits to the Services. At the same time, the Armed Forces have always recognized the need for dramatic license in military comedies and non-war films like De Laurentiis' *King Kong.*

Whether the audience regards the film as high or low camp, a Romeo and Juliet love story, or simply an escapist adventure, *King Kong* is first of all a special effects masterpiece which can be enjoyed as such. Consequently, the Defense Department could agree to cooperate without too much worry about its image. Nevertheless, if a flying saucer or super ape did suddenly threaten New York City or Washington, the Army, National Guard, and Air Force would be the logical organizations to respond to the emergency. If the Army has replaced the

Navy as the villain in the new version of the movie, at least the Air Force is happy because its jets did not serve as the instruments of Kong's death.

Notes

1. Interview with Donald Baruch, Chief, Motion Picture Production Branch, Directorate for Public Affairs, Department of Defense, October 27, 1976.

2. Ibid.

3. *Chicago Industrial Solidarity,* November 24, 1923.

4. Interview with Robert Wise, April 10, 1974.

5. Interview with Richard Fleischer, June 26, 1975. Interview with Harper Goff, July 21, 1975.

6. Interview with Wendell Mayes, March 6, 1974.

7. Interview with Stan Hough, July 1, 1975.

8. Interview with Robert Wise, April 10, 1974. Interview with Donald Baruch, March 31, 1975.

9. Interview with Donald Baruch, October 27, 1976.

10. Interview with Major Ron Gruchey, July 25, 1975. Interview with James Gavin, August 21, 1975.

11. Interview with Donald Baruch, October 27, 1976.

12. Ibid.

13. Department of Defense Instruction 5410.15, November 3, 1966. Letter from Donald Baruch to Jack Grossberg, April 6, 1976.

14. Interview with Donald Baruch, October 27, 1976. Letter from Donald Baruch to Jack Grossberg, April 6, 1976.

15. Letter from RKO Studios to Navy Department, December 13, 1932.

16. Unsigned memo attached to RKO letter, [N.D.]. Letter from Chief of Naval Operations to RKO Studios, December 21, 1932.

17. Orville Goldner and George Turner, *The Making of King Kong.* Ballantine Books, New York, 1976, pp. 167–69.

18. Except for the cited material, there is nothing in the Navy Records in the National Archives about *King Kong.*

19. Interview with Raymond Bell, April 8, 1975.

20. Letter from Donald Baruch to Kenneth Clark, August 16, 1963.

21. Ibid.

22. Letter from Edward Lewis to author, October 25, 1976.

23. *Look Magazine,* November 19, 1963, p. 94.

The Other Authors of *Gone with the Wind*

Rodney Richey

Originally appeared in vol. 5, no. 6 (November/December 1981)

The screenplay for the motion picture *Gone with the Wind* is, for all intents and purposes, a mosaic consisting of bits and pieces of script supplied by over a dozen writers working from the original novel under some of the most unusual circumstances imaginable; a tyrannical producer, an immense budget, a forgotten schedule, and an occupational duty to filmgoers to bring faithfully to the screen this famous Civil War story. Of course, multiple writers on a movie set are not out of the ordinary but the methodical hiring and firing of over fifteen different craftsmen is curious. One must wonder why this chapter in film history has been virtually ignored by critics and historians (save a few chapters in scattered books), especially since *Gone with the Wind* has remained a popular perennial for over forty years.

Soon after the galley proofs of Margaret Mitchell's novel were available for reading, producer David O. Selznick received from his story editor, Katharine Brown, a synopsis of the plot, in the event he would care to purchase the movie rights. He did not say "yes" immediately but vacillated for six weeks, unable to decide. The price of $65,000 seemed too rich for his blood, and he well remembered the hex that had plagued Civil War movies for years. Finally, in response to an overture from his company's chairman, John Hay Whitney, Selznick made a casual offer of $50,000. The offer was quickly accepted.[1]

Here the story begins, one which has fascinated filmmakers and filmgoers ever since. Selznick, a known perfectionist, decided almost immediately to produce a multi-million dollar epic the likes of which Hollywood had never seen. He would hire the best director (George Cukor), the best writer (Sidney Howard), and the best actors (Clark Gable, Olivia de Havilland, and Leslie Howard) to help him construct this epic, which would be funded by Selznick International Studios. He would spare no expense in bringing the story to the screen *his* way.

That last phrase, "his way," describes the primary problem that haunted the infamous production of *GWTW*, as it was later termed. Selznick was an artist dedicated to making great films and his track record was impressive. Yet he preferred to annoy his employees with incessant suggestions and ideas that he would strongly urge be put into the finished product. In fact, he plainly stated once that, "I have never had much success with leaving a writer alone to do a script without almost daily collaboration with myself."[2] His intrusions on the working time of his staff are legendary, and they make the story of the *GWTW* screenplay especially interesting.

Playwright Sidney Howard was hired to mill down the weighty Mitchell novel to a workable motion picture script. His first draft screenplay, which was a heavily edited version of the plot, would have constituted five and a half hours of screen time.[3] (It was once estimated that if the book had been filmed completely cover to cover it would have lasted 168 hours, or one week.)[4] Howard worked steadily and alone, as was his normal pattern. He completed his work in six weeks and turned it over to Selznick who delayed work on it in the excitement of getting production started. Although Howard occasionally visited Selznick for short dialogue conferences, he never again worked on the script. Shortly before the movie's premiere, Howard died on his Connecticut farm.[5]

Had Selznick used Howard's finished screenplay as the basis for the film, the story might have ended there. He did not, however, settle for that script; he ignored it for several months. While in Bermuda for a few weeks with scenario assistant Barbara Keon and scenarist Jo Swerling, Selznick ordered a new writer, Oliver H. P. Garrett, to begin laboring on the intimidating project.[6] It was a good thing Selznick hired Garrett at the time, for very little had been accomplished on the Bermuda junket, and time and budget were both very thin. Selznick, after letting Sidney Howard leave, now tried repeatedly to rehire him.

Although principal photography began in earnest on January 26, 1939, the screenplay was nowhere near being finished.[7] On December 10, 1938, "Atlanta,"—a long stretch of dilapidated backlot sets—had been burned to allow the carpenters to begin construction of Tara, the estate owned by the O'Hara family.[8] Even when filming came to an end on June 27, 1939, the call sheet for that day read "Script to come."[9] It had been two years since Howard had set down the first *GWTW* screenplay and a finished shooting script still did not exist.

Early in January, 1939—six months before the end of shooting—F. Scott Fitzgerald was recruited to work with Garrett. He enjoyed the Mitchell story but realized it resembled, in some ways, other Civil War stories that had seen the printed page. Although there was a certain fresh realism to it which he found interesting, he did not feel, as others did, that *Gone with the Wind* was the greatest novel in history.[10] Most of his major contributions were made in the form of cuts in the script as he thought that silence was one of the screenwriter's strongest tools. He also advocated the use of Margaret Mitchell's original dialogue wherever possible, since he found it much better crafted than the Garrett brand. He did not, however, appreciate Selznick's "suggestion" that every single line of dialogue be taken from the novel.[11] Fitzgerald's premature dismissal from the picture over a minor disagreement with Selznick started him on a long and difficult drunken spree which resulted in his death later the following year.[12]

Selznick now had three different screenplays: the Howard script, the Garrett-Fitzgerald script, and the extremely thin shooting script. He already knew that much of the first two versions would later be used in the third script, and he told his partner, Whitney, not to worry. According to Selznick, the film was fully realized in his mind.[13] Yet it was not realized fully enough for him to halt progress on the screenplay. Soon he hired veteran screen writer/novelist/playwright Ben Hecht, whose reputation for rapid script "fixing" was legendary. Hecht's autobiography reports that his salary for a week's work was $5,100. The week was supposedly spent editing and polishing previously completed scenes and laboring over the script eighteen hours a day with Selznick and Victor Fleming, who had replaced Cukor as director.

Before beginning his task, Hecht—who had never read the novel—listened as Selznick recited a synopsis of the plot. He almost backed out of the project, expressing the sentiment that the compacted and interwoven story was unworkable as a screen property. Selznick, desperate to get more finished pages into the shooting script, suggested using the original Howard script, which had been discarded. Hecht reports that he wrote for a solid week, overhauling the first nine reels.[14]

Historians tend to agree that Hecht's principal additions to the film were the title cards which were interspersed throughout the footage and superimposed over the action. The most famous title card introduced the movie:

> There was a land of Cavaliers and Cotton Fields called the Old South . . .
>   Here in this pretty world Gallantry took its last bow . . .
>   Here was the last ever to be seen of Knights and their Ladies fair, of Master and of Slave . . .
>   Look for it only in books, for it is no more than a dream remembered, a Civilization gone with the wind . . . [15]

The events surrounding the script had become so confused that Margaret Mitchell (who refused to participate in the writing of the screenplay) reportedly wrote, after hearing a list of famous writers who had been asked repeatedly to contribute to the patchwork script, that she would not be surprised if William Faulkner, Erskine Caldwell, and Groucho Marx had done writing stints on *GWTW*.[16] Admittedly, the skin of the producer's teeth was getting quite worn as the movie was terribly behind schedule. Two of the writers who came after Hecht—John Van Druten and John Balderston—rounded out a list of crafts-men who, in the end, totaled some seventeen people. This did not include Miss Mitchell, who, by nature of being the original author, was the principal contrib-utor. Richard Harwell, a Civil War writer and GWTW historian, acknowledges the following writers and editors as having done considerable work: Ben Hecht, F. Scott Fitzgerald, John Van Druten, John Balderston, Michael Foster, Oliver H. P. Garrett, Barbara Keon, Wilbur Kurtz, Val Lewton, Charles MacArthur, John Lee Mahin, Edwin Justus Mayer, Winston Miller, David O. Selznick, Donald Ogden Stewart, Jo Swerling, and, naturally, Sidney Howard.[17] (We will probably never know even a partial list of minor contributors, their names be-ing hidden in the tomb of legend.) Harwell's list of GWTW writers is the most complete available, as it contains the names of Keon, Kurtz, and Lewton, who were research associates hired by Selznick to supervise the accuracy of the script. They also helped him on occasion during early morning rewrites.

While the history of the script may be entertaining to some, for film scholars it is nightmarish. Because no one bothered to keep track of who wrote what, Sidney Howard received sole credit for the script, since it was his last. Selznick's disrespect for the dozen or so important and gifted writers he hired seems some-how unfair especially in the light of his claim that 80% of the final GWTW script was his own work.[18] If that claim is true, what were Howard and Hecht doing all those weeks and why did he bother to hire them?

The differences among historians as to the events of those two years, 1937–1939, make gathering the history about the film a formidable task. In his book Gone with the Wind: The Screenplay, Richard Harwell takes several pages in the introduction to dispel rumors and false information, such as Ben Hecht's contention in his autobiography, A Child of the Century, that he rewrote the first nine reels of the Sidney Howard script in a week. Harwell insists that the period was two weeks. Hecht's biographer, Doug Fetherling, estimates that Hecht took only three days to restructure an hour and a half of the script, which would be approximately nine reels.[19] Harwell points out that production had begun in 1937, so there is considerable doubt that Hecht asked for and received a copy of Howard's original script which was "discarded three years before."[20] He also adds that Hecht neglects to mention that few of his original ideas were used and that he did not so much "rewrite" as "edit" Howard's script.

Harwell's book on the screenplay itself is a vast improvement over other books such as Gavin Lambert's GWTW: The Making of Gone with the Wind or Roland Flamini's Scarlett, Rhett, and a Cast of Thousands. It does focus mainly on the writing of GWTW but does not do an adequate job of digging below the surface. The closest Harwell comes to evaluating or penetrating the history of the script is to disagree with others as to what happened, as in the case of

Hecht's autobiography. Harwell does not look at the motivations behind the actions. He elects to ride the crest, stopping only once to make vague guesses as to authorship of the play's various parts. His entire version of the story, with his comments—such as they are—fits loosely into the sparse introduction.

What is needed for *GWTW*, as with all major American films, is a volume discussing not the mere history of the film, but the film as it relates to screenwriting in general. Since *GWTW* is considered by many American filmgoers to be the greatest American motion picture ever made, it seems only logical that competent, enthusiastic, and effective research be done, if only to answer the multitude of questions surrounding the erratic writing of the screenplay of *Gone with the Wind*—the most confusing and bizarre script collaboration in film history.

Notes

1. Gavin Lambert, *GWTW: The Making of* Gone with the Wind (Boston: Little, Brown, 1973), pp. 16–17.

2. Rudy Behlmer, ed., *Memo from David O. Selznick* (New York: The Viking Press, 1972), p. 141.

3. Sidney Howard White, *Sidney Howard* (Boston: Twayne Publishers, 1977), p. 128.

4. Roland Flamini, *Scarlett, Rhett, and a Cast of Thousands* (New York: Macmillan, 1975), p. 197.

5. White, pp. 128–130.

6. Richard Harwell, *GWTW: The Screenplay* (New York: Collier Books, 1980), p. 19.

7. Harwell, p. 21.

8. Lambert, p. 47.

9. "Gone with the Wind," *Time*, December 25, 1939, p. 31.

10. Andrew Turnbull, ed., *The Letters of F. Scott Fitzgerald* (New York: Scribner's, 1963), pp. 49–50.

11. Aaron Latham, *Crazy Sundays: F. Scott Fitzgerald in Hollywood* (New York: Viking Press, 1971), pp. 215–217.

12. Lambert, p. 72.

13. Harwell, p. 24.

14. Ben Hecht, *A Child of the Century* (New York: Simon and Schuster, 1954), pp. 488–489.

15. Harwell, pp. 28–29.

16. Harwell, pp. 28–29.

17. Harwell, pp. 28–29.

18. Harwell, pp. 28–29.

19. Doug Fetherling, *The Five Lives of Ben Hecht* (Toronto: Lester & Orpen, Ltd., 1977), p. 142.

20. Hecht, p. 489.

Citizen Kane on the Drawing Board

John C. Tibbetts

Originally appeared in vol. 2, no. 6 (July/August 1978)

A look at the pre-production sketches and storyboards for *Citizen Kane* reveals some interesting correlations between the artists' original conceptions and the look of the finished film. I am indebted to Mr. Greg Brull, who provided these sketches. According to Mr. Brull, these drawings offer a tantalizing look into the visual source material behind Orson Welles' masterpiece. While the artwork is credited to Van Nest Polglase and/or his assistant Perry Ferguson, it is difficult to determine if they actually executed them, of if they were the products of assistants. Another question remains: *When* were they drawn?

As will be seen, in some cases the work postdates the shooting script; but in others (see especially the "Roman Sequence") it apparently predates that script, indicating that the storyboarding was being done while the script was still in its preliminary stages. This last point makes it particularly troublesome to determine just where a lot of the credit should go for the famous "look" of the finished film. The artists at RKO were possibly working in advance of either Welles or cameraman Gregg Toland. Their contributions, therefore, could be just as important when one considers how their notations for lighting, camera angles, and architectural details were carried through the set construction and the actual photographed film.

Certainly the implication is that artists were a powerful shaping force behind *Citizen Kane*. Anyone sensitive to the painterly qualities of the film's visual design probably knew that, anyway, but here are proofs that make that implication indisputable. There, in assessing the true Auteur of the film, one cannot only consider the director, scriptwriter, or cameraman, as did Pauline Kael in her *The Citizen Kane Book*. She attempted to compare the contributions of director Welles with the contributions of scriptwriter Herman Mankiewicz and cameraman Toland. In particular, Toland is given the lion's share of the credit for the visual schema, borrowing as he allegedly did both from his own deep-focus work

188

for William Wyler and from the work of James Wong Howe's *Transatlantic* (not to mention the whole Gothic Expressionist style that came from Germany to America in the late 1920s via the work of Paul Leni and G.W. Pabst).

The drawings on these pages are offered simply in the spirit of suggestion, i.e., that the RKO artists had a profound impact on the visual aspect of *Citizen Kane*. Their contributions, whatever their extent, have been unjustly neglected. Clearly, assigning the responsibility for them is enormously complicated. To what degree Polglase himself was responsible is debatable. In the instances of the classic Astaire-Rogers films, claims historian Arlene Croce, Van Nest Polglase was primarily a supervisor and that the real set designs were the contributions of many others, including Carroll Clark and Perry Ferguson. John Baxter's *Hollywood in the Thirties* grants Polglase more credit, while Ellen Spiegel's indispensable article, "Fred and Ginger Meet Van Nest Polglase," in *The Velvet Light Trap* (Fall 1973) gives much credit to unit director John Mansbridge and designers Allan Abbott and Maurice Zuberano.

A typical storyboard lays out drawings rather in the manner of a comic strip. They are arranged in horizontal sequence, left to right, top to bottom, indicating not only the compositions, but the character dispositions, camera angles, and lighting sources. Thus, they provide the preliminary groundwork for visually relating event, action, light, and architecture. This technique, which was developed to an art form in itself in the pioneering work of the Disney studios, was absolutely essential in the era of the studio films, when films were literally built up from the ground for story conferences. Thus, comparing the storyboards in these pages with the various stages of the script—treatment, shooting script, cutting continuity—reveals not only the inevitable changes that occur from drawing to finished photography, but also the close correlations that remain between the original art and the finished films. Yes, Welles, Mankiewicz, and Toland made their own changes; but also, they proceeded upon a clearly articulated visual groundplan of these drawings.

The Thatcher Library Scene

These four angles of the interior of the Thatcher Library are good examples of the eloquence of their relatively simple execution. They show how stark contrasts in lighting dominated *Citizen Kane* from the very beginning. The Expressionist style is seen in the oblique lighting—note how the bars of shadow and light fall in a diagonal line in all four drawings—and the resolution of masses into opposed contrasts of light and dark German Expressionist lighting often employed these stark and dynamic contrasts. Backgrounds and secondary characters were obscured through strong key lighting or strong backlighting. The lack of fill light would increase the ratio between key and fill and result in a frame with rich, dark shadows. The *Kane* drawings almost insist upon this lighting style. Note that the figure of the reporter remains totally undefined (see frames 1 and 5). He is only a mass of shadow against the white of the book page (frame 3). Likewise, in the film, all the newsmen remain similarly ill-defined. The Thatcher Library, incidentally, shares much with the other set pieces of the film, i.e., the nightclub, Xanadu, the Opera House, in that it is starkly bare, virtually devoid of human presence, distorted oddly by the crazily angled light, chilling in its stiff and stony appearance.

1

2

3

4

5

Kane Meets Susan Alexander

There are many differences between this preliminary storyboard and the cutting continuity of the final release print:

a. In the cutting continuity, Kane meets Susan Alexander after he is dashed with water from the wheels of a passing wagon. She offers to clean his clothes and takes him to her apartment. Kane, now at his ease, charms Susan into forgetting her toothache by playing some parlor games. She sings for him at the piano. This preliminary storyboard illustrates an apparently earlier script version: both Kane and Alexander are doused when Kane steps on a loose board (see frames 1–6).

b. In the ensuing conversation between Kane and Susan, she invites him into her apartment to get cleaned up. In frame 12 we see one of Kane's amusing shadow-tricks, although there is no indication of the many bits of additional business what would appear in the finished film.

c. Entirely absent from this storyboard are cues to the dialogue in the shooting script and release print to the effect that Kane's nocturnal errand was "a search for my youth."

d. Frame 14 contains a reference to a landlady present during the piano sequence. The cutting continuity of the released film omits this character.

e. In the finished film, Kane is clad in a simple pin-stripe suit. In the storyboard, however, he wears evening dress. The change of clothing was doubtless necessitated because the more informal clothes were more consistent with Kane's avowed purpose in visiting the warehouse. This detail reinforces the notion that at the time of these drawings, the script did not call for Kane's errand. That was added later in the shooting script.

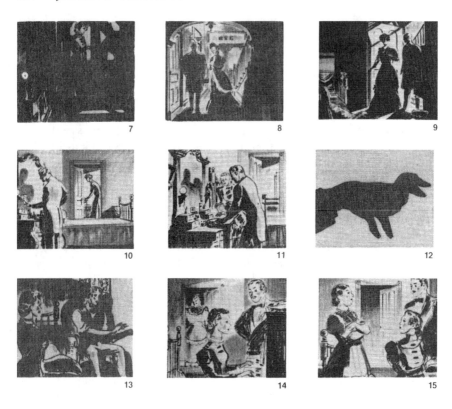

The "El Rancho" Nightclub

One of the most famous shots in *Citizen Kane* is the crane shot that moves from a high angle outside the glass roof of the "El Rancho" café down through the glass to a tight shot of the seated Susan Alexander. The shooting script describes the action this way: "Camera moves close to the skylight. We see through the skylight down into the cabaret. Directly below at a table sits the lone figure of a woman, drinking by herself." The cutting continuity of the release print describes it similarly: "Camera moves through sign to skylight below—rain pouring down, thunder heard, lightning flashing—Susan seen below at table . . . camera moves up to her—headwaiter comes on at right—Thompson coming on at right—Susan bows head on her arms on table—coughing—two men look at her." These drawings, superbly envisioned, capture all the requisite low-light lighting and moody intensity of the drama. The subsequent photography would carry out their schemas with remarkable fidelity. Frames 1–4 indicate the crane movement downward and the isolation of Alexander's bowed figure. The three-quarter aerial perspective would also remain in the subsequent photography. Frame 4 closely resembles the accompanying frame enlargements from the film, save for the absence of the waiter in the latter. Frame 6 is strikingly similar to the accompanying frame enlargement. Note that each drawing presents only the simplest arrangement of masses and light source.

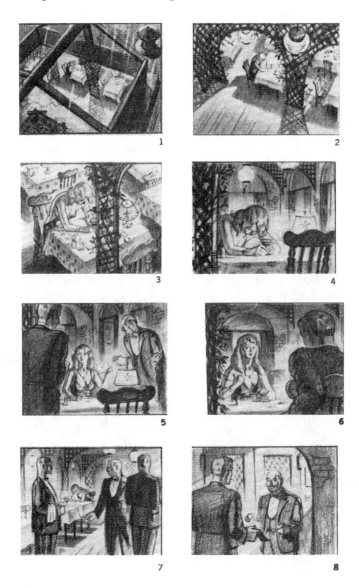

Kane's Xanadu

"Legendary was Xanadu, where Kubla Khan decreed his stately pleasure dome," intones the voice of the "News on the March" newsreel near the beginning of *Citizen Kane*. The sets created for Xanadu, with its fabulous menagerie of animals, statues, cavernous rooms, bounding grounds, eclectic architectural styles, stand at the core of the story. The two drawings here display artists' conceptions of both interior and exterior views of Kane's palace. The exterior drawing captures the flavor of the exotic, with its elegant, plumed bird and fountain in the foreground and spectacular towers and stairways of the mansion in the background. Note the Eastern architectural motifs in the façade, the minaret, the arabesques, the domed structures. The interior drawing carries these motifs inside, as seen in the arched corridors—save that the sense of emptiness and the forbidding entrapment of space prevails now. Both drawings appear to be more highly detailed than they really are. The artist knew how to suggest much from just a few lines. Thus, they are probably sketches for later, more elaborate architectural renderings that were more suitable for the set designers and architects. The essential contrast of both drawings resides in the exotic opulence of the one and the claustrophobia of the other.

The "Roman Sequence"

Tracing the evolution of *Citizen Kane* through the storyboards reveals that at least one scene was envisioned but never photographed. Pauline Kael hinted at this when she stated, "The scandals in the long draft—some of it set in Italy during Kane's youth, are startlingly like material that came to the screen twenty years later in *La Dolce Vita.*" Perusal of Mankiewicz's first draft script, called simply "American," reveals that a "Roman Sequence" was to have taken place in Kane's "Renaissance Palace" in Rome, when the Thatcher and the American ambassador visit him. It is here that the twenty-five-year-old Kane first learns of the existence of the newspaper, *The Inquirer.* Kane appears "in a dandified velvet costume of his own design." He is surrounded by sumptuous furnishings and a group of dissolute Europeans. The incident was to have been related by both Thatcher (in his memoirs) and Bernstein (in his interview with the reporter).

1   2   3

Needless to say, such an episode does not appear in the release print. It also seems safe to say that no footage was shot of it, either. Robert Wise, the film's editor, confirmed this in a letter to the author: "Regarding the storyboard sequence of *Citizen Kane* that was laid in Rome, I never have heard of this before. Certainly it was never shot when Orson made the picture. That doesn't mean that it might not have been included in an earlier script with preliminary storyboarding from that version. However, to repeat, no such sequence was ever shot for the picture or came into my cutting room." (letter of April 3, 1978)

The storyboard is ample enough proof that Mankiewicz's Roman sequence went far enough into production to be storyboarded. It must stem from the recollections of Thatcher, since it begins with a title care from the *Memoirs* perused by the reporter in the Thatcher Library, and ends with Thatcher driving away in the carriage. Bernstein, who remained with Kane, would have filled in the subsequent conversation during *his* recollections. It is, more importantly, possibly the only visual link we will ever have to a sequence that was never filmed. Fleshed out by the artist in terms of scale, décor, camera angle, light, and character disposition, it follows Mankiewicz's verbal exposition perfectly: We move from the written word "Rome" (frame 1), to Thatcher and Parker's arrival at Kane's palace (frames 2–8), to Kane's appearance in his "dandified" clothes (frame 9), to the dialogue with "The Duchess" (frame 10), to the conversation among Kane and Thatcher and Parker in the Library shortly afterward. Indications of dialogue are absent, but we know from Mankiewicz's script that the interchange with the Duchess was to have consisted of merely snippy society remarks; while the dialogue in the Library was concerned with Kane's decision to take over the *Inquirer.* That the sequence would have been consistent with the rest of the film is seen in the clever scene transition indicated in frames 6–7 and in the expressionist lighting in frames 2 and 13. Regard this for a few moments. It is as if we, years after the film's release, are uncovering a part of Kane's past, another piece of the jigsaw puzzle that is Charles Foster Kane.

A Word about the Artwork

Examinations of these storyboards reveals artists at work who with but a few lines and masses suggested quite complex schemas. Such work is reminiscent of that of the illustrators who earned their spurs working for newspapers in Chicago, Philadelphia, and New York. Just before the turn of the century—artists like Everett Shinn, William Glackens, and John Sloan. They conveyed with the greatest economy the maximum of information, whether it be atmosphere or factual content. Moreover, they had little to work with beyond their own highly developed "visual memories." And their equally developed "visual imaginations." As much as they reported the news in their drawings, they also invented it. As Robert Henri, an important artist at the time, described the work of the newspaper illustrators:

> One of the chief benefits to be derived from newspaper work is the development of the inventive faculty, or, to follow more closely the language of the artist, the cultivation of the image. The newspaper artists . . . is constantly called on to draw things he never saw . . . The fact that . . . only a meager description was at hand was no obstacle; it gave the artist's imagination all the more play.

Similarly, the RKO artists—indeed all the designers and sketch conceptualizers of the Hollywood studio film—had to utilize their own imaginative resources to visualize scripts that at best were limited in the descriptive cues. They also had to execute their work in the swiftest, most economical way possible, conveying action and visual sense at the same time. As for designing *Citizen Kane*, the RKO artists never saw Xanadu; they never saw the El Rancho Café, the Chicago Opera House, the Kane warehouses with their exotic clutter. They never saw these, save through Mankiewicz's scripts. Better than seeing them, however, they *invented* them. Truly the traditional artistic priorities of invention and imagination are at work in the cinema; in the case of *Citizen Kane* certainly, they shaped its verbal clay into graceful images as surely as if the artists had turned the camera crank themselves.

Val Lewton's *The Ghost Ship*

UNCHARTED WATERS

J. P. Telotte

Originally appeared in vol. 7, no. 3 (May/June 1983)

Cat women, body snatchers, witch cults, and zombies were not the whole story behind the notable series of horror/fantasy films Val Lewton produced for RKO in the mid-1940s. *The Cat People, I Walked with a Zombie, The Body Snatcher,* and *The Seventh Victim* were indeed most uncommon films. As Carlos Clarens describes them in his history of the genre, they were like "chamber music against the seedy bombast of the claw-and-fang epics of the day."[1] Their lurid titles (assigned arbitrarily by the RKO brass) lured audiences into the theaters of wartime America, but it is their unconventional yet effective eeriness which keeps them alive today. In Lewton's hands the horror film became a commentary not so much upon ghosts and ghouls but upon human nature itself. Jacques Tourneur, Lewton's first director, has noted that Lewton thoroughly worked out each detail of the scripts, even spending his nights "rewriting what we had been doing all day,"[2] and the result was an almost unbroken string of successes, now seen as classics of the genre.

In the case of *The Ghost Ship*, though, the jury seems still out. The reason is that it almost sank without a trace after its initial release in 1943. Virtually the only detailed descriptions of the film up to now could be found in Manny Farber's short tribute, written on the occasion of Lewton's untimely death, and in Joel Siegel's study of his career.[3] Only recently has the film again become available, and on viewing it seems to add reason to our appreciation of Lewton's work.

Raising Anchor

Certainly a rather strange offering for any Christmas season, *The Ghost Ship* first reached audiences in late December 1943 and garnered favorable reviews. Critic

199

Bosley Crowther, in keeping with the season, termed it "a nice little package of morbidity all wrapped in gloom."[4] Perhaps because of this promise of success, the film became the target of a plagiarism charge, brought by two men who had submitted manuscripts to Lewton's office on similar seafaring material. According to Lewton, the material had been returned unread—the policy for all unsolicited work. And actually, the film took much of its shape from the usual studio circumstances—namely the need to fashion a story around a large ship set standing from a previous film and to create a suitable role for Richard Dix, then finishing his contractual obligations to RKO. Rather than settle out of court as both the studio and plaintiffs wished, though, Lewton fought the charge, only to have the court rule against him, finding he could *possibly* have had access to the material in question, and awarding damages of $25,000 and directing that *The Ghost Ship* be withdrawn from circulation. Since then the film has seldom been seen, although several prints reached television stations in the 1950s when RKO went bankrupt. The original 35mm negative, along with those of the other entries in Lewton's RKO series, has been restored by the American Film Institute.

As one might expect, *The Ghost Ship*, once seen, clearly belies its title. It offers no ghosts, only those darker, murderous spirits man has always been able to conjure up from within himself. Its story is a fairly simple one, clearly drawing on the themes of several famous works on seafaring, notably London's *The Sea Wolf* and Conrad's *The Secret Sharer*. The main action springs from the encounter between a young man on his first voyage (Tom Merriam) and the ship's disciplinarian-philosopher captain. Fresh from the Merchant Marine Academy, Merriam joins the crew of the *Altair* as a replacement for the third mate who died under mysterious circumstances. The crew is a motley, international group. Captain Stone is an experienced officer who allows no challenges to his authority, claiming that as captain he has "the right to do what I want with the men." When other deaths occur, Merriam concludes that Captain Stone is responsible, but he can find no one who will listen to his charges. When he persists, he is at first ostracized, then strapped to his bunk (as had been the previous third mate) as if he were insane. Finally, Stone tries to kill the helpless Merriam, only to be done in himself by one of the sailors (the Finn) who has been sympathetically watching Tom's situation. With that murderous force vanquished and Tom vindicated, the *Altair* concludes its voyage and a voice-over notes that "all is well."

In structure *The Ghost Ship* is a classic "initiation" tale. The young hero is thrust into a new and threatening situation where he learns about the complexities of human nature and is then returned home to bear the burden of his new awareness. Some narrative complexity arises from an initially detached perspective on events and characters, coupled with a curious voice-over from the mute Finn, the sailor who saves Tom. Adding to this intricacy is the rather roundabout construction of the tale, whereby a number of scenes initially seem little concerned with furthering the plot. Farber suggests that this approach typifies the Lewton films, is his usual "shorthand method,"[5] and director Mark Robson admits that *The Ghost Ship* "broke many of the rules of story telling," being "much freer" in construction and following "very few dramaturgical rules."[6] That unstable narrative, however, is quite effective, for it heightens tension and creates a sense of unease in the viewer who is forced to witness the threats of the world into which Tom is plunged without the comfort of detachment.

Setting a Course

Visually, the film offers little reinforcement for the ominous atmosphere we at first expect. Certainly in comparison to Lewton's films made under Jacques Tourneur's direction—*The Cat People, I Walked with a Zombie,* and *The Leopard Man*—it seems undistinguished, lacking the careful compositions and striking images which mark those works. In their place we find, save for a few long tracking shots, mainly a static camera and repetition of the typical conversation two-shot. Robson, directing only his second film, admits to some fault here, noting that Tourneur, Lewton's previous director, "had a rare, gifted eye," a flare for the visual which Robson lacked.[7] Still, one can be impressed by several of the images in *The Ghost Ship*, especially the manner in which it "brought out the voluptuous reality of things, such as a dangerously swinging ship's hook, which was inconspicuously knocking men overboard like tenpins."[8]

Predictably, according to Robson, those images were spelled out by Lewton in the shooting script. The opening scene, for instance, establishes two focal points— a blind beggar in the foreground singing a happy sea chanty and a storefront of the Seaman's Outfitting Company in the rear. The latter provides a sober visual counterpoint to the former's vocal invitation—"Come all ye young fellows who follow the sea, with a yo ho, blow the man down"—with its cache of supplies one needs to "follow the sea": row upon row of vicious-looking knives. That image suggests what Tom will require to survive in a seafaring life, and it foreshadows the climactic knife fight in which his life is saved. Moreover, this ironic counterpointing of a buoyant song with those menacing instruments invokes a threatening atmosphere and prepares the way for the subsequent tension infusing the film.

By establishing that sense of menace in this way, though, Lewton did more than simply follow a typical formula of horror. In the following scene, Tom boards the *Altair* and meets the Finn who is slowly and carefully sharpening his own long knife, pointing up a pattern of misdirection at work here, undercutting many of our immediate assumptions. As we later learn, the Finn is actually the most sympathetic character on board—the one who, with that very knife, risks his life to defend Merriam. What is established early on, then, is the complex and problematic nature of this world: an environment where appearances are deceiving, where man himself is often the most dangerous element, and his needs and intentions the most difficult items to decipher.

Despite the initial menacing atmosphere, the environment Lewton evokes is not a threateningly naturalistic one of "nature red in tooth and claw." The fog, night, and the sea, we soon see, hold relatively little danger, much less, in any case, than Captain Stone who feels that most men "are worthless cattle and a few men are given authority to drive them." That ethic too is finally refuted with the captain foundering on the rocks of his shallow deterministic views. In its place Lewton asserts a vision more hopeful than that found in his previous films, one marking *The Ghost Ship* as a pivotal movie in his career.

Lewton knew that no affirmation would be meaningful or convincing unless the precariousness of the human world and values was first established. The blind beggar whom Merriam initially encounters helps to establish this situation by warning Tom that the *Altair* "is a bad ship" and that he should expect "nothing but bad luck and bad blows." Before the cruise is hardly under way that prophecy haunts Merriam, as he learns how the previous third mate died and, at roll call, finds another man dead. "You can't tell about ships," Tom had told the blind man, implying a need for caution in judging this new world. The deaths which ensue bear out his skepticism, for neither the ship nor the sea itself is at fault, despite the captain's efforts to make it seem otherwise. Those menaces have a clearly human origin, which makes them all the more ominous, but also reassures us that they can indeed be dealt with by right-thinking men.

Robson claims some credit for this note of affirmation, as he asserted that "I'm optimistic as a person and I've tried to show this. I think that the struggle to improve the world is important and I believe that if you try hard enough you can make some dent in the wall that imprisons us."[9] Starting with *The Ghost Ship*, that affirmation plays an increasing role in the Lewton series and might arguably be seen as one of Robson's personal signatures. We might note, however, that this potential underlies Lewton's own conception of horror. All of his films underscore that the true source of evil and chief danger to man are, despite contrary appearances, nothing external like ghouls or monsters, but problems lodged in the self. These threats are, as a result, remediable, so that one only needs to become aware of them; in some cases, though, they seem so deeply ingrained in human nature that they might never be rooted out.

Mustering the Crew

From the very start of the *Altair*'s voyage we are shown that the men aboard are all essentially alone, isolated by their different cultures and experiences, bound together only by their common duties. In the Finn's case it is clearly an unwilling estrangement, caused by his muteness, and his choric voice-over reveals the anguish of such an enforced isolation. On first seeing Merriam, the Finn laments that "this is another man I can never know, because I cannot talk with him. I am cut off from other men in my silence. I can hear things they never hear, know things they never know." And what he especially knows is the pain of that human estrangement. All the Lewton films develop this sense of isolation, often showing how commonplace it is, while also suggesting that it is not inevitable.

On the *Altair* the majority of the crew seems willing to accept that condition, however, since it makes few demands. The captain emphasizes this trait when he refers to his men as "sheep." This characterization recurs when we learn that the *Altair* regularly carries sheep and wool as cargo, and that the ship virtually reeks with the smell of sheep. When it docks in the port of San Sebastian and Tom goes looking for aid, his chances of finding help are ironically undercut as he is repeatedly framed in long shot with random groups of sheep rambling through the streets. Ultimately, it is the casual way that the crew accept the mysterious deaths of their fellows that completes this motif, for their animal-like stolidity reinforces their estrangement from each other and demonstrates how similar they are to sheep being led to the slaughter.

What Lewton apparently sought to underscore in this metaphor is a common tendency to avoid those responsibilities we have to others and to ourselves. It is this abdication which is often one of the most frightening of human experiences. The *Altair*'s first mate particularly—aptly named Mr. Bowns—feels that he should strictly observe certain "bounds" of concern. When Tom tries to convince him that the captain murdered a sailor who had protested his treatment, Bowns refuses to listen, warning Tom against any action that could be seen as mutiny. Sparks the radio operator—Tom's best friend on board—also excuses himself, indicating that he believes in "keeping my nose clean, really clean." Although he sees merit in Tom's charges, he admits, "I like my job and I want to keep it." An even more telling clue to Sparks' sense of "bounds" occurs when Tom finds him dancing about the radio shack with his headphones on, waltzing to music only he can hear. That image speaks much about Sparks' character: he apparently finds comfort in an internal music only he can tune in and prefers to substitute that pleasurable isolation for human interaction. While the *Altair*'s other officers are practically anonymous, appearing in only a few scenes, they too demonstrate this tendency to abdicate responsibility. Their announced concern is solely with the internal workings of the ship, with keeping the engines running. When the captain appears, they typically rush off to their own little purgatory, the *Altair*'s engine room which they term "the Black Hole of Calcutta." When confronted with evidence of the captain's murderous actions, they deny their involvement, informing Bowns that "you deck officers have a problem";

and they are not moved by his assertion that the problem concerns "you fellows as well . . . we've got to do something about this. After me, you're next in rank and you've got to help." Wisely, Lewton leaves the full effect of that comment ambiguous, interposing other actions which save them from having to make an uncharacteristic moral commitment.

Tom Merriam is the catalyst for the moral awakening with which the film is concerned. An orphan and newcomer to seafaring on his first ship, Tom seems the archetypal innocent, eager to learn about ships and human nature. Like Lewton's previous leads, Russell Wade plays Merriam as a supremely ordinary figure: not overly handsome, strong, or even intelligent. In fact, he seems quite gullible at first, quick to accept the captain's explanations for his actions—or for his failure to act. Yet that simplistic nature makes Tom's predicament all the more human and natural, while innocence and weakness call out for assistance, underscoring a common need for others, for help.

Merriam is, though, endowed with some important strengths of character. Not content to remain a stranger in a world of strangers, he tries to make friends; and when the one black member of the crew is accosted by a gang of sailors on shore, Tom comes to his aid—only to be beaten for his efforts. Such concern, however, helps explain why he is able to piece together the incidents surrounding the death of a sailor found crushed to death in the ship's chain locker shortly after complaining to the captain. Tom connects this "accident" to Stone's previous remarks on discipline and his later comment that now there will be "no more insolent remarks, no more danger to the authority of the ship." What truly distinguishes Tom from the others is that he refuses to ignore this evidence; he recognizes that what happens to his mates inevitably affects him too. He thereby demonstrates a basic moral imperative here; as he tells Sparks, "If something's wrong, I've got to do something about it."

Captain Stone, against whom Tom is played off, seems driven by a much more primitive impulse—a desire for power. He is not so much concerned with others as he is with extending "authority" over all. He has hired Tom sight unseen he says, because of certain similarities to his own life: "Your history could have been my own at your age—orphaned, serious, ambitious. . . ." In Tom he sought "a man who'd think as I think," someone to whom he could teach what he terms "the great lesson" of authority.

Because of that pattern of misdirection, however, the full implications of the captain's attitude are not immediately seen. In fact, a note of sympathy is initially struck, Tom seeing Stone as a father figure. Consequently, when Sparks snidely questions the captain's comments on authority, Tom comes to his defense, noting that, "he's the first older man who's ever treated me like a friend." The fact that Lewton never knew his own father may add a further touch of irony to this point.

Behind the captain's sternly benevolent image is a violent and dangerous nature which firmly believes that "authority cannot be questioned or defied." When Tom first boards the *Altair*, we note a motto in Stone's cabin which reads: "Who Does Not Heed The Rudder Shall Meet The Rock." As we later see, that phrase functions as a warning to the crew that they must heed his every command or suffer the consequences. As captain of the ship, Stone tells Tom, "I have the right to do what I want with the men because their safety does depend on me. I stand ready at any hour of the day or night to give my life for their safety and the safety of this vessel. Because I do, I have certain rights of risk over them." Immediately, a scene follows which tests that philosophy, as Stone is called upon to operate on one of his sailors suffering from appendicitis. He freezes, however, and Tom is forced to handle the operation. Although Stone later explains away his lapse, noting that he is "not afraid of anything but failure," and that a ship's captain also has the right to refuse to act, Sparks remarks to Tom that "he's a smooth man with the words, the captain."

Stone basically demonstrates how flimsy is that reason we depend so heavily upon to organize and demystify our world. This theme has been incorporated in all of the prior Lewton films, as secondary characters like Dr. Judd of *Cat People* and Dr. Galbraith of *The Leopard Man* espouse simple rationales for the horrors plaguing their worlds, only to demonstrate by their actions how wrong and even misleading those explanations can be. Stone finally retreats behind this facade of authority and reason and teeters on the edge of insanity. Rationalizing additional murders seems to pose less and less a problem, especially since he sees his crew as "worthless cattle" who are, as he informs Tom, "too lazy, too cowardly, too disinterested" to care what happens to anyone else.

Final Soundings

From this point the film demonstrates the worth of the more humane attitude represented by Tom. He tells Stone that he cannot prove people are such pitiable creatures, "not even with a gun. I know people aren't that way. They're good, kind; they help each other. It's only hard to get them to understand." And after repeated appeals and denials, Tom does get a few "to understand" and offer help, first Sparks whom Stone immediately kills, claiming that he was "lost overboard in heavy seas," and then Mr. Bowns, who explains to the other officers that they must act. Ironically, though, the final burden of that affirmation falls on the least likely candidate, the mute Finn. Cut off from his shipmates by his condition, the Finn is also illiterate, so he cannot read a note Sparks leaves, proving Stone's murderous intentions. Still, he quietly watches, apparently feeling some sympathy for one who, under different circumstances, has also become a pariah, unable to communicate with his fellow men. Through his voice-over reflections, we learn of this inexpressible sympathy and of his suspicions: "I know this man's trouble. I've seen the captain's hatred. I know and I will watch."

In subtle reworking of the film's opening, then, the Finn saves Merriam through a bloody knife fight with Stone. Instead of a blind beggar singing a sea chanty, it is the crew, gathered on deck, singing a similar song of how the sailor's life "is the life for me," who seem blind to what is happening. Their lighthearted song creates a nicely ironic contrast, as those threatening knives which formed the first scene's backdrop are put into the hands of Stone and the Finn who silently slice each other up while Tom watches helplessly. That small, human buffer between Stone and his intended victim works in this case, so the film leaves us with a sense of just how vital human relationships are.

Horror, as Lewton saw it, was essentially inherent in the normal—the daily events of our lives. It could spring from within man, often as he tried, like Captain Stone, to avert chaos at all cost. What that human measure of horror forces us to see is how tenuous that order and how commonplace those threats to it ultimately are, and that only our capacity to recognize these human failings and effectively respond to them enables us to maintain that fragile world we inhabit. Lewton's combination of high seriousness and entertainment value in films like *The Ghost Ship* demonstrates how accurate James Agee's assessment of his talents was: "few people in Hollywood show in their work that they know or care half as much about movies or human beings as he does."[10]

Notes

1. *An Illustrated History of the Horror Film* (New York: Capricorn Books, 1968), p. 111.

2. See Joel Siegel's interview, "Tourneur Remembers," *Cinefantastique*, 2, No. 4 (1973), 24.

3. Farber's "Val Lewton: Unorthodox Artistry at RKO" is included in *Kings of the B's*, eds. Todd McCarthy and Charles Flynn (New York: E.P. Dutton, 1975), pp. 105–8. Joel Siegel's monograph is entitled *Val Lewton: The Reality of Terror* (New York: Viking Press, 1973).

4. "Review of *The Ghost Ship*," *New York Times*, 25 Dec. 1943, p. 19, col. 4.

5. "Val Lewton: Unorthodox Artistry at RKO," p. 107.

6. See Dennis Peary's interview, "Mark Robson Remembers RKO, Welles, and Val Lewton," *Velvet Light Trap*, No. 10 (Fall 1973), p. 37.

7. "Mark Robson Remembers," p. 36.

8. "Val Lewton: Unorthodox Artistry at RKO," p. 107.

9. "Mark Robson Remembers," p. 36.

10. *Agee on Film* (New York: Grosset & Dunlap, 1969), p. 192.

Knockout in Paradise

AN APPRAISAL OF *THE SET-UP*

James M. Welsh

Originally appeared in vol. 2, no. 6 (July/August 1978)

In his book *The American Cinema* Andrew Sarris points out that among Val Lewton alumni the director Robert Wise occupies "a middle position between Jacques Tourneur at the top and Mark Robson at the bottom." Sarris goes on to pontificate that "after *The Sound of Music* and *The Sand Pebbles* the stylistic signature of Robert Wise is indistinct to the point of invisibility." The fact remains that up to *Sand Pebbles* Wise had directed some thirty-odd pictures, some of which are very good indeed. A few of them are truly outstanding, especially Robert Ryan's climactic fight sequence in *The Set-Up* (RKO, 1948).

During the span of his directorial career, Wise has moved with facility among the major and minor genres—particularly the Horror Film (*The Body Snatcher*, 1945, and *The Haunting*, 1963, e.g.), the Musical (*The Sound of Music*, 1965, and *West Side Story*, 1961), Science Fiction (*The Day the Earth Stood Still*, 1951, and *The Andromeda Strain*, 1971), the War Film (*The Desert Rats*, 1953; *Run Silent, Run Deep*, 1958), the Western (*Blood on the Moon*, 1949; *Two Flags West*, 1950; *Tribute to a Bad Man*, 1956), and the Fight Film (*The Set-Up*, 1948; *Somebody Up There Likes Me*, 1956). He has also made films, such as *The Curse of the Cat People* (1944), that resist classification.

As an early experiment in the genre of the Fight Film, *The Set-Up*, made in 1948, is still a Knockout. That same year another Val Lewton protégé, Mark Robson, made *The Champion*, starring Kirk Douglas. During the '50s Wise directed Paul Newman as Rocky Graziano in *Somebody Up There Likes Me*. And of course the genre has resurfaced in the '70s with Martin Ritt's *The Great White Hope* (starring James Earl Jones, 1970) and the recently acclaimed *Rocky*.

In certain key elements *The Set-Up* is important as a "classic" demonstration of the Fight Film. It sets a very high standard indeed for the genre. It is especially remarkable for its creation of atmosphere in the noir tradition, the murky, soiled world of small-time boxing arenas, ruined athletes, sadistic fans, corrupt managers, and vengeful gangsters. It is remarkable also for the psychological understanding it conveys of an on-the-skids middle-aged boxer (played by Robert Ryan, convincing in the role partly, no doubt, because of his experience as a collegiate boxer), his wife (played by Audrey Totter), whose only desire is to see her husband retire from the Ring, and the bloodthirsty audience of Grotesques drawn to the ringside for the brutal spectacle it promises.

The Set-Up is seventy-two minutes long, exactly the period of time consumed by the action represented. When the action begins after the credits, it is 9:05 p.m., screen time; the last clock Wise shows us at the end reads 10:16 p.m. (The rest of the running time is reserved for the credits, superimposed over a fight sequence. One of the boxers in this montage is knocked to the floor just as "Directed by Robert Wise" completes the credits, demonstrating that the film is exquisitely structured in small ways, too.)

All the way through the film Wise makes us aware of Time and of time passing by the presence of clocks of varying kinds that repeatedly appear in the frame. At one key point in the film the action itself is reflected through the glass covering the face of a clock in Thompson's hotel room. This iconic fascination with Time is thematically justifiable because the boxer whose story this is, Stoker Thompson, is a man whose time is running out. He is getting too old to box, on the one hand; on the other, he is unwittingly double-crossing the gangster who has paid fifty dollars to "fix" what proves to be Thompson's last fight. Inevitable consequences therefore await him.

The film is tightly structured in terms of time, space, and action. Particularly striking in the continuing sense of Time Wise creates is an awareness of how long three minutes can be for a fighter who is taking a beating in the Ring, a brightly lighted confined space of twenty by twenty-four feet. The basic brutality of the sport is emphasized by a number of three-minute rounds filmed, unrelentingly, in their entirety. Time, then, is important in its psychological and existential dimensions, serving as more than simply a structuring principle. *The Set-Up* is confined to a given locale so that a calculated Unity of Place is also carefully created. Almost all of the action takes place in a one-block radius in a rather grimy neighborhood. On one corner is the "Cozy Hotel," where Stoker Thompson and his wife live; diagonally across the street is "Paradise City," the boxing arena. With only one exception, all of the action occurs in the hotel room, the dressing room, and, later, the Ring of the boxing arena; subsidiary action occurs in a penny arcade (called "Dreamland") and bar ("The Ringside Cafe") next to the arena, where Thompson's manager, Tiny (George Tobias), and trainer, Red (Percy Helton), accept the fifty-dollar bribe, then decide not to tell Thompson what the "set-up" is, assuming, wrongly, as it turns out, that he hasn't a chance of winning against his opponent, Tiger Nelson, a much younger boxer who is on his way up just as Thompson is on his way down. At the conclusion the locale is tightly constricted into the dingy alley where, finally, Thompson is badly beaten for his refusal to throw the fight.

The one movement away from this area is not a substantial violation of the film's Unity of Place. Mrs. Thompson, unable to force herself to enter the boxing arena, takes a walk through the night streets, and the camera follows her to her destination, a bridge where she presumably contemplates suicide. Slowly and thoughtfully she tears up her ticket, casting its shreds to the wind—a fine emblem of hopelessness. As the torn pieces of the ticket float, confetti-like, to the streetcar tracks below, an eerie sense of despair and finality is created, purely in visual terms, for not a line of dialogue or recorded thought is conveyed. This nighttime walk, however, takes us no farther than a few blocks from the Ring where her husband is desperately fighting for his pride and self-respect.

There is also a Unity of Action at work in this film, which focuses entirely upon the last fight of Stoker Thompson, an innocent man caught up in a corrupt world. Stoker thinks only of the present, not of the future. He is out to prove that he is still capable of fighting and winning. Of course it is not until after the fight that Stoker realizes that it was meant to be rigged. Stoker gauges his opponent, then turns the match into a test of endurance. After taking his beating, the worst that his opponent can deliver, Stoker then goes to work on the younger man, outlasting and finally defeating him. Slowly, as the crowd realizes what is happening, their allegiance shifts from the younger boxer to Stoker. But this is a fickle Mob, and their allegiance, ultimately, means nothing.

Though Stoker wins by the rules of the conventional American success myth; he has, without intending to, broken the Code of the Underworld. For this transgression he must be punished, and the second beating he takes in the alley is his final "reward." Wise therefore provides a bitter twist that is doubly ironic since Thompson is, as a result of that second beating, rendered incapable of fighting again. Thus, though he is saved from the dismal future and humiliation an overaged boxer must face, he is also denied the advantage of ending his career in the limelight of unqualified success. He does score a moral victory, however, an existential triumph that depends upon his own sense of self-respect, and not upon those less-worthy creatures that would only cheer him on when they saw that his winning the match was inevitable.

Characters in this film fall into three groups: 1) the boxers themselves, the exploited; 2) the fans who support and exploit them, buying their pain and grief; and 3) the fixers, hoodlums led by the appropriately named "Little Boy" (Alan Baxter), whose corruptive influence extends to the managers and trainers. The most admirable and sympathetic characters are the boxers, most of them deluded by dreams of fame and success, all of them plagued by fear and self-doubt but ambitious—or desperate—enough to continue going into the Ring. The fans are another matter, almost all of them lusting after blood, a fickle Mob that changes its allegiances capriciously and for dubious reasons. There is a middle-aged woman, for example, who protests before entering the arena that she doesn't like boxing; but once the matches begin she turns out to be the real fight fan, as her husband is sickened by the spectacle and embarrassed by her comments. Most disgusting is a blind man, whose escort describes the action ("Nelson's working on his kidney") for the blind man's vicarious sadistic enjoyment: "Why doesn't he work on his eye?" the blind man queries. "The other eye, Nelson," he urges, "close the other eye!"

Even more disgusting than anyone in the brutish group of spectators is the gangster "Little Boy," a metaphoric foil to Stoker Thompson's Man. "Little Boy" appears to be a sadistic, cowardly homosexual who enjoys intimidation. When threatened after the fight, Thompson protests his innocence honestly. Tiny had not told him about the "set-up" because, clearly, Tiny was not willing to share the fifty-dollar bribe with his fighter. But Little Boy will hear none of this; he wants only his revenge. When later trapped in the alley and held by three men (one of them is Tiger Nelson, whom he had earlier beaten fairly in the Ring), Thompson still manages to strike Little Boy in the face, only to have the offending hand broken so that he may never fight again.

Then there are the boxers, victims of the fight game. Only one, a Black named Luther Hawkins (intelligently played by James Edwards), seems to have much natural ability and the confidence necessary to win. The most pathetic of them is a boxer named "Gunboat" Johnson, who is obviously too old to be in the Ring. A doctor checks his body before allowing him to fight, but his mind, which has been ruined, is ignored. ("Guess you can only stop so many," the dressing-room attendant says of him.) He is later floored in the second round of his match. When revived in the dressing room, he cannot even remember who he is, contending instead that he is who he wants to be, his hero, Frankie Manila, Middleweight Champion of the World. In him Thompson can see a reflection of his own ultimate fate.

Bill "Stoker" Thompson is thirty-five years old (Robert Ryan is perfect for the part); his opponent, "Tiger" Nelson, is only twenty-three, cocky and confident, a "popular" favorite. But Stoker is not yet over the hill. As Red, his trainer, tells Tiny, his manager, "Stoker can still punch," and indeed he can. Regardless, the psychological odds are against him. He knows his wife wants him to quit the Ring, and he is well aware that she is not in her seat in Section "C" when the fight begins. Moreover, the dressing-room conversation has reminded him of his age and of the pointlessness of his profession. At one point after Tiger Nelson floors him, he stumbles to his feet woozily and notices a billboard at the back of the arena that asks, pointedly, "over 35?" And yet he wins the fight by a knockout two minutes and fifty-eight seconds into the 4th Round, not because of his skill as a boxer, but because of his strength, his courage, and his experience. He

wins on brute determination, but he needs his wife later to interpret the significance of his victory. "Julie, I won tonight . . . I won!" he tells her after his hand
has been crippled. She adds, "We both won," which seems to stress his moral
victory as well as the fulfillment of her desire for her husband to quit the sport.
And this is where Wise leaves him at 10:16 p.m., beaten and maimed on the
street, but reunited with the woman he loves, surrounded by an ignorant Mob
of curious passersby. As an ambulance arrives, the camera withdraws in a long
departing crane shot, reversing the movement and direction of the film's opening shot—the perfect ending for a carefully planned and tightly structured film.

The film's greatest impact lies in the director's genius for creating atmosphere and his sensitivity of nuance and gesture.

The atmosphere of this motion picture is solidly in the tradition of film noir,
a visual style that cuts through a number of different American genre pictures of
the '40s and '50s. Though primarily, of course, a boxing film, The Set-Up also
marks a confluence with another genre motif, the gangster film. Stoker Thompson is a "framed innocent" in this film; Little Boy represents the psychopathol-
ogy of the criminal mind—cruel, vindictive, and aberrant in his behavior. The
outcome of the action realistically shatters what noir critics would call "the com-
placency of the American Dream." (See especially John S. Whitney's "Filmography of Film Noir" in Journal of Popular Film, Vol. V, Nos. 3–4, pp. 321–322.)
Although Stoker Thompson is an Innocent, at the age of thirty-five he surely has
seen enough of the prizefighting milieu to know that it is a corrupt world that
preys upon bloodlust and savage instinct, that it is morally bankrupt, frequently
rigged, and manipulated by gangsters like Little Boy. In his definition of film
noir, John Whitney notes two traits that certainly are present in The Set-Up: 1)
"a passion for the past and a consequent fear of the future" (Stoker's confidence
about his future as a contender is never convincing; beneath this confidence it is
clear that he can only live and fight for the present), and 2) "the protagonist's use
of professionalism and style as a means of submerging doubts, insecurities and
neuroses" (Journal of Popular Film, V:3–4, p. 321).

In The Set-Up Stoker Thompson lives in a nighttime world of shadows. The
film begins just after night has fallen, just as Thompson, a denizen of the night,
is waking up. In the boxing arena he is put under the spotlight as his strength
and courage are tested, but it is not his individual effort that converts the crowd
to his side; rather, it is the psychology of the Mob that dictates that they align
themselves with a winner. No matter how valiantly he fights, he cannot win their
allegiance without winning the bout. His greatest victory and most severe test,
ironically, comes later, after the Mob has dispersed. No one but the movie audience witnesses his superb demonstration of courage when he strikes Little Boy in
the face in that dark alley. But even here the response and the instinct is partly
that of a trapped animal. We see fear in his eyes as he realizes that he is entrapped

in that dark cul-de-sac, and we realize that he would flee if he could. He clearly understands, as any reasonable man might, that he is vastly outnumbered.

Stoker Thompson is no large melodramatic Hero. He is a Man, flawed and self-deluded, but courageous and, finally, capable of learning from his experience. The film is allegorical, as genre vehicles frequently tend to be. It can be seen as the story of an Innocent who falls through Pride, and is rewarded by Vainglory, only later to be expelled from "Paradise." Stoker Thompson is first a metaphorical icon for Adam, then becomes an icon for Christ, the "second Adam." He falls from Paradise into the soiled world of common existence. After he has lost his innocence, he loses his bearings as the doors of Paradise slam shut behind him. He gropes his way through the darkness of the alley after his Passion, and in the arms of a Good Woman he is reborn into a new life—a higher existence. Some may protest that I am attempting to "read" too much into what appears to be a "simple" story, but it is the very nature of allegory to be deceptive and concealed—to be entertaining on one level and to be instructive on another, where it works on mythic layers of the subconscious. And it seems to me that The Set-Up works in this way.

John Ford's *Wagon Master*

RITE OF PASSAGE

James M. Welsh

Originally appeared in vol. 4, no. 2 (Winter 1980)

John Ford directed so many good Westerns during his long career that some are likely to be overlooked. Two in particular, I believe, have commanded more than their share of attention —*Stagecoach* (1939) and *My Darling Clementine* (1948), both of which are superb genre pictures that may reasonably be considered "classics." *Clementine* has been justly admired for its treatment of legend, for its economy of structure, for its richness of characterization. *Stagecoach* was set forth by André Bazin as the model "classic" Western that established a critical standard for artistic achievement with the genre. Others have measured it against its source, Ernest Haycox's story "Stage to Lordsburg," attempting to show how it surpasses its literary origins. One writer, David Clanfield, has even meticulously analyzed the patterns of names the film presents in an essay entitled "The Onomastic Code of *Stagecoach*" that appeared in the Spring 1977 issue of *Literature/Film Quarterly*.

Links to Other Films

John Ford's *Wagon Master*, which resembles *Stagecoach* structurally but comes later in the director's career, has not enjoyed this kind of comprehensive and painstaking critical attention, though it has not been altogether ignored. J. A. Place, in her fine study *The Western Films of John Ford* (Citadel Press, 1973), rightly claims that this "deceptively unpretentious film is in many ways the high point of Ford's Westerns." Certainly in its symbolic use of music and dance it is not inferior to *Clementine*, though the frequent use of music here *is*, perhaps, more heavily stylized (though not to the same degree as in *Rio Grande*, Ford's next Western after *Wagon Master*, which also uses the music of the "Sons of the

Pioneers" symbolically). Like *Stagecoach*, *Wagon Master* employs a picaresque journey of a group of people, a journey fraught with danger.

The grouping of characters in *Wagon Master* is also very similar to *Stagecoach*. Both are populated with flawed characters and untested innocents— cowpokes with shady dealings in their past and derelict professionals. A dancehall girl named Dallas in the one film blends into one named Denver in the other; both names reverberate with experience. Each film involves the process of integrating "respectable" and disreputable people who are allowed to prove themselves in a ritual process of rejuvenation.

Perhaps the biggest difference between the two films is that the heroic Ringo in *Stagecoach* is played by John Wayne, whereas Travis, his counterpart in *Wagon Master*, is played by Ben Johnson, whose quiet dignity and competence is more low-keyed; his function as leader is shared by Ward Bond, while his heroic function is shared by his sidekick Sandy (Harry Carey, Jr.). Even more so than *Stagecoach*, *Wagon Master* involves an ensemble demonstration of heroics and courage. If Ben Johnson fails to dominate the action in the way that John Wayne does in *Stagecoach*, that is entirely a consequence of Ford's collective design.

Tribulation and Regeneration

The Mormons of *Wagon Master* are good, decent, God-fearing, and innocent people, people who need protection from the denizens of hell. Their passage through hell becomes a test of their patience and resolve, their courage, their endurance. By passing the test, they prove themselves worthy of entering the Promised Land. They *are* worthy, but they need help. Their leaders, therefore, are men from the world at large, men who have known temptation, men who have reformed and entered the community of God's chosen people. Such a man is Elder Wiggs (played by Ward Bond). He has integrity—to the point that he will not lie, even when a cocked and loaded pistol is at his back. Equally important, he has wisdom and tolerance. He readily invites the medicine show people whom they find on the desert, stranded and seemingly degenerate, with nothing to drink but "Lightin' Elixir," to join the wagon train, despite the objections of Brother Perkins and some of the other Mormons.

In their dedication to the communal effort, and through their communal labors, each member of the group becomes sanctified and inspired. It is a process of regeneration through work and sacrifice that this film is out to demonstrate. Perhaps the most obvious example of this regeneration is Dr. A. Thorndyke Locksley Hall (Alan Mowbray), the medicine man who first is called upon to remove a bullet from Uncle Shiloh Clegg's shoulder in a do-or-die situation, then later volunteers to take his wagon over the final mountain after the first wagon to try has failed and turned over. Both acts require him to draw upon forgotten reserves of courage. Fleuretty Phyffe (Ruth Clifford) calls him a "big ham," but his actions speak louder than her words. She chooses to ride up the mountain with him. At the end they both have been regenerated.

Crystal City, with its intolerance and mistrust, represents a stratified and close-minded civilization that has downright rejected or labeled as undesirable all of the people we see in the wagon train—the Mormons for their religion, Sandy and Travis for their horse-trading (for the line between horse traders and horse thieves would seem to be a thin one), Locksley Hall and his troupe for their theatrical way of life, and the Cleggs, who, of course, are outlaws. All of these "outcasts," save the Cleggs, are capable of redemption, and even the Cleggs are given a chance to reform. The communal experience, for all the others, breeds a respect and concern for their fellow men, and out of this respect comes a willingness to sacrifice. The Cleggs refuse to think of anyone but themselves. In their selfishness, then, they prove themselves to be unworthy. They are totally incapable of gratitude. That the medicine-show "doctor" has repaired Uncle Shiloh's wounded shoulder is quickly forgotten. All that is remembered is the fact that one of Uncle Shiloh's "boys" was whipped for having raped or molested a Navaho maiden.

The wagon train, in short, takes civilization beyond Crystal City, both geographically and spiritually. The community of the wagon train is ennobled by its tribulations and suffering. And it is the communal responsibility of facing hardships that unites them; an existential unity is therefore established that transcends the close-knit community of the religious sect. In the "Wilderness" the Mormons learn tolerance and exercise it much more liberally than the "civilized" citizens of Crystal City had done.

The film's overall pattern is that of the legendary Quest—the steady and determined progression towards the Promised Land. Beyond this general pattern, the structure is determined by a specific pattern of trial, celebration, and advancement (physical and moral), introduced, then complicated by particular variations. The film's opening presents a series of vignettes whereby the characters are introduced and defined. The Cleggs are presented before the film's titles appear, economically by means of a wanted poster, then a demonstration of their psychotic vengeance in a tavern shoot-out, foreshadowing their menacing presence throughout the film. Travis and Sandy are introduced next in a more leisurely fashion (as fits their natures), wanderers in the wasteland whose lives have no real purpose. They are then counterposed against the Mormons (in Crystal City), whose lives have a definite and strongly felt purpose, zealously in pursuit of a goal.

The temperamental and experiential similarities between Travis and Elder Wiggs are suggested visually when, in an extended sequence, both men stand side by side in medium shot, whittling. The older man has found a purpose for his existence. In asking Travis to lead the wagon train, he is not only requesting a favor, but inviting the younger man to join the community and dedicate his services to a higher goal. Travis is reluctant to accept this responsibility and commitment and to sacrifice his freedom. But his human compassion for the Mormons and the hardships he knows they will encounter without proper leadership and guidance wins him over. Sandy's motivation is more simple, but no less human: He is interested in Miss Prudence, a Mormon maiden. In the larger scheme of events, however, both of these young men are guided by Prudence and Providence.

Three Tests

This establishing "prologue" is then followed by a carefully designed pattern of "tests." The initial test is relatively uncomplicated in that a single action is represented. This is necessary, for it clearly introduces the structural pattern that will govern the entire film. The initial trial, of course, involves crossing the desert. The strain and the lethargy imposed by this trial is suggested in terms of movement and music—both of which are slowed down almost to the point of stasis until the watering hole is discovered, at which point the pace quickens into a breakneck race of men, horses, and wagons towards the source of water and physical regeneration.

This reversal of fortune is then followed by the celebration of the joyous square dance, a celebration that is interrupted by the arrival of the Cleggs. Uncle Shiloh's first line uncannily describes the situation and the participants: "Whenever there's singin' and dancin' you can be sure there's Christian folks." This is a Christian community governed by basic human decency that requires charity and compassion—qualities that these barbaric aliens do not possess. With the arrival of Uncle Shiloh and his "boys" (the most degenerate family grouping in all of the Ford films I know), the "singin' and dancin'" naturally ceases. In this character grouping the line between good and evil is simply and clearly drawn, but the polarization is deceptively simple. The mode is allegorical, and though personifications may populate the narrative, questions of meaning and value are much more complicated than they at first seem to be.

The second trial involves a confrontation with the Indians. The Cleggs' instinct is to shoot without any deliberation, but they are prevented from doing so by the Mormons, who will avoid gunplay at any risk. By facing the Indians bravely, the Mormons are protected, for it turns out that the Navahos know and respect Mormons, recognizing them to be more honorable than other frontier white men in general. This trial is then concluded with a second celebration as the Mormons are invited to join a Navaho Squaw Dance. Once again, the festivities are disrupted by the intruding Clegg family as one of the "boys" attempts to rape a Navaho woman. The festivities are halted for all to witness his punishment.

The third trial combines hardship with menace, the rigors of the landscape with the irrationality of the Cleggs. The final challenge is to get the wagon train—the grain wagon in particular—safely over a dangerous mountain ridge, the last physical obstacle that stands between the Mormons and their goal. Through determination and hard work a ridge is dug over the mountain to anchor the wagon wheels. The first wagon to attempt the passage overturns. Ford's set-up for the reaction to this misfortune polarizes and isolates the good and evil groupings of characters. The Mormons and the others who have integrated their community are horrified and sickened by what they witness. These characters—Wiggs, Travis, and Sandy in particular—are isolated in the right foreground of the frame. The Cleggs, still the alien intruders who have not become integrated into the community of the wagon train and who have no sense of communal responsibility, respond with derisive laughter as addlepated Luke observes, giggling: "He didn't make it, Uncle Shiloh." The Cleggs are segregated in the left background of the frame. Ford's blocking of characters, therefore, is arranged according to moral categories and thematic principles—a visual representation of psychological separation.

The complications of the third trial are as much psychological as physical. Sheer determination must be supported by moral resolve and courage. When the Cleggs first intrude upon the community, they interrupt a celebration; as the music stops, all activity is brought to a point of stasis, emphasized by a visual caesura, a montage of reaction close-ups, first among the Cleggs, then among the Mormons. This is done in order to evoke tension and to establish the division between the small malicious group that threatens the larger peaceful one. A variation on this idea is worked later when the Cleggs disarm the Mormons and assert their leadership. At the point of stasis here we see all the Mormons with their hands raised, standing utterly motionless. The danger of the Cleggs can only be overcome by a group effort, and Ford's camera isolates a small boy with a concealed revolver, which he passes on to his sister, Miss Prudence, who later gives it to Sandy. In this way the group prepares itself for the final confrontation.

Finally, after all the other wagons have crossed the ridge, all attention turns towards the task of moving the wagon filled with grain seed, the Mormons' prized possession, over the mountain. At this point Uncle Shiloh decides it is time for his family to avenge the whipping of their peccant "boy." The dynamics of the situation are as follows: Sandy, who now has the hidden revolver, is not a gunfighter; he has admitted to Travis that he has never shot a man. Nor is Travis a violent person, though he is a more experienced one. Travis has earlier stated that he has never drawn on a man, "only on snakes." According to Ford's moral categories, however, the Cleggs are snakes rather than men.

In order to exact his revenge against the Mormons who have aided and protected him, Uncle Shiloh has decided that Elder Wiggs shall take the grain wagon across the ridge, but at a dead run, and without the advantage of the rut the Mormons have dug. It is a suicidal mission, but one that Elder Wiggs accepts bravely and stoically. Uncle Shiloh has already shot Brother Johnson off the wagon, which serves to demonstrate that this final confrontation can only be settled by violent means. Just as Wiggs is about to whip up the horses, however, Sandy uses his gun and is immediately aided by Travis, who retrieves a revolver from the fallen Clegg. In a matter of moments, all of the younger Cleggs are dispatched. Uncle Shiloh is spared momentarily to lament the loss of his "good" boys, then is shot down as he attempts to avenge them. True to the genre formula, therefore, Ford provides us with a climactic shoot-out, a violent expedient to protect the non-violent, to maintain justice, and to reestablish communal harmony.

Characterizations

The characters of this film in particular will be better understood if analyzed in comparison to their counterparts in other Ford films. If Joanne Dru's Denver here resembles Claire Trevor's Dallas in *Stagecoach*, for example, Sandy and Travis are soon to be reincarnated, not only as horse traders, but as horse traders with similar names in Ford's next Western, *Rio Grande*, where Ben Johnson's Travis is presented as a wanted man, seriously implicated in a killing in Texas. In *Rio Grande*, however, the Ben Johnson character is in the background rather than in the foreground and is far subordinate to John Wayne's Lieutenant Colonel Kirby Yorke, who of course dominates the film. The story of the Ben Johnson character is not the main one to be told in *Rio Grande*; but because he represents a well-defined character type for those familiar with John Ford's Westerns, he immediately strikes a responsive chord and the viewer's understanding is enhanced. One knows at once that such a character is in his own way "heroic" and that he can be depended upon despite his questionable past. Ford makes use of such expectations in the way he manipulates plot, structure, and audience in his films.

The Clegg family in *Wagon Master* represents such a baroque ornamentation of a familiar Ford idea that they can only be taken seriously with effort. They initially seem to be caricatures rather than characters, overdrawn nearly to the point of parody. Not only are they moral monstrosities; they are also, some of them, retarded, as if to equate evil impulses with ignoble stupidity. When

Luke first becomes aware of the Indians, for example, he says: "Kin I shoot one, Uncle Shiloh? I never killed me a Navaho before!" The "boys" therefore seem to be genetically disordered, and Hank Worden's Luke is only marginally inferior in intelligence to his demented and hulking brother Floyd (played by James Arness).

The Clegg family must be taken seriously in this film, however, and, exaggerated as they are, they do nonetheless convey a convincing sense of irrational menace. To say that Charles Kemper's Uncle Shiloh Clegg is the "brains" of the family would be a major (and risible) understatement. The mold for his character in the cinema of John Ford was mythically formed by Walter Brennan's Old Man Clanton in *My Darling Clementine* some six years earlier. But the Clantons in *Clementine* are mythic figures in a legendary conflict—the battle at the OK Corral. The process of *Wagon Master* in contrast is allegorical rather than legendary, and the allegorical mode both demands and sanctions exaggerated characters who are usually shallow personifications.

If the larger pattern that governs *Wagon Master* is allegorical, that is why the film seems so deceptively "simple." God's chosen people have passed through the wilderness and, chastened by the experience, are found worthy of passing into the Promised Land. Finally in this allegory of good and evil and of salvation and redemption, the serpent who has attempted to mislead them and block their successful passage is slain by a weapon that has passed through Prudence to their protectors and champions. This is a film that is large on heroics but rather limited in its deployment of individual heroes. What is found here is the heroism of the common man, a democratized heroism that Ford surely sees as a necessary component in the "winning" of the West. *Wagon Master* is the story of a worthy and courageous community, whose victory depends upon determination, initiative, and unflinching moral resolve. It is entirely appropriate that the film should end with a song of celebration.

"I Want Stone-Age Faces!"

A BEHIND-THE-SCENES LOOK WITH HARRY CAREY JR., PATRICK FORD, AND WES JEFFERIES AT THE MAKING OF JOHN FORD'S FAVORITE FILM

James V. D'Arc

Originally appeared in vol. 4, no. 2 (Winter 1980)

The John Ford persona has over the years attained an auteurist image as winsome and sentimental as one of his own films. However with the recent publication of grandson Daniel Ford's *Pappy: The Life of John Ford* (Prentice-Hall), some of the cumulative aura has been stripped away revealing more of the man, but in no way diminishing one's respect for the Fordian genius. That film is a collaborative art is perhaps the most overused descriptive artifice by those talking about film, but even as John Ford was an ardent devotee of the one-man-one-film school, his films were nevertheless a unique blend—clearly his own—of the efforts of many.

In this piece, with that collaborative emphasis, I'd like to delve into the behind-the-scenes making of Ford's classic *Wagon Master*, which along with *Young Mr. Lincoln* remained his favorite film. In so doing, my search has taken me to three most interesting sources who, while vastly different in their personalities and involvement in the film, speak from vantage points untainted by the pressures of a director or producer responsible for the film. On their words hang the burden of blame for failures or in rarer cases the glow of both public acclaim and critical esteem.

The first is Patrick Ford, gravelly voiced, immensely likeable, and candid screenwriter son of John Ford. It was he who first passed Ernest Haycox's story "Stage to Lordsburg" onto the "Old Man" which was subsequently made into *Stagecoach*. Pat, with Frank Nugent, conceived the story and wrote the screenplay to *Wagon Master*. He left Hollywood and producing films some fifteen years ago to raise horses—his lifelong interest—in Southern California. Next is Harry

Carey, Jr., son of the man who helped give John Ford his start as a director and who played Sandy Owen (the horse trader who, with Ben Johnson and Travis Blue, proved to be the wagon masters for the Mormon trek). Finally there is Wes Jefferies, costume supervisor for *Wagon Master* and later Ford films, whose keen reminiscences are matched by an always ready camera responsible for the candid location photographs.

The beginnings of *Wagon Master* date back just after World War II when Ford and movie financier and innovator Merian C. Cooper formed Argosy Pictures. The new company entered into a three-picture agreement with RKO, then owned by Howard Hughes. The pictures agreed upon were *She Wore a Yellow Ribbon, The Fugitive,* and only a title with as yet no subject matter specified—*Wagon Master.* Patrick Ford, having been mustered out of the Navy and since departing a good writing job at M-G-M, joined the *Yellow Ribbon* company as technical advisor on cavalry drills in southern Utah's Monument Valley, by then a Ford landmark. "I had time on my hands," remembers Pat, "and I got to know some of the rough old Mormon pioneer descendants who were riding and supplying horses for us. They fascinated me. They wore leather clothes, and they had a hardness about them, a frontier hardness. They were the real McCoy, not Hollywood extras, which are a flaky bunch to begin with and don't look like anything but Hollywood extras on film. We rarely had Sundays during shooting, but when we did I would listen to stories of how their people got into that country in the 1880s, quite a while after the more illustrious of the Mormons to the Salt Lake Valley in the 1840s, and they would talk about the old Escalante Trail followed by the Catholic fathers through this country in the 1770s."

With shooting completed, Cooper, familiar with Pat's writing skill, called him into the office one day and said, "I have this *Wagon Master* thing to produce; we have a time schedule and Hughes is screaming to get it underway. Can you think of anything?" Pat responded, "I had been reading about the trek of the Boers in South Africa away from the British but quickly scratched that idea since Britain was one of our strongest markets. So we brought in Frank Nugent, a film critic for the New York *Herald* who didn't know much about screen writing but had some good ideas. So he and I in the middle of the summer of 1949 holed ourselves up in a cramped office at the old Selznick Studio in Culver City and began throwing ideas around. The stories told to me about the Mormons coming into the San Juan area by a Mormon Bishop Perkins in Blanding, Utah stuck to me. Soon, Frank was hooked, although being from the East, the only thing he knew about Mormons was that they had a lot of wives. We both read the *Book of Mormon* and began going around with Mormons in Los Angeles to get the feel and flavor of these people who made their pilgrimages to Utah not for greed or gold, but because of their religion. It took about ninety days from the time we started with the story outline to the finished screenplay. We hadn't written in the Alan Mowbray part of Dr. A. Locksley Hall, the drunken Shakespearean actor/medicine barker; but the Old Man really liked Mowbray and wrote him into the film."

The location for filming, according to Pat, was chosen in response to John Ford's demand, "Go where these people came from." The sleepy little southern Utah town of Moab had never seen such activity as when the Ford company came to town in October of 1949. Wes Jeffries, who was on the chartered DC-3 with Ford, recalls their arrival: "The walls of this canyon-rimmed country were so narrow it looked like the wings of the plane would scrape them any moment. Below us were about 100 of the townspeople at the small airstrip and a six-piece band reception committee. No one, including the publicity man, knew that there would be such a reception. Initially, Ford didn't want to leave the plane and be festooned by all of these people."

Accommodations were certainly in keeping with the theme of the film, re-members Jefferies: "With only one small hotel in town most of us lived in tents with butane heaters all the time we were there. And it was cold. The Mormon meetinghouse was converted into a dining hall where we ate our meals. The nearest place to relax was a small bar down the road that served 3.2 beer. Cast calls were about 6:00 or 6:30 a.m. We met at one point in town where a lo-cal driver took us the 25 or 30 miles north of the town—which because of the roads took us about an hour to an hour-and-a-half—to the George White Ranch where most of the shooting took place. Ford wouldn't arrive until about 8:30 or nine o'clock, and then he would hunt for a suitable location for the day's shoot-ing. But when he found the right spot, we'd work at breakneck speed and get in a full day's shooting."

Harry Carey Jr. recalls that the 45-day allotted shooting schedule went sur-prisingly smooth and, for the most part, unruffled. "Never was there a day on *Wagon Master* when it wasn't like a vacation," he remembers. Apparently part of the vacation was an amusing incident involving stock company favorite Ward Bond. "It was the scene where Don Summers, playing a straitlaced Mormon, thinks I'm going to say a swear word. Ben and I in the film weren't Mormons, just horse traders, and I was in love with Summers's girl in the film and that kicks it off and we get into a fight. There were these two dogs on the set—some of the local people brought their dogs out for the filming—and off camera these dogs would fight and kick like you've never seen when we'd be tussling before the cameras. When Bond, as the Elder, broke up the fight, one of the dogs tore out across the desert and the other lit out straight for Bond and ripped a big slit up his pant leg. John Ford, in a rare moment to us, burst out in laughter, while simultaneously chewing out the camera operator for not getting the moment on film. Look closely at the film and you'll see Bond's pant leg ripped and it's never revealed in the film how it got that way."

There was an undercurrent of frantic activity to keep things going at an even pace. Jefferies recalled a story with a happy ending, only because of some creative thinking, cross-country flying, and enlisting about a dozen Navajo women as on-the-spot costume seamstresses. "Ford had on the film a military technical advisor, Don Hatchwell, who approved among other things the costumes for the film. I knew, however, in one incident that Hatchwell wanted Indian costumes that Ford wouldn't like. Lowell Farrell, the assistant producer, told me not to fight it, that Ford trusted Hatchwell implicitly, 'you'll see.' Well, the day came on location, finally, when I dressed up the Indians, brought up from Monument Valley, in these Hatchwell approved outfits. The Old Man came over and carefully inspected the braves, then really tore into Hatchwell, his close friend, right in front of all of us. In more colorful language than this he said, 'These costumes are all wrong, you've put us back a day in shooting and I don't know what you'—and he was pointing right at me—'are going to do about it.' Well, I had to think fast. All of the costumes were in Los Angeles, I was in the middle of nowhere and we had to shoot tomorrow. After much difficulty, I managed to find someone in the area who had a phone that worked. I called Western Costume in Hollywood to send up some costumes on a commercial flight to Grand Junction, Colorado. Then, with the help of the local driver I located a couple of men who had small planes. I hired one of them to fly out to Grand Junction to meet the plane with the costumes that night and instructed him to meet me the next day at sunrise in Moab. Next, I got Lee Brady, the Indian agent in the area, to go with me and the other pilot, fly down to Monument Valley some 200 miles south and get some Indian jewelry, which he got from the pawn shop the Indians have down there, and round up about a dozen old Indian women to sew up some buckskin Indian outfits, of a style not particularly suited for the Indians in this area, but what I knew Ford wanted. We spent all night on this and at daybreak, exhausted, flew out of Monument Valley and up to Moab. Shortly after landing, in came the other pilot with the costumes flown in to Grand Junction some 150 miles to the east. Quickly I fit the Indians into their costumes in the barn at White's Ranch and Ford came down for the inspection. Believe me, I was sweating this one out as he nonchalantly walked up and down the line like a general reviewing his troops. When he came to me at the end, he simply leaned over to me and whispered into my ear. 'It's great. But how did you do it?' When I told him, he could hardly believe it."

Pat says *Wagon Master* made a lot of money, not only in the United States, but particularly in Europe where it was a big hit. "The film was made for just under a million dollars and grossed worldwide a little over four times that amount. I still get residuals on it."

Pat Ford feels his father's greatness is due partly to his stubbornness on using people who genuinely fit the film. "'These are the people I want,' the Old

Man would say as I showed him photographs in Hollywood of the people in the Moab area. Because he was a perfectionist, he wouldn't get a Hollywood extra if he could do otherwise. He wouldn't use a Hollywood Indian when there was a still a real Indian alive. His term was 'I want stone-age faces. I want faces of men and women who have seen people die of snake bite, whose women and babies die in childbirth, and whose men die from being bucked off horses, just the life of primitive people.'"

Ford, although he looked for the "stone-age" face, had a special affection for the Mormon people whom he had first known while filming on location in western Utah and Nevada for *The Iron Horse* (1924) and in Cedar City, Utah for *Drums along the Mohawk* in 1938. "They were good, honest people," recalls Pat, "who wouldn't cheat you, or show up bombed-out drunk after the first pay-day like what happens everywhere else you go, and once they've committed to you, they're not going to go out and hang you." Interestingly enough, Pat continued, it was not Ford who dressed up the Mormons in the Mennonite-Calvinistic dress which made them seem so archaic and aloof, in the film: "It was Howard Hughes. For some reason he insisted they be dressed that way. And when he's holding the purse strings you do it. Ford protested because he knew Mormons were different than that, but Hughes wouldn't budge."

Pat also credits Ford with an instinctive visual consciousness of what works on film. "When Frank and I wrote the screenplay, we tried to absorb the spirit of these people by a lot of reading and while on location I mingled with the locals. But the Old Man didn't need to do that. He was a brilliant man. He was single-minded, he only cared about pictures, the visuals. It may have been that he saw without having to sit and talk. He saw an awful lot that I didn't see, and I had to sit and talk to get it. For example, it could be that just watching an Indian family with a travois behind their horse carrying a stove, he'd immediately understand the situation, but I'd have to contrive a way to get somebody to translate and ask the Indian why he had a stove on a travois, why he didn't have a pick-up, a wagon or something to carry it in. But John Ford would get the whole picture and its meaning. Maybe that was it. Maybe when we were in Moab he just absorbed the spirit of these people by just looking at them and watching them. He didn't bother sitting down, he was busy, busy, busy."

John Ford remarked often of his love for *Wagon Master*. "His favorite film was *Wagon Master*," Pat concluded. "It was his favorite Western. His favorite 'Eastern'—that was the term he always used—was *Young Mr. Lincoln*." Looking past me, Pat's voice became a bit more soft-spoken as he focused his eyes seemingly on the wood grain of the table. "You know, *Wagon Master* was pure of heart, and simple and good, and Frank Nugent and I were pure of heart and simple and good when we wrote it. And maybe John Ford was too."

Project RXM

John C. Tibbetts

Originally appeared in vol. 3, no. 6 (July/August 1979)

Donald Wollheim once wrote a wonderful story about a crew of space travelers stranded on an asteroid from Saturn's outer ring. They discover a spaceship, a remnant of a vanished civilization, which has been perfectly preserved. They succeed in jerry-rigging it so that it will fly once again and they make their escape in it. In its way the story is typical of much science fiction; it is even profound in that it reveals science fiction's predilection for the imaginative reconstruction of new worlds from old. And, as always, flight, contact, and escape are its basic actions.

Now listen to the story of "Project RXM," about a modern day crew who has also found a spaceship, a relic of past glories. They too have tooled it up for one more flight. The spaceship is the "RXM," a silver arrow that sometime around 1950 left the earth headed for the moon, was deflected in its course and headed for Mars, and finally disappeared during the return flight. Thanks to the efforts of a new generation of visionaries, the RXM has been located and its story has begun all over again.

Of course I'm talking about a film, a science fiction film, the prototype of all subsequent space travel epics. Since *Rocketship X-M*'s initial release in 1950, dozens and dozens of such films have followed in all sizes, shapes, colors, budgets, and types. The cinematic heavens have swarmed with more celestial bodies than can be imagined this side of "Doc" Smith. And it has gotten difficult, over the years, to spot the real thing from the imitation. Rocket ships are like used cars in that respect—unless you can kick the tires every now and then, you may get conned. Maybe that is why *RXM* has been forgotten by so many: it was sold for junk to television long ago and relegated to a tiny image in the playroom before it disappeared altogether.

But Wade Williams, a Kansas City producer, has remembered it ever since he wandered away from his first viewing of it convinced it would change his life. Maybe it has; it's difficult to gauge such things. At any rate he has helped recover it for the rest of us. It had been misplaced while for the last two decades technically bloated, carnivorous science fiction films have eaten alive audiences, special effects budgets, and ulcered producers. But Williams, like his literary brethren the historians Sam Moskowitz and Brian Aldiss, is helping us all rediscover the glories of a more naive, perhaps, but young and vital period of science fiction. The science fiction films of the 1950–56 period constituted something of a "golden age" of the genre, not at all unlike the classic era of the pulps in the years between the wars. Now you can define "golden age" any way you want, but for this writer it is any period where imagination precedes calculation, where inventiveness takes priority over self-consciousness and imitation. Thus, the two periods in question ushered in outstanding, intuitive talents like Frank R. Paul, Chesley Bonestell, "Doc" Smith, Jack Williamson, Kurt Neumann, George Pal, and so many others with their eyes and ears tilted toward the romance of the spaceways. Even if the narrative formulas were often all too familiar, and all too obviously borrowed from the already time-worn genres of the western and gangster forms, the locales, the characterizations, the hardware were wildly imaginative and bizarre.

⅋

Even the most cursory examination of the classic literary works and the classic films cannot fail to detect the ties that bind them. The titles of these swashbuckling books and films fairly roll off the tongue—Doc Smith's "Skylark and Lensman" series with their wonderfully improbable space wars, Jack Williamson's "Legion of Space," C.L. Moore's sagas of Northwest Smith, the string of George Pal films like *Destination Moon, When Worlds Collide,* and *Conquest of Space,* and, of course, the film that started the cycle, *Rocketship X-M.*

The ingredients that bind all these titles together constitute a peculiar alchemy all their own. They include an unabashed need to spring out of earthly restraints (as was the case with Burroughs' John Carter), a sprinkling of aliens, lost civilizations, and ancient technologies (heavily influenced by Rider Haggard's 19th century romances), a blend of seriousness and fun that transcends the comic book quality of Flash Gordon, a dazzling array of gadgetry that nonetheless does not swamp the story (as, again, Burroughs understood), and, above all, those wonderful spaceships that seem to be all fin and rocket exhaust, like the terrestrial brethren of the '50s, the Cadillac.

Take the example of *RXM.* It was first produced in 1950 and just beat its rival, George Pal's *Destination Moon* (based on Heinlein's *Rocket Ship Galileo*) to the box office. It told the story of the first expedition to the moon which, because of equipment malfunction during a meteor shower, finds itself instead heading straight for Mars. It carries a five-person crew, portrayed by, variously, Lloyd Bridges, John Emory, Hugh O'Brian, Noah Beery, Jr., and Osa Massen. Miss Massen finds herself the most misunderstood of the group as she alternately tries to defend her position on the crew (even though she is a woman), keep amorous swains like Lloyd Bridges at a distance, and contact her own awakening sense of romance and poetry (the film really is perhaps as much a story of inner discovery as it is of outer exploration). They land on Mars and discover the remnants of a near-vanished civilization, apparently destroyed by nuclear holocaust. The site of a huge city lies buried in the arid wastes while scattered artifacts mutely attest to the waste and desolation that overcame the planet. They set out to explore the terrain but are suddenly attacked by the planet's only survivors, a tribe of savage, blind mutants. In scenes of mounting terror, several of the crew are killed while the others stagger back to the ship and hurriedly liftoff back to earth. But it is discovered that there is not enough of the precious fuel to insure their reentry to earth, so they transmit a radio message describing the conditions and the message of the tragedy of Mars. Now, only two members of the crew left, the film ends with . . . well, not now, in case some readers may not have seen it and are not aware of the film's extraordinary climax.

Perhaps no other science fiction film has achieved such a cult following as *Rocketship X-M*. Many people active in science fiction films today credit it as their initial inspiration, enthusiasts circulate newsletters and can recite entire stretches of dialogue at the drop of a hat, and producers like Wade Williams devote much of their waking hours to bringing it back to today's audiences. So what is it about this film that has survived the years while so many other titles have long since disappeared? Some of the reasons, at least, are obvious. From hindsight it seems remarkable that so many top names came together for a film budgeted at less than a hundred thousand dollars, especially at a time when the science fiction genre was still tainted by a comic book atmosphere. For instance, its cameraman, Karl Struss, was already a legend, acclaimed as a top artist in still photography and in the movies (his credits began with such classics as Sunrise in 1927); composer Ferde Grofé was already famed for his suites like *The Grand Canyon* and *Mississippi Suite* and his work of long standing for such jazz greats as Paul Whiteman and George Gershwin; director Kurt Neumann had a solid background in astronomy and science behind him and retained the enthusiastic spark of the dedicated science fiction buff; and the cast had its own special qualities—Lloyd Bridges and Hugh O'Brian were just beginning their careers, while Morris Ankrum and John Emory lent weight and authority to their roles; above all, the lovely Osa Massen reversed one of science fiction's more unfortunate tendencies—the sexist stereotyping of females—and portrayed a woman who was both tough and vulnerable, a dedicated professional still sensitive to the more poetic aspects of space travel. Miss Massen would soon drop out of movies altogether (today she resides in Beverly Hills and has been involved with the Motion Picture Academy) and today views with some bemusement the legions of fans who have seen her in this picture and have never forgotten her. . . .

The results are harder to pin down. For one thing, it is a film of unusual power and seriousness. It has a message and employs no nonsense in getting it across. In fact, in this age of Three Mile Island, the holocaust that destroyed Mars in the film is more relevant today than ever. For another, there is a surprising amount of time devoted to characterizations of the ill-fated crew. We come to care about these people and project ourselves into their places. Except for some tediously predictable jokes from Noah Beery, Jr. about the size of Texas, moreover, the dialogue is crisp and functional. For instance, in the scene between Massen and Bridges as they stand before a porthole through which the moon's receding orb is glimpsed, they speak casually of their past lives, and the romance of space as opposed to the detachment of science and technology. Pretty pretentious stuff, one would suppose from this description, but it's all carefully injected into deceptively simple and terse snatches of dialogue. The wonder is that such dialogue is there at all, after one has viewed so many other hack efforts where such talk would be totally out of place amid the bug-eyed monsters and papier-mâché planets.

There is a disturbing kind of quietness about the film too. This is most effective, perhaps, in those scenes just prior to the first attack of the mutants, where the deep focus frame reveals their movements beyond the unsuspecting figures of the crew. The film seems determined not to yield to petty sensationalism. Even the romantic exchanges between Massen and Bridges are underplayed.

Effective moments come from the film's exceptional musical score, too, particularly during the liftoff and later during the Martian sequences. It is a collaboration of composer Grofé, conductor Albert Glasser, and theremin player Samuel Hoffman. The sound mix is altogether unworldly, decidedly "advanced" for a commercial entertainment. Grofé need not have worried about composing "down" to film audiences; indeed, it could be argued that the score is superior to some of his other, supposedly, more serious works, such as the *Death Valley Suite* and *The Hudson River Suite*. (Recently this score has itself been resurrected due to the untiring efforts of Williams and publishers Kerry O'Quinn and Norman Jacobs of *Starlog* magazine.)

And yet for all of this *RXM* was marred with some flaws. Chief among them was the unfortunate use of V-2 rocket footage intercut with shots of the RXM. In 1950 the only footage of rockets available were those of the V-2s that the United States had seized during the war and had later fired off at White Sands. Because *RXM* did not have a big budget, and because outer space special effects crews were still unheard of in those days, the producer Robert Lippert ordered the V-2 footage used. That the V-2 design is entirely different from that of the RXM is painfully apparent in the initial liftoff sequence and, later, in the takeoff from the Martian surface. At the same time, there are no exterior shots of the rocket in flight in space, only interiors.

The desires to correct these problems as well as to get the film back into general circulation for today's audiences were prime motivations in the long-standing efforts of Williams and others to "refurbish" the picture. The "new" *RXM* is slated to premiere in May of 1980, on its 30th birthday.

Williams had obtained the rights to the film some seven years after tracking it down for years. "The picture had been sold by Lippert to the Victor organization," he recalls. "All rights had been sold. Warners had bought it for foreign distribution in Germany in 1958. I bought the rights to the film from the television distributor, who owned the United States rights. He had no more use for it for theatrical or non-theatrical [such as for rental libraries and video tape or disc]. The original 35mm negative had been on nitrate cellulose and had already decomposed, but Warner Brothers had made up a fine-grain 35mm positive, from which you can make a decent negative. We located that print and struck a new negative. Precision-Deluxe, a lab in New York owned by 20th Century Fox, made the negative."

But simply owning a film doesn't insure its profitable re-release in theatres. "I had tried this with *Invaders from Mars*," Williams explained, "and I knew what it would cost. It's not just owning the picture, it's the cost of the accessories—from one-sheets to trailers. Just because you have a picture and a negative, doesn't mean it's ready to go into the theatres, because you have to accessorize it. That's why a lot of the old pictures aren't released on a wide scale theatrically. It just costs too much money."

ॐ

Elements of color would also be added to the film. A process called "Auramation" is described by Williams as a toning process which can take a black-and-white film and on new printers, with a series of colored gels, can translate the various gray shades into appropriately varied hues. This works especially well on special films, Williams reports, such as horror and science fiction where the mood is so dependent upon lighting and shadows. "Toned black-and-white films can be quite beautiful; it's a shame they are not done today. We're keeping the Martian scenes red but we're pulling out different shades of the color as well as pulling whites out for the clouds. So it's not like looking at the scenes through rose-colored glasses, but like looking at actual contrasts of colors. The spaceship interiors will be done in pale blues."

Much of the process shooting was done at nights in the CPC studios in Los Angeles, where Ron Seawright and Dave Stipes coordinated the interior effects shooting. "The new version will include, among other things, a spectacular shot of the RXM lifting off of the Martian surface—just a few seconds worth of footage, but time-consuming to do. Both camera and ship model have to be animated for the shot. The mattes were made in the camera and there's no way you can see any matte lines; it looks absolutely legitimate."

When asked about the possible disapproval of *RXM*'s fans to its refurbishing, Williams pauses a moment and finally shrugs. "If we hadn't given a facelift to this picture, it probably wouldn't have gotten any new bookings. For one thing, theatres rarely book a black-and-white picture, especially when so many wouldn't have seen the picture in the first place to be able to criticize it. You have to tailor it to the people who do the booking. It's a film with a good story and which develops characters, and today very few action films do that. For the most part, today's films are done by television directors who have to develop a climax every seven or eight minutes. *X-M* builds throughout the whole film. I don't know if today's audiences will find this dull by comparison with something like *Star Wars* or not. But we have not changed the mood and pacing; I don't think there will be any complaints."

There are virtually no precedents for "Project RXM." Certainly there are many examples of films that have been taken off the shelf, dusted off, and re-released in slightly altered form. *Gone with the Wind*, to cite the most obvious example, was released ten years ago in a new wide-screen ratio, much to the consternation of its most die-hard fans. When Robert Youngson re-released the 1929 *Noah's Ark* in 1958 he added newsreel footage of the film's premiere and some bridging sequences, but the original film itself was untouched. When the last *Flash Gordon* serial was released, to choose an example closer to home, it contained borrowed sequences from Leni Riefenstahl's 1931 *The White Hell of Pitzpalu*, a famous German "Mountain" film. But generally, few films are re-released at all with much success. Their tendency to "date" does not help, and in the case of science fiction classics, it is disastrous. *Destination Moon*, for instance, was famous in its time for its wealth of gadgetry and effects. Today it all looks dated, like a story from *Popular Science*, the human element and romance were never there.

But Project RXM is a different matter. New scenes are incorporated into the old footage so that an amalgam of past and present results in which one is indistinguishable from the other. One generation reaches out to another and joins hands, so to speak. The project itself becomes a metaphor for the whole course and aim of science fiction, wherein successive generations inspire one another, building upon one another, so that past and future history are welded into a timeless continuum where only ideas and imagination of the head and the heart are significant. Only a film of unusual substance and energy can do such a thing. One can only wonder what future generations will find of significance in *RXM*. Perhaps they too will be inspired and the film will once again be adapted to another time and place. Like the adaptable life forms in Clifford Simak's classic "City" stories, it will seek and adapt to new environments, some perhaps not even of this world.

Part VI

FILM HISTORY

Charlie Chan Meets OWI

RACISM IN WORLD WAR II FILMS

Gregory D. Black

Originally appeared in vol. 3, no. 2 (November/December 1978)

"The screen portrayal given Charlie Chan will contribute nothing to American-Chinese relations. It cannot . . . be recommended by us for overseas distribution!" So lectured the United States propaganda agency, the Office of War Information (OWI), to the Monogram Pictures Corporation during World War II. Convinced that Hollywood entertainment films could help sway American and foreign audiences to support American war aims, OWI began to carefully screen Hollywood products for their presentation of the war, the home front, the issues, the United Nations, and the enemy. Of the 1,210 scripts the agency examined from mid-1943 through mid-1945, 500 were changed in various ways to reflect the propaganda agency's interpretation of the war. OWI was especially concerned that the image of China, a member of the United Nations, not be reduced to racial stereotypes.

OWI was also determined that Hollywood eliminate any implication of racism from its productions. The agency did not believe American minorities or millions of non-White foreign nationals would be convinced of the superiority of the American system of government if Hollywood presented either individuals or the war in racial terms. To their horror, however, OWI discovered that the industry had grafted the war to its traditional cliché-ridden, stereotyped version of the world. Blacks were menials; Latins were playboys or dancing girls; Asians were sly and spoke in riddles; and foreigners of all types were inferior to good old Americans.

The Office of War Information was formed by an executive order on June 13, 1942, that consolidated several prewar information agencies. President Franklin D. Roosevelt instructed OWI to implement a program through the press, radio, and motion picture to enhance public understanding of the war; and to act as the intermediary between federal agencies and the radio and motion picture industries. Elmer Davis, a popular radio commentator, was named director. A basic assumption that dominated the agency was that entertainment films, which had achieved a staggering degree of world-wide acceptability, could play an effective role in selling the war. Mincing no words, Davis wrote, "The easiest way to inject a propaganda idea into most people's minds is to let it go in through the medium of an entertainment picture when they do not realize that they are being propagandized."

But while the industry reached millions of people, its productions had never been known for historical accuracy or commitment to social issues. Studios avoided "message films" for box-office proven musicals, comedies, or murder mysteries. Only a small percentage of the films produced during the period from 1935 to 1941 dealt with the growth of fascism; many of these were playful spoofs. When Mussolini's armies invaded Ethiopia, an excited friend asked a producer, "Have you heard any late news?" Yes, the agitated mogul replied: "Italy had just banned *Marie Antoinette!*"

In an effort to uplift the industry's conception of the war, OWI's Hollywood office prepared a "Manual for the Motion Picture Industry." The document asked producers to present the war as a "people's war," not a "national, class or racial war." Movies were urged to show democracy at work. Minorities, the manual stressed, "have as much to win or lose" in this war as anyone else. Fascism was the enemy, not hatred toward a particular personality or people. "It is far from sufficient to characterize the enemy as a strutting, heiling Nazi, or as a little buck-toothed treacherous Jap." The war, OWI wrote, was a "United Nations campaign of thirty nations fighting together. Don't overplay America's role by inadequate coverage of our Allies. Above all, avoid disparaging portrayals of Allied types." The manual concluded: show our allies as people, not stereotypes.

The propaganda agency was especially concerned about the image that Hollywood films presented of the Chinese. The issue of the Chinese seemed clouded by the fact that one oriental race, the Japanese, was an enemy, while the Chinese were an ally. *Time* magazine believed its readers were so confused on this matter that they published a guide, complete with photographs on, "How to Tell Your Friends from the Japs." The Chinese, *Time* reported, are relaxed in appearance while the Japanese are stiff. Facial expression was also a good clue to racial differences: "The Japanese are dogmatic and arrogant, while the Chinese expression is kindly and placid." Lastly, the news magazine sagely observed "most Chinese avoid horn-rimmed spectacles."

Despite this confusion, the Chinese were allies. Anything that implied racial stereotyping OWI feared would insult the Chinese government and undermine the American effort to build China into an equal ally. OWI, therefore, attempted to have Hollywood films present China as a modern unified nation, cooperating with the United Nations in its battle against Japanese aggression.

Hollywood, however, had its own version of China and the Chinese. China traditionally had been a place of mystery. There were evil mandarin villains, inhuman warlords who terrorized women and children, but who were easily disposed of by Western heroes. It was a nation teeming with people who spoke in riddles and lived in extreme poverty. Backward, unfamiliar with modern science and technology, China was conceived of as a nation and people who needed American help to survive. Obviously, the interpretations put forward by D. W. Griffith's *Broken Blossoms* to *The Good Earth* would not be acceptable to America's propaganda agency.

OWI found a great deal of racial stereotyping toward Asian allies in Hollywood war films. A re-release of *The Good Earth* was judged objectionable for creating "a false impression" of the Chinese people. *China* has Alan Ladd single-handedly wiping out an entire Japanese division. OWI shuddered; "Hollywood trumpery," declared Bosley Crowther. In *China Girl*, the Chinese can only fight effectively if led by Americans. Racial slurs were also common. In *So Proudly We Hail* the only Chinese was a typical Hollywood stereotype. The original script called for an American girl to address the Chinese in pidgin English. When the Chinese replies in perfect English, the startled girl huffs: "Okay, I'll do your laundry." OWI had the scene removed and reminded Paramount that not all Chinese were laundrymen.

Any evaluation of the image of the Chinese in American films must take into consideration the most famous of all Chinese, the venerable Charlie Chan. Hollywood produced 99 feature films between 1931 and 1945 that had some aspects of China as a major theme. Thirty-one of these were Charlie Chan mysteries. During the war years, twenty-five features on China were produced—six were Charlie Chans. The rigors of total war required that OWI subject the inscrutable detective to its own meticulous investigation.

Charlie Chan in the Secret Service (1944), starring Sidney Toler, was typical of the wartime versions in the series. The thin plot revolves around the mysterious murder of George Metton, an inventor, and the theft of his top-secret blueprints for a new powerful secret weapon. Chan, now a detective in the Secret Service for the duration, is called in on the case. In all too familiar fashion, Chan, somewhat hindered by his children, solves the murder, uncovers a German espionage ring, and recovers the valuable blueprints. To most observers, this was simply another harmless Chan mystery designed to satisfy the constant demands of his fans. *Variety* labeled it as "stodgy."

Yet to OWI, Charlie Chan presented a serious propaganda problem. When Monogram Pictures first presented the script of *Charlie Chan in the Secret Service* to OWI for review in 1943, the agency began to exhibit serious concern over the entire series. The film upset the propaganda agency for several reasons. It obviously dragged the war needlessly into a conventional series and would contribute nothing to an improvement of American-Chinese relations. While Chan might be a folk hero among millions of Americans, OWI found him a bland and inscrutable Oriental whose pidgin English and cryptic proverbs would "appear to the Chinese as an American caricature of their race." The agency was also convinced that the Chinese would take offense to the role played by Chan's children. The propagandists noted that Iris and Tommy appear "bumptious and irresponsible." Although Tommy spoke of becoming a bombardier, OWI was upset because he showed "no awareness of the war except as an opportunity for adventure." This might imply to the Chinese that the American-Chinese were unaware of the war. The characterization of the Americanized children as rather inept might, in OWI's opinion, "raise grave doubts on the part of the Chinese people as to the value of a Western [American] upbringing."

The film also used every opportunity to make gag jokes of Confucius, the Chinese use of chopsticks, and Chan's large family. On a more serious side, OWI bristled that Menton Moreland, a famous Black actor of the period, was used for comic relief. In typical Hollywood fashion, Chan's servant was presented as an ignorant, superstitious person whose basic fears were only overcome by constant trips to the bar. In a letter to Phil Krasne of Monogram, OWI reminded the producer that the role played by Moreland is a "characterization offensive to all dark-skinned peoples throughout the world since it suggests that Americans consider peoples of other races as inferior human beings." Of course, most Americans did consider peoples of non-white races as inferior and Monogram was simply presenting a timeworn Hollywood version of Black Americans. This was no longer acceptable in a world at war.

To OWI any racial inferences would prove detrimental to the American war effort. The agency also believed that Hollywood could play a major role in convincing both American and world-wide audiences that America represented a superior system of government—one worth fighting for. This struggle, as much a struggle for men's minds as a battlefield encounter, was so important that even Charlie Chan films must take into account the heightened sensitivity of World War II. As a liberal agency within the Roosevelt administration, OWI was determined to use American entertainment films as propaganda. As the agency observed:

> The motion picture industry has an important job to do in helping create the better understanding between all peoples necessary to establish a just and lasting peace. To caricature the Chinese, as this film does [*Charlie Chan in the Secret Service*], retards that understanding.

In fact, OWI was so upset over the images in *Charlie Chan in the Secret Service* that members of the reviewing staff recommended "that the studio be urged to abandon not only this film but the entire Chan series." Happily, calmer heads in the agency prevailed and no attempt was made to have the Chan series cancelled. After several meetings the agency decided to attempt to have Monogram tone down its characterizations of ethnic minorities in the series. If the images of minorities and Chinese were seen as unacceptable, OWI could use its authority to prohibit an export license for the offending film. This would, in effect, take away the profit margin from the film. Since OWI was never given total censorship powers, the agency could only negotiate with studios for cooperation. Failing that, OWI could restrict distribution overseas, but was powerless to prevent its domestic distribution.

OWI followed the Chan series closely through the remaining war years. In a script review of *Charlie Chan in the Mystery Mansion* (1944), the agency again made violent objection to the characterization of Blacks in the film. "This stereotyped treatment of a Negro in an American film is most offensive to colored audiences . . . because of the implication of American acceptance of the doctrine of racial superiority." The film was not recommended for overseas distribution.

The Scarlet Clue (1945) had similar problems. In this film, Chan must solve the mysterious murder of a secret agent, a radio executive, and two actors. He does this in his typical style while the befuddled "cops" look on. OWI had several objections to *The Scarlet Clue*. When Monogram first submitted the script to OWI for approval, the agency raised serious objections to the use of the word "radar" in the film. The subject was *top secret* and any discussion, even of the concept, had been banned by the government. OWI advised Monogram not to make any discussion of "radar" central to the film.

The agency was somewhat relieved when the final print of the film was screened in March, 1945. OWI described the film as another "dull detective story" which dealt with enemy agents who were after American radar blueprints. While that subject was generally forbidden, the Chan presentation was "so implausible and the sets involving electronics so unrealistic that they cannot be called dangerous."

OWI was pleased to notice some small improvement in the characterization of Blacks in the film. While far from perfect, the main Black character was at least played in a sympathetic nature. The general impression of the film was still judged as unacceptable for overseas distribution.

The last Chan film that OWI reviewed was *The Shanghai Cobra* (1945). Chan, again playing a government agent, is called from Washington to help solve three poison murders. Chan quickly attributes the crimes to the archvillain Cobra, Jan Van Horn. Chan is interested in the murders and the appearance of the Cobra because he is responsible for the safety of several million dollars' worth of government radium. All of the murders have taken place near the radium storage area. Again a typical vehicle for Charlie Chan.

This time around OWI objected to the film because the film implied that lawlessness was a major problem in America. The propaganda agency did not believe that foreign nationals would look up to America if they were given the impression that America was a land of crooks. In a letter to Monogram, OWI summed up its view: "The portrayal of organized crime and the considerable lawlessness inherent in this story naturally makes it a questionable projection of America for overseas audiences."

The Chan series might have been bad propaganda but they were good entertainment films which delighted millions of fans. As Dorothy Jones observed in her study, *The Portrayal of China and India on the American Screen*, "Charlie Chan was an American tribute to China['s] wisdom and antiquity." Reviewers of the Chan series remarked how delighted audiences were with Charlie's "gems of wisdom." Charlie, with his broken English, his Confucian logic ("Theory, like mist on eyeglasses, obscures fact"), was above all oriental. He proved his superiority time and time again by solving baffling mysteries that left Western "cops" befuddled. This was not a social comment on the American system of justice or police efficiency nor should OWI have taken it as such.

Nor should the role played by his children have upset OWI. Charlie Chan, on the one hand, is calm, all-knowing, and always one step ahead of everyone. His son, on the other hand, while obviously well educated and ambitious, is inept. But the relationship is one of mutual respect. Thus the films recognize the traditional wisdom of China and mock the modern lifestyle which the son so desperately wants.

And these points were quite clear to oriental audiences. While OWI worried that Orientals would take offense of the role of Charlie Chan—they did not. In fact, the series was extremely popular in the Far East long before the war. OWI should have been aware of this and viewed the series in that light. The Chan films implied that oriental methods were superior to Western methods; and that America was willing to poke fun, not only at Orientals, but also at itself. This was a fact the bureaucrats of the propaganda agency could never understand or appreciate.

OWI, for its part, was certainly correct in trying to convince Hollywood to eliminate offensive stereotypes from its films. The experience with the Charlie Chan series showed how totally insensitive Hollywood was. They could only conceive of the character played by Menton Moreland as comic relief—ignorant, superstitious, scared of his own shadow. The industry which poured millions into script development was incapable of revising that stereotype.

But clearly OWI was overreacting to the role it believed Hollywood films could play in the propaganda field. Serious drama might well make effective propaganda but the millions of people who flooded to see Charlie Chan would not accept their detective hero as a propagandist for American democracy. To expect Tommy, as OWI did in *Charlie Chan in the Secret Service,* to show a serious concern about the state of total war would be to change the nature of the series, or to have our detective hero address himself to the philosophical differences between fascism and democracy, as OWI would have liked, would mar the popular appeal of Chan. Charlie Chan was harmless entertainment and it so remained despite the interference of America's propaganda agency.

Disney Out-Foxed

THE TALE OF REYNARD
AT THE DISNEY STUDIO

John Cawley Jr.

Originally appeared in vol. 3, no. 6 (July/August 1979)

Walt Disney is best known as a pioneer and master in the field of animation. In reality, he personally lingered over the drawing board for only a brief period in his early career, turning his attention toward the area where his greatest talents lay: direction and story. It was a fortunate development: no film mogul possessed a keener eye—or a sharper editing scalpel—when it came to making the most of the slimmest of story concepts. In both animated and live-action features, Disney's native instinct for sound storytelling remains unequalled.

1937 put this instinct to a crucial test.

Snow White was now a part of history, its success the stuff of myth in the industry. What next? The search began; few popular stories or books were neglected, though fewer still ever made it past Disney's mental screen and on the movie screen. Stories that didn't hold up very well—stories that didn't have the right feel, the special touch of Disney magic waiting to blossom—were quickly dispatched. Those with some kernel of potential lived on, sometimes seeing the light of projection over twenty years after their first consideration.

Out of this muddled torrent of story selection and work, one name surfaces and stays afloat: Reynard the Fox. Many prospective works, like a Salvador Dali film and dozens more, were never completed by Disney in the rush of time and changing interests of genius, but Reynard seems to have dug a little foxhole in some corner of the Disney imagination, provoking numerous forays over the years, to little end. The fox returned time and again in various guises of the highest quality, yet nothing came of it. How did this craftiest of creatures manage to elude the master story-huntsman and his crew?

Meet Reynard: he goes back a long way. Arising in 12th-century Germany, his story begins as a beast epic, the only known, set in a kingdom of animals.

When Reynard does not show up one day in court, the affronted King sends messengers after him. The first, Bruin the Bear, is tricked into going after honey and gets badly stung. Next is Tibert the Cat, who is badly beaten chasing mice and loses an eye. It is Reynard's cousin who finally brings in the fox.

In a bid for self-preservation, Reynard tells of a treasure, piquing the interest of the King. Reynard, the Ram, and the Hare are commissioned to fetch the treasure. Reynard kills the Hare and gives the Hare's head to the Ram in a bag, telling him to present it to the King. The apoplectic King demands Reynard's own head in response.

Again Reynard comes to court and again saves his neck with a tale of treasure. He is pardoned, but the Wolf demands satisfaction. In the resulting duel, Reynard wins through trickery and wits and is made advisor to the King.

In some versions, Reynard is killed in the end; but all contain episodes of accusation, apprehension, confrontation, and general outwittery, with the fox usually coming out on top. Appearing in poems (the Goethe version is most known and read), fables, novels, and almost every other form of literature, Reynard and his kingdom of animals have played everywhere, from moral tales for children to biting satire for adults.

This intriguing subject could not long go unnoticed by Disney. The first treatment for the prospective feature was under consideration less than two months after the release of *Snow White*. Its authors were Dorothy Ann Blank, fresh from her story work on *Snow White*, and Al Perkins.

This first stab remains faithful to the characters of the traditional stories, portraying Reynard as sly and basically crooked. As one commentator put it: for Reynard, any means justify the ends. Reynard exists in the "kingdom of beasts," where the animals are either "selfish, or vain, or greedy, or foolish, or stupid, or full of envy." Reynard was a paragon compared to the rest of the cast.

As in the Goethe version, this treatment begins with Reynard absent from court. The King sends out his guards to capture the Fox—who actually is at court in, literally, sheep's clothing. Reynard's friend Petunia, a skunk, defends the Fox to no avail. In an interesting scene, the King's men spy on Reynard at Reynard's castle, watching him play with his children. As the children jump from the mantle, he catches them—until the last time, when he lets them fall. "That's the first thing children must learn in this wicked world—to trust no one—not even their own father," says Reynard.

Reynard outwits the guards, and the angry King sends Petunia for him, who brings him back to court where he is sentenced to be hanged. On the gallows, Reynard confesses his father once tried to overthrow the King with the help of the Wolf (who happens to be Reynard's principal accuser), and that he has hidden all of his father's wealth. Naturally, the King is suddenly willing to spare Reynard in order to gain directions to the treasure. The Wolf is thrown in jail.

The King and his subjects head off to the volcano where the treasure is supposedly hidden. The volcano erupts; many are killed, and the King barely escapes. The King returns and frees the Wolf, who demands satisfaction, as in the traditional version. Reynard wins the duel, of course, and demands that a ball be thrown in his honor. That night, when all the animals are at court, Reynard steals all the wealth of the Kingdom. When confronted, he again claims that the treasure is hidden in the volcano. No longer prey to Reynard's deception, the King banishes Reynard himself to the volcano, Reynard begging for mercy (a la Br'er Rabbit and the briar patch). Arriving at the volcano, he looks down at the village with a smile and proceeds to dig up all the treasure.

The treatment may have paralleled the original tales, but it took obvious liberties with the Disney image—a point much discussed at a subsequent story meeting. Attending the meeting were such story people as Bill Cottrell (*Pinocchio, Saludos Amigos, Alice in Wonderland, Peter Pan*), Ben Sharpsteen (*Snow White, Pinocchio, Alice, Ichabod and Mr. Toad*), and Otto Englander (*Snow White, Pinocchio,* and *Fantasia*). Fortunately notes of this meeting still exist.

"I see some swell possibilities in Reynard, but is it smart to make it?" asks Disney at the start. "Our main character is a crook, and there's nothing about him having a 'Robin Hood' angle. *That* was different, because they built up these land barons and all that, but can you do this here? To begin with, it wouldn't be Reynard."

The satire angle was floated. "Too sophisticated." Someone suggested showing Reynard to be a good guy pretending to be bad. "Sounds very involved to me," responded Disney. At first Disney concentrated on the negative aspects, becoming enthused only when he began to envision specific settings. "I'd like to see some scenes in a dive underground . . . and the way he has to get into things—back passages, like the sewers of Paris."

Disney suggested showing the fox to be a victim of his past life. "We've always accused the fox and maybe we could prove that he is really not that type— started out all right, and then we show how he goes wrong—really innocent, but the law has always been after him and he's had to use his wits." It was Reynard's wits that most fascinated Disney. No doubt Disney's own history of having overcome multiple hardships with his cleverness endeared this trait to him.

Discussing various plans, from a series of short vignettes to tying the whole project to Aesop in some way, Walt declared, "The idea is to write a book. You know, you can read some books and see there's a story in it right away." Books he got.

By 1945 another synopsis had evolved, and another debate. Clifton Johnson, the author, even takes time out before the treatment to talk over the situation. He felt that the basic premise of the characters (all animals) and the locales (woods, castles, secret passages) were ideal. His character description of Reynard ("very wicked, sly, self-sufficient, clever, orator") included the statement, "Perhaps the story has more undesirable qualities than desirable ones for picture purposes."

This second treatment is even closer to the traditional version, to the extent that Reynard causes the Cat to lose an eye, eats the Rabbit, and allows the Ram to take the Hare's head back to the King. This orgy of un-Disneylike violence—along with bringing Reynard's footloose freedom to an end by making him High Chancellor—was a surprising follow-up to the milder concept created earlier.

1947 was the year of the fox: no less than three treatments were submitted. Along with this mass of writing was a flood of reading. The Reynard books in the Studio library were increasing in number and usage. Walt himself checked out a copy of *Rogue Reynard* by Andre Norton.

The first synopsis, dated 1/28/47, is uncredited. The tone is much lighter than the earlier versions, suggesting a possible connection with the hands who made the contemporaneous *Song of the South*.

A "Charles Boyer–type" narrator opens the story. The King, still unadmirable, has become a comedic figure, continually combing his mane while gazing in a hand mirror. This tale makes use of a "conspiracy" angle: the Wolf, Bear, and Cat are all in some sort of plot against the King—mostly an assault on his treasure.

When the Wolf tells the King of the many complaints against Reynard, the King demands that the scoundrel be brought in. The Cat and Wolf send the Bear, a bumbling slow-thinking carbon of Br'er Bear. Reynard is depicted as a "free spirit" whose only concern is having a good time by making sport of the Bear. Whether tricking him with honey or disguising himself as a woman, the Bear proves no match for Reynard's vulpine wit.

The Wolf tells the King that only the royal Lion is smart enough to catch the Fox. Flattered, the King is fooled into going after Reynard in disguise (the Wolf plans to kill the King and blame Reynard). When the King is attacked, Reynard comes to the rescue, but in the confusion he is accused of leading the attack himself. On the gallows, he is able not only to clear himself, but prove the guilt of the three villains.

The bear/fox tangles have much the feel of the bear/rabbit encounters in *Song of the South*. Both are loaded with sly humor and cleverness. The scene in which Reynard, disguised as a woman, takes the bear to his hiding place only to quickly sneak out of the Bear's hug and appear as Reynard (shouting "my wife"), whereupon he pummels the Bear with a club, is extremely funny. Also amusing is the "Reynard is everywhere" concept, even showing him on the canopy of the King's bed while the Lion and Wolf are in private conference.

This quick and happy version may have caught Disney's eye, for the next two versions are equally light, though less clever. The prior version, in which the King says, "That Reynard, always getting in my hair!" is noted as "too punny."

Both later 1947 versions appear over two weeks' time from Norm Ferguson, the excellent animator of Pluto. He evidently made little use of the many books in the Studio, basing his stories more on the earlier treatments and characters. As in the previous version, the Wolf, Cat, and Bear are in league against the King.

In Ferguson's first story, mysterious crimes have been committed with an "R" left at the scenes. The court convenes, expecting that the guilty party will be absent. Reynard's absence is defended by his friend, a badger. Meanwhile, there is another court in session, consisting of the small animals, birds, mice, insects, etc., in a large cavern. In the wall of the cavern is a throne carved out of solid rock, and on the throne is Reynard. He tells his subjects that he is aware of the crimes and the "R"s and will try to uncover the perpetrator.

In this version we have the first mention of a song, "It's Reynard," to be sung by his subjects.

The story shifts from court to court with the usual string of accusations, disguises, attempted captures of Reynard, and upon his arrival, the promise of treasure. This time, though, the treasure ploy is only used to finally flush out the guilt of the conspirators.

The constant disguising and additional characters in the two courts may have been the reason for the failure of this version to reach a further point. In his next treatment, Ferguson tries less plot and more humor, structuring the story around flashbacks.

This synopsis starts at the gallows with Reynard about to be hanged. The wolf comes up and lists the crimes done to the Bear, Cat, Ram, and Hare. The crowd, and even Reynard, applauds after the Wolf's oration. Then it is Reynard's turn to give his last words.

Adjusting the noose around his neck like a tie, Reynard proceeds to tell the "truth" about the Ram and the Hare and the treasure they were to bring back. The riches included a magic ring for the King and a mirror for the Queen. The sequences in which Reynard presents the advantages of the objects were humorous segments that included numerous gags.

Soon the entire crowd is begging for more information. Reynard responds with some "Aesopian" tales pointing up the loyalty of the Wolf, Cat, and Bear by implication. He then tells of his father's conspiracy involving the treasure and those three animals.

The Wolf demands that the hanging proceed, but the King can only think of the conspiracy. He asks the crowd to decide the guilty party, and the Wolf, Cat, and Bear are chosen for hanging. As the hanging ceremony thus continues, the King asks Reynard about the treasure, and, winking to the audience, he promises again to return it.

This version contains new infusions of humor plus a more sophisticated portrayal of Reynard, who is seen as an "English gentleman." It also contains a proposed song "We're Hanging Reynard Today," which, one suspects, would not have had quite the universal appeal of "Whistle While You Work." Once again the treatment seemed to miss the mark.

Animator Frank Thomas remembers that at the time there was talk about the Reynard feature. Many wondered whether Reynard, *Alice*, or *Cinderella* would be slated as the next animated feature. History shows that *Cinderella* got the nod, with *Alice* a close second.

Reynard did not die, though, for he turns up again in perhaps his most natural setting: among pirates and thieves. Along the lines of *Song of the South* and *So Dear to My Heart*, Disney considered adding three animated segments to the live-action feature *Treasure Island*.

The script called for Long John Silver to recite tales of Reynard to Jim Hawkins to gain the boy's confidence. The first fable was to be "Reynard and the Golden Apple," which would show that even though Reynard had stolen the King's golden apple and treasure, it was to protect it from the real thieves. The moral: things are not always what they seem.

The story then continues much along the lines of the released film, with the addition of a second, "phony" map. When Jim is captured by the pirates, Silver averts Jim's death by telling the pirates the story of "How Reynard Saved Grimbert's Life," suggesting that the pirates, by killing Jim, would be making their own deaths a certainty.

The final fable was to come at the end, when Silver, captured, had proven to be less honest than Jim had hoped. Silver tells of "Reynard's Death and Confession," showing that one should always use one's wits for good, not evil.

It's a shame that these segments were not used, for Reynard's epic is basically a series of short adventures, and this form would no doubt fit the purpose of retaining Reynard's villainy in the face of the Disney sweeteners.

Treasure Island lost its fox, becoming Disney's first all live-action feature.

With feature production back in full swing, the early fifties saw another surge of interest in Reynard. The books in the Studio library show extensive use of story men Ralph Wright (*Bambi, Lady and the Tramp, Song of the South, Peter Pan*), Bill Cottrell, Bill Peet (*Dumbo, Cinderella, Alice, Peter Pan*), and several others.

This work seems to have resulted in neither scripts nor story notes. All that is extant are some storyboard sketches from 1956 by Ken Anderson. There is no real story line, only some scenes of Reynard on the gallows and several character studies. Bill Peet also reportedly did some sketches at this time.

Finally a script did come into existence during 1980 by Ken Anderson, known mostly for character designing. However, this project was not entitled *Reynard*. The villainous Fox had taken a back seat to one of the "good" characters of the tales, *Chanticleer*. This treatment tells how Chanticleer, head rooster of the barnyard, is brought down by Reynard and his gang.

Luckily, a storyboard also exists showing Chanticleer in top hat and tails while Reynard (with a moustache) is in striped shirt and beret. In fact, the whole visual concept of the film is a sort of Parisian spoof. There are to be musical numbers a la the Folies Bergere, an underground of characters (". . . like the sewers of Paris . . ."), and a clear-cut definition of good and evil. Not only do we find the usual Disney stock plot devices of love between the classes, duty versus desire, and hero versus villain, but they are enacted in a creative manner that almost suggests some psychological affinity with the real world. One clever touch is that Reynard and his gang are portrayed by creatures of the night while Chanticleer (who brings up the sun) and his barnyard fellows are daylight creatures.

Even as downright villain, though, the wily fox continued to elude the Disney staff. It is likely that Walt's declining interest in making animated features was one factor in keeping this project on a back burner. Ken Anderson, however, periodically kept the project alive up until his recent retirement (summer 1978).

But Reynard in his many disguises (a blind man, a woman), tricks (stealing rings by kissing the King's hand, outwitting the Wolf), and adversaries (an egotistical and greedy Lion), did finally make it to the screen, after a fashion. All these items appeared in the animated *Robin Hood* in 1973.

Ollie Johnston, one of the original "nine old men," explains that the studio wanted to use a property with an all animal cast. Someone came up with Robin Hood, and the idea caught hold. "We used a lot of the story and character designs from Reynard in formulating *Robin Hood*." During production of the recent feature *The Rescuers*, a list of possible future projects included *Chanticleer* and *Reynard the Fox*. *The Fox and the Hound* is currently being animated, but its vulpine hero is quite the antithesis of the roguish Reynard.

Next on the Disney agenda is *The Black Cauldron*, a more adultish feature than the Disney animated product of recent years. Perhaps the time is ripe for the amoral if not immoral, fox to sneak onto the scene. The books are still in the library. Every now and then, they still get checked out.

Of course, Walt's central concern still remains: "The whole central character is a crook. That's what I'm afraid of." However, time shows that few things in which Walt Disney every expressed an interest were allowed to die. Even his dream of EPCOT is coming true.

Perhaps we should give Reynard the final word, looking down at the palace from atop a volcano at the end of the first script version: "Have no fear. I'll come back. I'll *always* come back."

Alice's Looking Glass

THE MOVIE ADVENTURES OF LEWIS CARROLL'S ALICE

David and Maxine Schaefer

Originally appeared in vol. 5, no. 5 (September/October 1981)

On a "golden afternoon" in July of 1862 a mathematics professor at Oxford University took three small girls on a rowboat ride down the Isis River. During this excursion the story that became *Alice's Adventures in Wonderland* was told by the extraordinarily imaginative professor, Dr. Charles Dodgson (Lewis Carroll), to his crew, who begged him "to begin it" and hoped "there will be nonsense in it." One of the children, Alice Liddell, urged the storyteller to write down his tale. He did—and in the process made the book, little Alice, and himself famous.

Lewis Carroll was a proper Victorian English gentleman with a fertile imagination and an absorbing interest in new "inventions." He was an accomplished photographer. His surviving photographs show an originality and style in the way he posed and clothed his subjects. He experimented with the use of an "electric pen," the typewriter, and other modern conveniences of the late 19th century. The first attempts at motion pictures were begun in the 1880s (Carroll died in 1898), and it seems logical that he would have had an interest in these new "moving pictures." Yet, there is no evidence that he did. His diaries, which he meticulously kept, made no mention of "moving pictures." Perhaps, being a snobbish English gentleman, he was unaware of the movies that the common folk were viewing at the time.

Ever since the publication of *Alice's Adventures in Wonderland* in 1865 and of *Through the Looking Glass and What Alice Found There* in 1872, the "Alice" books have been widely quoted, translated into over fifty languages, imitated, condensed, parodied, and analyzed. The "Alice" books' wide appeal has not escaped the attention of the motion picture maker. Over fourteen motion picture versions of *Alice in Wonderland* have emerged, each one trying in its own way to describe Alice's experiences.[1] All these known "Alice" films are happily in existence and viewable.

The fantastic happenings, the clever manipulation of words, the ingenious use of puns, the outlandish humor, the convoluted logic, and subtleties of Carroll are attributes that immortalize the "Alice" books. The poetry in the books has a lilt and meter that enriches the delicious nonsense. The classic illustrations of John Tenniel add their own brand of the fantastic to the tales. The books are a mild, humorous tale of a simple, literal-minded, Victorian girl. In reviewing the "Alice" movies, it is only logical to examine how well or poorly the filmmaker has brought these qualities of the books to the screen.

In the 1890s, film exhibitors in England discovered that Thomas Edison had neglected to take out foreign rights on his new invention, the Kinetoscope, and it wasn't too long before they began to manufacture their own machines. In retaliation, Edison refused to sell his Kinetoscope films to such entrepreneurs. Undaunted, Englishmen began making their own Kinetoscope films. Thus England's movie industry began. Among these early producers was Cecil Hepworth. By 1903, Hepworth was producing a hundred motion pictures a year for exhibit in nickelodeon-type theatres. In his villa at Walton-on-Thames, a dynamo operated in a scullery, a developing machine perched in the drawing room, drying films were draped over wires in the bedroom, and the cutting room was located in the bathroom. Among Hepworth's 1903 films appeared the first *Alice in Wonderland*.[2]

This remarkable 16-scene film compresses the book into ten minutes! The film has scenes of Alice shrinking, growing, and dissolving into nothingness. The sophistication of this technique for 1903 is surprising. It must have been the first time a human changed size by means of special effects on the screen. There are original, contrived segments such as underground scenes of Alice pursuing the rabbit through the small cramped burrow and scenes of the Duchess' baby turning into a lively black pig. The film does an exemplary job of portraying the astounding aspects of the books. The puns and the humor of Carroll, however, are missing. Not one line from the book appears in any of the captions. The production ends with a chase—Alice being chased by the children of Hepworth's employees (dressed as cards). It should be pointed out that the "Alice" books do not contain any chase scenes with Alice as the prey. However, many subsequent movie versions contain a similar chase scene—chase scenes being the "in thing" of the motion picture industry. In spite of its accentuating only the astounding aspects of the tale, the film was a success. Strange happenings were enough to keep box offices happy on both sides of the Atlantic.

The second effort at depicting "Alice" was produced by the Edison Manufacturing Company at their Bronx studios in 1910.[3] The fall down the rabbit hole simulates a ride on an amusement park slide, and size changes blatantly reveal the technique of film superimposition. Hepworth had done a more skillful job seven years earlier. A confusing scene, foreign to the books, shows the Knave of Hearts at a royal party, stealing the tarts. The only moments of Carroll's humor are captioned lines from the poem, "Speak Roughly." However, the film has some delightful touches, such as a miniature White Rabbit scurrying around Alice's feet in the Hall of Doors. Nonetheless, the film did poorly. Midwest agents, in fact, refused to distribute the film.[4] They complained it was too long (ten minutes) and uninteresting. The film is available today only because it was rendered onto 22mm format for home viewing.

In 1915 an hour-long version of *Alice in Wonderland* was produced by a gentleman named W.W. Young—a newspaperman who had never before made a motion picture.[5] The film, surprisingly, has no size changes, but still, moments of the fantastic abound. Lobsters in striped pants emerge literally from a pounding surf, a king-sized caterpillar sits on top of his oversized mushroom, and a woeful Mock Turtle sings "Soup of the Evening" atop a rock at the seashore. The fantastic is skillfully brought out through the use of elaborate costumes based on the Tenniel drawings, while beautiful outdoor locations provide the proper contrasting environment for these creatures. The humor of Carroll appears not only through the action of the film but also through extensive use of Carroll's dialogue in the title cards. Midgets were employed to portray the animals so that Alice would always be larger than her friends—an example of the meticulous care taken in the production of this film. Testimony to its acceptance is shown by the fact that it was still on display as late as 1921, and it was remade into two films for re-release in 1928.

Alice reached the sound screen in 1930 in the person of a young and beautiful Joan Bennett in a short, "Wonderland" dance sequence in the film *Puttin' on the Ritz*. The fantastic is heightened with a glamorous chorus line of cards—a spectacular entry into a new film era![6]

The first sound feature production of *Alice in Wonderland* (or to use its advertising phrase—the first *articulate* Alice)—was presented to audio hungry children during the 1931 Christmas season.[7] This film, produced in New Jersey, has no special effects, and Alice appears to have utilized a convenient mop as a wig! Articulate it is, however, with Carroll's lines spewing forth in a never-ending torrent. The tables are turned from the silent "Alices"—now the fantasy is gone, motion is nonexistent, and the dialogue overwhelmingly boring. The primitive stationary sound cameras dictated that there could be no actor mobility and no outdoor scenes. Even with these precautions, the thumping sound of the camera is often audible. The ultimate demerit of the film, however, is a scene that stretches even the bounds of Wonderland. Here, the White Rabbit confesses he stole the tarts to give to his love—the Duchess! A plethora of Carroll's words on a soundtrack cannot put Humpty Dumpty together again!

In 1933 Hollywood found *Alice*.[8] Paramount mobilized its stable of stars for bit parts, while it handed the starring role to young lady named Charlotte

Henry, "the final choice from 6,000 candidates for the part." *Movie Classic* magazine of January 1934 proclaimed Henry, their cover girl, the "luckiest girl of the year." Her future was in fact a different story. In good "Looking-glass" fashion, she started at the top and rapidly "progressed" down the ladder from starring roles in Grade A movies to supporting roles in Grade B ones. In the early 1940s, she abandoned Hollywood. In 1980 she died at age 67, still remembered by *Time* magazine's obituary as the girl who had played Alice with Cary Grant, Gary Cooper, and W. C. Fields in supporting roles.

The 1933 production remains the classic *Alice* motion picture. It utilized the most sophisticated techniques of the day to bring out the unreal and unexpected. There are four size changes, the near-perfect illusion of Alice going through the mirror, conversations with a leg of mutton and a pudding, and the use of live flamingoes as croquet mallets. Carroll's words are utilized, although many of his themes are left undeveloped. Charlotte Henry was too old for the part, and her interactions with her eccentric acquaintances do not have the force of that of the very young and proper Alice in the books. W. C. Fields as Humpty Dumpty, however, does bring out the full Carroll character, whose words mean exactly what he wants them to mean, "nothing more, nothing less," and Gary Cooper's White Knight has the pathos, humor, and the inability to stay on a horse of Carroll's original.

The Paramount Alice is an example the maturing of the motion picture industry. The talents of such notables as designer William Cameron Menzies and composer Dimitri Tiomkin are combined with those of the best actors and technicians. They took Lewis Carroll's story in hand and used their professionalism to create an entertaining version of the classic. However, it should have been better. The lighthearted, eye-twinkling spirit of the book doesn't make it to the screen.

The Paramount production includes an animated version of "The Walrus and the Carpenter." No credits are given for this cartoon, but it may well have been made by the Fleischer brothers, whose studio was controlled by Paramount. In any event, a scant four months after the release of the Paramount *Alice*, the Fleischer Studio released a cartoon that cast Betty Boop as Alice! Entitled "Betty in Blunderland," the influence of the New York locale of the Fleischers is evident with the route to Wonderland being via a subway station, and with shrinking occurring in a tavern selling "Shrinkola."[9] The fantastic is present throughout the production. Although Carroll's humor is nowhere to be found, the "What's going to happen next" spirit of the books does shine through.

Walt Disney had already called his early cartoon series "Alice in Cartoonland." So far as is known, however, none of these productions ever used any of Carroll's episodes. Disney's first attempt at animating Lewis Carroll's stories was a 1936 Mickey Mouse cartoon entitled, "Thru the Mirror." Disney had a field day combining Carroll's concepts with his own embellishments. Mickey climbs through a mirror, meets a talking telephone, eats walnuts and shrinks to the size of a (real) mouse, and is rescued from the King of Hearts by a gallant electric fan. The outstanding portion of the film is the dance of the cards. Here Mickey finds himself in the middle of a deck as the cards are shuffled and reshuffled in a brilliant display of animation. Carroll's characters have all been changed, but the essence of Alice's different world is retained, while Carroll's theme of humanized playing cards is carried forward by Disney to an unparalleled height. "Thru the Mirror" doesn't display Carroll's use of language—but the fantastic spirit of *Alice* is intact, and the film is outstanding.

The motion picture industry has always had trouble deciding how to represent characters that populate Wonderland. For the animal parts, do you use actual animals? In the Hepworth *Alice* the Cheshire Cat is a real cat, and the pig-baby is a very lively black pig. In the Paramount *Alice* the croquet mallets are live flamingoes. No one, however, has been able to inveigle a real rabbit to wear a coat and vest and look at his watch. Rabbits are costumed humans or an animated character. But in 1948 a new medium was introduced into the *Alice* film saga. Lou Bunin, a French puppeteer, had Alice an actual girl but the characters around her were puppets.[10] The concept should have worked—if only Mr. Bunin hadn't made each and every puppet a grotesque and evil-looking figure.

Disney tried to stop the showing of the Bunin *Alice* when it was exhibited just before his own feature-length Alice was to open. A sensible judge ruled that "Alice" was public property, and that anyone could display their "Alice" motion picture. Disney needn't have worried. The Bunin film did poorly and was no match for the ebullient Disney production.

Disney's 1951 feature film presents a Wonderland even madder than Carroll's.[11] Every scene is wilder that its predecessor. Seen one at a time, the Alice sequences are amusing—the growing episode in the Rabbit's house is a good example. Carroll's humor, however, is never really developed. In the Mad Tea Party, for example, Carroll provided a long discourse on the treatment of time. You shouldn't waste it, because it's a *him*. You shouldn't beat *him*—but be good to *him*—it will always be tea time. All Disney could get out of this was a watch that goes mad, shoots its insides out like missiles, and expires when stuffed with butter, mustard, and lemon.

There is humor in Disney's *Alice*, but it's Disney's humor, not Carroll's. The character that comes closest to Carroll's type of humor is the Door Knob ("one good turn deserves another"), ironically a character that is not a part of any of Carroll's work, but in tune with the talking telephone and rescuing fan of Disney's "Thru the Mirror." The fantastic in the film cannot be savored for all the commotion. Even Alice's changes in size come on in a raucous, tumultuous frenzy. The film ends with a frantic chase.[12]

A Popeye cartoon (made after the Fleischers had departed Paramount) has "Swee'pea" marching through a looking glass and falling down a golf hole.[13] The Alice character (Swee'pea) and the Rabbit ("Eugene the Jeep") are in constant jeopardy—a distorted reflection of Carroll's mild tales.

A visually beautiful motion picture version of *Alice* was produced in England in 1972.[14] The sets reverently follow the Tenniel drawings, while most of the dialogue is straight from the books. The film, however, suffers from major maladies—the irritatingly slow pacing of the production, and the ever-present ponderous, sugary sweet songs. Another malady concerns the costuming of the animal characters. To allow for the play of facial expressions and to provide a means for audience identification of actors (such as Peter Sellers), extensive facial makeup was substituted for the use of facial masks. The result is not the desired presentation of animals with human characteristics, but rather the presentation of bizarre humans.

The film is not humorous in large part because of its slow pacing. The presentation of the fantastic does not succeed. The lovable characters of the book now simply emerge as creepy humans, and Carroll's linguistic genius becomes submerged in a sea of abysmal songs.

The Bicentennial year produced the ultimate—a sexually aware Alice![15] The old story is hard to recognize in its new (un)dress, although most of the characters are there, unusual activities keep occurring, and much of the lighthearted spirit of the books is present. Relating this Alice to the little girl in Queen Victoria's England, however, requires an effort greater than "Believing six impossible things before breakfast."

A film, already released in Europe and surely heading for our shores, is a current Anglo-Belgian-Polish production entitled *Alice*.[16] The film is a very contemporary version of the classic and is completely characterized by humans. The White Rabbit is a jogger, the Queen is the Godmother of the Mafia, and the Lobster Quadrille evolves into a sensuous disco dance. A first reaction is a panning by the *London Daily Mail*. The United States may well find it great!

In adding up the score on how well the motion picture industry, in seventy-seven years of trying, has been able to bring Carroll's genius to the screen—the conclusion is that no one has really succeeded. Why? The motion picture's flexibility should provide the perfect platform for showing the humorous and the fantastic. Lewis Carroll could closely relate to children throughout his life. Perhaps the reason for the failure of motion pictures to successfully transfer the book to the screen is because no director of these films has retained the heart of a child. Our formula for the producer and director of the next "Alice" motion picture is to

"Fill up the glasses with treacle and ink
Or anything else that is pleasant to drink;
Mix sand with the cider and wool with the wine—
And welcome Queen Alice with ninety-times-nine."[17]

Notes

1. For a complete listing of film and television versions of the works of Lewis Carroll up to 1973, see "The Film Collectors' Alice: An Essay and Checklist," by D.H. Shaefer, in *Lewis Carroll Observed*, edited by Edward Guiliano (Clarkson N. Potter, 1976).

2. *Alice in Wonderland.* Produced and directed by Cecil Hepworth. Alice is played by May Clark, the White Rabbit and Queen of Hearts by the producer's wife, and the Frog Footman by the producer.

3. *Alice's Adventures in Wonderland (A Fairy Comedy).* Produced by the Edison Manufacturing Company. Alice is played by Gladys Hulette. The film has fourteen scenes. Edwin S. Porter is often incorrectly listed as the director.

4. Memorandum to H.C. Plimpton, Manager of Negative Production at the Bronx Studios of the Edison Manufacturing Company, from the Kinetograph Department, dated September 8, 1910. This correspondence is on file at the Edison National Historical Site, West Orange, New Jersey.

5. *Alice in Wonderland.* Produced by Nonpareil Feature Film Company, directed by W.W. Young, "picturized" by Dewitt C. Wheeler. Alice is played by Viola Savoy.

6. *Puttin' on the Ritz.* Starring Harry Rickman and Joan Bennett, produced by John W. Considine, directed by Edward H. Sloman, music and lyrics by Irving Berlin.

7. *Alice in Wonderland.* Commonwealth Pictures Corporation. Screen adaptation by John E. Godson and Ashley Miller. Directed by "Bud" Pollard. Alice is played by Ruth Gilbert. Produced at the Metropolitan Studios, Fort Lee, New Jersey.

8. *Alice in Wonderland.* Paramount Pictures, produced by Louis D. Leighton, directed by Norman McLeod, screenplay by Joseph L. Mankiewicz and William Cameron Menzies with music by Dimitri Tiomkin. Alice is played by Charlotte Henry. Supporting cast includes W. C. Fields as Humpty Dumpty, Edward Everett Horton as the Mad Hatter, Cary Grant as the Mock Turtle, Gary Cooper as the White Knight, Edna May Oliver as the Red Queen, May Robson as the Queen of Hearts, and Baby LeRoy as the Deuce of Hearts.

9. "Betty in Blunderland." Directed by Dave Fleischer. Animation by Roland Crandell and Thomas Johnson.

10. *Alice in Wonderland.* Produced in France at Victorine Studios by Lou Bunin. Directed by Marc Maurette and Dallas Bowers. Alice is played by Carol Marsh. Voices for puppets by Joyce Grenfell, Peter Bull, and Jack Train. The prologue has Pamela Brown as Queen Victoria.

11. *Alice in Wonderland.* Walt Disney Productions. Production Supervisor, Ben Sharpsteen. Alice's voice is that of Kathryn Beaumont, the Mad Hatter's is that of Ed Wynn, and the March Hare's that of Jerry Colonna.

12. This film was not a financial success at the time of its initial release. When re-released in 1974, the film had a better response, in part due to the college crowd's psychedelic interpretation of the *Alice* stories.

13. "Swee'pea Thru the Looking Glass." King Features Syndicate. Executive Producer, Al Brodax. Directed by Jack Kinney.

14. *Alice's Adventures in Wonderland.* Executive Producer, Joseph Shaftel; Production Designer, Michael Stringer; Producer, Derek Horne. Written and directed by William Sterling. Music by John Barry, lyrics by Don Black. Alice is played by Fiona Fullerton. Peter Sellers is the March Hare, Dame Flora Robson the Queen of Hearts, Dennis Price the King of Hearts, Sir Ralph Richardson the caterpillar, and Peter Bull the Duchess.

15. *Alice in Wonderland: An X-Rated Musical Comedy.* Produced by Bill Osco. Alice is played by Kristine DeBell.

16. *Alice.* Directed by Jacek Bromski and Jerzy Gruza, with Jean-Pierre Cassel, Sophie Barjac (as Alice), Suzannah York, and Jack Wild.

17. *Through the Looking Glass and What Alice Found There.* Chapter IX.

The Singing Screen

REMEMBERING THOSE MOVIES THAT NOT ONLY TALKED BUT *SANG* . . .

David L. Parker

Originally appeared in vol. 7, no. 2 (March/April 1983)

M-G-M's 1982 production of *Yes, Giorgio,* starring Luciano Pavarotti, a comedy about an Italian singer who falls in love with an American woman, marked an attempt to bring back that long-gone Hollywood era which began with Grace Moore and ended with Mario Lanza—the era of the opera singer films.

Before Grace Moore's popular breakthrough in 1934, there were several attempts to establish singers with operatic voices as screen idols. The first Metropolitan Opera star to work in Hollywood was baritone Lawrence Tibbett, who pioneered the acceptance of the American-trained singer in an arena dominated by the European-trained singer. An accomplished singing actor with phenomenal clarity of diction, Tibbett scored a personal success in *The Rogue Song* (1930). In this operetta—aided by deserts, palaces, a thieves' market, and Laurel and Hardy in M-G-M's first all-Technicolor film—the energetic Tibbett played a curly-headed Russian bandit costumed in olive green who sings of his love for the princess, even while being stripped to the waist, hung by his wrists, and lashed by Cossacks in front of her window. "Not only does the distinguished baritone endow the cinema with an important musical talent," wrote film critic Andre Sennweld, "but he also brings . . . a vigorous personality and an engaging acting gift." For his performance in *The Rogue Song,* Tibbett received an Oscar nomination for Best Actor in a leading role.

Although Tibbett was virtually the only singing member of the cast in *The Rogue Song,* in another of his 1930 films, *New Moon,* his co-star was the blonde soprano Grace Moore, who had achieved some success at the Metropolitan, on Broadway in an operetta, and in an Irving Berlin Music Box Revue. She had already made films such as the slyly titled *A Lady's Morals,* in which she, encased in high-waisted dresses with enormously full skirts, portrayed the legendary opera singer, Jenny Lind, "the Swedish Nightingale."

Great versatility was demanded of a singer who assumed a starring role in a film. Grace Moore wrote in her autobiography that her M-G-M bosses of 1930 assumed because she was trained in singing that she automatically was equally proficient in film acting and dancing. Moore's experience at M-G-M is similar to that of Evelyn Laye. After appearing in a British film version of Johann Strauss Jr.'s *Die Fledermaus,* Miss Laye, a soprano, was signed by M-G-M to play a ballerina in *The Night Is Young.* A dancing double was used for her in the long shots, but she undertook an agonizing crash course in ballet in order to look credible in the close shots.

At different times, in different films, Tibbett and Moore would be important in establishing the singer film in Hollywood. But their film together was released at the end of the first cycle of musicals when audiences were surfeited with filmed singing, and although *New Moon* received favorable reviews, it was not a success.

Neither was the film debut of the beloved lyric tenor, John MacCormack (after Caruso, the most famous tenor of his time). He was paid $470,000 in 1930 for 10 weeks of work in Fox's *Song O' My Heart.* In addition to oratorio and opera arias, used only in the foreign version, MacCormack sang songs chosen by the readers of *Photoplay.* Predictably the winners were Irish songs, which had sold well all over the world in MacCormack recordings—"I Hear You Calling Me," "The Rose of Tralee," and eight others. Records were available of MacCormack singing nearly all the songs in the film, and network radio, then in its infancy, was also used successfully to publicize the title songs of the singer films. The director, Frank Borzage, once cut away from MacCormack singing and did the sentimental "Little Boy Blue" as an illustrated song, but most of the film consisted of MacCormack being given a song cue and then singing. When the film was not a success, Hollywood decided that MacCormack "lacked sex appeal."

An endlessly repeated plot followed the vicissitudes of an attractive American nobody with a glorious voice who rises from obscurity to conquer Europe on the way to a triumphant debut at the Metropolitan Opera. The most successful use of this plot occurred in the comedy romance, *One Night of Love,* starring Grace Moore. It ranked fourth in popularity among all films released in 1934 and launched the operatic film cycle.

It was not an easy film to convince Columbia to produce. Harry Cohn's initial lack of courage was not unexpected. Popularity of a film with generous helpings of opera scenes are unprecedented. After having refused *The Merry Widow* at M-G-M in a dispute over top billing, Moore was rumored to have invested her own money in *One Night of Love* to convince Columbia to produce it. She appeared at her best in a role that emphasized her sense of humor and energetic personality. Her attractive appearance didn't hurt, either. As *Variety* observed,

"Grace Moore looks well singing in close-ups, and that's plenty." Academy Award nominations went to Moore, the film's musically knowledgeable director, Victor Schertzinger (who was also a composer), and to the picture, which was nominated as the best of the year. It was approved by many desirous of finding something to praise as an alternative to the risqué comedies and crime films to which they objected. Grace Moore was awarded a gold medal by the Society of Arts and Sciences for ". . . conspicuous achievement in raising the standard of cinema entertainment."

Prompted by Moore's box-office power, studios devised vehicles for other sufficiently glamorous divas with figures suitable for posing for publicity pictures in swimming suits. Paramount engaged the handsome brunette mezzo-soprano, Gladys Swarthout, and soprano Helen Jepson; Universal took an option on the services of Marta Eggerth; RKO put under contract the petite French coloratura, Lily Pons. Pons's first film, RKO's *I Dream Too Much* (1935), portrays a singer who forsakes her opera career for home and husband and ends the film singing to a toddler she is bouncing on her knee. On the way to this ending, Pons sings music from Verdi's *Rigoletto* at an audition, operetta songs by her composer-husband (Henry Fonda), which were actually written for the film by Jerome Kern, and the exacting aria "The Bell Song," from Delibe's *Lakmé*, which first brought stage fame to Pons. The bare midriff of her Indian costume revealed a moment that was truly visual: Pons's well-trained abdominal muscles rapidly working like a bellows to produce an elaborately decorated "vocal line."

Pons's demeanor exuded a sense of humor, which was exploited in her subsequent RKO films. As *That Girl from Paris*, an opera star who is a stowaway on an ocean liner, Pons sings a spirited swing version of "The Blue Danube" (which also gets the swing treatment in a Gladys Swarthout movie). In the now-obligatory ending, she triumphs in *The Barber of Seville* at the Met.

In the 1937 farce, *Hitting a New High*—actually an E-flat note above high C—Pons played a singer who attempts to launch her opera career by allowing herself to be discovered in the jungle as "Ooga-hunga, the bird girl." Wearing a feather skirt to obvious advantage, Pons also sings a showy aria from Thomas' *Mignon* and the "Mad Scene" from Donizetti's *Lucia di Lammermoor*, in which her flute-like voice is touching. But the scene RKO chose for the "Mad Scene" was a "big white set" which seemed to have come from a Fred Astaire–Ginger Rogers musical.

In her debut film, Paramount sensitively cast Gladys Swarthout—the epitome of chic—in a musical western derived from an old stage melodrama, *Rose of the Rancho*. Despite its ingratiating refusal to take itself seriously, it broke no records at the box office. Swarthout's second film, *Champagne Waltz*, debuted at Radio City Music Hall to celebrate Adolph Zukor's silver anniversary in the movie business. Her union with an American jazz band leader (Fred MacMurray) was symbolized by the simultaneous playing of "The Beautiful Blue Danube" and "Tiger Rag" in one of Billy Wilder's earliest U.S. scripts. The film was a box office flop.

Swarthout later was teamed with Jan Kiepura, a tenor of daunting vigor, who was already popular from films made in Europe, in which his heavy makeup made him resemble a robust Bela Lugosi. Choosing a title suspiciously similar to that of Grace Moore's pioneering success, Paramount launched Kiepura and Swarthout in *Give Us This Night* (1936). With its script drastically cut by the time of release, the musical marked a "first," in that all of the music in it (of an opera of *Romeo and Juliet*) sung by Swarthout and Kiepura was written for the film by Erich Wolfgang Korngold in an attempt at a compromise between pop and classical idioms. While Swarthout's acting style was flat, Kiepura's was scenery devouring. As a team, they proved to be no threat to Jeanette MacDonald and Nelson Eddy.

What makes *Give Us This Night* memorable today are scenes like the one of Kiepura as a jailed fisherman, belting out an aria to the sole accompaniment of an impromptu chorus of townspeople instantly assembled outside the jail. As a fisherman (or the taxi driver or tour guide he impersonated in earlier films), Kiepura kept his cap on. Whatever the correctness of etiquette of keeping his hat on while singing, it saved him the nuisance of wearing a wig over his bald spot.

True to form, Kiepura wears a cap as Romeo in a balcony scene with Swarthout as Juliet. Apparently she has been directed to gaze at Kiepura in silent admiration—although she stays so far away from him that it looked more like terror—as he widens his magnetic eyes and bellows high notes in his "bel-canto" style, as if portraying Red Buttons on amphetamines.

Swarthout's third film, *Romance in the Dark* (1938), showed her comfortably in an aria from one of her opera house successes, Bizet's *Carmen,* and in a duet with porcelain-voiced John Boles from Rossini's free operatic adaptation of the Cinderella story, *La Centerentola.* Although almost two-thirds of her drastically shortened film with Kiepura had singing scenes, in her final film of her Paramount contract, *Ambush*—a bank robbery "B" picture for which her salary represented a fourth of the budget—Gladys Swarthout did no singing at all.

༃

But my story is getting ahead of itself. All this activity concerning opera on film brought to a head a concept that had been practiced in the movies since their very inception: exploiting the talents and the reputations of "legitimate" singers in the more dubious vehicle of the film entertainment. Opera singers appeared in sound films as early as the Paris International Exposition of 1900. By 1903 in Britain and by 1906 in Brazil, France, and Germany, producers were making films of less than ten minutes duration of singers in arias from *Tosca* and *Mi-*

gnon with the accompanying sound on disc or cylinder. When the opera-loving Edison showed his Kinetophone publicly in February, 1913, he included a scene from one opera, *The Chimes of Normandy,* and a duet from *Samson and Delilah.* Although Edison's films did not prove lucrative, in October of the same year a film industry trade paper reported that San Antonio audiences liked sound films of snippets of *Carmen* and *Faust.*

Three years later, in the spring of 1916, Webb's Singing Pictures offered an act from Gounod's *Faust* with the world-famous bass, Leon Rothier. Webb's second film presentation in January 1917 included an act from *Carmen* in which the diminutive baritone, Guiseppe Campora, repeating one of his most successful stage roles, sang the "Toreador Song." In the audience was the world's most famous tenor, Enrico Caruso, who had been seen in a 1908 sound film himself. With both Webb's *Faust* and *Carmen* the recorded voices of the singers were accompanied by an orchestra present in the theatre.

Kellum's Talking Pictures premiered in May, 1921 at New York's Town Hall to good reviews and a two-week run with a program of shorts, which included a tenor singing an aria from Flotow's *Martha* and a bass singing an aria from Gounod's *Faust,* and also the surefire number of the minstrel show *basso profundo,* "Rocked in the Cradle of the Deep." This not only allowed the singer to show off his ability to hit low notes (an acrobatic feat attempted by only the most intrepid), but also demonstrated the sound system's ability to reproduce them. When the great Viennese bass, Emmanuel List, was first heard in a sound film, it was not in the music of Wagner for which he was famous, but in another minstrel show bass standard, "Many Brave Souls Are Asleep in the Deep," which he may have sung in vaudeville.

Another bass, Leon Rothier, also sang for Phonofilms, a sound-on-film system which debuted in 1923. Among its single-camera performances were solos by two sopranos, Marie Rappold and Bernice de Pasquale, "late of the Metropolitan," and *Rigoletto* arias sung by Luella Paikin. Phonofilm's competition, the ultimately victorious Vitaphones, were produced in great numbers. Among hundreds of 10-to-20-minute offerings, was one Mary Lewis, a "soprano of the Metropolitan Opera," singing "Dixie" in a southern mansion garden setting. An elegant Warner Bros. advertisement of the time, labeled "Stars of the Vitaphone," put a portrait of world-famous opera singers such as Beniamino Gigli side by side with one of Rin Tin Tin.

Competing in kind with Vitaphone's sound-on-disc were the short-lived Vocalfilms, which debuted in June, 1927 with lyric tenor Guido Ciccolini, formerly of the Chicago Opera, who had made recordings for Edison and Victor, and the longer-lived M-G-M sound-on-film "Movie Acts." By 1930, more than 50 of them had been filmed, many in the Cosmopolitan studios in New York. The shorts, part of a program of variety acts supporting the feature, included some featuring Italian bass Tino Ruffo, singing from Verdi's *Otello* and Russian soprano Marie Kurenko singing an aria from *Faust*.

Jesse Lasky, in charge of production at Paramount at the time of the first boom of sound musicals, in 1929, hired Nino Martini, a tenor who could hit a high 'F' above 'C.' Martini appeared as a gondolier in a color sequence in the revue film, *Paramount on Parade* and then in a 1931 short. When film musicals lost their appeal, Lasky did not renew Martini's contract. By the mid-thirties, the movie opera boom reached such a frenzy that Lasky placed Martini under contract again and built three films around him, the best of which was undoubtedly *The Gay Desperado* (1936).

Rouben Mamoulian, who directed *The Gay Desperado*, offered this romp as an alternative to *Faust*, which Lasky had proposed for his tenor star. The film was a delightful comedy about an ineffectual tenor pitted against a Mexican bandit (Leo Carillo). The bandit emulated Chicago gangsters by terrorizing the populace in an ancient touring car, and by kidnapping a sister singing act (which visually suggested Kate Smith times three) from a radio station.

Mamoulian had staged opera in Rochester, New York, before working in movies, and he kidded established conventions of the singer film, as when audiences of extras and bit players are emotionally moved by a singer's performance virtually to the point of epilepsy. An obviously Russian Mischa Auer improbably impersonated a Mexican bandit, who suffered exquisitely each time Martini sang, whether it was the almost-inevitable "Celeste Aida" or songs appropriate to the setting such as "Estrellita" and "Ciento Lindo."

Jeanette MacDonald's opera career came years after she made films in which she sang opera: *Romeo and Juliet* in *Rose Marie* and *Faust* in *San Francisco* (1936). Her usual co-star, baritone Nelson Eddy, a former member of the Philadelphia Civic Opera, looked upon his film career as promotion for his concert tours, which he never let filmmaking conflict with. His film acting style is understandable, if one sees it in the stance of a recitalist, standing in the curve of a grand piano, pressing his elbows to his sides, as if to protect broken ribs. His ringing baritone emanates from a military uniform worn so rigidly that one imagines it conceals a corset.

Another, more affable baritone who starred in the first film released by the new Twentieth Century Fox, *Metropolitan* (1935), was Lawrence Tibbett. His voice was called by *Time* as "Still the best vocal instrument Hollywood has presented." And the review went on to claim that Tibbett was heard to better advantage in it than when he had been in *The Rogue Song* and *Cuban Love Song* in the early thirties. *Metropolitan* didn't tax Tibbett's acting abilities, but let him sing arias from *Faust, Carmen,* and *I Pagliacci,* and recital encores associated with him such as the spiritual, "De Glory Road." *Time*'s review of *Metropolitan* went on to praise its "lighthearted, literate" screenplay, but warned: "till opera movies can be written about persons other than the opera singer, the form will remain affected, feeble, monotonous." The *New York Times* critic wrote similarly of a James Melton film of the same season: "It merits praise chiefly for its failure to fawn completely upon the [Metropolitan Opera]" and objected to the obsequiousness of the operatic film cycle: "Opera, when placed in the fellowship of Sacred Cows, can be made very dull indeed." The warning proved justified. Although 1937 was a banner year for opera singer films in Hollywood with nine major releases, not one of them was among the most popular of the year and production sank to one to two a year.

The success of *One Night of Love* had led to a Grace Moore series in which she was teamed with such leading men as Melvyn Douglas or Cary Grant; and she sang everything from Mendelssohn's "On Wings of Song" to Cab Calloway's "Minnie the Moocher." These films were not greeted with the universal applause which followed her at first. Earlier her ebullient personality and pleasant voice had made her a favorite with movie audiences throughout the world but by 1938 Columbia would pay her a settlement rather than risk making another film starring her.

Tibbett refused such a settlement from Fox and was cast instead in a "B" movie, *Under Your Spell*. It was an indifferently written screwball romantic comedy in which Tibbett sang arias from *Faust, The Barber of Seville*, and the title song. It was the first American film directed by the newly arrived Otto Preminger.

There soon was a backlash in Hollywood against the plethora of opera in movies. A *Merrie Melodies* cartoon, "The Woods Are Full of Cuckoos" (1937), depicted such celebrity caricatures as "Lily Swans" and "Grace Moose." Scriptwriters had opera singers murdered in *Find the Witness, Moonlight Murder*, and *Charlie Chan at the Opera* (the latter casting Boris Karloff as an opera basso). Later Karloff murdered opera singers himself in Universal's Technicolor horror film, *The Climax* (1944), inspired by the success of the studio's remake a year earlier of *The Phantom of the Opera*. In *Goin' to Town* (1935) Mae West was amusingly subversive as the widow of a cattle rustler trying to break into society by singing the female lead in a fashionable production of Saint-Saëns' *Samson and Delilah* (for which Paramount exercised its film rights to the opera).

Producer Joe Pasternak developed the European film formula of opera-singing teenage girls into a greater success in America with his discoveries: Deanna Durbin, Jane Powell, and Kathryn Grayson. It was he who produced *The Great Caruso* (1951), the last real success of the singer film to date. In this quasi-biography, which ran for 10 weeks at Radio City Music Hall, arias from 18 operas were sung by Mario Lanza, a cherub-faced tenor who achieved stardom by singing 23 times during the film's 109 minutes.

A group of prominent opera singers of the time lent an aura of authenticity to *The Great Caruso* (1951). They included Dorothy Kirsten (who appeared as herself in a benefit show cameo number in a Big Crosby vehicle, *Mr. Music*, the same year) and Blanche Thebom, a Metropolitan Opera mezzo who had already appeared briefly with baritone Leonard Warren in one of those typical forties pseudo-biographies of songwriters, *Irish Eyes Are Smiling* (1944).

Lanza's success also prompted one of the last of the vehicles showcasing an opera singer, *Melba* (1953). It begins with the American Met opera star, Patrice Munsel, as the famous Australian soprano. She begins with an Australian song, "Comin' Through the Rye" for Queen Victoria and ends with Mendelssohn's "On Wings of Song." In the trifling flashback story between these—a throwback to the Grace Moore films of the thirties—she sings arias from eight operas and a popular song. In the early fifties M-G-M built films around the former Metropolitan bass Ezio Pinza, who had become a mature sex symbol as the male lead in *South Pacific* (1958). M-G-M cast him as an opera star romancing Janet Leigh in *Strictly Dishonorable* (1951) and a foreign ruler courting Lana Turner in *Mr. Imperium* (1951), but was unsuccessful in turning Pinza into a film star.

Paramount fared no better casting Met baritone Robert Merrill as the city slicker in *Aaron Slick from Punkin Crick* (1951), who sang "Marshmallow Moon" to Dinah Shore. The period of Hollywood musicals with opera singers as principals ended with the major change in the public's musical taste in the mid-fifties. Nevertheless, the singer films contain some repertoire that was never otherwise recorded by the artist—Wagnerian soprano Helen Traubel singing "Stout-hearted Men" and "The Leg of Mutton Dance" in *Deep in My Heart*.

Such productions have left us visual and aural documentation of many interpretations by many artists worth preserving, capturing the visual aspects of the individual singer's art, appearance, bearing, use of dramatic mime, and unique personality. Among them were the brave pioneers who risked jeers from their peers to participate in motion pictures, and through the movies—arguably the most influential form of communication of the time—to introduce millions to classical music.

Red Alert

IMAGES OF COMMUNISM IN HOLLYWOOD

J. Thomas Brown

Originally appeared in vol. 2, no. 3 (January/February 1978)

American films over the years have portrayed Russians as either mad, misunderstood, heroic, or menacing. Wars and "cold wars" have greatly contributed to these varying images. This article examines these shifts in attitudes within the context of the entertainment film.

ॐ

Between 1930 and 1950, Hollywood alternately manipulated its portrayal of the Russian and periodically ignored him as the need arose. These needs were determined not so much by the movie industry itself, but by responses to larger forces which influenced the industry: public opinion, finance capitalism, and government policy. Exemplifying the flexibility of this portrayal is the distinction between a "Russian" and a "Communist" which the Hollywood films maintained during this period. Superficially, a Russian lived in Russia, was usually a simple man of the earth, and despite the governmental system of Russia, he loved his motherland. The Communist, however, lived in the Soviet Union, was dedicated to the party, and was motivated by an unthinking loyalty to an ideology. While distinctions became more elaborate and were altered to suit individual story plots, these character portrayals remain consistent in Hollywood's stereotypic treatment of the Russian and the Communist between 1930 and 1950.

To the American public, Russian society was largely an unknown quantity. There were no cultural ties or traditions which linked the two peoples; and certainly, the antagonisms of the governments had not aided in clearing the perceptions of one people toward the other. An American history text of the period, analyzing the position of the Soviet Union during the inter-war decades, mentioned the success of the first Russian Five Year Plan and noted that the United States had extended diplomatic recognition to the Soviet Union in 1933. These were events of noteworthy importance, yet the author continued, "still, Russia

263

was far off and could be discounted as a bit oriental in its ways and values." Indeed, Russia was "far off" and more than alien to a majority of the American people, as well as the Hollywood movie industry.

There were few films made during the inter-war period which dealt with the Soviet Union. American films which were produced were largely studio made and employed German actors to provide a Russian environment for the Hollywood stars of the film. Cinematic depictions of Russia, while they did not ignore the disasters of Tsarist rule, hardly embraced the victory of the Bolshevik Revolution. Plots of the notable films of the period were remarkably similar. Each of these movies culminated in a romance between a Russian Communist and his or her class enemy which drove home to audiences the humanly destructive aspects of the Bolshevik's class hatred. *Mockery* (1927) was a melodrama concerning Russian life in Siberia at the time of the Russian Revolution. The plot revolves around Sergei, the hero, who briefly falls under the revolutionary influence of the Bolsheviks, but finally surrenders his life for his "class enemy," the Countess Tatiana. In *The Tempest* (1928), a Bolshevik soldier once scorned by his love, Princess Tamara, for his peasant origins, saves Tamara from execution during the revolution, kills his Bolshevik leader, and escapes the country with his love. Yet another contribution of the period, *The Last Command* (1928), was "inspired by the experiences of a Russian general who fled to this country after the revolution in his own land." After a melodramatic biography of this broken man who once had achieved the height of power and prestige in Tsarist Russia, the movie ends with the old general dying in the belief that the Russia that once was had returned to power again.

These early "historical" portrayals of Russia have very real consistencies, not only in plot, but also in the portrayal of characters and personal values. Inhuman class hatred transcended by love is present. Recurring themes in *Mockery*, *The Tempest*, and *The Last Command*, are their setting in revolutionary Russia and the subsequent disasters, both political and social, reaped by the Bolshevik Revolution on the population. These produce a universal desire by the heroes or heroines of these films to flee Bolshevism, even at the expense of leaving the homeland forever. The revolution and Bolshevism are portrayed as being illegitimate and a "good" Russian will not succumb to either. It is this "Russian" portrayed to the cinema audience which represented all that was good and desirable about Russia.

Formal diplomatic recognition of the Soviet Union by the United States for the first time since the old regime was toppled in 1917 produced no radical transformation in the public attitude toward the Soviet Union. However, directly related to this recognition, subtle changes did occur in the film industry's portrayal of Russians and Communists. Certainly, official government policy toward the Soviet Union softened at the diplomatic level, but Communism remained the subject of criticism in the Hollywood film. Yet a light, often satirical skirmish with the Communist was substituted for the early more blatant attacks on the Bolshevik Revolution. Now the "mad Russian" who was overly fond of music, ballet, and vodka was added to the list of stereotypes. In addition, this list included fixed concepts of a Soviet Union which consisted of collective farms, the secret police, and purges. Despite the Motion Picture Production Code of 1930, Americans were still presented with distorted portrayals of Russians and Communists which violated the spirit and intent of the code. Soviet society was depicted in a less than favorable light despite the efforts of the Hollywood industry at self-regulation. The feature film was designed to entertain, and there was little entertainment value or profit potential in films which dealt with the Soviet Union, or any other substantive concern of the period. Entertainment directed at achieving the broadest popular appeal was the goal which the Hollywood industry strove for in the production of the feature film. The serious depiction of a contemporary event or the confrontation of an issue might very well result only in the alienation of a segment of a potential audience.

As a result of this practice, Hollywood's treatment of contemporary events, notably the rise of fascism in Europe, was disappointing at best. The predominant European political movement of the century was virtually ignored by the Hollywood movie industry. Minor anti-fascist films were released by independent producers, but it wasn't until 1939, when, *Confessions of a Nazi Spy* was released that Hollywood committed itself to a major production depicting the increasing international threat of fascism.

The split in, and indecisiveness of, the public mood accounts in large part for Hollywood's evasiveness. Even after the Munich crisis of 1938, when the fascist dictatorships were recognized as threats to world peace, American filmmakers were reluctant to deal substantively with portrayals of the growing threat. Isolationist sentiment in the United States, international pacifist groups, and the American government's policy of neutrality all acted as restraining forces. No major Hollywood film company acted outside the sanction of national policy or its assessment of public sentiment.

In the spring of 1940, only after the fall of France and the United States government's announced commitment of "all aid short of war" to England, did the Hollywood industry rally to the Allied cause. Through the industry's creation of the Motion Picture Committee Cooperating for National Defense was the government able to encourage and stimulate production for the national emergency. As events in Europe and the North Atlantic brought the United States closer to war, the early objectivity and neutrality which newsreel producers had maintained began to crumble. The United States army and naval authorities brought pressure to bear on motion picture producers to delete anti-war sentiment from films which employed army or navy backgrounds.

As the Hollywood industry made its first halting attempts to deal with the political and social concerns of the day, both the Russians and the Communists continued to be slighted on the screen. Barraged by more than a half century of radical attacks in politics and in the media, the public's knowledge and perception of Communists and Communism remained highly distorted. Anti-Communism had played a significant role in American political rhetoric since the Bolshevik Revolution and peaked in the declaration of the Nazi-Soviet Pact in 1939. Despite the conditions which molded the American public's assessment of the Soviet Union, the serious portrayal of the Russian and the Communist remained conspicuously absent from the pre-war Hollywood film. During the period from 1939 to 1941, the dominant issue confronting Americans was the question of neutrality or intervention in the European conflict. For the moment Russians and Communism were not issues of immediate concern.

The notable pre-war exception to this hands-off attitude Hollywood maintained was the release of *Ninotchka* in 1939. The movie was described as an "amusing piece of raillery," which depicted Marxist trained Russians who succumb to the temptations of the Western world. The story revolves around three Bolshevik agents who are sent to Paris for the purpose of selling confiscated royal jewels. These are simple men who are unaccustomed to the West. Naturally, they quickly surrender to the decadent temptations of Paris. Their superiors send a fourth agent, Comrade Ninotchka, to take charge after learning of the misconduct of the original mission. Ninotchka is mannish in behavior, cold in temperament, and dedicated to the revolution. However, she too falls to the lure of Western life, aided by the love of a Western capitalist who transforms her into a woman.

This Hollywood portrayal of Communists in a Western environment demonstrated to audiences the natural openness and feeling of the West in contrast to the repression and denial of human emotion in Soviet life. Billed as a light satirical comedy, *Ninotchka* received rave reviews with only token objections voiced about the film's content. The film poked fun at the unfashionable Russians in gay Paris, and in the process reinforced traditional stereotypes of the period: Communism was a failure because it couldn't produce human beings or stylish clothing. Moreover, the Russian was more buffoon than beast, and the Soviet state could hardly be taken seriously as a world power.

When critics of Hollywood films policies, Senator Bennett C. Clark and journalist John T. Flynn, complained to a Senate committee that Hollywood had produced anti-Nazi films (*Confessions of a Nazi Spy*, and others) of a serious melodramatic nature depicting the German as a formidable enemy, but no anti-Communist films; Nicholas Schenck of Loews leapt to the defense of the industry by pointing to *Ninotchka*.

This pattern was maintained in a series of films produced in which Hollywood continued to ridicule the Communist and his alleged lifestyle. *He Stayed for*

Breakfast (1940), "a gay spoof of Communist camaraderie that flourished in Paris before the war," is the story of the male lead, a Communist, and the female lead, a capitalist, meeting when the hero flees the Parisian police and hides in the glamorous woman's apartment. On the basis of this weak plot, the film's finale shows the hero renouncing Communism: "a government without people," according to the heroine who won him over. *Public Deb No. 1* (1940) was critiqued as being even less artless than *He Stayed for Breakfast.* The plot focuses on a young heiress who is indoctrinated into the Communist fold by her butler. At the conclusion of the film, it takes the love of the hero and the invasion of Finland to bring her back to capitalism. Finally, *Comrade X* (1940), a "satire which takes malicious delight" in running down the Communist system, is based on the story of an American who falls in love with a streetcar conductor in Moscow, convinces her of the evils of her country, and flees the Soviet Union with her to the hope and promise of the free world. This film was to be the last anti-Soviet film released for several years. Within six months the Soviet Union and the United States would be allies in arms, fighting international aggression and tyranny.

While American public opinion was not immediately swayed, Hitler's June 21 attack on the Soviet Union effected an overnight revolution in United States policy toward that country. On June 21, Stalin had been a ruthless, cynical, self-seeking aggressor; on June 22, Stalin was an ally. President Roosevelt promptly unfroze credits that had been held in the United States to keep them out of Soviet hands. He declined to invoke neutrality legislation so that American ships could transport provisions to the Soviet Union. Not only were sweeping promises of aid made to Stalin, loans became immediately available to the Soviet Union. On November 6, 1941, after having determined that the defense of the Soviet Union was essential to the security of the United States, Roosevelt announced a grant of Lend-Lease aid to the new allies.

To many Americans outraged by the brutality and inhumanity of fascism, the Soviet Union immediately acquired some measure of moral legitimacy simply by being an ally in a larger anti-fascist coalition. From 1942 until the end of the war the Hollywood film industry would serve as a potent instrument of United States foreign policy. After the United States' entry into the war, Americans began to focus their attention on the differences, rather than similarities, between Hitler's Germany and Stalin's Russia in a popular effort to cement the wartime alliance between the two peoples. This effort was exemplified by the emphasis on assertions that the United States and the Soviet Union were in many respects similar; both were anti-imperialist and both had a revolutionary past.

A new Soviet Union was to emerge from the mobilization of the United States film industry. Russia was depicted on the Hollywood screen as an essentially progressive, economically innovative society which was still in the process of overcoming the chaos of the revolutionary and depression periods of the previous decades. The fighting determination of the Russian people contributed to the belief that the government held the allegiance of the populous, and that the government was essentially guided by the popular will. Generally, Americans were informed by the media that despite censorship, poverty, and lack of political freedom, life in the "new" Soviet Union seemed to be improving after the upheavals of the 1930s. The Soviet system was demonstrating that it could perform well under stress, and that a bright future lay ahead. The Hollywood industry was even encouraged to emulate and respect the wartime model provided by the new Soviet ally.

The fact that the Hollywood studios drastically altered their portrayal of Communism and saluted the Russian alliance was not surprising given the direction of the OWL. Soviet Communism, the purges, and the Molotov-Ribbentrop Pact were forgotten in the name of the alliance, as were the traditional stereotypic portrayals of Russians. As films about Russians, their role in the war, and the "united nations" theme of the alliance began to appear in American theatres, audiences learned of brave Russian women soldiers, happiness in the villages and collective farms, and how the dictator Stalin had become lovable old "Uncle Joe." Americans were exposed to a wide range of very favorable images of the Soviet Union which totally overshadowed critical themes and issues.

The Russian military performance was, by far, the single most powerful factor in the development of a favorable Russian image in the United States. The reports emanating from the Soviet Union, as well as the screen portrayals of Hollywood actors, uniformly depicted a heroic Russian resistance to the Nazi aggressor. Notable contributions to this "brothers in arms" category include: *North Star*, *Mission to Moscow*, *Song of Russia*, and *Battle of Russia*, as well as numerous B films of lesser importance.

৵৽

The most notable wartime depiction of the new Soviet Union came in the film *Mission to Moscow* (1943). The movie plot followed the book of the same title by former Ambassador to the Soviet Union, Joseph E. Davies. Real characters were portrayed and real names used in the film to give the appearance of a trustworthy documentary newsreel. The film portrayed the Soviet government in a favorable light. Within this context the film alluded to the hint of romance between Davies' daughter and a dashing Russian officer, as well as offered Davies' explanation of the infamous Soviet purge trials of the 1930s (they rid the Russian nation of subversive pro-German and pro-Japanese sympathizers) as an authentic and justifiable domestic policy. The movie took gross liberties with the reality of Soviet life, but it was nonetheless an important social document for wartime America. It was the first genuinely sympathetic screen portrayal of the Soviet allies, and as such marked a major reversal in cinematic perceptions of the Russian state. Yet, despite the movie's release and the billing of an all-star cast, the film was not a box office success.

North Star (1944) was a movie which paid tribute to Russian resistance to Nazi aggression. Specifically, the film alleged to portray the events surrounding the Nazi occupation of a typical Russian village. Highlights of the film included Russia's maintenance of a scorched earth policy, and Russian children fighting as guerrillas against the Nazi occupier. Samuel Goldwyn of MGM maintained that the film demonstrated that the average Russian was very much like an American. This was amply demonstrated by the character portrayal of Walter Brennan, who played a "homespun, earthy philosopher . . . (with a) counterpart in every American town."

Played against the background of war torn Russia, *Song of Russia* (1944), a musical "scored" by Tchaikovsky, told the story of an American symphony conductor's marriage to a beautiful Russian girl and all the trials and tribulations of their wartime romance. Within the context of Hollywood's world war, Russia was depicted as happy, well fed, and religious in this feature film which offered pleasant vistas of life in the land of Russia. Finally, a "Why We Fight" film made for the army and entitled, *Battle of Russia*, was released to the American public in 1943. The film briefly outlined the Russian people's flight for freedom from the 12th century to the 20th century. Film critic Bosley Crowther found the movie to be a brilliant documentary, full of "grim and moving scenes."

World War II ended abruptly with faith in the wartime alliance between the Soviet Union and the United States peaking in 1945 as the war came to a decisive conclusion. However, there remained a variety of explicit as well as implicit pre-alliance attitudes and perceptions deeply rooted in the American consciousness. American fear and distrust of the Soviet Union (the government and the ideology of Communism) was never completely eradicated by the media's wartime portrayals of the "new" Russia. Prior to the war's end, a number of highly placed Americans, both in and out of government, were suggesting that the Soviet Union would be the new enemy; a threat to peace and successor to Germany as an international aggressor.

Attitudes and animosity hardened rapidly after the victory in 1945. Post-war policy confrontations between the United States and Soviet Union in Europe heightened tensions between the two powers. The political inflexibility of both nations produced the cold war and imperiled the peace and post-war cooperation between the two allies.

Cold war foreign policy necessitated that Russia be labeled the enemy by America's leadership. The American people were encouraged to transfer their hatred of Hitler's Germany to Stalin's Russia. Stalin became the new Hitler, dictatorial, ruthless, and easily capable of ideological (if not armed) confrontation. The firm but likable "Uncle Joe" of the wartime alliance became a cold war tyrant. As had been the case in years prior to the war (particularly 1939–1941), Americans once again began to casually and deliberately distort similarities between the Nazi and the Communist. Their ideology, Soviet and German policies, authoritarian controls, trade practices, and most importantly, the personalities of Hitler and Stalin were perceived as being one and the same.

Russians all but disappeared from the American screen from 1945 to 1948. The Soviet Union's absence from the post-war film, remarkably similar in nature to their pre-war absence, was a phenomenon unique to the movie industry. The cold war controversy, particularly concerning American foreign policy toward the Soviet Union, was the subject of widespread and intense national debate. The film medium alone did not reflect the mass obsession with cold war foreign policy toward the Soviet Union in the American media.

Once the issues in the cold war conflict between the Soviet Union and the United States were safely identified, Hollywood, as it had in 1942, atoned for its inactivity by enthusiastically joining the cold war battle, only this time it produced numerous exposés of the "Communist menace." Unlike the "brothers in arms" films produced during the war, these post-war exposes did not deal with Russia or the Russian people. Instead they emphasized the alleged ideology of Communism in the Soviet Union and concentrated on the nature of the international Communist menace. Actors portraying the Russian were no longer representing the common Russian folk, but were the Communist party elite, espionage agents, or dupes of the Communist conspiracy. The Communist was portrayed as, and intimately identified with, the most negative reference groups available to the American film audience: the violence-ridden underworld of organized crime, gangsterism, and the Nazis.

Fears of Communist infiltration were reinforced by the domestic environment of 1947. Labor disturbances in the movie industry produced charges that they were "Communist inspired." The Motion Picture Alliance for the Preservation of American Ideals had been formed in 1944 by Hollywood writers and actors in order to prevent the growing impression "that the industry is made up of, and dominated by, Communists, radicals, and crackpots." A board member of the Alliance, actor Adolphe Menjou, charged that Hollywood was one of the major centers of international Communist activity in the United States, and that a number of Hollywood films had been influenced by Communists within the industry. Prompted by charges from outside, as well as from within the industry, the House Committee on Un-American Activities proceeded to investigate the Hollywood movie industry for evidence of alleged Communist infiltration or activity. Despite a brief and feeble attempt to resist this investigation, the film industry as a whole correctly concluded that public opinion would not support (ideologically or financially) an uncooperative attitude by the movie industry.

In October 1947, Adolphe Menjou publicly urged the Hollywood producers to begin a concentrated effort to distribute anti-Communist films, erroneously predicting that these would be both popular and financial successes. The Hollywood industry, cognizant of the public's awareness of the HUAC hearings (as well as those of the Tenny Committee in California), had developed a very keen sense of its own vulnerability. In an effort to respond to this organized pressure, the industry moved quickly to clear itself of charges of radicalism and Communist influence. Studio owner, Louis B. Mayer, told the HUAC in November of 1947, that MGM was already in the process of preparing an anti-Communist film entitled *Vespers in Vienna*. Although this film wasn't released until 1949 (under the title of *The Red Danube*), Mayer also reported that the studio was preparing to reissue its pre-war "anti-Communist" film, *Ninotchka*.

The anti-Communist thriller which in all probability had the largest impact on the American public was *The Iron Curtain*, a film which dealt with the Igor Gouzenko spy case. Released in 1948, the film is notable not for the subject of its message, but because it was the first attempt by Hollywood to venture into the realm of anti-Communist propaganda. The release of the film indicated that American public opinion had emerged from a controversial stage to favor a tougher stand against the Soviet Union. Hollywood had determined that this type of entertainment would be accepted by a majority of the moviegoing public. Soviet officials in the film were portrayed as ruthless totalitarians who were obeyed by mindless dupes. The movie was, "an out and out anti-Soviet picture," in which "entertainment seems a secondary concern," and whose message was to "hate the Red." Moreover, the similarities between *The Iron Curtain* and *Confessions of a Nazi Spy* were significant. Both were spy thrillers based on allegedly factual events, both were based on scripts by the same author, and both were narrated in a documentary fashion.

These anti-Communist films contained their own message, and to a limited degree a unique story line. Each film made its own assessment of the nature of the "threat" and the "enemy." In *Walk a Crooked Mile* (1949), an American scientist gathers top secret data for the Communists, while the FBI is portrayed as being ineffectual. The film gives the impression the United States' counter measures against Communists are weak and ill prepared. In the spy thrillers, *I Was a Communist for the FBI* and *Big Jim McLain*, the American Communist Party is depicted as being run by a gang of clever hoodlums. The leaders are in close touch with Moscow, and were contemptuous of native party members. Communists were indeed willing to commit murder in order to demonstrate their methods to wavering comrades (*Woman on Pier 13*), or for asking awkward questions at study meetings. In *Whip Hand* (1951), Communist agents were able to maintain a huge sanitarium full of human guinea pigs. Communists were cold and calculating, as depicted in *I Was a Communist for the FBI*, and did not display any emotion or guilt. They were not expected to form any personal attachments, and as a discipline of party membership they were expected to establish a personal isolation from outsiders. This cruel inhuman social behavior was depicted in the films *Whip Hand* and *Woman on Pier 13*, where as a function of discipline even love was not tolerated. Consistently throughout these films, audiences were impressed with the contention that in one way or another, all Communists were neurotic and many were pathologically vain with "martyr complexes."

One critic of the new anti-Communist film was "exasperated by the rosy, ritualistic domesticity of the films . . . where Mom is in charge, and Uncle Joe is doing all those terrible mean things simply to spite her." These movies were cheaply produced routine thrillers which demonstrated no real intellectual animosity toward an ideology or a political system. After all, the industry, despite the nature of the crusade, was producing a commercial commodity whose success depended upon entertainment appeal, not its message.

Hollywood existed on a highly visible pedestal with a great potential to exert influence on public attitudes. This pedestal, however, was extremely vulnerable and kept the Hollywood industry conscious of markets, foreign policy, and public opinion. Fear as well as shared conviction produced the anti-Communist films of the post-war period. Hollywood attempted to establish its loyalty in the face of mounting criticism of the industry by producing these propaganda vehicles which were neither successful nor profitable. But government pressure and public attitudes necessitated productions which conformed to the national mood.

Popular opinion toward the Russian created by the movies, other media, and governmental policy both reflected public attitudes and helped form them. On the other hand, it is essential for Hollywood to determine the limits of public opinion in order to achieve commercial success and maximum market potential for each film. The Hollywood film, only after the bounds of public opinion have been safely identified, offers a commercial product which visually reinforces stereotypes and images that conform to what a majority of Americans want to see.

On the other hand, social scientists and social commentators have long attested to the power of the motion picture medium to influence the attitudes, values, and opinions of a viewing audience. Undoubtedly the manner in which Russians and Communists were portrayed in the Hollywood feature film affected the way in which the American public perceived these people. Despite the relatively unorthodox nature of the material, the commercial feature film provides an invaluable source of information for the historian who is interested in Soviet-American relations. The Hollywood film was a product which was particularly important to the American public, because it graphically portrayed the rest of the world to a uniquely insular and isolated American community in the years prior to 1945. Before the aggressive post-war role assumed by the United States and the growth of international communication and media networks, Hollywood quite often served as the "window on the world" for millions of American who attended movies.

The Rise and Fall of the California Motion Picture Corporation

Geoffrey Bell

Originally appeared in vol. 5, no. 3 (May/June 1981)

Born of a wide-eyed enthusiasm, the California Motion Picture Corporation began in San Francisco in the forward-looking year of 1913. The rich potential of the new medium attracted Comstock mining heir Herbert Payne, whose tastes were formed by the best of Broadway, advertising entrepreneur Alex Beyfuss, who envisioned a financial bonanza, exposition organizer George Middleton, whose background was steeped in California history, and beautiful actress Beatriz Michelena, who drew all three men into her skein. Even though their California Motion Picture Corporation studio is virtually unknown today, and its history is little noted in movie annals, it was a company initially able to compete successfully with the very giants of the industry.

The new company made an impressive entry into the theatrical feature film field in 1913 with its first major motion picture, *Salomy Jane*. Hailed as "America's Greatest Picture Play," the film was greeted by accolades from the press. "A Winner!" headlined a glowing review in the *New York Dramatic Mirror,* which went on to praise the "reel after reel of gorgeous scenes—undulating rows of hills, towering mountains threaded with winding roads, rivers breaking their way through primal forests . . . This is creating an environment in the best sense," the *Mirror* continued, "for . . . it is as if the director adopted the most plausible of all means of convincing an audience that his people really lived in California in the 'Days of '49.'" San Francisco critic Walter Anthony could hardly contain his enthusiasm: "If seven years of dramatic reviewing is competent to qualify judgment," Anthony wrote, "I will not hesitate to say that in theme, dramatic treatment, and in cumulative, growing and finally thrilling interest, *Salomy Jane* is a masterpiece of picturesque dramatic construction." The outdoor camerawork for this adventure movie romance greatly improved on the painted backdrops, net foliage, and canvas rocks which the theatre used to represent outdoor scenes. Capturing nature itself, the camera placed its characters squarely in their environment, prompting the critic of New York's *Motion Picture News* to declare: "Photographically the whole production is of the highest order," and to crown *Salomy Jane* as "a bright star" among "the lesser constellations." The persuasiveness and grace of Beatriz Michelena in the title role also won compliments from the press, as did the stalwart contribution of the leading man, House Peters, well known for his appearances opposite Mary Pickford and other major stars. *Salomy Jane* also launched the career of Jack Holt, who daringly rode a horse over a high cliff into a rushing torrent!

Hopeful Prospects

In New York, at this time, a group of hopeful unknowns—Jesse Lasky, Cecil B. DeMille, and Samuel Goldfish (later Goldwyn)—formed a film company and attempted, with difficulty, to raise a mere $26,500 to get started in the business. In San Francisco, however, the CMPC, backed by prominent leaders in the financial and social worlds, asked for one million dollars—and got it! Ironically, Lasky and DeMille, sharing experiences with popular audiences, had considerable on-the-spot working knowledge of show business; Lasky in vaudeville and DeMille on the legitimate stage, whereas the organizers and the board of directors of the new CMPC were totally inexperienced in either the theatre or motion pictures. The producer-director, George Middleton, had been active in mounting automobile shows. The general manager, Alex Beyfuss, came from the commercial calling of promotion and publicity, with a sideline in accounting—as well as in the mysteries of double-entry bookkeeping. The president of the CMPC, Herbert Payne, came from a non-business background, giving as his occupation "clubman," and sometimes "Capitalist." The trio initially had been drawn together by business interests in real estate and automobile sales, then became attracted to the motion picture as an advertising medium for their enterprises and later for its exciting opportunities for themselves. Being where they were, it was natural that the romance and colorful history of their state should provide the themes and motifs for their company, hence the epithet, the "California Motion Picture Corporation," and also that they should be enthused by the advantages of the San Francisco Bay area for motion picture production. Within a close radius lay a wide variety of photogenic scenery which could represent sites the world over. San Francisco itself was a flourishing theatrical center. Its numerous legitimate, stock, musical, and vaudeville theatres provided a plentiful supply of trained actors and stage technicians. There was a literary tradition extending from the time of Robert Louis Stevenson and Mark Twain to the more contemporary Frank Norris and Jack London which could supply story material attractive to the masses about California and the West, as well as a European heritage in painting, architecture and decorative arts to provide artistic visual effects.

The new company, then, in addition to the evident natural, economic, and cultural advantages of central California, had the other necessary assets—the bank account of Payne, the ambitious drive of Beyfuss, and the persuasiveness of Middleton—to make it a leader in motion picture production. Still ahead for the CMPC staff was that final issue all filmmakers have to face: *distribution.* Marketing movies and getting them into theatres to earn continuing profits was the ultimate test of every producer. He must sell his product—or be vanquished. Yet, officials of the CMPC, with all the exuberance of youth, proudly emblazoned on their logo: "Our Trade Mark, we have determined, shall, whenever flashed on the screen, immediately connote the ultimate achievement in picture producing art."

Buoyed by such ideals, it was of utmost importance to secure a high-calibre technical staff. To aid Middleton in the production and direction of theatrical films, the company engaged stage-trained professional actors and directors William Nigh and Earle Emlay. Another associate was Edwin B. Willis (later of M-G-M), whose background in theatre design gave him the professional expertise to weave available visual components with striking effectiveness. The photographic consultants were Frank Padilla, together with Robert Carson and Arthur Powelson, whose knowledge and understanding of the camera, together with the employment of the finest equipment, enabled the CMPC to achieve the highest quality photographic image. Perfect cinematography was by no means common then. In fact, eyestrain had been a common complaint of earlier nickelodeon patrons in their attempts to follow a hodge-podge of murky shadows, glaring light flares, mismatched exposures, and out-of-focus scenes.

Location Shooting

The next task was to find the ideal location on which to build their studio. After scouting the entire state, the team of Middleton, Willis, and Padilla found their site in Marin County, one of the choicest areas in central California. Its coastal mountains ran down among valleys, meadows, and woodlands to the many islands, sheltered coves, and inlets of San Francisco Bay to the east, and to the rocky headlands and sweeping beaches of the Pacific Ocean to the west. To the south lay the Golden Gate, beyond which San Francisco gleamed like a mirage between sea and sky. With nature at its most prodigal, Marin County could provide an unrivaled variety of locations for motion picture work, as it was an easy distance to vast evergreen forests, the great Central Valley with its plains, rivers, and lakes, and beyond, the titanic Sierras mantled with eternal snow. With the advantages of these scenic resources at hand, the CMPC built their production plant with spacious stages to take advantage of natural light, plus offices and dressing rooms, a professionally equipped laboratory, projection and editing rooms, and outlying buildings to shelter the rolling stock. The lot had ample space for exterior sets, and in addition, the CMPC technicians designed and constructed a highly authentic, three-dimensional set in the Big Tree country of the Santa Cruz mountains, just south of San Francisco. This was one of the first movie "Western Street" sets, and was so convincing that it was later used for exterior scenes by producer Thomas H. Ince, directors Cecil B. DeMille and Marshall Neilan, and stars Mary Pickford, William S. Hart, and Douglas Fairbanks.

In preparation for its "California" themes of the old West, the studio staff consulted university and museum archives to insure historical accuracy in settings, furniture, props, and costumes. They assembled genuine Indian artifacts, equipment from early mining days, original ox carts, Spanish carettas, and prairie schooners. Nor did they overlook that vehicle which was to become classic in the movie Western: the Wells Fargo stagecoach. A veteran Wells Fargo driver, Dan Bart (or Barth), was hired to handle the reins, while equestrian events were supervised by Don Nicholas Covarrubias, a bonafide descendant of the conquistadores, who in his earlier days had been a real U.S. Marshall.

Old Californiana and the new studio's organization and equipment were first combined in a newsreel series, "The Golden Gate Weekly," under the direction of Earle Emlay. Of its many insights into California life and activities, one issue was of unusual anthropological interest —a film record of the indigenous Indian, *Ishi,* the last of his tribe, who had lived with nature, completely apart from the white man.

Feature Films

"The Golden Gate Weekly" was useful as an initial exercise, but the important task ahead was to channel the Company's entire energies into the making of feature-length films. The setting for its photodramas of early California was already established. Similar themes from the old West were being filmed with success by a neighboring company across the Bay in Niles, Alameda County, by the Essanay Film Manufacturing Company. The Essanay Westerns, however, were only one reel in length and were aimed for the nickelodeon trade; whereas the CMPC were designing five-reel productions for high-class legitimate theatres. Even so, the feature-length film, running from sixty to seventy-five minutes, as contrasted with the one-reel film of between ten to fifteen minutes, represented an enormous gamble for the producers of 1913–1914. Both investors and exhibitors questioned whether the feature film's greatly increased costs, with its diminished audience turnover, could produce profits comparable to the short, inexpensive, nickelodeon pictures. At this time of uncertainty, it was inevitable that moviemakers would look to successful theatre forms for their models. Sustaining audience interest for an entire performance of well over two hours, establishing an immediate bond between performers and patrons, and reaching the hearts of wide audiences had, from earliest times, been among the special artistries of the legitimate stage.

"Long before the movies . . . live stage performances provided Americans with virtually all their entertainment," wrote theatre historian Robert C. Toll in *On with the Show* (1976). Between 1850 and 1920, Toll observed, "Drama belonged to the people, the common people. It reflected their desires, needs, tastes. . . . And in small towns all around the nation people gathered to have traveling performers make them laugh, cry, shriek with fear, gasp with incredulity, and sigh with longing." The plots of popular plays might already be well known, and the audiences never tired of seeing reenactments, in terms larger than life, of the triumph of the human spirit—of life, not as it is lived, but as it *should* be lived. A performance by Joseph Jefferson in *Rip Van Winkle* at some rural "opera house" could well be the theatrical highlight of an entire year. Families might economize on a diet of bacon drippings and grits for a month in order to purchase their precious tickets to the gallery to hear, in *The Count of Monte Cristo,* Edmund Dantes triumphantly proclaim, "The World is Mine!" or to feel the nobility of self-sacrifice as evidenced by the downtrodden in such spectacles as *Quo Vadis?* and *Ben Hur.*

These performances depended on the spoken word, not available to filmmakers of the silent era, yet the special form of the melodrama had other gifts for the movies. In addition to themes of proven audience appeal, it could demonstrate means of achieving attention-getting visual effects and eye-appealing spectacle; it could offer plots told less by dialogue than by action and pictorial episodes; it could provide examples of appealing characters; and it could show how to link scenes so that they built to rousing climaxes.

The CMPC management had yet to avail themselves of all the advantages offered by melodrama, particularly for the movie Western, when it made its first venture into the still undefined feature film format with *The Pageant of San Francisco.* An episodic series of photographed tableaux, its picture of the frontier West was enlivened with caballeros led by Don Nicholas Covarrubias, bands of Indians, processions of monks, Yankees in broad-brimmed hats, and senoritas in mantillas. This piece, adroitly combining in one package the appealing virtues of patriotism, religion, and nostalgia, was actually only a preparation for an even grander production based on the momentous discovery of gold in California.

Yet, the ambitious plan to produce *Gold!* was abandoned.

The board of directors evidently was reluctant to risk the expense of a production on an epic scale if it were based on a script by an unknown writer. In addition, reconstructions of early Sacramento and San Francisco during 1848 to 1949 and large crowd scenes would tie up an enormous amount of capital. Here was the company's initial confrontation with the moviemaker's dilemma: the desire for artistry versus the high costs of materials and labor.

A sure-fire source of immediate earnings from box office returns lay in the star system. In central California, a constellation of talent was available from the many theatres, vaudeville houses, and cabarets operating in San Francisco, Oakland, San Jose, Sacramento, and other cities. San Francisco's Alcazar Theatre alone could boast a galaxy of stars of international renown, including such favorites as Theodore Roberts, Marjory Rambeau, Bert Lytell, Bessie Barriscale, Forrest Stanley, Laurette Taylor, Edmund Lowe, Alice Brady, Mary Boland, and Lon Chaney, all of whom went on to notable careers in motion pictures. Others in the area, yet to be "discovered," could have included the likes of Ruth Roland, Jean Hersholt, Lois Wilson, John Gilbert, Monte Blue, Irene Rich, Aileen Pringle, Frank Fay, Lou Holtz, Al Jolson, or Eric von Stroheim.

Yet out of all these stellar personalities, the one making the biggest impression on the CMPC management was "The California Prima Donna," Beatriz Michelena. This Latin-American *artiste* had been successful primarily in musical comedy. Her father and dramatic coach, Fernando Michelena, had been a leading tenor with San Francisco's Tivoli Opera Company (although it was whispered that Beatriz was not really his daughter but his "protégé"). Michelena also recently had married director Middleton, whom she had captivated when she sang at one of his automobile show entertainments. On Middleton's not impartial urging, her screen test proved to be in all ways photogenic, disclosing—in addition to her evident Latinate beauty and grace—that quality which might well be that *rara avis,* an emotional actress of magnetism, intensity, and passion.

This raven-haired enchantress soon assumed all CMPC female starring roles and in time became virtually the studio manager. As a result, the company scrapped its initial plans for historical scripts in favor of romances. All the early California historical material of museum quality became mere background props for love stories. Projects originally designed to advertise the attractions of the state were redesigned to advance the career of the "star." Thus, instead of action-adventure stories bursting with the power and energy of California's lumbering, mining, shipping, or farming operations, the CMPC pictures became idylls of the wooing of a wistful maiden by a gallant suitor amid the flowers and sunlight of an idealized "Golden West." To obtain such stories, the CMPC turned to an eminent author, one whose short stories about Gold Rush days in California (the period in which the CMPC had heavily invested) could provide suitable story material—Bret Harte. Already one of his stories had been dramatized as the well-received stage play, *Salomy Jane*, (in the mold of the Broadway success, *The Girl of the Golden West* (1905) by San Francisco–born producer David Belasco). With this as a model, the Company negotiated exclusive rights to all of Harte's work. To insure authenticity, they engaged his daughter, Jessamy, as historical consultant.

Stories of Old California

Enthused by this new story source (supplying that quality known in the trade as "class") and by the presence of Michelena (adding that attribute known later as "sex appeal") the company embarked on its first Bret Harte adaptation, *Salomy Jane*. On the wave of the success of this pictorially handsome Western, Michelena and co-star House Peters went on to appear in other CMPC pictures, but strangely, Jack Holt, whose work was so dashingly executed, so ideally suited for the role of the Western hero, and with so much box office potential, went totally unnoticed by the management. But then, the CMPC was not looking for a rip-roaring action-adventure hero, but rather a romantic type to pair with Michelena.

Salomy Jane's triumph with the critics meant that it set the standard and style for future CMPC stories of old California: *The Lily of Poverty Flat, The Rose of the Musty Pool, A Phyllis of the Sierra, The Passion Flower, The Heart of Juanita, Just Squaw, The Flame of Hellgate*. Beatriz Michelena starred in every one of these feature films, and their feminine titles indicate that they depicted a romanticized old West and events whose outcome hinged ultimately on the matrimonial fate of the heroine. Bret Harte seemed ideal as a source of story material in view of his skill in evoking the atmosphere of California's "Days of '49" and in creating picturesque character types. Yet, he wrote short stories, not novels, and this genre rarely had the breadth of vision, the texture, or the complex plot development of the full-length drama. Harte, in fact, had attempted to write plays, but only one, *Sue*, ever reached the stage and that had only a limited run. His *Salomy Jane* owed its success on the stage to the crafting of playwright Paul Armstrong. With its story material confined to adaptations of short stories by Harte, the CMPC Westerns tended to be drawing room romances set in sylvan surroundings. For all their technical artistry, they never attained the box office appeal of the movie Westerns made by the neighboring Essanay studio in Niles.

Other Films

The CMPC operated as an acting group, alternating its performers in a succession of different plays and in different characterizations. This stock company system provided opportunities for ensemble playing and unified style, at the same time enabling the players to appear in a wide variety of roles. For example, Michelena was able to balance her portrayal of the Western heroine (a wholesome, guileless, straightforward "girl of the golden West") with other, more complex types, such as a youthful street dancer of central Europe, a New York evangelist, a maiden of feudal Germany, a flirtatious Italian diva, and a typical American housewife. For example, in *Mignon* (Autumn, 1914), based on a poem by Goethe, Michelena played a teenage waif who fell in love with an 18th century nobleman. In *Salvation Nell* (Summer, 1915), she appeared as a battered woman of the Bowery in a film version of Ned Sheldon's famous play. This emotional drama set forth an outcast's struggle from out of the depths of degradation to the heights of religious redemption. *Faust* (early 1916) represented another big change in style, for Michelena played Marguerite—a symbol of virginal purity—in this adaptation of another Goethe classic. In *The Woman Who Dared* (Spring, 1916) the actress switched to playing a coquette—a Princess of Italy—in a spy thriller of international intrigue. *Mrs. Wiggs of the Cabbage Patch* (December, 1914) provided Michelena with the role of the demure ingenue, Lovey Mary. *The Unwritten Law* (Autumn, 1915), on the other hand, was a story of family heartaches and the star appeared as a young American married woman torn between love and duty. Michelena's performances, then, brought to the screen some of the rich acting tradition of the repertory theatre, presented with the technical virtuosity of film.

The expressive, even tragic, quality of her acting justified the CMPC's original expectations of Beatriz Michelena as "The Bernhardt of the Screen." The critics were at one with their praise, judging her performances as the equals of the greats of the New York stage. The *New York Dramatic Mirror* critic felt her portrayal of "Salvation Nell" gave "the character the force it had in Mrs. Fiske's remarkable portrayal. That it has such force is our compliment to Miss Michelena." The same journal, reviewing *Mignon,* found it "hard to imagine a person more estimably fitted to portray the difficult character of this wild child of nature and to do it in such a manner as to subtly suggest the heritage of noble lineage."

Emotional roles also were the forte of Nazimova at Metro and of Pauline Frederick at Famous Players, yet even with the competition of their expensively advertised films, Michelena's *The Unwritten Law* more than held its own in the affections of audiences by virtue of the star's tour de force performance. "Miss

Michelena's work on the witness stand . . . is the most real and convincing emotion I have ever seen in pictures," wrote playwright Edwin Milton Royle, "so free from exaggeration that it approaches artistic perfection. It is a very great triumph." Other critics raved about her talent and the flawless quality of the CMPC movies, which a London reviewer felt was as good as the best produced anywhere. "The Italian atmosphere hovers over every situation," he wrote, "and the actors, particularly Beatriz Michelena, impart additional color to this remarkable illusion. Her acting throughout the film is marked by extraordinary 'grip,' and a full appreciation of the dramatic possibilities of her part. She plays with all the Southern fire and intensity. The story . . . is first-class entertainment, excellently presented—a long, sustained thrill."

Why It Failed

The CMPC soon found itself out of step with the maturing movie business. Reveling in such reviews as: "To sum up, this is a picture in which there are no flaws. It is wonderful. It goes into the exclusive class which we can recommend to any exhibitor, anywhere, as an absolutely certain success," the studio management expected to continue production on a sound financial basis, proceeding on the assumption that if their films excelled in photographic quality, artistic *mise en scène,* and acting authority, their photoplays also would equal those of their competitors in earning power. Yet, while the CMPC films were extensively—and expensively—advertised in the leading trade journals, they were not being exhibited at the popular showcase movie houses, which were now almost entirely monopolized by the big-studio New York–Hollywood combines. The studio also faced growing competition from the new movie capital to the south and the new types of movie fare Hollywood found most profitable.

The CMPC, in its deference to the theatre, tended to rely too much on traditional dramatic pieces, so that even its contemporary stories were several seasons old: *The Woman Who Dared* (1916), a story of pre–World War I days in Europe, already was dated by the time it was released during the War when audiences were beginning to demand fare like *To Hell with The Kaiser,* which capitalized on newspaper headlines. *The Unwritten Law* (1915), a contemporary story of domestic conflict, made a good profit, but lacked the smashing box-office appeal of such artistically inferior films as Cecil B. DeMille's *Don't Change Your Husband,* or *Why Change Your Wife?,* concoctions that bordered on the salacious, and as historian John Fell observed, "combined social comedy with scanty costume." So while Hollywood was learning to crank out money-making films about divorce and other mildly controversial subjects, the CMPC expended previous funds on such esoteric adaptations from the classics as *Mignon*

(1915), and *Faust* (1916), both written by a German using German themes at a time of great anti-German hysteria during the War.

With its artistic level and technical competence on a parity with rival film companies of the day, although lacking in Hollywood-style stories and stars, the CMPC had the will and the energy to survive. Its greatest nemesis—and one which haunt every filmmaker then and now—was the business of having their films widely distributed and repeatedly exhibited to generate box office profits. In forming the CMPC, Middleton, Beyfuss, and Payne expected, as independent producers, to enjoy artistic autonomy. Making the films was one thing, but there was still the thorny problem of finding a sure means of having their films exhibited on a national basis. An earlier producer in the San Francisco Bay area, Gilbert M. Anderson, had a sure market for his Essanay "Broncho Billy" pictures because of his company's strong ties with major national distribution combines. The CMPC had gambled that superior pictures would automatically result in wide audiences. In their innocence, they allowed Lewis J. Selznick, general manager of World Film Corporation in New York, to convince them that he could distribute their pictures so effectively that they would be playing in the best show houses from coast to coast. Unknown to Beyfuss and the management of the CMPC, however, Selznick's position with World Films was by no means as important or as secure as he made it out to be. Selznick may have been a super salesman, but he was no match for other, far more experienced movie distributors. Movie tycoons Adolph Zukor, William Fox, or Carl Laemmle, for example, all had begun in the business, not by making films, but by showing them. They had learned their trade from the ground up, working in penny arcades, nickelodeons, and storefront movie houses. Through this actual, day-by-day contact with the public, they had gained a keen sense of what audiences would pay to see. In contrast, Selznick had little show business experience, while his promises of widespread and lucrative distribution far exceeded his ability to deliver. The aspiring CMPC could not have foreseen that Zukor's, Fox's, and Laemmle's small-time operations would prosper mightily and grow into the powerful Paramount Pictures, Twentieth Century Fox, or Universal Studios; and that Selznick's vaunted World Film Corporation, the exclusive distributor for the CMPC pictures, would be forced out of business within a few years. As a result, the company, operating as an independent, with no assured markets for its products nor a dependable national distribution system, was in a fatal predicament. Beyfuss, out-maneuvered at the movie marketplace, lost the CMPC bankroll and was axed. But not in time.

Like other similarly disadvantaged independent film producers, Middleton attempted to market each release separately after the Beyfuss-Selznick fiasco. This marketing system was called "states rights," which meant that state or area distributors acquired for a flat fee the right to show the movie in their territory.

If the picture was popular, the distributor, not the studio, reaped the profits. Such limited returns were not enough to maintain the studio operation. The last hope of the CMPC was a Western, *The Flame of Hellgate* (filmed, Spring of 1917), but when director Middleton called "Cut" on its final fade-out, the Company's whirring cameras were silenced forever.

The ultimate concession to fate came later when a devastating vault fire destroyed the total production of the CMPC—thus depriving future generations of that superior body of work which distribution problems had closed to the public of its time. Long search, however, has brought to light some film footage from *The Flame of Hellgate*, which was incorporated into the documentary film, *Those Daring Young Film Makers by the Golden Gate*, directed by the author. The film clip depicts a parallel action sequence. In one progression of events, "Forty Niners" organize a rescue posse, while simultaneously in a cabin, hero William Pike battles menacing Andrew Robson, as heroine Michelena escapes from the fray. These bits of live action are all that remain today to bring, across the years, glimpses of some of those whose lives were lifted up and given special significance because of their part in the initial definition of the feature film.

The story of the CMPC presents insights into just what it meant to make a film at a time when the many small independent studios, often in areas other than Hollywood, were striving for expression . . . studios that were a little different than those which later came into prominence under the astute guidance of a Zukor, Fox, or Laemmle. The events surrounding the rise and fall of the CMPC also can give some understanding of the commitment and professionalism required to sustain a motion picture career. Those in the company who viewed the CMPC as a commercial enterprise found that the movie business is a stern taskmaster demanding more than a lust for quick profits. Both clubman Payne and opportunist Beyfuss found themselves cut out of any glittering financial spoil; both, in time, were reported suicides. Middleton resiliently bounced back, utilizing his talents and imagination to further an expanding and less chancy automobile business. That Circe, early career-woman—or a bit of both, Beatriz Michelena withdrew to Iberia, sustained by remittances from her American bank accounts.

However flawed, the California Motion Picture Corporation had a sense of destiny. Its initial work contributed significantly to the format of the full-length feature film (only later defined following the acceptance of D. W. Griffith's *Birth of a Nation*; its Westerns brought to the screen, as rarely seen before, the freshness, space, and authentic beauty of the great West; and its production values placed it high among those pioneers whose work elevated the movies from a mere arcade pastime to the status of a new and lively art.

Walt Disney and "The Gremlins"

AN UNFINISHED STORY . . .

John Cawley Jr.

Originally appeared in vol. 4, no. 3 (Spring 1980)

During the World War II years, Disney developed a number of films that explicitly faced modern times and had a firm foundation in the contemporary world. Among these were features such as *The Three Caballeros, Victory Through Air Power*, and *Saludos Amigos*; shorts in the mold of "The New Spirit" and "The Spirit of '43"; and various training films.

Fantasy, of course, did not die; it adapted. Disney chose this period to plan a timely feature that would also be a timely fantasy: *The Gremlins*.

What are Gremlins? Their origin is as mystery-shrouded as their habits. During World War II they sprang up in the vocabulary of the British RAF. As one press release described them: "If he can ride the wings of your dive bomber tearing at 400 miles an hour toward a target; if he bores holes in your petrol tank and freezes your machine gun when you are about to bring a Nazi to bay; or if he uses your compass for a merry-go-round, then he's a Gremlin."

These imaginary imps, latter-day offspring of the homeland of leprechauns, Robin Hood, and Merlin, were first brought to Walt Disney's attention while he was preparing his personal propaganda film, *Victory Through Air Power*. In July of 1942 an unpublished story entitled *Gremlin Lore* was sent to Walt by a member of the British Information Services. Its author was young Flight Lieutenant Roald Dahl (later to become known as a popular author of children's books, a screenwriter, and the perpetrator of those remarkable short story collections—*Kiss Kiss* and *Someone Like You*), serving at the British embassy in Washington, DC.

It may have seemed natural to Dahl that the movie producer renowned for magic would be a likely prospect for turning Dahl's story into film. Recognizing a problem—Gremlins were little known outside the RAF and the British populace—Disney was taken with the idea and plunged into preparation. By September of '42, the studio was at work both on the proposed film and on the American popularization of Gremlins. But even as Disney began to work on the Gremlins, the Gremlins began to work on Disney. Problems developed.

In a letter dated September 1st, Dahl mentions some ideas on illustrating his story, which was to appear in *Cosmopolitan* as part of the Disney drive for greater Gremlin publicity on this side of the Atlantic. He states that his "chief," Air Commodore H.N. Thornton, would be visiting the Studio to discuss control of the film. It seemed the Air Ministry was insisting on "the RAF having the power to say no to anything that is done." As Disney did not enjoy being told how to make movies, this caused friction. But given Disney's interest in the film, and the fact that profits from all merchandise and promotions would go to the RAF, the provision became Clause 12 of the contract, signed in October of that year.

Then came a more surprising problem: Gremlins became a fad. Virtually unknown in July, September saw Gremlin articles springing up everywhere. It started with *Newsweek, Time,* and *The Christian Science Monitor;* by the end of the year, *Collier's, The American Weekly,* and even *The Reader's Digest* were featuring articles. And to increase the dispersion, Disney realized that he did not own the sole rights to the imps.

Not since Oswald the Rabbit had Disney found himself with a creation that he couldn't protect from massive use by others in the media. Many of the new articles carried pictures of what Gremlins looked like—a particular vexation, since the studio had not yet developed the feature's visual concept.

In a call to the art editor of *Cosmopolitan,* Disney asked for some extra time to develop illustrations for Dahl's article. The director asked for sketches by Sept. 15th, to which Disney responded, "We couldn't possibly set the character in so short a time." Walt noted that everyone seemed to have his own idea of what Gremlins looked like. He mentioned a recent newspaper article reporting Gremlins "riding on our Flying Fortresses—in other words, there is an American branch of Gremlins."

This problem of visual conception became more apparent when, in an interview, Dahl told the *Washington Daily News* that "Disney has tried 12 times to draw the right picture and hasn't gotten it yet. But it will come."

By October, the world knew that Disney and Gremlins were going to join in a new feature film, maybe. Louella Parsons announced that it was going to be a "fascinating movie." Bob Hope, joking about how Gremlins ruined his recent *They Got Me Covered,* responded when asked what Gremlins were: "Didn't you read about the Gremlins? Disney is going to make a movie out of them." As if association with Disney was description enough.

On October 21st, real work began with the opening of a story charge number at the Studio. This now meant that the film would start having serious money spent on it. Disney also set up plans to go to England to get firsthand knowledge of the Gremlins for the film (a trip that never took place). It was also, confusingly, announced that the "Gremlins" would be a segment of *Victory Through Air Power*, not a feature on its own.

Work progressed in November. Sketches of the characters were being shot for publicity purposes. Also, Dahl flew out to the Studio to assist in planning. As stated in a Studio press release: "Dahl is an authority on these little fellows, who wear suction boots so that they can ride the wings of planes doing 400 miles an hour, and will give Disney benefit of his knowledge of them gained from personal experience as well as that of scores of other RAF pilots."

In a quote from an interview with Virginia Wright of the *Los Angeles Times*, Dahl commented that "He comes onto the Disney lot with very definite ideas about the appearance of Gremlins. Their make-up is not to be left to the imagination of Disney artists." This interview also provides the first hint as to the type of film: a live action film in which "only the little fellows themselves will be animated."

This gauche reminder to Disney that his control was limited came at a bad moment, for that same month Cecil B. DeMille announced that he was putting a Gremlin sequence in a film he was currently working on, adding yet more pressure to a production that was mounting up costs as fast as problems.

One bright spot was the generally good reception to the test reel done in November. Those who remember the reel recall that it was mainly live action footage of planes with Gremlins running about. Another plus point was that United Artists had expressed an interest in releasing *Gremlins*, after having signed to release *Victory Through Air Power*. So the Studio had a charge number, and advisor, a test reel, and a releasing agent. The minor detail of a story remained.

Cosmopolitan's January issue appeared in December and featured "The Gremlins" by Roald Dahl. At last the public could get some idea of what sort of film the Disney production would be. The story did manage to name every character possible and set up the basic plot: a pilot, named Gus, does not believe in Gremlins until he befriends "Gremlin Gus," through whom the hero learns about lady Gremlins (Fifinella) and baby Gremlins (widgets) and why they all hate pilots (airplane factory construction tore up their homes). Gus naturally explains that this was done to save their homeland, England, and Gremlin Gus agrees to train the Gremlins to be good. The training is of a sort practiced by modern behaviorists: the Gremlins are tricked so that when they do something bad to a plane, they get hurt. When they do something good, they are rewarded. Soon, a spirit of patriotic co-operation holds sway. Sadly, Gus is injured in an accident and can no longer pass the flier physicals; the Gremlins aid him with their magic. The moral of the tale: the only ones who have anything to fear from Gremlins are those who don't believe in them.

The rather slim story caught on quite well and soon was published in book form by Random House. With the release of the article "with illustrations by the Disney Studio," the full publicity campaign began. Stills and announcements were sent by both RKO and Disney (odd, since UA had been negotiating for the release) to publications and trade papers. Walt even wrote a small piece called "Low-Down on Gremlins."

But there was still outside pressure to contend with. On December 8 it was reported that Disney had to make "some costly changes" in *Gremlins* because of "the disapproval of British flyers over the levity with which the Gremlins were being treated in the picture." RKO also began demanding more artwork for publicity purposes. Adding the ridiculous to the merely ludicrous, the Gremlin fad brought about the debut of "Gremlin hats" for the ladies, and still more articles on the creatures.

A newspaper headline seems best to represent the early part of 1943: "Gremlins Appear in Alaska Now." The Gremlin bandwagon was filling fast. Count Basie recorded "Dance of the Gremlins." A daily comic strip, *The Gremlins*, also began in January. And to make matters worse, Warners, M-G-M, Universal, and Columbia all announced motion pictures based on Gremlins.

To fight this deluge of Gremliniana, a memo was sent down to push the "Gremlin Gus" character in all publicity and drawings, thus making him/it the property of Disney. Roy Disney also got into the act in the role he played best: businessman. He contacted the various studios to personally discourage Gremlin films. Most of the studios were sympathetic, and the competing films were all eventually dropped. Two that did get out (cartoons from Warner Brothers) were already too far in production to stop, but the titles were changed so that no mention of Gremlins would endanger the Disney project (now running to about $50,000).

By February it appeared that all the forces on Earth were fighting the completion of the film. Polls showed that filmgoers were tiring of war theme pictures. An Associated Press article titled "Gremlin Stuff is Getting Tiresome" echoed many media columnists when it stated that "They've been whimsied to pieces," and that "very soon any member of the general public who ventures to wax coy about them will run the risk of getting his itsy-bitsy block stoved in."

In March an aviation magazine editor also complained about the constant attention to Gremlins. The problem was not so much the overabundance of material, but the image they gave the RAF: "Surely the greatest flying and fighting service is not going to ape Sir James Barrie at his worst." Also in March, Disney wrote to Dahl stating that the feature would be totally animated, rather than half live-action.

In May a finished script appeared. It is basically the same story as Dahl's, with the addition of large chunks of narration and a dose of patriotic exhortation concerning the need to join together to fight a single enemy. This script abandons a sample idea worked out in late 1942 by a story person about the Gremlins having their own Hitler and having to fight him before they help the RAF fight our Hitler.

June saw Bill Justice (animator on such wartime films as *Fantasia, Victory Through Airpower,* and *Three Caballeros*) draw several Spandula (high flying Gremlins . . . part of the lore) for planned publication in a book for the Air Corps. The Gremlins also turned up on a large number of war insignia designed by the Studio for various fighting units.

It became obvious that the project was quickly winding down. In July, Disney wrote Dahl saying that he was now going to make *Gremlins* a short. He also re-mentioned that he did not like the RAF having the final say. After a story conference in August, Walt wrote again to Dahl saying that he just couldn't get any enthusiasm for the project and was going to drop it. He added that he would get in touch with Dahl if a good way of doing it ever cropped up.

In September 1943, one year after the first burst of Gremlin mania, the charge number was closed and the word was sent down to stop all tests on *The Gremlins.*

Of course, not every project that Disney started work on made it to the finish line (hundreds didn't), but it seems odd that Disney would give lack of staff interest as the official reason for suspending the project. When challenged earlier by such "problems" as the addition of sound, color, or expanding to feature length, he was able to inspire even his worst critic with his enthusiasm.

The real problem may have been that Walt lost that enthusiasm. The clause giving a major role to the RAF was a burr in his side. And, additionally, the oversaturation of the Gremlin market had a damaging effect on the film's financial prospects.

Ward Kimball, one of Disney's top animators, said that the frustration of not being able to visualize the characters or create a real plot weighed heavily. After all, Disney was the archetypal man of vision; he could not direct a project that gave him little opportunity to use it.

Oddly enough, Frank Thomas, another veteran animator, remembers that when he left for military service in later 1942, the project was already considered dead by most of the staff. The reason? At the time Frank did not know, but while researching with fellow animator Ollie Johnston, he and Ollie interviewed T. Hee, who worked closely on the project. Hee remembered that the final Gremlin to jinx the project was the RAF pilots themselves. Walt had taken several animators and story men (Hee among them) to meet a group of RAF pilots who were visiting Los Angeles. At this ill-fated meeting Walt discovered that the pilots didn't really believe in Gremlins; they were just a "big joke."

This insincerity rang the death knell of the project, according to Hee. Frank Thomas had to agree, remembering that Walt even waited on doing *Darby*

O'Gill and the Little People until he'd been to Ireland to see if people really believed in the wee folk. Walt took fantasy seriously and firmly believed that the public could not be expected to believe in the Gremlins if the pilots themselves didn't.

The Gremlins, mischievous imps who took the rap for everything from downing pilots to misdirecting buses in Chicago, finally sabotaged Disney's '40s attempt to mix the timelessness of fantasy with the timeliness of a world at war. It was only later, near the end of his career, that modernness again appeared in his films.

In a way, the Gremlins can be thanked for keeping Disney deep in traditional fantasy for another couple of decades. They couldn't keep him there forever—but Gremlins are not known for their reliability.

Appendix: List of *American Classic Screen* Feature Articles

In each issue of *American Classic Screen,* the magazine contained original articles and interviews, as well as regular columns, and occasional quizzes, crossword puzzles, etc. The following is a list of main articles that appeared in the magazine through its entire run (1976–1983). Some issues did not indicate the publication date either on the cover or on the masthead, but we have determined these dates based on the Vol. and issue No.

Note that some article titles have been renamed for purposes of clarification in American Classic Screen *Interviews, Profiles,* and *Features.* The original article titles appear below.

Vol. 1, No. 1 (September/October 1976)

Cover Portrait: Ginger Rogers
"Ginger Rogers: Still the Spice of Life" by Roger Holden
"Remembering the Glad Girl: An Appraisal of Five Mary Pickford Films [Part 1]" by John C. Tibbetts
"Rouben Mamoulian: An Exclusive Interview [Part 1]" by William Hare
"The World of Hollywood: Robert Alda Discusses His Career" by Robert Kendall

Vol. 1, No. 2 (November/December 1976)

Cover Portrait: Alice Faye
"Alice Faye: Sweetheart of the Musical Cinema" by Robert Kendall
"Remembering the Glad Girl: An Appraisal of Five Mary Pickford Films [Part 2]" by John C. Tibbetts
"Rouben Mamoulian: An Exclusive Interview [Part 2]" by William Hare
"One of America's Great Memorabilia Collections" by Randy Neil

Vol. 1, No. 3 (January/February 1977)

Cover Portrait: Charlie Chaplin
"Sir Charles Chaplin in 1976" by Robert Kendall
"Rouben Mamoulian: An Exclusive Interview [Part 3]" by William Hare
"Chaplain and Fairbanks: The Story of a Friendship" by John Tibbetts

Vol. 1, No. 4 (March/April 1977)

Cover Portrait: Mervyn LeRoy
"Mervyn LeRoy Interview" by William Hare
"The Film Industry Cherishes Its Traditions at the Motion Picture Country
    House" by Randy L. Neil
"From Silence to Sound: The Transformation of the Motion Picture Industry"
    by Rosalind Rogoff
"The Face Is Familiar, but the Name . . . ?" by Fred Putnam
"*Love Me or Leave Me*: Shots on an M-G-M Soundstage" by Randy Neil

Vol. 1, No. 5 (May/June 1977)

Cover Portrait: Mickey Rooney
"Mickey Rooney" by William Hare
"Preserving Our Palaces: A Job for All of Us" by Randy Neil
"Irving Thalberg: Important Words from a Film Pioneer at the Beginning of
    the Era of Sound"
"Rouben Mamoulian: An Exclusive Interview [Part 4]" by William Hare

Vol. 1, No. 6 (July/August 1977)

Cover Portrait: Buster Crabbe
"Buster Crabbe: Still Moving" by John Tibbetts
"*King Kong* and the Military" by Lawrence H. Suid
"The Outspoken Don 'Red' Barry: Interview" by William Hare
"The Way They Might Have Been" by Andrew Laskos
"The Birth of a Sex Symbol: Jayne Mansfield" by James Robert Haspiel

Vol. 2, No. 1 (September/October 1977)

Cover Portrait: Judy Garland
"A Visit with Irene Dunne" by James Bawden
"A Garland of Memories: A Rare Look at Judy Garland from the Collection of
    Nancy Barr" by Nancy Barr and Randy L. Neil
"They Killed King Kong" by Robert F. Wilson Jr.
"How a Superstar Was Born: The Screen Testing of Kim Novak" by James
    Robert Haspiel
"The Matthews' Musicals: Enduring Young Charms" by Dan Navarro
"*The Jazz Singer*: A Commentary on the Film's 50th Anniversary" by Rosalind
    Rogoff

Vol. 2, No. 2 (November/December 1977)

Cover Portrait: Marilyn Monroe
"Taking Stock" [Anne Baxter] by Doug McClelland
"How a Cinema Legend Was Born: The Screen Testing of Marilyn Monroe" by
    James Robert Haspiel
"The 1977 National Screen Heritage Award: Miss Rita Hayworth" by John C.
    Tibbetts
"Roscoe 'Fatty' Arbuckle: Filmdom's Forgotten Funnyman [Part 1]" by Bob
    Young Jr.

Vol. 2, No. 3 (January/February 1978)

Cover Art: Hollywood Goes to War
"Red Alert: Images of Communism in Hollywood" by J. Thomas Brown
"Innocence Abroad: *Hearts of the World*" by James M. Welsh
"The Midland Celebrates [Theatre Preservation Monitor]" by John C. Tibbetts
"World War II . . . The Girls Who Stayed Home" by Jack Ketch
"*The Big Parade*: A Standard for the Future" by Larry Suid

Vol. 2, No. 4 (March/April 1978)

Cover Portrait: Jean Harlow
"Coming to Light: The Celebrity Portraits of Orval Hixon" by John C. Tibbetts

"Revival! Tom Copper and the Return of the Revival House" by Dan Navarro
"The Screwball Satirists: Wheeler & Woolsey" by William M. Drew
"Roscoe 'Fatty' Arbuckle: Film's Forgotten Funnyman [Part 2]" by Robert
   Young Jr.

Vol. 2, No. 5 (May/June 1978)

Cover Illustration: Mickey Mouse
"Of Mouse and Man" [Mickey Mouse and Walt Disney] by John C. Tibbetts
"Joan Fontaine: A Recent Interview" by Doug McClelland
"Frank Capra: The Forgotten Films" by John C. Tibbetts
"The Paper Chase" [DeMille Archives] by James D'Arc
"Bowing Out: Roscoe 'Fatty' Arbuckle: Film's Forgotten Funnyman [Part 3]"
   by Robert Young Jr.

Vol. 2, No. 6 (July/August 1978)

Cover Portrait: Jeanette MacDonald
"Jeanette MacDonald: Super Star [Part 1]" by Clara Rhoades and Tessa Wil-
   liams
"Knockout in Paradise": An Appraisal of *The Set-Up*" by James M. Welsh
"*Citizen Kane* on the Drawing Board" by John C. Tibbetts
"*The Set-Up / Champion* Controversy: Fight Films Go to Court" by Richard
   Keenan

Vol. 3, No. 1 (September/October 1978)

Cover Portrait: Fred Astaire
"Fred Astaire: The Gentleman Is a Champ" by Dan Navarro
The Lady of the Screen: Norma Shearer" by Albert B. Manski
"Bernard B. Brown: A Profile of Mr. Hollywood" by Larry Leverett

Vol. 3, No. 2 (November/December 1978)

Cover Portrait: Bing Crosby
"A Day with Bing" by Fr. Robert Murphy
"Charlie Chan Meets OWI: Racism in World War II Films" by Gregory D. Black

"The Fighting O' Quinn: An Encounter with *Starlog*'s Editor, Kerry O'Quinn" by John C. Tibbetts

"Jeanette MacDonald: Super Star [Part 2]" by Clara Rhoades and Tessa Williams

Vol. 3, No. 3 (January/February 1979)

Cover Portrait: Errol Flynn and Olivia De Havilland

"'Perfect Manners': An Interview with Olivia De Havilland" by James V. D'Arc

"Film Copyright Infringement: A Handful against the Multitude" by Randy Neil

"Glen MacWilliams: Following the Sun with a Veteran Hollywood Cameraman" by John C. Tibbetts

"America's Boyfriend: The Early Years" [Charles "Buddy" Rogers] by Stan Singer

Vol. 3, No. 4 (March/April 1979)

Cover Portrait: Christopher Reeve

"Man and Superman—Then and Now: Flight As the American Dream" by James M. Welsh and John C. Tibbetts

"The MacMurrays at Home: A Double Portrait" by Dan Navarro

"Dear Beulah: Reflection on the Long and Distinguished Career of Beulah Bondi [Part 1]" by Dr. Frank A. Aversano

Vol. 3, No. 5 (May/June 1979)

"Innocence Protected: Will Rogers and *Steamboat 'Round the Bend*" by Peter C. Rollins

"Dear Beulah: Reflection on the Long and Distinguished Career of Beulah Bondi [Part 2]" by Dr. Frank A. Aversano

"That Beautiful Brat: A Visit with Jane Withers" by Dan Navarro

Vol. 3, No. 6 (July/August 1979)

Cover Illustration: Rocketship X-M

"Project RXM" by John C. Tibbetts

"Frank Capra: A Lighthouse in a Foggy World" Interview by William M. Drew

"Hugh O'Brian Talks about RXM" by John C. Tibbetts
"Disney Out-Foxed: The Tale of Reynard at the Disney Studio" by John Cawley Jr.

Vol. 4, No. 1 (Fall 1979)

Cover Portrait: Katharine Hepburn
"Cukor and Hepburn: The Story of a Creative Partnership That Has Spanned Forty-Seven Years" by Gene D. Phillips
"Seastrom: The Hollywood Years" by Herman Weinberg
"Siren Song: The Tragedy of Barbara La Marr" by Jack Marston
"Howard Hughes and That Tussle with Russell: Some Alarms and Excursions in Hollywood" by Dick Sheppard
"The Film Career of George M. Cohan" by Audrey Kupferberg

Vol. 4, No. 2 (Winter 1980)

Cover Portrait: Tom Mix
"The Wellman Westerns: An Appraisal" by Frank T. Thompson
"John Ford's *Wagon Master*: Rite of Passage" by James M. Welsh
"I Want Stone-Age Faces!' A Behind-the-Scenes Look with Harry Carey Jr., Patrick Ford, and Wes Jefferies at the Making of John Ford's Favorite Film" by James V. D'Arc
"Roy Rogers: First Days at Republic" [Excerpt from *Happy Trails* (Word Books)] by Roy Rogers
"Pauline Moore: Girl of the Golden West" by Doug Moore
"Westward the Stars! Tom Corbett: Space Cadet" by Frankie Thomas
"Walt Disney and 'The Gremlins': An Unfinished Story . . . " by John Cawley
"Kubrick, *Killer's Kiss*, *The Killing*, and Film Noir" by Gene D. Phillips
"In All Its Splendor . . . The Nelson Theatre, 1907–1972" by James M. Welsh
"Seymour Stern: American Film Critic, Guardian, and Prophet" by Ira H. Gallen
"Sam Peckinpah and the 'Post-Western'" by Joseph A. Gomez
"Murder Will Out: A Life and Death of William Desmond Taylor" by Robert Young Jr.

Vol. 4, No. 3 (Summer 1980)

Cover Portrait: Greta Garbo
"Uncensored Garbo" by Charles Affron

"Hollywood Visited and Revisited" by Milton Plesur
"William Wellman: The Paramount Years (1927–1930)" by Frank Thompson

Vol. 5, No. 1 (November/December 1980)

Cover Portrait: Lillian Gish
"Silent Screen Heroines: Idealizations on Film" by Jocelyn Tey
"Visions of Dracula" by James M. Welsh and John C. Tibbetts
"Truman and Reagan: 'The Winning Team'" by Don Walker
"*The Birth of a Nation*: An Assessment" by Seymour Stern

Vol. 5, No. 2 (March/April 1981)

Cover Portrait: Paul Newman
"Twenty-Five Years with the Golden Boy" by Chuck Sack
"Marilyn: A Personal Reminiscence" by Del Burnett
"An Interview with Kevin Brownlow" by John C. Tibbetts
"Hollywood Goes to Court: The Trial of Mary Dugan" by Al Manski and Dan
    Navarro

Vol. 5, No. 3 (May/June 1981)

Cover Portrait: Bette Davis
"Bette Davis and Claude Rains" by Anne Etheridge
"The Rise and Fall of the California Motion Picture Company" by Geoffrey Bell
"Beatriz Michelena in *Salvation Nell*" by Geoffrey Bell
"I'll Never Forget Warner's Ohio" by Doris McClure Humphrey)
"Souls Aflame: D.W. Griffith and Seymour Stern" by Arthur Lennig
"The Lost Movie of Errol Flynn" by Wade Ward
"A Visit to the Will Rogers Memorial" by Jack Ketch

Vol. 5, No. 4 (July/August 1981)

Cover Illustration: Silent Film Posters
"The Right Image: Revisiting the Golden Age of the Hollywood Movie Poster"
    by Anthony Slide and the Editors of *ACS*
"Those Busby Berkeley and Astaire-Rogers Depression Musicals: Two Different
    Worlds" by Rocco Fumento

"*Napoleon* Conquers America" by James M. Welsh
"Esther Ralston Interview" by William M. Drew
"Frontier Families: John Ford/Sergio Leone" by Dr. Lane Roth

Vol. 5, No. 5 (September/October 1981)

Cover Illustration: Lon Chaney, Charlie Chaplin, Greta Garbo, etc.
"Alice's Looking Glass: The Movie Adventures of Lewis Carroll's Alice" by David and Maxine Schaefer
"Hollywood Royalty: Conversations with Henry King" by Gene D. Phillips
"Kicking Away Gravity: The Saga of Four Great Hollywood Stuntmen" by David Wilson
"The Final Legacy of Max Steiner" by James D'Arc and the Editors of *ACS*

Vol. 5, No. 6 (November/December 1981)

Cover Portrait: John Barrymore
"The Search for John Barrymore: The Quest Is Elusive for the 'Lost' Barrymore Films" by Spencer Berger
"The Other Authors of *Gone with the Wind*" by Rodney Richey
"Bigger Than Life: Episodes in the Erratic Career of 3-D Technology" by Roxanne Meuller
"Charles T. Barton: An Informal Profile" by Frank Thompson

Vol. 6, No. 1 (January/February 1982)

Cover Portrait: Robert Redford
"Eleanor Powell: Born to Dance" by Lisa Capps
"Winton Hoch: 'Master of Technicolor'" by John Gallagher
"Robert Redford: A Lesson in 'Taking Charge'" by Jocelyn Tey
"Living with Father: Remember the Blondie Films" by Dr. Judith Cornes
"Surviving Mother Hollywood: Diana Serra Cary ('Baby Peggy') Speaks Out . . . " by Betty Dodds

Vol. 6, No. 2 (March/April 1982)

Cover Portrait: Natalie Wood
"Mike Mazurki: Hollywood's Favorite Tough Guy" by Bill Kelly

"Natalie Wood: A Life on Film" by John C. Tibbetts

"Kidflicks: The Western Films of Fred Thomson" by Bruce M. Firestone

"Will Rogers: The Story Behind His First Talking Picture" by Reba Neighbors Collins

Vol. 6, No. 3 (May/June 1982)

Cover Illustration: William Shatner, Leonard Nimoy, and Robert Wise

"*Star Trek: The [First] Motion Picture*: Looking Back . . . 'Thataway!'" by Richard Keenan

"Dyan Cannon: An Interview" by John C. Tibbetts

"Uncle Sam: Family Reminiscences of One of Hollywood's Most Beloved Character Actors, Laird Cregar" by Elizabeth Hayman

"In the State of California: De Havilland, Plaintiff vs. Warner Bros., Defendant" by J. L. Yeck

Vol. 6, No. 4 (July/August 1982)

Cover Portrait: Elizabeth Taylor

"View from the Bridge: George (Sulu) Takei Discusses His Career and the New *Star Trek: The Wrath of Khan*" by John C. Tibbetts

"Walter Plunkett" Always in Fashion" by John C. Tibbetts

"Lana Turner: Authentic American Glamour Queen" by Gene Sheppard

Vol. 6, No. 5 (September/October 1982)

Cover Portrait: Vivien Leigh

"Robert Preston Talks about Typecasting, Cecil B. DeMille and *Victor/Victoria*" by John C. Tibbetts

Walter Plunkett: Dressing Right for *Gone with the Wind*" by John C. Tibbetts

"Woody Allen Talks about His New Feature Film, *A Midsummer Night's Sex Comedy*" by John C. Tibbetts

"'I Never Saw a Mountain I Wouldn't Climb': Hollywood Cinematographer William H. Clothier" by John Gallagher

Vol. 6, No. 6 (November/December 1982)

Cover Portrait: Cornel Wilde

"That Man Called Bond" by Brian Hughes

"George [Bancroft]" by Raymond G. Cabana Jr.

"Cornel Wilde: The Complete Filmmaker and Man of Action" by Gene Sheppard

"Walter Hill: Talking Shop with One of America's Finest Young Directors" by John Gallagher and Sam Sarowitz

Vol. 7, No. 1 (January/February 1982)

Cover Portrait: Joan Crawford

"Ron Howard: From Child Star to 'Complete' Filmmaker . . . a Running Commentary" by John C. Tibbetts

"Warner Baxter" by DeWitt Bodeen

"Those Lovely Ladies" by Tony Gray

"The Elusive Cecil B. DeMille: An Appreciation of a Hollywood Legend" by James V. D'Arc

"'Mister Electricity': The Multi-Volted Career of Kenneth Strickfaden" by William Ludington

"Ralph Bellamy" by James Bawden

Vol. 7, No. 2 (March/April 1983)

Cover Portrait: Boris Karloff

"A Great Year for Sidney Lumet" by James M. Welsh

"Boris Karloff: An Affectionate Memoir of the Gentleman of Terror" by DeWitt Bodeen

"The Singing Screen: Remembering Those Movies That Not Only Talked but Sang . . . " by David L. Parker

"The Twilight World of Roland West: A Forgotten Master of the Macabre" by Scott MacQueen

Vol. 7, No. 3 (May/June 1983)

Cover Illustration: Broadway Musicals

"Lord Love a Duck! Fifty Years with Donald . . ." by Fr. Robert Murphy

"Sister Act: Molly O'Day, Sally O'Neil, Remembering Two Irish Lasses from Those Days of the Silent Screen" by DeWitt Bodeen

"In Step with Hermes Pan: An Interview with a Hollywood Dance Legend" by Lenna DeMarco

"An Interview with David Cronenberg" by Dan Crutcher
"Lois Wilson: Interview" by William M. Drew
"Adventures in Film History with William K. Everson" by John C. Tibbetts
"My Friend Bing Crosby" by Fr. Robert Murphy
"California Dreamin': Chasing Rainbows in Hollywood with Gary Berwin" by
    John C. Tibbetts

Vol. 8, No. 1 [duplicate Vol./No. of above] (March/April 1984)

Cover Illustration: The Wizard of Oz
"Margaret Hamilton" by Gregory J. Catsos
"Lyle Talbot: Breaking in to Hollywood" by John C. Tibbetts
"Stanley Donen: A Noted Film Director Discusses His Career and His Return
    to the Screen with *Blame It on Rio*" by John C. Tibbetts
"A Countess in Hollywood: Elyssa Landi" by John Roberts

Index

About the Editors

John C. Tibbetts was educated at the University of Kansas (B.A., Ph.D.) and has worked as an artist, illustrator, editor, writer, teacher, and broadcaster; for eight years he was editor-in-chief of *American Classic Screen* and sat on the board of the National Film Society. He is an associate professor of film and theater at the University of Kansas and the author of several books, including the two-volume *The Encyclopedia of Filmmakers* (2002), *Composers in the Movies: Studies in Musical Biography* (2005), and *All My Loving? The Films of Tony Palmer* (2009).

James M. Welsh is emeritus professor at Salisbury University in Maryland and was educated at Indiana University, Bloomington, and the University of Kansas (M.A., Ph.D.). The founder of the Literature/Film Association, and the co-founding editor of *Literature/Film Quarterly*, Welsh was East Coast editor of *American Classic Screen*. He now serves on the editorial board of *The Journal of American Culture* and *The Journal of Adaptation in Film and Performance*, published in Britain. His most recent books are *The Pedagogy of Adaptation*, co-edited with Laurence Raw and Dennis Cutchins, and *The Francis Ford Coppola Encyclopedia*, co-edited with Rodney Hill and the Rev. Gene D. Phillips, S.J., both published by Scarecrow Press in 2010.

About the Contributors

Charles Affron is an essayist, critic, and professor of French, New York University, since 1965. Author of *Star Acting: Gish, Garbo, Davis* (1977); *Cinema and Sentiment* (1982); *Divine Garbo* (1985); *Fellini's 8½* (1987); and *Sets in Motion: Art Direction and Film Narrative* (1995), he served as general editor of the Rutgers Films in Print Series.

Geoffrey Bell was a San Francisco filmmaker featured at the 1981 Movie Expo in Los Angeles; his films to that point included *The First Motion Picture Show* (a documentary on the pre-history of film), *Movies Go West* (a documentary about the Essanay Company), and *Those Daring Young Film Makers by the Golden Gate* (a documentary about early Bay filmmakers).

Spencer Merriam Berger (1917–2002) was an artist, film historian, and chairman of the board of the former Berger Brothers Company of New Haven, Connecticut, as well as a leading authority on the Barrymores. His film collection is now part of the Spencer M. Berger Collection at the Film Study Center and the Beinecke Library at Yale University and the Cinema Archives at Wesleyan University.

Gregory D. Black, professor of the Communications History Department at the University of Missouri, Kansas City, helped Randy Neil and John Tibbetts get *American Classic Screen* off and running. He is author of *Hollywood Censored: Morality Codes, Catholics, and the Movies* (1994) and *The Catholic Crusade against the Movies, 1940–1975* (1997).

J. Thomas Brown wrote his "Red Alert" essay from research completed for a doctoral dissertation written for the University of Kansas, Lawrence.

John Cawley Jr. worked for five years at Walt Disney Productions, including one year in the Disney Archives in Burbank. He edited the magazine *Private Screenings* (1975–1977) and was appointed animation editor and columnist for *American Classic Screen* in 1981.

Reba Neighbors Collins was curator of the Will Rogers Memorial Museum in Claremore, Oklahoma.

James V. D'Arc is curator of the Harold B. Lee Library Archives of Brigham Young University in Provo, Utah, and was also a contributing editor of *American Classic Screen*. The Lee Library at BYU houses the Cecil B. DeMille papers.

William M. Drew is an independent scholar whose work has been published in film-related periodicals, such as *Take One* (Canada), *Literature/Film Quarterly*, and *American Classic Screen*. He is the author of *D. W. Griffith's* Intolerance: *Its Genesis and Its Vision* (1986) and *The Last Silent Picture Show: Silent Films of the 1930s* (Scarecrow Press, 2010).

Rocco Fumento is the author of two published novels and a college textbook, *Introduction to the Short Story* (1962). When he taught English at the University of Illinois, Urbana-Champaign, and wrote for *American Classic Screen*, he edited the screenplay of *42nd Street* for the Wisconsin/Warner Bros. Screenplay series in 1980.

James Robert Haspiel worked early for *American Classic Screen*, providing profiles of Jayne Mansfield and Kim Novak.

Roger Holden served as president of the Kansas Film Institute and president of a robotics company called Holden Gentry Systems. He designed an animation computer system that allowed Centron Films of Lawrence, Kansas, to film fourteen episodes of animation for the nationally broadcast PBS series *Reading Rainbow*.

Scott MacQueen was fortunate enough to have worked at the Walt Disney Company Archives.

David L. Parker is the co-author of *Guide to Dance in Film* (1978) and the former technical officer of Motion Picture Section, Prints and Photographs Division of the Library of Congress in Washington, D.C.

The Rev. Gene D. Phillips, S.J., a prolific film scholar, teaches English and film at Loyola University in Chicago. He was a member of the *American Classic Screen* editorial board, has published books on several major literary figures (such as Graham Greene, whom he interviewed) and film directors he was also privileged to know, such as Alfred Hitchcock, Stanley Kubrick, John Schlesinger, Ken Russell, and Billy Wilder. He is the co-editor and co-author of *The Francis Ford Coppola Encyclopedia*, recently published by Scarecrow Press.

Rodney Richey taught in the English Department of Ball State University in Muncie, Indiana.

Rosalind Rogoff served as a contributing editor to *American Classic Screen* while pursuing a graduate degree in cinema studies at the University of Southern California.

Peter C. Rollins retired as Regents Professor of English and American Film Studies at Oklahoma State University after serving as editor-in-chief of *Film & History: An Interdisciplinary Journal of Film and Television Studies*. His many books include *The Columbia Companion to American History on Film* (2003) and *The West Wing: The American Presidency as Television Drama* (2003), co-authored with John E. O'Connor.

David and Maxine Schaefer were dedicated, long-term collectors of *Alice in Wonderland* memorabilia.

Seymour W. Stern, a film critic, established a column, "Kaleido-scopia," in 1926 in the *Greenwich Village Quill*. In 1929 he wrote *Six Principles of Camera Montage*, which became required reading at Universal Pictures. His major obsessions were the life and work of D. W. Griffith, the future of artistic cinema, and the development of a responsible yet impassioned film criticism in America. His magnum opus to be titled *Griffith: Master of Cinema*, announced in 1938, remained uncompleted at his death in 1975.

Lawrence H. Suid, a military historian, is the author and editor of several books, including *Sailing on the Silver Screen, Guts & Glory: The Making of the American Military Image in Film*, and *Stars and Stripes on Screen* (Scarecrow, 2004).

J. P. Telotte is film genre authority and professor of literature, communication, and culture at the Georgia Institute of Technology; his many books include *Dreams of Darkness: Fantasy and the Films of Val Lewton* (1985), *Voices in the Dark: The Narrative Patterns of Film Noir* (1989), *The Cult Film Experience* (1991), *Replications: A Robotic History of the Science Fiction Film* (1995), and *A Distant Technology: Science Fiction Film and the Modern Age* (1999).

Irving Thalberg (1899–1936), dubbed the "Boy Wonder" by studio magnates at Universal and M-G-M, acquired in his lifetime a reputation for astute script sense and tough business practices. His early death in 1936 robbed Hollywood of one of its most intelligent and sensitive film producers. Thalberg was allegedly the inspiration for the lead character of F. Scott Fitzgerald's novel *The Last Tycoon* (1940).

Frank T. Thompson has worked as an editor, archivist, and television writer in Los Angeles, Chicago, Atlanta, and elsewhere. An awesome and informed film buff, Thompson has written several books, including *William A. Wellman* (1983, with an affectionate foreword by Barbara Stanwyck, Wellman's favorite actress), *Robert Wise: A Bio-Bibliography* (1995), *Lost Films* (1996), and *The Alamo: A Cultural History* (2001). Frank also appeared in Todd Robinson's documentary *Wild Bill: Hollywood Maverick* (1995), along with Robert Wise, Robert Redford, Robert Mitchum, Robert Stack, Clint Eastwood, Martin Scorsese, Tony Scott, and his pal, John Gallagher.

Wade Ward, a member of the National Film Society, worked as a newspaper-man in Hoisington, Kansas.

Joanne L. Yeck is an essayist, lecturer on humanities and film at the Art Center College of Design, Pasadena, and co-author (with Tom McGreevey) of *Movie Westerns* (1994).